DRAGONFLIES
THROUGH
BINOCULARS

Field Guide Series
edited by Jeffrey Glassberg

Butterflies through Binoculars: A Field and Finding Guide to
   Butterflies of the Boston-New York-Washington Region
by Jeffrey Glassberg

Butterflies through Binoculars: A Field Guide to Butterflies
   of Eastern North America
by Jeffrey Glassberg

Butterflies through Binoculars: A Field, Finding, and
   Gardening Guide to Butterflies in Florida
by Jeffrey Glassberg, Marc C. Minno, and John V. Calhoun

Dragonflies through Binoculars: A Field Guide to Dragonflies
   of North America
by Sidney W. Dunkle

Butterflies through Binoculars: A Field Guide to Butterflies of
   Western North America
by Jeffrey Glassberg

DRAGONFLIES THROUGH BINOCULARS

A FIELD GUIDE TO DRAGONFLIES OF NORTH AMERICA

Sidney W. Dunkle

OXFORD
UNIVERSITY PRESS
2000

OXFORD
UNIVERSITY PRESS

Oxford   New York
Athens   Auckland   Bangkok   Bogotá   Buenos Aires
Calcutta   Cape Town   Chennai   Dar es Salaam   Delhi
Florence   Hong Kong   Istanbul   Karachi   Kuala Lumpur
Madrid   Melbourne   Mexico City   Mumbai   Nairobi   Paris
São Paulo   Singapore   Taipei   Tokyo   Toronto   Warsaw

and associated companies in
Berlin   Ibadan

Copyright © 2000 by Sidney W. Dunkle

Published by Oxford University Press, Inc.
198 Madison Avenue, New York, New York 10016

Oxford is a registered trademark of Oxford University Press, Inc.

Library of Congress Cataloging-in-Publication Data
Dunkle, Sidney W., 1940–
Dragonflies through binoculars : a field guide to dragonflies
of North America / by Sidney W. Dunkle.
p. cm.   (Butterflies [and others] through
binoculars field guide series)
Includes bibliographical references.
ISBN 0-19-511268-7
1. Dragonflies—United States Identification.
2. Dragonflies—Canada Identification.   I. Title.   II. Series
QL520.2.U6 D87   2000
595.7'33'0973—dc21   99-34854

1 3 5 7 9 8 6 4 2

Printed in Hong Kong
on acid-free paper

Contents

Preface

Today I saw the dragon-fly
Come from the well where he did lie...
Thro' crofts and pastures wet with dew
A living flash of light he flew
—ALFRED LORD TENNYSON

DRAGONFLIES CAN INSPIRE THE POET IN A PERSON, as they did for Lord Tennyson. With their beautiful colors, unmatched symmetry, and bird-like behavior, they are watcher's animals *par excellance*. Thus it is incredible that until now no field guide has been available for the identification of the 307 North American species. While field guides with painted plates have advantages, an advantage of photographic guides like this one is that they show *exactly* what the creatures look like, without the intervention of the hand and mind of an artist. All but 14 North American dragonfly species are illustrated in this book by one or more photos, many whose images have not previously been published anywhere. Those not shown are identical in the field or nearly so to illustrated species.

Dragonflies do not sting, their bite if restrained is inconsequential, and most people appreciate that they consume as both flying adults and aquatic larvae vast numbers of pest insects, such as mosquitoes. Dragonflies are one of the most visible indicators of wetland diversity and health, and their population changes allow monitoring of environmental changes.

Although this book is intended to allow identification without capture, I wish to emphasize that collecting in moderation is essential for scientific documentation and progress. Over the years I have found many misidentifications of specimens in collections. Records from such specimens can be corrected, but similar data taken from sight records could not ever be verified. The book had to focus on field identification, and space limitations caused much interesting information to be (painfully!) left out. These items will have to await inclusion in a planned future book on the natural history of North American dragonflies.

I warmly thank all of the people, too numerous to mention, who have helped me with my dragonfly studies. A number of people answered a "last call for data," including A. Barlow, J. Daigle, T. Donnelly, R. Garrison, E. Gonzalez, C. Hobson, M. Holder, S. Krotzer, W. Mauffray, R. Novelo, R. Orr, K. Tennessen, S. Valley, C. Williams, and especially P. Brunelle and C. Shiffer. Special thanks are due to the photographers who allowed me to use their hard-won photographs. I greatly appreciate the computer help cheerfully given to me by D. McCulloch and T. McRae.

DRAGONFLIES
THROUGH
BINOCULARS

INTRODUCTION

Organization of Accounts and Maps

DRAGONFLY FAMILIES ARE SEQUENCED from those believed to be the most primitive to the most advanced. Within each family or other group, similar-looking species are placed next to each other wherever possible. Information that applies to all species in a group is given in the introduction to the group. Within each species account, the English name and scientific name are stated first. Then sections on field Identification, Structural Features and geographic Variation (where appropriate), Similar Species, breeding Habitat, flight Season, and behavioral and other Comments are given. For further details, see "About the Species Accounts," beginning on page 29.

"North America" as used in this book refers to the continent north of Mexico, shown on the maps opposite the plates. These are necessarily crude because the limits of many dragonflies' ranges are imperfectly known, and there are many undocumented gaps even within known ranges. Many species are local, with a spotty distribution. Some species' ranges, primarily stream and bog species, are decreasing due usually to development and agriculture, while some other dragonflies are expanding their ranges due to the building of ponds. Some southern species appear to be extending their ranges northward in response to global warming, and northern species can be expected to retreat farther northward. Nonetheless, the scientist within me cringed as I "connected the dots" and took leaps of faith across entire states to construct the maps.

Binoculars

There are really only two things one needs to know about binoculars for dragonfly viewing: (1) Get *close-focus* binoculars. You will probably not be satisfied with any binos that do not focus closer than 8 ft., and state of the art is 4 ft. (2) Buy the *best* binos that you can possibly afford. The pleasure you get from seeing crystal-clear, bright images will far more than compensate for the initial cost. Any of the standard bino 7–10× magnifications will be OK, with the lower powers giving a wider field of view (I settled on 8×). Eyeglass wearers should look for a *long eye relief* of 18–20 mm or more, and retractable or fold-down rubber eyecups. *Waterproof* binos (not "water-resistant" or some other euphemism) will save a lot of grief since they will not fog internally. Other suggestions are, at the present state of technology, to avoid rocker-type focusing, zoom magnification, and a very wide field (more than 525 ft. at 1000 yards). Useful literature on buying binoculars is published by Canon, Eagle Optics, Nikon, and by Christophers of Norman, Oklahoma.

Other field equipment can include a thermometer, altimeter, global positioning instrument, and stopwatch. A notebook or pocket tape recorder are essential for recording observations.

How to Identify Dragonflies

The reader should begin by finding the most similar appearing photograph to the dragonfly under observation, then read the appropriate species account, checking similar species, geographic range, and flight season. It may also be useful to review the genus and family accounts that include the species under consideration.

While some dragonflies, because of their size, wing pattern, unique behavior, or some combination of features, can be identified as far as they can be seen, others are identified in the field with difficulty, if at all. Besides keeping in mind whether a possible species is expected to occur in the area, habitat, and season, the following questions are all useful in arriving at an identification: Does it perch or fly most of the time? If it perches, is the body horizontal, oblique, or vertical, and what type of perch does it select? How big is it relative to other known dragonflies, or to other insects or objects? What sex is it, and if it is female does it have a visible egg-layer (ovipositor) near the tip of the abdomen? Can its age be estimated—for example, is it newly emerged with pale colors and shiny wings, a sexually mature territorial male, a mature egg-laying female? If it is involved in reproductive activity, note that only some dragonflies mate entirely while airborne, and only some lay eggs as a tandem pair. If you have time to systematically scan the dragonfly's body from face to tip of abdomen: Are the eyes widely separated, in contact at a point on top of the head, or widely fused together? What color is the face, forehead, and the tops of the eyes? What is the stripe or other pattern on the thorax? Is there any wing pattern, such as a small brown or black spot at the base of each wing (all dragonflies have a colored spot or stigma near the tip of each wing)? Does the thigh of the hindleg reach just to the base of the abdomen (short legs), or as far as the second segment of the abdomen (long legs)? How does the length of the abdomen compare to the length of a wing? Of the 10 abdominal segments (S1 at base to S10 at tip), which are narrowest or widest, and which bear spots or bands? For some of the most difficult to identify dragonflies, it may be necessary or advisable to scrutinize the shape of the male terminal abdominal appendages, the color of the chin, the color of the legs including the shins, the color of the back of the head, or even the pattern of wing veins.

How to Find Dragonflies

Since dragonflies breed in water, and the males of most species wait there for females, the key to finding a variety of dragonflies is to look at as many different aquatic habitats as possible, including seepages. At each habitat, check each available microhabitat. For example, at a pond take a look at the north and south sides, shady and sunny sides, inlet and outlet, emergent and floating plants, shallow and deep areas, areas of different bottom types, shores closer to or farther from forest, and lee and windy sides. The downwind side may be especially good on a very windy day and for seeing mating pairs. At a stream, look at different bridge crossings, rippling and still water, rocky and sandy shores, and grassy and shrubby shores. In particular, check prominent objects where a male dragonfly would be likely to perch with a good view of the water, such as the tip of an upright stick on the shore, or a rock in the water at the head of a riffle. Where possible, wading or cruising along the shore in a canoe is the best way to check dragonfly perches. The scarcer dragonflies are sensitive to environmental disturbance and pollution, and there will not be many stream-dwelling dragonflies in heavily developed or farmed areas. Ways to circumvent this are to look in large long-established parks, forested watersheds, and along larger streams near the entry of an unpolluted tributary.

Feeding dragonflies can usually be found by slowly walking the fields near appropriate aquatic habitats, especially along fencerows or forest edges. Those parts of a field out of a strong wind and in the sun are best. Such factors as proximity to roosting sites, flight lanes, humid areas where prey insects are most abundant, or the side of a hill where the sunlight was strongest the previous evening are worth checking next. Dusk-flying species are most likely identified by methodically searching the undergrowth in shady floodplain forest. Most dragonflies are active at an air temperature of 65°F or more. On cold, cloudy, or rainy days dragonflies hide in the vegetation and your time is better spent reading this guide and dreaming about the neat dragonflies you will see when the sun comes out.

What Is a Dragonfly?

A full classification of the term "dragonfly" as used in North America includes: Animal Kingdom, Arthropod Phylum, Insect Class, Odonata Order, and Anisoptera Suborder. Like other Arthropods dragonflies have an outer skeleton and jointed legs. Like most other insects, they have a head with two antennae, a thorax bearing 6 legs and 4 wings, and an abdomen. The Odonata ("toothy ones") Order includes three Suborders, the damselflies (Suborder Zygoptera), the Suborder Anisozygoptera of only two "living fossil" Asiatic species, and the drag-onflies (Suborder Anisoptera, with about 3000 world species). In much of the world, "dragonfly" refers to all Odonata. People who study dragonflies and damselflies are called odonatists or odonatologists, and the insects themselves are often called odonates.

Dragonflies are generally easily recognized by their tiny, bristle-like antennae, and wings held out to the sides. The hind wings are broader at the base than the forewings, and in most dragonflies the huge eyes come into contact on top of the head. Damselflies are smaller and more slender, with separated eyes, and have forewings and hind wings similarly shaped and usually held together over the

back. Male dragonflies use 3 appendages (2 cerci, 1 epiproct) at the
tip of their abdomen to grasp the female's head during mating, while
male damselflies use 4 appendages (2 cerci, 2 paraprocts) to grasp the
female's neck. Dragonfly larvae have stout-pointed appendages at
the tip of their abdomens, while damselfly larvae have 3 leaf-like
gills. The Anisozygoptera have wings and perching behavior like
damselflies, but adult body structure and larvae like dragonflies.

The only other insects much like dragonflies are in the Order Neu-
roptera, the owlflies and antlions, but these fold their wings rooflike
over their abdomens, and have clublike antennae. The larvae of all
Odonata differ from those of other insects by their greatly enlarged
lower lip, which is used to capture prey.

Dragonflies include a variable number of families, depending on
who is classifying them. Like other family names for animals, the scientific names of dragonfly families end in -idae (pronounced "id-
dee"). The classification used in this book provides 7 North American
families—namely, the Petaltails, Darners, Clubtails, Spiketails, Cruisers, Emeralds, and Skimmers.

Dragonfly Biology
Life Cycle

EGG

Dragonflies lay eggs in or near water, or in a place that will fill with
rainwater. Eggs are rod-shaped in Petaltails and Darners, round or
oval in outline and usually covered with sticky jelly in other families.
Freshly laid eggs are usually yellow to orange, but are green in Cruisers and some Skimmers. Fertile eggs turn darker a few hours after
being laid. Eggs hatch in about 10 days, or as soon as 5 days in temporary pool breeders, to as long as several months for some others that
must survive a cold winter or long dry season.

LARVA

The brown or green aquatic larvae are sometimes called nymphs or
naiads. Their uniquely enlarged and clawed lower lip can be shot out
in 1/100 second to as much as 1/3 the body length to capture prey. In
fact, dragonfly larvae are usually the top carnivores in freshwater

habitats without fish. Another remarkable feature is that their gills are located inside the rectal chamber, and they breathe in and out of their anus. This system protects the delicate gills internally, and when water is forced out under pressure the larvae become jet propelled. The sex of a well-grown larva can be told by looking for the developing male genitalia on the underside of S2, and the developing ovipositor of the female on the underside of S9.

A larva grows by molting its skin (nonliving cuticle) 8–17 times, depending on the species. The shed skin is called the **Exuviae** (singular and plural, like clothes). The time spent as a larva varies from a month to as much as 8 years, depending on species and temperature. In a full grown larva the developing wings are much longer than broad, and extend to about S4. As the time for adult emergence approaches, an internal metamorphosis occurs. The external signs of this are adult colors visible through the skin, the large adult eyes under the skin of the head, the swelling wings, and the adult lower lip retracted into the base of the lip-trap. For a few days before becoming adult, larvae cannot capture prey and do not eat. In many species the larvae move to the surface of the water and begin to breathe air.

At night, or in Clubtails often during the day, the larva climbs out of the water and hooks its claws into a support and prepares to change to an adult, a process called **Emergence** or **Transformation**. The dragonfly swallows air, and the resulting pressure splits the larval skin. As the adult continues to swallow air it rises out of the larval skin like a pale ghost. After the legs have hardened, the wings are inflated with a characteristic glistening sheen produced by the layer of blood between their upper and lower surfaces. The adult — called a teneral by entomologists—is soft, pale, and helpless at this time. (see Plate 45, no. 2). Tenerals could be mistaken for albinos, but no true albino dragonflies have been found. If the teneral is knocked off its perch by the wind, a wave, or a boat wake, it will die. The wings of a dragonfly are at first held together over the back, but at the end of emergence the wings are suddenly flicked out to the sides. Soon, often at dawn, the dragonfly takes its maiden flight and leaves the water until it is sexually mature. The dragonfly is now fully grown. Little winged dragonflies do not grow into big winged dragonflies.

ADULT

ADULT

The pre-reproductive adult between emergence and sexual maturity is termed in this book a **Juvenile**, a period that lasts about a week to a month, depending on the species, temperature, and food supply. The whole adult life span of many species of dragonflies appears to be approximately a month, up to 9 months for a few species. During maturation, pale markings may in different species become brighter, or they may become darker and be obscured. Especially in male Skimmers, various parts of the body or wings become covered with a waxy powder or **Pruinescence**, which is white or pale blue. Males of at least some species will patrol territories and can mate before their fully "mature" coloration develops.

Parasites

Dragonfly eggs are parasitized by tiny wasps, such as those of the family Mymaridae that can fly underwater to find the eggs. Wasps of the genus *Thoronella* (family Scelionidae) have been found riding (rarely—much more data needed) on female Darners in the eastern United States, probably waiting for the dragonfly to lay her eggs.

The most common external parasites are red or green mites (genus *Arrenurus*, see Plate 41, no. 2), sometimes in such numbers as to deform the body or create colored patches on the body. Females of a biting gnat, *Forcipomyia fusicornis* (family Ceratopogonidae), most abundant near the east coast, also suck blood, commonly from a wing vein even while a dragonfly is in flight.

Among the many predators of adult dragonflies, frogs, flycatchers, falcons, purple martins, spiders, robber flies, and sundew plants (*Drosera*) could be mentioned.

Behavior

PERCHING

Petaltails, Darners, and Cruisers usually perch or hang vertically. Clubtails generally perch horizontally on the ground or a leaf. Most other dragonflies perch obliquely on sides of stems, but some Skimmers perch horizontally on tips of stems. Many Skimmers fold their forelegs behind their heads and do not use them to hold a perch except in windy conditions. Skimmers and Clubtails may rest the sides of one or more legs against a perch and not use the claws, for an unimpeded takeoff. Different species perch at different heights above the ground or the water, and thus partition the airspace to some extent. Some Skimmers, called **Pennants**, allow the breeze to lift their wings, flaglike. Other Skimmers, called **Gliders**, perch little and feed while gliding on their widened hindwings. In this book "weed" is commonly used for perches, because there is no other commonly used short term for nonwoody plants.

TEMPERATURE EFFECTS

Most species of dragonflies seem "solar powered," because they disappear and reappear as the sun is hidden or uncovered by clouds, as if a switch was thrown in their brains. On cold days, dragonflies **Bask** by holding their bodies perpendicular to the sun, and species that do not ordinarily perch on flat surfaces may do so to bask. When temperature drops, many dragonflies become wary and will fly for cover at the least disturbance. Territorial males and egg-laying females of many species can prolong their stay at water by **Wing-whirring**, using the heat from their shivering flight muscles to maintain optimum flight capability. Some spring species of dragonflies are noticeably hairy on the thorax, which has some insulating function.

On hot days, some Clubtails and Skimmers raise the abdomen, a behavior called **Obelisking** (see Plate 10). The warmer the temperature, the higher the abdomen is elevated, like the needle on a gauge. The raised abdomen reduces the body surface exposed to the sun, as can be seen by the smaller shadow then. However, some King Skimmers raise their abdomens perpendicular to the sun to *gain* heat, and some dragonflies raise their abdomen as a threat or as part of their normal perching posture.

Percher dragonflies, those that spend more time perching than flying, mainly gain heat from the sun, but **Flyer** dragonflies also gain heat generated by their flight muscles. In hot weather flyers are most active early in the morning or in late afternoon, and they hover more during the cooler parts of the day. Varying temperatures during a daily cycle can produce a "Jekyll and Hyde" behavior. For example, the same dragonfly may perch on the bank early in the morning and be very wary then; later in the morning it may perch on sticks in the open, while in the hot afternoon it may perch in shade under overhanging branches and be unwary.

Some Darners can change body coloration as an aid to temperature control. Their blue markings are produced by tiny refractive granules in their skin cells that scatter light and help prevent overheating. Other dark granules migrate toward the surface of both bodies and eyes at cool temperatures and at night. The dark purple or gray color thus produced hides the dragonfly when it is not flying, and allows faster absorption of the sun's heat.

FEEDING

There seems to be a trend toward feeding on tiny prey in the more advanced dragonflies. Petaltails and Clubtails may capture large prey, Darners and Spiketails often eat medium-size prey, while Cruisers, Emeralds, and Skimmers commonly feed on aerial plankton. When large prey is taken, it is eaten head first. Perchers hunt from perches, often flying out to capture prey and returning to the same perch. Flyers may circle a limited area while prey lasts, or may cruise for miles, feeding along the way. Where prey is abundant, flyers can quickly gather in swarms to feed on it. Dragonflies in feeding swarms usually ignore each other, but some swarms are of males only, indicating that any female entering the swarm is likely to be mated instead of allowed to feed. Female-only swarms are not known.

MIGRATION

Our only migratory dragonflies are some species of Darners and Skimmers that breed in still water. They may fly in swarms, but appear to gather due to features of the landscape, and little interaction occurs between individuals, although some swarms contain tandem pairs. A swarm may form because of good breeding conditions, in which case its members are mostly juveniles. Northward migrations in the spring, usually behind warm fronts from late March to June, are far less noticeable than fall migrations. Migrations appear not to be due to prey shortages, but possibly are caused in some cases by restlessness due to internal parasites such as flukes. The most massive migrations are seen following cold fronts between late July and mid-October, peaking in September, usually along lakeshores and coasts, often on peninsulas, although some migrants cross the Gulf of Mexico! Migration is certainly an area of knowledge where amateur observers can make a great contribution, including collection of voucher specimens and a program of individual marking and relocating, as in banding birds. No North American dragonfly species routinely hibernate as adults.

TERRITORIALITY

Some perchers of either sex defend a feeding perch, and flyers sometimes defend a feeding area. Territoriality in dragonflies, though, applies primarily to a male defending three-dimensional mating space over the water. No examples of female dragonflies defending mating territories are known. Male dragonflies defend a territory mostly against other males of their species, but some defend it also against similar species, or even against all other dragonflies. The latter category, of course, excludes females of their own species, which are welcomed with open claws! As population densities increase, male territories may become smaller and more compressed, and each male defends his more fiercely. At very high population densities, none of the males can defend a zone and territoriality breaks down. Cruisers, Spiketails, and most Clubtails seem not to be territorial, while Regal and Swamp Darners do not wait for females at water at all. Some Striped Emeralds and Mosaic Darners apparently gather on tops of hills for mating, a phenomenon called hilltopping.

Males defending a mating territory may perch in the territory or may continuously fly over it, all day if they can, or only for a few minutes at a time. Species with short-term territories typically do not feed while on territory. Male Skimmers with a brightly colored abdomen often raise it in a threat display. Some Skimmers decide who deserves to hold a territory with high-speed parallel flights sometimes lasting several minutes. Male territoriality means that only a small fraction of males will have a chance to mate; most others are forced to disperse.

MATING

The only North American dragonflies known to have a courtship, in which a female has a clear choice of whether or not to accept a male, are the Amberwings, although the Neon Skimmer also has a rudimentary courtship. The Yellow-Legged Meadowhawk has a type of after-tandem courtship.

Mating among dragonflies is complicated and unique. The male flies above the female and grasps her head and thorax with his legs, then curves his abdomen to grasp the top rear part of her head between his terminal abdominal appendages (cerci and epiproct). He then releases his legs and the pair is now said to be in **Tandem**. The male curls his abdomen downward and forward, so that sperm from the pore on the underside of S9 can be transferred to his accessory genitalia on the underside of S2. This is called intramale sperm transfer, and males of some species do this before capturing a female. He then straightens his abdomen and the female bends her abdomen downward and forward to receive the sperm into her reproductive opening on the underside of S8. The pair is now said to be in the **Wheel Position** (see Plate 5), which lasts as little as 3 seconds in some species to more than an hour in others (much more data needed on time and location). For species that mate in flight, the male may raise his abdomen to bring the wings of the female into a more horizontal plane so that she can assist the flight. Rarely, chains of 3 or even 4 dragonflies are formed when two or more males clasp each other mistakenly by the head.

Just one mating probably provides a female with a lifetime sperm supply, but dragonflies provide one of the best examples of the phenomenon of sperm competition. The penis of male dragonflies is highly modified and can scoop out or push to the side any sperm already present in a female. Most of the time spent in "copulation" usually involves removal of sperm, with injection only at the end of the process.

GUARDING

Males of the Common Green Darner and some Skimmers, especially nonterritorial species, retain the female in tandem after mating, and travel with her while she lays her eggs. In this **Contact Guarding,** the male prevents other males access to his mate and acts like an aerial towtruck, doing most of the work of flying; he also picks the egg-laying sites. Females of species that usually lay eggs in tandem can also lay eggs alone when no male is present. In some other Skimmers, the male perches or hovers above the female as she lays her eggs, and drives away any other male that tries to mate with her. This is noncontact guarding, or **Hover-guarding,** which allows the male to defend his territory better and gives him the option of mating with a second female, should one appear. When males are too abundant, females cannot lay all their eggs, and may even be injured in a frenzied melee. Most dragonflies other than Skimmers have long mating times, and, after their first mating, the females of these families commonly attempt to sneak to the water to lay eggs without male interference.

EGG LAYING

Egg laying is also known as oviposition ("eggpositioning"—see Plate 5). In Petaltails and a few Darners the female egg-laying device (ovipositor) has blades and is used to insert eggs into the soil, but in most Darners the blades insert eggs into plant tissue. Although eggs deposited this way are well protected, they can be more easily found by parasites, and the stationary female is very exposed to fish and frog predation. Female Spiketails, and those Emeralds and Skimmers with spoutlike ovipositors, hover or fly slowly while poking eggs into mud or algae mats. Clubtails, Cruisers, and most Skimmers use flying contact egg laying, in which the female dips the abdominal tip to the water surface while hovering or flying, often at high speed. Female Skimmers with lateral flanges on S8 use splash egg laying to throw drops of water containing eggs onto plants or the bank. Rarer types of egg laying include noncontact flying egg laying, used by a few Clubtails and Skimmers; in this type of egg laying, the female drops eggs into the water from the air, usually as she hovers with an arched or bent abdomen. In some Meadowhawks and Tropical Dashers, the perched female drops eggs or deposits clusters of eggs on plants in or near the water. Female Baskettails have to make only one strafing pass at the water to lay an egg-filled jelly string.

Habitats

Flowing Water

Running water habitats form a continuum, but for the purposes of this book several types are defined below. Subtypes can be described by current speed, temperature, turbidity, and bottom type.

1. **Seeps.** Water oozing out of a slope.
2. **Trickles.** Definitely moving water collected from a seep.
3. **Rivulets.** Water collected from several trickles, in forest completely shaded.
4. **Streams.** Water collected from several rivulets, wide enough in forest to be sunny part of the day. **Riffles** are shallow areas over a rough bottom where the water visibly ripples. Riffles grade into **Rapids** where white-water waves form over boulders. Stream and river dragonflies are commonly attracted to riffles and rapids and tend to congregate there, especially where quiet water slides into the waves of a riffle.
5. **Rivers.** Water collected from several streams, in forested flatlands sunny most of the day.
6. **Big Rivers.** The biggest rivers, water collected from several smaller rivers, now commonly used as shipping channels.

Still Water

1. **Ponds.** Commonly have much emergent, floating, and submergent vegetation and no wave action. Temporary or semipermanent ponds may be fishless, allowing certain species to breed there. **Ditches** and **Canals** in which water has little flow are essentially linear ponds.
2. **Borrow Pits.** Ponds formed by human construction activities, with soil and rock "borrowed" for filling in other areas. New borrow pits form habitat for species that do not compete well against species of long-established ponds.

3. **Bogs and Fens.** Bogs are poor in mineral nutrients, and are partially filled by *Sphagnum* (peat) moss, which makes the water acid, restricting the vegetative structure and thus indirectly the species of dragonflies breeding there. Common in Canada, where large areas are called **Muskegs**, bogs become increasingly rare south of the northernmost United States. Southern bogs are usually in mineral-poor, sandy areas. **Fens** are grassy seepages that are less acid but have more mineral nutrients than bogs.

4. **Lakes.** Water bodies large enough for wave action to oxygenate the water.

5. **Marshes.** Water bodies nearly covered with herbaceous vegetation.

6. **Swamps.** Water bodies nearly covered with woody vegetation, such as bald cypress trees.

In the arid west, some species of dragonflies are not too fussy about their habitat, and will be found at nearly any open water. Successful breeding at a habitat is confirmed only by larval skins above water, or newly emerged adults.

Flight Season and Abundance

Some species of dragonflies emerge as adults all year as long as the weather is warm enough. These species, commonly called summer species, might have an all-year season in southern Florida but only a three-month season in the far north. Other dragonflies emerge during a period of only a few days, usually in the spring, so they are commonly called spring species. Many of the rarer species in the east fly in spring, while the best time to see most southwestern species is during the summer monsoon rains of August and September. Species of a few groups of dragonflies, such as Mosaic Darners, Hanging Clubtails, Striped Emeralds, and Meadowhawks emerge relatively late in the growing season. The best time to search for a particular species is about a third of the way through its flight season.

Often, the first individuals seen during the flight season of a species are males; at least in some species, they begin emerging earlier than females. Males also usually mature in fewer days than females. Generally, the last survivors in the flight season are females, partly because they probably can resorb egg yolk for sustenance during periods of inclement weather. Additionally, males of most species do not eat while they are on territory, and exhaust themselves in territorial battles.

If the habitat of a dragonfly is rare, then although the species may be common in small areas, the species is rare in the landscape as a whole; such species are termed **Local** in this book. **Stray** refers to species that are not known to breed north of Mexico. **Rare** species are usually those with a rare type of habitat, which may be due to human activity, and/or a small geographic range. In some species, larvae are common but adults are rarely seen because of their short flight season, furtive behavior, or habit of perching in trees. **Scarce** species are those for which a special search has to be made. **Uncommon** species are also noteworthy whenever found. An observer expects to see **Common** species, and **Abundant** species dominate common habitats. A species is usually much less common at the edge of its range.

Geographic Distribution

Dragonflies can be called eastern if they do not range much beyond the western border of the eastern deciduous forest, which occurs in part from eastern Kansas to eastern Texas. Many southeastern species range far to the north, to about New Jersey, along the Atlantic Coast. Southeastern stream-breeding species do not range inland much beyond the fall line, where the Piedmont hills give way to the coastal plain, because of faster water currents and rockier bottoms above the fall line. Northern species occur primarily in the boreal forest biome, but extend southward at high elevations in the Appalachian or Rocky Mountains. Western species generally occur from the Rocky Mountains westward, with a few species restricted to the Pacific Coast states. Other species are typical of the hot and arid southwest, from about central Texas westward. A few dragonfly species occur in smaller areas, such as New England, the Great Lakes area, the northern Great Plains or the southern Great Plains, and some are found in only a part of one state. A number of tropical species barely enter our area in southern Florida and along the Mexican border.

Canadian and Alaskan dragonflies are generally the same as in the northern contiguous states of the United States. Only 5 species, all inhabitants of cold northern bogs, have not been found south of the U.S./Canadian transcontinental border: Whitehouse's, Muskeg, and Treeline Emeralds, Azure Darner, and Canada Whiteface. Some species barely enter Canada from the south, in southernmost British Columbia or southern Ontario. In the far north, no dragonflies breed in the large rivers, and seldom in the tundra. No dragonflies are known from the Aleutian or Pribilof Islands, or Greenland, and any capture of a dragonfly there would be of great scientific interest.

Conservation

About 15% of North American dragonfly species are at risk of extinction in the foreseeable future, at least outside of reserves. The Pacific Coast, Florida, the New England Coast, and the Central Gulf of Mexico Coast each contains concentrations of species endemic to those areas. Some of the habitats most worthy of preservation include pristine streams, arid-land streams and ponds, sand-bottomed lakes, bogs, and fens.

A few human activities benefit some dragonflies, such as pond building. Newly created ponds help certain species that cannot compete well with species of long-established ponds. On the other hand, people typically introduce fish into ponds, which greatly reduces dragonfly populations (up to 80-90% in some studies), and eliminates some species entirely. "Cleaning up" a pond by mowing its borders and removing all the aquatic vegetation pretty much sterilizes it for most dragonflies. If to this is added a flock of ducks augmented by artificial feeding, you can forget about having dragonflies breed at that pond. A problem in some areas are oil ponds, which are even more attractive to dragonflies than water ponds, and which trap large numbers of dragonflies.

Stream dragonflies have been much more severely affected by human activities than have pond species. Pesticides kill dragonfly larvae, and sewage and organic wastes from industries cause bacterial growth, which reduces the oxygen content of the water. Fertilizer runoff from farmlands and lawns causes algae to grow that use excessive oxygen at night, and shade out submerged plants during the day. In this process of eutrophication the water changes from clear to green, and the bottom becomes muckier as the algae die and decompose.

Silt from eroding land changes bottom characteristics and blocks light from plants. Siltation and even destruction of the streambed is especially severe where livestock are allowed to graze the banks, forest is clear-cut to the banks, or fields are plowed to the banks. Dredging, ditching, and channelization pretty much destroy a stream biologically. A buffer zone of forest 100-plus ft. wide on each side of a stream will help prevent erosion. General deforestation of the watershed of a stream leads to reduced water-holding capacity of the land, resulting in alternating floods that wash away dragonfly larvae, and droughts that reduce the area in which they live. Dam construction results in rare stream dragonflies being replaced by common pond species. The worst habitats are reservoirs with fluctuating water levels, which prevent aquatic plants from growing at the edges. Also, below dams the strong, even current over the years creates a rockier bottom for hundreds of miles downstream. The larger a stream, the greater the cumulative effect of the above influences.

Special dragonfly habitats, such as forest seeps or bogs, should be protected from lumbering, grazing, or development, although they might need periodic burning after the flight season. The drying of springs due to excessive pumping from underground aquifers is a big problem in the arid west. Fortunately, a sanctuary of just a few acres may be enough to protect a population of rare dragonflies and associated plants and animals. However, the sanctuary must encompass not only the breeding habitat of the species concerned but also its feeding and overnight roosting requirements. Extensive sanctuaries just for dragonflies have been developed in the United Kingdom, and especially in Japan.

The effect of boat traffic on dragonflies has not been studied, but a boat wake at the wrong time could kill many dragonflies that were emerging along the banks. Boat traffic also increases the turbidity of the water, affecting the growth of water plants, so no-wake zones are a good idea where channels are narrow. Heated water from power stations (thermal pollution) sometimes interferes with the life cycle of dragonflies by causing larvae to transform to adults at inappropriate times.

The dragonfly conservation action plan (Moore, 1997) stated that "... any nation which protects significant examples of all its main habitat types will succeed in conserving most of its dragonfly species." and "The risk of doing the wrong thing through lack of scientific knowledge is much less than the risk of delay."

Backyard Ponds for Dragonflies

A garden pond for dragonflies should be sunny, as large as possible, 2-plus ft. deep, with a shallow berm with emergent vegetation and perching sticks along the edges, and **fishless** if you wish dragonflies to actually breed in the pond. Other vertebrate predators, such as ducks and large frogs, are also best kept out of a dragonfly pond. If mosquito larvae become a problem, they can be controlled by a *Bacillus thuringiensis* ("Mosquito Dunk") cake, which is said not to harm dragonfly larvae. Your backyard pond is virtually certain to attract some common dragonfly species, but is unlikely to be a habitat for rare species. However, some partially shaded backyard ponds in Texas have attracted the "Purple Martin" of the dragonflies, the uncommon and brilliant red Neon Skimmer. Creation of a backyard bog is worth a try.

Photography

Most of the photographs in this book were made with a 35 mm single-lens-reflex (SLR) camera with a 55 or 105 mm macro lens for close-ups. This type of camera uses the same lens for viewing, focusing, and light measurement. A 200 mm macro lens or a 300 mm telephoto with a screw-on close-up lens is good, except that a tripod must usually be used. A tripod is necessary to obtain the sharpest photos with any size lens, but is inconvenient and time consuming to set up. A leg of the tripod regularly bumps the vine that is connected to the perch on which the dragonfly is sitting. Bracing a stick against the camera to use as a monopod can work well. I find it easiest to preset the focus for the size image I want, then slowly and smoothly approach the dragonfly with the camera at my eye until it is in sharp focus, then press the shutter. During the approach it is usually best not to let your shadow cross over the dragonfly. Any subsequent adjustments or advancing the film are made with slow, smooth movements. Some photographers prefer a motor drive to eliminate the thumb movements of advancing the film. If you can get close enough to a dragonfly, so as to blot out a third or so of its field of view, it regards you as a distant tree line or cloud bank, and your movements are no longer very threatening.

As film speed or sensitivity to light increases—from ISO 25 to 400, for example—the film gets grainier, resulting in fuzzier images. I find ISO 100 a good compromise between speed and graininess. Using ISO 100 film in full sunlight, I use a shutter opening of about f8 at 1/125 second, or f5.6 at 1/250 second if I am in a shaky position or if there is a breeze. An electronic flash (best is a flash dedicated to your camera and Through-the-Lens (TTL) light metering) solves the problem of camera shake, allows the use of fine-grained film, and allows great depth of field. Unfortunately flash seldom looks as natural as sunlight. If the background is not close, it will not be lit by the flash and will appear black.

The most challenging thing in dragonfly photography is to get both head and tip of abdomen in focus at the same time. A depth-of-field preview button on the camera is a useful feature if you have time to use it; it allows you to see before the shutter is triggered how much of the subject and background will be in focus. For good photos of dragonflies, you also need to pay attention to the background, ensuring that it is contrasting but not too confusing, and that dark body parts do not blend with shadows. Since dragonflies may not be quite up to speed when they first become active in the morning, that is often the best time to photograph them. It is difficult to get everything right for a photo of a wild dragonfly; therefore, many of the photos in this book were posed. Sometimes a dragonfly is stunned by the net during capture and will allow a photo or two, or it can be cooled in a refrigerator or ice chest and a couple of photos can be taken—perhaps, before it leaves. The most essential ingredient in all dragonfly photography is patience.

Dragonfly Societies

The International Odonata Research Institute (IORI) has some books and supplies for sale, and information on the societies is listed below. Its current address is: International Odonata Research Institute, c/o Florida Division of Plant Industry, 1911 SW 34 St., Gainesville, FL 32608; e-mail: iori@afn.org; Web site (links to many other good sites): http://www.afn.org/~iori/ Directions for collecting techniques and specimen preservation are given on the IORI and other Web sites, and in Dunkle (1989).

An e-mail list, **ODONATA,** was established in 1999. To enroll, contact D. R. Paulson at: dpaulson@ups.edu

You may wish to join the International Dragonfly Society FSIO (Foundation Societas Internationalis Odonatologica). Members each year receive 4 issues of the journal *Odonatologica* and 2 issues of the smaller journal *Notulae Odonatologicae*. The society is currently headquartered in The Netherlands, and dues fluctuate with the value of the guilder (Hfl) relative to the U.S. dollar.

The Worldwide Dragonfly Association (WDA) currently has its headquarters in Germany, publishing *The International Journal of Odonatology* (= "*Pantala*"), and its twice-yearly newsletter *Agrion*. Dues with the journal are about $45.

The Dragonfly Society of the Americas (DSA) publishes the quarterly newsletter *Argia* and the journal *Bulletin of American Odonatology*. Current DSA annual dues are $15, plus $15 for the Bulletin.

The Ohio Odonata Society (OOS) publishes a newsletter *The Ohio Dragon-flier*, as does the Michigan Odonata Survey (MOS), which publishes the newsletter *Williamsonia*.

Dragonfly Body Parts

In the text below, the scientific term for a structure is given in parentheses following the term used in this book. **Dorsal** refers to the back or top side, **Ventral** to the underside or bottom. **Anterior** means toward the front, **Posterior** toward the rear. **Lateral** refers to right and left sides; in this book, lateral usually refers to one side of the body, what would be seen in a side view. These words can be combined—for example,

PARTS OF A DRAGONFLY
(MALE FINE-LINED EMERALD)

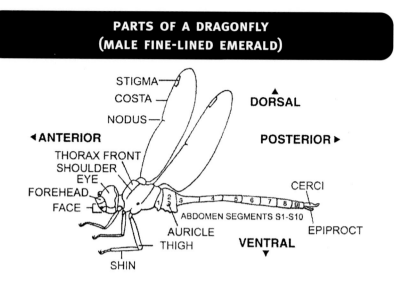

STIGMA
COSTA
NODUS
▲ DORSAL
◀ ANTERIOR
POSTERIOR ▶
THORAX FRONT
SHOULDER
EYE
FOREHEAD
FACE
CERCI
ABDOMEN SEGMENTS S1-S10
AURICLE
THIGH
EPIPROCT
VENTRAL ▼
SHIN

dorsolateral—to designate intermediate locations. **Stripes** extend along the longitudinal axis of a body part; **Bands** and **Rings** lie perpendicular to the longitudinal axis. In describing coloration, the second color is the main one; thus yellow-green means more green than yellow.

Head

The large eyes (compound eyes) of dragonflies consist of many small eyes fused together, forming facets on their surfaces. One can tell how good a dragonfly's vision is in different directions by looking into its eye and observing the size of the largest black spot (pseudopupil). The larger the spot, the better the insect's vision in that direction. While some dragonflies feed until late in the evening, no truly nocturnal dragonfly is known, probably because such a dragonfly would become bat food. The dorsal facets in the dragonfly eye are larger and usually darker in color than the ventral ones. In this book, eye color refers to the dorsal eye color unless stated otherwise. Clubtails and Skimmers often rapidly rotate their heads to scan moving objects. Dragonflies can see all the colors we see, plus ultraviolet light and polarized light, and can detect the flickering of light at twice the rate that we can (80 versus 40 per second). Presumably, they use these abilities to see ultraviolet color patterns invisible to us, navigate by the pattern of polarized light in the sky, and see the pattern on fast-beating wings. Still-water dragonflies probably find water by its ultraviolet horizontally polarized reflection, stream dragonflies by the shimmering of ripples and waves. Sometimes female dragonflies mistake a shiny car for water and lay eggs on it. In addition to the 2 large compound eyes, dragonflies have 3 small "simple" eyes (ocelli) set like jewels into the dorsal anterior part (vertex) of the head. A comb of flat bristles on each front leg is used to brush dust and water off the eyes.

The tiny antennae of dragonflies indicate that they have a poor sense of smell, but the antennae probably function as airspeed sensors. Dragonflies are apparently deaf and do not respond to sounds, so talking will not disturb them.

The **Forehead** (dorsal surface of the frons) is often colored differently from the **Face** (labrum, clypeus, and anterior surface of the frons), and is used to recognize potential mates in face-to-face encounters. The toothy jaws, which move side to side, are enclosed by an upper lip (labrum) and a 3-lobed lower lip or **Chin** (labium). Dragonflies appear to catch most prey directly in the mouth, but larger prey is caught by the bristly legs, then stuffed into the jaws (see Plate 6). That tiny prey has been caught is revealed when the jaws are chomping after a dragonfly returns from a foray. Dragonflies drink by flopping into the water 3 times; for unknown reasons, they rarely do this more or less than 3 times. They use the same flopping behavior for cooling and cleaning—for example, females often wash off any remaining eggs after egg laying in this way.

The dorsal posterior part of the head, ridged crosswise in most dragonflies, is called the **Occiput**. This is commonly modified in females, because the male abdominal appendages fit over it during mating. In female Clubtails, spines may occur on the top of the head, occiput (**Occipital Horns**), or rear of the head behind the eyes (**Postocular Horns**).

Thorax

The thorax consists of 3 segments, each with a pair of legs, but the first segment (prothorax) is small and necklike. The term **Thorax** in this book refers to the fused second and third segments (synthorax), form-

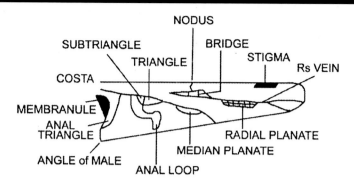

ing a backward-slanting box with pairs of forewings **(FW)** and hind wings **(HW)**. The slant of the thorax allows the dragonfly to reach a vertical stem with its legs while the wings are free of contact for a quick takeoff. The anterior sloping surface (mesepisterna) is the **Front** of the thorax; the "corners" (humeral sutures) at each side of the front are the **Shoulders**. A full series of dark stripes on the thorax would include, from anterior to posterior, the **Midfrontal, Anterior Shoulder, Posterior Shoulder, Anterior Lateral, Posterior Lateral,** and **Lower Rear**.

The wings are a double layer of membrane supported by a network of veins, which are tubes carrying blood, air ducts, and nerves. The membranous parts of the wing between the veins **(Cells)** are also alive, as indicated by the white wax deposits that accumulate on the wings of some species of King Skimmers. At the base of the hind wing outside the veins is a narrow strip of membrane called the **Membranule**, which may be white or brown but is not counted as a wing marking. The strong anterior vein of each wing is called the **Costa**. Near the middle of the wing the costa joins other large veins at a slight notch called the **Nodus** (pronounced *"node-us"*). Near the base of the hind wing a loop of veins, the **Anal Loop**, is usually present, and this is of different shapes in different families. At about 1/5 length of each wing is a **Triangle** (or discoidal cell) of veins, bordered on the side nearest the base by another triangle of veins, called the **Subtriangle** (often absent in HW). Narrow areas of the wings known as the **Median Planate** and

Radial Planate are useful in identifying a few species of Skimmers by noting whether they contain 1 or 2 rows of cells. The median planate is basal of the nodus, the radial planate beyond the nodus. Each wing has a blood-filled blister called the **Stigma** (pterostigma) near the tip. The stigma is often brightly colored and used in signaling mates or rivals.

Each leg consists of several segments, the longest being the **Thigh** (femur) and **Lower Leg** (tibia), and ends in 2 claws. The outer surface of the lower leg is called the **Shin** in this book. During flight the forelegs are folded up behind the head, while the other two pairs are folded parallel with the longitudinal body axis. The legs of all of our dragonflies except some species of Clubtails and Skimmers are brown or black.

Abdomen

The abdomen consists of 10 segments, denoted in this book from S1 at the base to S10 at the tip. S1 and S10 are often short, while S2 and S3 are somewhat inflated. S7, S8, and S9 are enlarged in some species and form a **Club**. It is often easiest to identify abdominal segments by counting forward from S10. Many species are narrowed at S3, which makes a convenient starting place to count rearward. The designation "spots on S4-S7 or S8" is read as "spots on S4 to S7 or S8", and means that there are spots on all segments beginning with S4 and ending on either S7 or S8. In some Skimmers the basal segments of the abdomen are transparent dorsally, probably allowing the sun to warm the intestine and gonads, which are insulated by air sacs, by a greenhouse effect for faster digestion and sexual maturation.

Sex Differences

Females usually are larger, and their abdomen is stouter, more cylindrical, more bluntly tipped, and has larger pale markings, especially on the sides. In species with abdominal clubs, the club is relatively smaller in females. The egg-laying devices of females are called **Ovipositors** ("oh-vee-*pos*-it-ores"). The ovipositor of Petaltails and Darners contains 2 pairs of sawlike blades that are housed in a ventrally bulging sheath on S9. While dragonflies do not sting, occasionally a female Darner will try to lay an egg with a painful jab into the leg of someone wading in the water. Female Spiketails, and some others, have a spikelike or triangular spout-shaped ovipositor extending from the underside of S9. Also on S9 of females are a pair of tiny ventral feelers (**Styli**, "style-eye"), which provide sensory information for egg laying. Female dragonflies "without" an ovipositor have it reduced to a **Subgenital Plate** (also called a vulvar lamina or vulvar scale), which is usually notched or split in the midline, attached to S8, and extends posteriorly under S9. Species with long plates tend to accumulate a large mass of eggs while they are perched before flying over water. (While only females have ovipositors and subgenital plates, expressions like "female ovipositor" are used in the text to alert the reader that the discussion has changed to females only.) Females of some Skimmers have lateral flaps on S8 that they use to help splash eggs onto the shore.

Females have a pair of appendages at the tip of S10 called **Cerci** ("*sir*-see"; singular: **cercus**, "cir-cus"), which may be small and pointed or large and leaflike. In some Darners the female cerci routinely break off during egg laying. Males have larger cerci plus a ventral **Epiproct** ("*ep*-ee-prahkt") used like a set of vertical claspers for holding the head of the female during mating. The epiproct fits on top of the female's head, and the two cerci press against the rear of her head. In certain species, mostly Darners and Clubtails, spines on the male appendages gouge the females' eyes or even punch holes in their heads. The exact shape of the male appendages, and sometimes the contact points on the female's head, are often used in hand-lens identification of species. The epiproct is present in females as a small tab between the cerci. Except in Skimmers and Green Darners, males have a nonmovable lateral flap (auricle) on each side of S2, and the hind wing base is "cutout" to clear the flap, forming a basal corner on each hind wing. The auricles are used by the female to help achieve proper orientation during mating.

Male dragonflies have a set of accessory genitalia on the underside of S2 and S3. Seen from the side, the lower margin of S2 makes a definite angle with S3 in males. In Petaltails, Clubtails, and Spiketails, a full set of accessory genitalia is present that some authors have compared to a Swiss army knife. These include two pairs of hooks, the **Anterior and Posterior Hamules** ("*ham*-yules"), plus a penis guard and a four-segmented penis, which has an expanded **Hood** at its base. The forward edge of the genital pocket under S2 is called the **Anterior Lamina** (*"lam*-in-ah"). In Darners the posterior hamules are vestigial, while the anterior hamules are adapted to clamp and hold the sharp blades of the female ovipositor. In Cruisers, Emeralds, and Skimmers the anterior hamules are vestigial or absent, but the ventral-posterior corners of S2 are expanded as **Genital Lobes**.

Skimmers often have different body coloration between males and females, or even a different wing pattern. As in many birds, mature males are usually more brightly colored than females and juvenile males.

ABOUT THE SPECIES ACCOUNTS

Names

Practically no common names are used by the public for individual species of dragonflies. Thus this book uses English names, newly standardized by the Dragonfly Society of the Americas. Many scientists will not know these names, so to communicate with them it is better to use scientific names. "Common" in English names means that a species is widespread rather than uniformly common throughout its range. Scientific names consist of two words, italicized to make them stand out from the rest of a text. The first word is capitalized and is called the genus ("*jean*-us", plural genera, "jen-ur-ah"); the second word is the species ("*spee*-sees") adjective. Some species have subspecies, denoted by a third word. In a few cases, the concept of a subgenus, indicated by a name in parentheses, is useful. For example, the name *Gomphus (Phanogomphus) cavillaris brimleyi* arises from the situation that the genus *Gomphus* has 38 North American species, including 17 species of the subgenus *(Phanogomphus)*, including the species *cavillaris* with its subspecies *brimleyi*. Where a full name is clear from its context, it is permissible to abbreviate the first words, as *G. (P.) c. brimleyi*.

Identification

The size range of North American dragonflies is approximately 1 to 5 inches in body length, measured from the face to the tip of the abdominal appendages, and subjectively categorized in this book as very small, small, small-medium, medium, medium-large, large, and very large. Size is given as an average length, and is usually stated only numerically and without adjectives for medium-size species, and for species whose size is typical of their group. Measurements in inches are easily converted to millimeters (mm) by multiplying by 25. For species with a long flight season, generally the largest individuals emerge first, and the size of individuals decreases slightly as the season progresses. The standard postal abbreviations are used for U.S. states. The Identification section generally includes only those features that are visible through binoculars at a distance of a few feet or farther. Phrases like "Cannot be told from . . ." means *in the field* without capture, unless implied or specified otherwise.

Structural Features

For species that are difficult to identify in the field, extra information in case a specimen can be handled is given.

Variation

If a species has geographic variation, such as subspecies, that information is stated here.

Similar Species

This section usually includes only the few most similar species, discussed in order of decreasing similarity.

Habitat

Refers to the breeding habitat, where males wait for females in most dragonflies.

Season

Flight seasons are highly variable, depending on latitude, yearly weather, and elevation above sea level.

Comments

Miscellaneous information, but especially what to look for when the species is away from water, and behavior of males at water, including, in sequence: naming; perching, feeding, and other activities away from water; territoriality and other behaviors of males at water; and extralimital range. Space limitations usually prevent adding data (when known) on overnight roosting, food, maturation time, mating, guarding, and egg laying, unless particularly unusual in some way.

SPECIES ACCOUNTS

Petaltails
(family Petaluridae)

Mostly black or gray large dragonflies usually seen perching on tree trunks. They show a unique combination of characteristics: widely separated eyes as in the Clubtails, a female ovipositor with blades as in the Darners, and long parallel-sided stigmas. The male cerci are expanded and flattened, like a flower petal, particularly in Old World species. These are ancient dragonflies, with only 10 surviving species scattered around the world, of which we have 2, one eastern, one western.

Gray Petaltail
(genus *Tachopteryx*)

This genus contains the single fascinating species below.

Gray Petaltail *Tachopteryx thoreyi* Plate 1

IDENTIFICATION   3.0 in., eastern, local. Our only large mostly gray dragonfly, and one of the few that routinely perch on tree trunks. Thorax gray with black stripes, and abdomen black with gray blotches. Note separated eyes and linear stigma. Eyes dark brown, becoming gray at maturity.

SIMILAR SPECIES   None.

HABITAT   Hillside seepages in deciduous forest.

SEASON   Early March to mid-June in FL, early June to mid-Aug. in NJ. About 2 months at any locale, primarily before trees leaf out in spring.

COMMENTS   Takes large prey. Males perch in sunny spots on anything substantial near seeps to defend a one-day territory and wait for females. They also search for females by flying up tree trunks one after another.

Black Petaltails
(genus *Tanypteryx*)

This genus includes only the species below and the Japanese Petaltail *T. pryeri*.

Black Petaltail *Tanypteryx hageni* Plate 1

IDENTIFICATION	2.3 in., northwestern, local. Medium-large, body black with small yellow spots. Eyes brown and widely separated, and stigma linear.
SIMILAR SPECIES	Pacific Spiketail has yellow thoracic stripes and aqua eyes. Female Mosaic Darners have eyes in wide contact.
HABITAT	Sunny, permanent, trickling, mossy fens and bogs at up to 6800 ft.
SEASON	Mid-May to early Sept.
COMMENTS	Juveniles are wary and perch on tree trunks, while mature males are unwary and perch on anything in the bog except leaves but including people. Males are present in bogs from late morning to evening shade, and defend small territories for 10–30 min. against all other dragonflies.

Darners
(family Aeshnidae)

Darners include our largest dragonflies, carrying abdomens long and slender beyond the base, like darning needles. They are flyers, but perch by hanging vertically. Most are brown or black, striped and spotted with blue, green, or yellow, while the eyes are large and meet in a seam on top of the head. In many species scars can be seen on the females' eyes, showing where the males' epiproct held her during mating. Females have an ovipositor with blades, used in most species to deposit eggs in plant tissues up to the length of the abdomen below the waterline. Each HW bears a rounded anal loop, while the maximum wing pattern among our species is a small brown spot at the base of each wing. Known life cycles are usually 1 year, up to 6 years in the far north. Of the nearly 500 species worldwide, 39 occur in North America.

Green Darners
(genus *Anax*)

This group includes nearly all of our Darners that have an unmarked green thorax. Males differ from all our other Darners by lacking auricles on S2 and the correlated inner angle on the HW. Of the 28 species worldwide, 4 are North American.

Common Green Darner *Anax junius* Plate 1

IDENTIFICATION 3.0 in., the most common and widespread Darner in the U.S., ranging into southern Canada. Males easily recognized by all-green thorax, and abdomen with wide blue lateral stripes is carried straight in flight. At cool temperatures the blue becomes purple or even green, remaining blue last on S2. Top of S2 blue in males, brown in females. Abdomen usually has sides gray-green in females, reddish brown to reddish violet in juveniles. The scarce **Blue Form** female has a mostly blue abdomen. A black spot enclosed by a blue semicircle forms a target- or bull's-eye-like mark on the forehead. Additional field marks are the yellow posterior rim of the eyes, and white base of S3. Overhead, note yellow-tinted wings and comparatively thick abdomen. It is our only Darner that lays eggs in tandem, and it is the only Darner other than Mosaic Darners in western Canada.

BODY FEATURES Male cerci each have a pointed spine at outer corner, versus cerci without spines and broad at tips in male Giant Darner and with paper-thin upturned tips in male Amazon Darner. Female Common Green our only Darner with a pair of blunt teeth on occiput.

SIMILAR SPECIES Giant Darner of the southwest appears twice as large in flight; male carries abdomen arched and has rear halves of S3–S7 brown. Amazon Darner has side of abdomen blotched. In the east check Comet Darner, and in south FL check Mangrove and Blue-Faced Darners. Great Pondhawk of the far south is much smaller, with a banded abdomen.

HABITAT Most still, marshy waters, including temporary or slightly brackish habitats, particularly fishless ones.

SEASON All year in south FL, mid-April to mid-Oct. in Canada. Migrants are often the earliest dragonflies to appear in the north.

COMMENTS Often perches and roosts low in weeds. Active from early morning to dark, often gathering in swarms where prey is abundant. Males sporadically patrol irregular territories at a height of about 3 ft., and have been filmed ramming or torpedoing other males flying in tandem with a female. Our only Darner that lays eggs in tandem. Recorded from every state in the U.S., the FL Keys and Dry Tortugas, ranging south to Honduras, including Baja California, and in Hawaii, Bahamas, Bermuda, and the West Indies southeast to Martinique. Strays also recorded from Tahiti, the east coast of Asia, and Britain.

Giant Darner *Anax walsinghami* Plate 1

IDENTIFICATION Our largest dragonfly, male 4.3 in., female 3.7 in. Southwestern, uncommon. Resembles Common Green Darner, but easily recognized by huge size alone. Its abdomen is longer than a wing; wings and abdomen are of equal length in the Common Green Darner. Blue abdominal markings become purple at cool temperatures, remaining blue longest on S2. Females have the abdominal markings tan, or in the **Blue Form**, blue.

SIMILAR SPECIES Compare with Common Green Darner.

HABITAT Spring-fed streams, ponds, and marshes in open arid country up to 4300 ft. elevation.

SEASON Mid-May to late Aug., most common spring and early summer.

COMMENTS The awesome males hold their abdomens in an arched posture as they fly low, slow, meandering, long beats of 300 ft. or so. Male Common Green Darners in the same circumstances fly with a straight abdomen on short beats that are higher, faster, and more direct. Male Giants patrol mostly in the morning, beginning about 8 A.M. under bright sunlight. From 6:30 to 8 P.M. both sexes may feed in swarms over water. It ranges south to Honduras, including Baja California.

Comet Darner *Anax longipes* Plate 1

IDENTIFICATION 3.2 in., eastern, uncommon, scattered northward. Spectacular males unmistakable, our only Darner with red markings, and our only dragonfly with a green thorax and red abdomen. In females the abdomen is green at the base, red-brown with dull green to tan spots beyond. Juvenile males have a pale orange abdomen, juvenile females have pale blue abdominal spots. Eyes gray in juveniles, becoming green in males and dark blue in females. Other field marks are the all-green forehead, and very long legs. It has the narrow stiff wings of the fastest-flying dragonflies.

SIMILAR SPECIES Common Green Darner has striped abdomen. Female and juvenile male Comets resemble female Commons, but the latter are smaller, with stubbier abdomens, bull's-eye marks on their fore-heads, broader wings, and shorter legs. In south FL check Mangrove and Blue-Faced Darners. Great Pondhawk of the far south is much smaller and has a banded abdomen.

HABITAT Borrow pits, and semipermanent, usually grassy, ponds, with low or absent fish populations.

SEASON Late Feb. to late Nov. in FL, early May to early Sept. in NJ.

COMMENTS Cruises far and wide to feed on insects as large as medium-size dragonflies. Males patrol with a free steady flight in beats up to 150 ft. long, from about 9 A.M. to late afternoon.

Amazon Darner *Anax amazili* Plate 1

IDENTIFICATION 2.8 in., rare stray to south. Similar to Common Green Darner but abdomen has large spots instead of stripes, the spots dull blue in juveniles but green at maturity. Sides of S2 green in both sexes, and blue semicircle of forehead target mark is incomplete at its middle.

SIMILAR SPECIES Compare with other Green Darners. Common Green has striped abdomen, side of S2 blue in male and Blue Form female, and complete forehead target mark. In south FL check Mangrove and Blue-Faced Darners. Great Pondhawk is smaller with complete green bands on S3–S6.

HABITAT Weedy ponds, lakes, and ditches, apparently including brackish waters.

SEASON June and July in U.S., wet season in tropics.

COMMENTS Feeds until dark on prey such as termites, often rather high. Males patrol over shoreline vegetation about 6 ft. up. It normally ranges from Mexico and the Antilles south to Argentina and the Galápagos Islands.

Pilot Darners
(genus *Coryphaeschna*)

These expert aviators are large dragonflies with long abdomens and short legs. Ours have a black forehead T-spot, mostly green thorax, and black abdomen with green markings. Juveniles have green eyes, which turn blue in females. Juvenile females of eastern species have the wings brown-orange at the base and transparent beyond, and long cerci, but with maturity the wing coloration reverses and the cerci break off. Of our 4 species, 3 are southeastern, 1 southwestern. In tropical America live 8 other species, including some all red ones.

Regal Darner *Coryphaeschna ingens* **Plate 2**

IDENTIFICATION One of our largest dragonflies, 3.6 in. Southeastern, common. Recognized by its size, green thorax with wide brown stripes, and narrow green abdominal cross-lines. Eyes green, becoming pure blue in mature females. In juvenile females wings brownish orange in basal 1/6, and long streaming cerci are longer than S8–S10. In mature females wings become clear in basal 1/6 and brownish orange beyond, and cerci break off. Some females become thinly pruinose and appear pale blue at a distance.

SIMILAR SPECIES Mangrove and Blue-Faced Darners of south FL have only narrow brown lines on thorax. Swamp and Cyrano Darners have a brown thorax with green stripes, and blue eyes in both sexes. When soaring overhead, wings of the equally large Swamp Darner are tinted yellow in the central portion in both sexes. Phantom Darner is much smaller, abdomen is constricted at S3, and mature males have blue basal abdominal spots.

HABITAT Densely vegetated lakes, ditches, and slow streams.

SEASON Early Feb. to mid-Oct., most common in spring, but a few emerge in the fall.

COMMENTS Juveniles of this splendid species sail languidly about in clearings, occasionally hanging from twigs or weed stems, but with maturity they fly mostly at treetop height. They often fly near vegetation to flush small prey. Feeding swarms are usually all males. Males are not territorial and do not patrol over water. Egg-laying females shift locations with their abdomens curled downward, signaling that they are not ready to mate at that time. It ranges through the FL Keys and Dry Tortugas to Cuba and the Bahamas.

Mangrove Darner *Coryphaeschna viriditas* **Plate 2**

IDENTIFICATION 3.4 in., southernmost FL, possibly LA, rare in U.S. Like Regal Darner but thorax has narrow brown lines instead of wide brown stripes.

SIMILAR SPECIES Blue-Faced Darner is smaller, with a blue face in mature males, and back of head blue in both sexes. Green Darners have large pale markings on sides of thicker abdomens.

HABITAT Ponds and ditches, often on fringes of Mangrove swamps.

SEASON Late March to mid-Aug., but possibly all year.

COMMENTS Formerly incorrectly named *C. virens*. Habits apparently like those of Regal Darner, including no male patrols over water. It ranges south to Paraguay, and in the Greater Antilles.

Blue-Faced Darner *Coryphaeschna adnexa* **Plate 2**

IDENTIFICATION Smallest of our Pilot Darners, 2.7 in. South FL, uncommon.

Similar to larger Mangrove Darner, but mature males have a sky-blue face and blue ventrally in the eyes. Both sexes have rear of head pale blue. Lateral spots of S5–S10 in mature females may be crimson.

SIMILAR SPECIES   Green Darners have large pale markings on sides of thicker abdomens. Great Pondhawk has wide green abdominal rings.
HABITAT   Weedy lakes, canals, and marshes.
SEASON   All year.
COMMENTS   Feeds in large irregular beats 3–6 ft. up in clearings. Males patrol short beats over water, especially over channels in marshy vegetation. Not discovered in FL until 1980, it ranges south through the Greater Antilles and Mexico to Argentina.

Malachite Darner *Coryphaeschna luteipennis* **Plate 2**

IDENTIFICATION   3.2 in., southeastern AZ, uncommon. Easily identified in its range by its large size, grass-green thorax with wide brown stripes, and black abdomen bearing a row of small blue-green dorsal triangles. Female cerci short, only as long as S10. Eyes of both sexes tinted blue. Face pale blue in males, green in females.
SIMILAR SPECIES   Other southwestern Darners lack brown thoracic stripes, or have brown stripes as wide or wider than green ones.
HABITAT   Weedy lakes, ponds, streams, and ditches.
SEASON   Early July to late Aug., monsoon season in AZ, all year in the tropics.
COMMENTS   Sometimes classified in the genus *Remartinia*. Males patrol and hover alertly about 1.5 ft. above emergent plants during short visits to the breeding habitat. It occurs in Baja California, and south to Argentina.

Three-Spined Darners
(genus *Triacanthagyna*)

Females are our only dragonflies with 3 ventral spines on S10. Only 1 species occurs in our area, while 5 others are tropical American.

Phantom Darner *Triacanthagyna trifida* **Plate 2**

IDENTIFICATION   2.6 in., far southeastern, common FL Peninsula, scarce northward. Smallest of the dusk-feeding Darners in the far southeast. Thorax green with brown stripes, abdomen narrowed at S3 and brown with small green spots. Eyes green, becoming deep blue in males, brown in old females. Mature males have blue spots between wings and on S2–S3. Wings tinted yellow, deepest in basal half of HW in male, between nodus and stigma of FW in female. Ribbonlike cerci of female, longer than S8–S10, eventually break off, and in old females wings become dark brown. Usually seen as juveniles, mature males appear in October.

SIMILAR SPECIES   S3 of Phantom Darner is narrowed much more than in any similar species. Regal and Swamp Darners are much larger, and Swamp has green thoracic stripes narrower than the brown. Mangrove and Blue-Faced Darners have only narrow brown thoracic lines.

HABITAT   Temporary forest pools.

SEASON   Early July through winter to mid-Feb. Most abundant in wet years, can survive several frosts due to its forest habitat.

COMMENTS   Hangs in forest undergrowth most of the day, but sometimes hunts along stems in the afternoon. They flit about in the open, phantomlike, to feed in the last 2 hours before nightfall, often holding to a beat a few yards in diameter until prey is exhausted there. Mature males swiftly patrol over muddy forest depressions, or hang over dry ponds that will fill with rainwater. It is found south into the FL Keys, Dry Tortugas, Bahamas, and Greater Antilles.

Swamp Darner
(genus *Epiaeschna*)

This genus contains only the very large, broad-headed species listed below.

Swamp Darner *Epiaeschna heros* Plate 2

IDENTIFICATION   One of our largest dragonflies, 3.4 in. Eastern, common southward. Dark brown with blue eyes, green thoracic stripes, and narrow green abdominal rings. Female cerci elongate-oval and leaflike. Wings tinted yellow in central 3/5 in juveniles, becoming progressively brown from tip toward base.

SIMILAR SPECIES   Regal Darner has thorax mostly green, blue eyes only in mature females, and narrower female cerci. Cyrano Darner is smaller, has a striped abdomen, and flies little in the open. Mosaic Darners have spotted abdomens.

HABITAT   Shady woodland ponds and slow streams, including swamps and temporary ponds.

| SEASON | Late Feb. to early Nov. in FL, early June to early Sept. in Canada. Most common spring and early summer. |
| COMMENTS | Feeds widely over the countryside at any height. Hangs from shady tree branches, and may enter buildings. Swarms containing both sexes quickly gather to feed on winged termites and ants. Males do not hold territories or patrol over water. Females lay eggs in mud or stems up to 6 ft. above waterline, or in dry pond bottoms. It migrates along the Atlantic Coast, and strays to Mexico and the Bahamas. |

Cyrano Darner
(genus *Nasiaeschna*)

Only 1 strange dragonfly is classified in this genus.

Cyrano Darner *Nasiaeschna pentacantha* **Plate 3**

IDENTIFICATION	2.7 in., eastern, common southward. Males easily recognized by tapered abdomen and distinctive patrol flight. Eyes dark blue, thorax dark brown with green stripes, abdomen with mid-dorsal and lateral interrupted blue-green stripes. Abdomen tapers from base to tip in males but is stout and cylindrical in females. Greenish-blue forehead projects forward 1/3 length of head. Cerci short, in both sexes slightly longer than S10. Coloration dull, may appear gray at a distance.
SIMILAR SPECIES	Regal and Swamp Darners are much larger, with ringed abdomens, and cerci longer than S9 + S10. Regal also has a mostly green thorax, and green eyes except in mature females. Phantom Darner is much more slender, with a spotted abdomen, mostly green thorax, and green eyes except in mature males. Green Form female Mosaic and Springtime Darners have spotted abdomens which are swollen at base and narrowed at S3.
HABITAT	The larva clings to sticks in swampy streams, lake coves, and ponds.
SEASON	Early March to late Dec. in FL, early June to late Aug. in IN.
COMMENTS	Named for long forehead, reminiscent of nose of literary character Cyrano de Bergerac. Stays in or close to forest, and does not forage in the open or in swarms. It commonly hunts with a slow flight along and through branches overhanging a stream. The mesmerizing male territorial patrols, usually seen in morning sunlight, are diagnostic. They fly slowly to and fro with the con-

tinuously flickering wings held up at an angle, suddenly darting at invading dragonflies. A second uncommon type of patrol is low through shade to examine water-soaked logs where females lay eggs.

Pygmy Darners
(genus *Gomphaeschna*)

The 2 species in this genus are eastern North American. They have a mottled green camouflage pattern, and are some of the few dragonflies seen more easily on windy days, when swarms gather to feed in the lee of trees. Female cerci are short, about as long as S10.

Harlequin Darner *Gomphaeschna furcillata* **Plate 3**

IDENTIFICATION One of our smallest Darners, 2.2 in. Eastern, scarce. Taper-Tailed is our only other Darner as small. Male has abdomen cylindrical beyond S3, green spots on S2–S9, and bright green eyes (gray in juveniles). Females have white lateral spots on middle abdominal segments, rusty orange dorsal spots on S2–S6, and usually an orange cloud between nodus and stigma of FW.

BODY FEATURES Harlequin has 2 bridge cross-veins, narrow wings (width of HW at nodus less than distance from nodus to stigma of FW), and male cerci separated by 2 times width of a cercus. Taper-Tailed Darner has 1 bridge cross-vein, broader wings (width of HW equal to distance from nodus to stigma of FW), and male cerci separated by width of 1 cercus. Males of both have 2 features unique among our Darners, a deeply forked epiproct, and the penis base extends ventrally as hamule-like blades.

SIMILAR SPECIES Taper-Tailed Darner is more dully colored, the male abdomen tapered and with obscure posterior spots, and eyes with only a green sheen. Female Taper-Tailed has rusty orange lateral spots on middle abdominal segments, rusty orange dorsal spots just on S2–S3, and sometimes an orange cloud at middle of FW. Our only other Darner with a mottled green thorax is the Mottled Darner, a large late-season species. Phantom Darner is larger with a mostly grass-green thorax, and mature male has blue markings. Baskettails and Striped Emeralds lack dorsal spots on middle abdominal segments. Clubtails have separated eyes and usually perch horizontally. Swift Setwing perches on twig tips with a raised abdomen.

HABITAT   Bogs, and swamps of bald cypress, alder, or cedar.
SEASON   Early Jan. to early Aug. in U.S., late May to early July in Canada.
COMMENTS   Feeds along forest edges, traveling long distances or on long beats at any height, hovering or gliding occasionally. Swarms mostly males but may include a few females. Usually perches on tree trunks, but occasionally hangs under branches, or rarely perches on the ground or grass stems. During mid-day, males continuously patrol for an hour or more 10 inches above small areas in bogs or swamps, hovering for long periods but turning to face another direction every few seconds. Sometimes they also patrol over land. Females lay eggs in wet wood about 6 in. above water level.

Taper-Tailed Darner *Gomphaeschna antilope* **Plate 3**

IDENTIFICATION   Eastern U.S., rare.
SIMILAR SPECIES   See Harlequin Darner.
HABITAT   Swamps and bogs.
SEASON   Late Feb. to early June in FL, late May to late July in NJ. Most common in late spring, about a month later than for Harlequin Darner at each locale.
COMMENTS   Perches on tree trunks in sun or shade, and hangs under small branches. Feeding swarms apparently contain only males. Feeding in the lee of trees, they fly downwind fast, then move slowly back upwind with minimal wing action to hover at points about 1.5 ft. apart. Males have been seen patrolling over land, but not water. Females lay eggs in wet wood above waterline.

Two-Spined Darners
(genus *Gynacantha*)

Only 2 species are North American, but about 90 others live in most tropical regions. Females have a large ovipositor adapted for laying eggs in mud, aided by 2 ventral spines on S10.

Twilight Darner *Gynacantha nervosa* **Plate 3**

IDENTIFICATION   3.0 in., far southeastern, common FL Peninsula, possible south TX. Our only Darner with sides of thorax all brown. Body slender, plain brown and dull green (red-brown in sunlight), without blue markings. Abdomen of male slightly constricted at S3, not constricted in female. Eyes brown in juveniles, becoming green with a horizontal blue bar across middle. The wide wings develop a brown tint, starting along front edge. Female cerci as long as S9 + S10, but quickly break off to half that length. Male epiproct more than half as long as cerci.

SIMILAR SPECIES All are smaller. Phantom Darner has a striped thorax, Spotted Darners have 2 yellow lateral thoracic spots, and Mocha Emerald is darker brown with red-brown to brilliant green eyes. Bar-Sided Darner of south TX has abdomen narrowed at S3, blue markings on S1–S3, and usually a brown costal stripe on each wing.

HABITAT Shaded fishless temporary pools, especially with emergent plants.

SEASON All year, most abundant in Oct. Because of its forest habitat, adults often survive frosts.

COMMENTS Usually seen feeding in the open during the last 30 min. before nightfall, but they also fly at dawn, and in cool weather often hunt in forest undergrowth during the day. They often feed in a small area while prey lasts, and must be a major predator of mosquitoes. During the day they hang in shady forest undergrowth, such as under Cabbage Palm leaves, or occasionally in buildings. It occurs in the FL Keys, Bahamas, West Indies, and from Mexico to Bolivia.

Bar-Sided Darner *Gynacantha mexicana* **Plate 3**

IDENTIFICATION 2.8 in., southernmost TX, rare in U.S. Like Twilight Darner but in side view shows a wide dark brown lower rear thoracic stripe or bar. In top view note constricted S3, especially contrast in male between swollen S2 and narrowed S3. Markings blue from S1 to base of S3, and blue spots between wing bases. Eyes dark brown to dark green above, with green anterior reflecting area. Female cerci longer than S9 + S10, male epiproct less than half as long as cerci. Wings may or may not have a definite brown stripe along front edge of each.

SIMILAR SPECIES Twilight Darner has no thoracic stripes, slight constriction of S3 in male and none in female, no blue body markings, shorter female cerci, longer male epiproct, and no definite brown costal stripes.

HABITAT Temporary pools.

SEASON Known late Oct. in TX, all year in tropics.

COMMENTS Behavior like Twilight Darner. Ranges south to Brazil.

Spotted Darners
(genus *Boyeria*)

Our 2 species of this genus are eastern, with 2 diagnostic yellow spots on each side of the thorax. Both eyes and wings are exceptionally wide. S3 is narrow, while S10 is often paler than the rest of the abdomen. In Eurasia, 4 other species occur, some with banded abdomens or green markings.

Ocellated Darner *Boyeria grafiana* Plate 3

IDENTIFICATION
2.6 in., eastern, fairly common. Gray-brown with 2 yellow lateral thoracic spots, and rows of yellow abdominal spots. Wings with tips tinted brown, but only a touch of brown at bases. Eyes brown in juveniles, green at maturity, becoming blue anteriorly in female. Female cerci short, as long as S10.

SIMILAR SPECIES
Fawn Darner is browner and more slender, with more brown at wing bases, smaller abdominal spots, and longer female cerci. Spotted Form of Variable Darner has 4 spots on each side of thorax. Shadowdragons are much smaller and thorax is not conspicuously marked.

HABITAT
Rocky rapid forest streams and rocky lakes.

SEASON
Early June to early Oct.

COMMENTS
More shade-loving than Fawn Darner. Hangs in dense shade during day, becoming most active in late afternoon and continuing until dark, but may fly all day in cool weather. Males patrol a little faster than Fawn Darner close to rocks or the shore.

Fawn Darner *Boyeria vinosa* Plate 3

IDENTIFICATION
2.6 in., eastern, common. Similar to Ocellated Darner but browner and more slender, with smaller dotlike abdominal spots, and a noticeable brown spot at base of each wing. Also, face is darker, and frontal green stripes of thorax are poorly developed or absent. Eyes olive-brown, becoming green in both sexes. Female cerci usually longer than S10. Wings become brown with age, in males often darkest at tips.

SIMILAR SPECIES
Compare with Ocellated Darner. Springtime Darner has pale thoracic stripes. Twilight Darner has no pale thoracic markings.

HABITAT
Shady forested rivulets, streams, and rivers. In the north sometimes lakes which have relatively bare shores. May fly with Ocellated Darner.

SEASON   Mid-March to early Dec. in FL, late June to late Sept. in Canada.

COMMENTS   Hangs under twigs, or sometimes on rock faces, in dense forest undergrowth most of the day, although in the far north it may fly all day in sunshine. Just after alighting it sometimes swings its body forward and back a few times, like a loose twig in a breeze. Males patrol most actively in the afternoon, but in the south may not begin until the last 30 min. before nightfall. They flutter with raised wings and abdomen without hovering or gliding, in shade and usually low and close to shore, inspecting each object that they encounter.

Springtime Darner
(genus *Basiaeschna*)

This genus contains only 1 species, which looks like a small Mosaic Darner, but unlike most of those, it flies in the spring.

Springtime Darner *Basiaeschna janata* **Plate 4**

IDENTIFICATION   2.4 in., eastern, common. Note brown thorax with 2 narrow straight yellow to white lateral stripes (upper ends may be green), a small dark brown spot at base of each wing, and dark blue eyes. Abdomen of male and **Blue Form** female has blue spots (gray at cool temperatures); **Green Form** female has green spots. Female cerci as long as S9 + S10. At a distance males may appear as a dark slender dragonfly with an olive green thorax and blue base on the abdomen.

SIMILAR SPECIES   Spatterdock Darner is larger, with blue or green lateral thoracic stripes, and male has sky-blue eyes.

HABITAT   Rivers and streams with a gentle current. Also forested lakes, preferably those with little shore vegetation, and oxygenated ponds.

SEASON   Mid-March to late May in NC, mid-May to mid-Aug. in NH.

COMMENTS   Feeds in fields, over water, and in open woods. Often perches near the ground on grass or sticks, but also hangs in trees. Males patrol without a definite beat over still or moving water, flying fast and erratically, either along shore or shifting from bank to bank. Although they patrol mostly at midday, they often fly in shade and until nightfall.

Mosaic Darners
(genus *Aeshna*)

Males of these Darners have rows of blue spots (green in Eastern Shadow and Turquoise-Tipped Darners) on the abdomen in a Mosaic pattern. In some species the blue spots become darker at cool temperatures. Many species look alike and present a difficult challenge for field identification. All of our species have a black T-spot on the forehead, and 11 of 20 have a black line across the upper part of the face. Identification without capture usually requires a close side view of a perched individual to see the shape and coloration of the lateral thoracic stripes, which are straight in 13 species, bent in 6, and irregular in the Mottled Darner. Males of 5 species, all with straight lateral thoracic stripes, have their cerci expanded at the tip, with the inner edge of each twisted downward, thus looking wedge-shaped in side view.

Most of our Mosaic Darners have 2 or 3 female color forms. Newly emerged females have blue abdominal spots, which remain blue in Blue Form females even after they mature. In Green Form females yellow pigment blends with the blue to produce green, while in Yellow Form females yellow pigment eventually masks the blue. Generally, the Green Form is most common, the Yellow Form the rarest, known in only 5 of our species. Many females are intermediate with a medley of colors, especially between the Green and Blue Forms; these usually have green dorsal spots and blue lateral spots on the abdomen. Female cerci of Mosaic Darners are leaflike, and do not normally break off except in the Shadow Darner. Frontal pale thoracic stripes are smaller (or lacking) in females compared with males of the same species. Mating usually occurs in bushes or trees, near or far from water in different species, and takes 50–75 min.

The Mosaic Darners include more than half of our Darners, and most dwell in the north and have a late flight season. They are absent from the southeastern Coastal Plain. Our 20 species include 3 eastern, 7 western, and 10 transcontinental. At least 7 species may occur at the same bog. In most of the west the only other Darner present is the Common Green Darner. About 80 species of Mosaic Darners occur worldwide.

Shadow Darner *Aeshna umbrosa* Plate 4

IDENTIFICATION   2.9 in., widespread, common. Male has wedge-type cerci. Lateral thoracic stripes straight and narrow, greenish yellow below, green to blue above. No face stripes, and pale spots of S10 obscure or absent. Female cerci usually break off, and wings become brown with age. **Green Form** female has green abdominal spots, rare **Blue Form** female has blue spots. Intermediate females have green dorsal spots, blue lateral spots. Lower rear surface of head is tan, diagnostic, but hard to see; pale spots on underside of abdomen brighter than in other Mosaic Darners, also hard to see. It darkens in color at cool temperatures.

BODY FEATURES
Diagnostic for males is that sides of S7 and S8 are concave inward in their anterior halves in ventral view. Female lacks hair tuft at tip of ovipositor sheath.

VARIATION
Eastern Form (*A. u. umbrosa*) has S3 elongate with spots posterior to S3 small and green, **Western Form** (*A. u. occidentalis*) has spots posterior to S3 larger and blue as in most Mosaic Darners. Posterior dorsal abdominal spots on each segment are larger and bluer in the far north, while those spots are absent in the Vancouver Island population.

SIMILAR SPECIES
Eastern Form males are identified by a combination of overall brown appearance, yellow-looking thoracic stripes, behavior, and habitat. Only other Darner in the east with wedge-type male cerci is Lance-Tipped, which has normal blue abdominal spots. Male Shadow Darners typically patrol shady stream banks, the Lance-Tipped flies in open sunshine. Of eastern females, the Sedge Darner of the far north has wider thoracic stripes and black facial cross-lines. Female Lance-Tipped and Black-Tipped Darners have longer abdomens that are notably constricted at S3.

In the west, male Shadow Darners are most like Paddle-Tailed Darners, which usually have a black facial cross-line, slightly wider thoracic stripes, a pale vertical streak on S1, blue spots of S9 fused, and blue spots on S10. Walker's Darner is also very similar but has lateral thoracic stripes white below, and is a foothill rather than a mountain species. Lance-Tipped Darner has blue spots on S10. Females in the west can seldom be distinguished from females of several other Mosaic Darners, but have S10 unspotted, narrow bandlike posterior lateral abdominal spots, no face stripes, and rear of head brown.

HABITAT
Primarily forest streams with a slow current, also shaded ponds, ditches, lakes, bogs, fens, and swamps, including beaver ponds.

SEASON
Late April to mid-Nov., most abundant in late summer and fall, one of the latest seasons among dragonflies.

COMMENTS
Most active in shade, thus feeds primarily at dusk in the open at any height, sometimes swarming with other Darners. Patrolling males hover close to the bank, periodically darting forward a few yards.

Lance-Tipped Darner *Aeshna constricta* Plate 4

IDENTIFICATION 2.8 in., southern Canada/northern U.S., common. Male with wedge-type cerci. Lateral thoracic stripes yellow-green below, blue above, the anterior nearly straight, slightly notched on both front and rear borders, the posterior expanded dorsally. Face without stripes, and S1 without a vertical streak. Male has abdominal spots sky blue, with spots on S9 not fused. Female abdomen longer and more slender, and more constricted at S3, than in most Mosaic Darners. Female has largest ovipositor among our Mosaic Darners, so S9 is longer than S8. Female also has pale spot of S9 wrapped ventrally to the ovipositor, and pale spots of S10 are vestigial or absent. **Blue Form** female has blue abdominal spots, **Green Form** has green spots, **Yellow Form** has all markings bright yellow. Especially in Yellow Form, wings may be tinted orange-brown from base to stigma.

SIMILAR SPECIES Only other male Mosaic Darners with wedge-type cerci within its range are Shadow and Paddle-Tailed. The male Paddle-Tailed of the west is extremely similar, but a black facial cross-line is usually well developed, blue abdominal spots are generally large with spots of S9 fused, and S1 bears a vertical pale streak. The male Shadow Darner has S10 black, or occasionally with small spots, and in the east has small green abdominal spots.

Female Black-Tipped Darner is similar, but has posterior thoracic stripe not widened above, S9 not longer than S8, and pale spots of S9 do not wrap ventrally. Other female Mosaic Darners with nearly straight lateral thoracic stripes have thick nearly cylindrical abdomens with small ovipositors; most have pale spots on S10, some have black face lines, and some have short frontal thoracic stripes (full length in Lance-Tipped).

HABITAT Marshy ponds and slow streams in the open below 1000 ft., including small temporary ponds, and sometimes bogs.

SEASON Late May to early Nov.

COMMENTS Our only Mosaic Darner that habitually hangs among low plants, although it will hang in trees and bushes. They hunt until dusk over open fields and marshes, sometimes forming swarms. The male patrols like the Canada Darner, but they fly more slowly, are warier, hover less, and go down into the vegetation less. Females usually lay eggs up to a yard above the water in cattails or sweet flag stems, sometimes in seasonally dry areas.

Paddle-Tailed Darner *Aeshna palmata* Plate 4

IDENTIFICATION 2.8 in., western, common. Male with wedge-type cerci. Lateral thoracic stripes nearly straight, S1 with pale vertical streak, S10 with pale spots, and usually a black facial cross-line present. Lateral thoracic stripes yellow below, green to blue above. Males have large sky-blue abdominal spots, often fused across midline on S9. Female of uncommon **Blue Form** has blue abdominal spots. **Green Form** has thoracic stripes and abdominal spots greenish yellow; some females are intermediate, with thoracic stripes blue above and abdominal spots green. This species does not darken when cool.

BODY FEATURES Male practically identical to male Lance-Tipped Darner, but ventral plate (sternum) of S1 usually extends posteriorly to edge of S1, anterior lamina is shorter with spines usually curved more dorsally, and hamules are more robust. Female lacks hair tuft on tip of ovipositor sheath, and cerci are oval, widest across the middle. Female Walker's Darner has cerci widest near their tips, and posterior spots fused on some abdominal segments. Ovipositor sheaths of Paddle-Tailed in side view concave before the tip, those of Variable Darner straight-edged, and with usual hair tuft at tip.

SIMILAR SPECIES Male closely resembles 4 other western Mosaic Darners with straight lateral thoracic stripes and wedge-type cerci. Lance-Tipped lacks facial stripes and pale lateral streak on S1, and S9 spots are separate. Walker's of the far west has narrow lateral thoracic stripes that are white below, and S1 and S10 are dark with vestigial pale marks, if any. Shadow Darner lacks face lines and pale streak on S1, and usually lacks pale spots on S10. Persephone's Darner of the southwest has wide yellow lateral thoracic stripes, and S10 is black or nearly so. Females are inseparable from some other Mosaic Darners.

HABITAT Partly shaded ponds, lakes, and slow streams in forested areas, or sometimes arid areas. Also breeds in bogs and fens, except in far north, where it is restricted to warmer lakes with marl bottoms and edged by sedge clumps.

SEASON Late May to early Nov., most common in late summer. Some can survive a snowfall.

COMMENTS Often hunts low and slowly along edges of thickets on short beats until dusk. Males patrol shorelines, particularly near trees, usually in the sun but occasionally in shade and until late evening. Females lay eggs in grass blades up to a yard above water.

IDENTIFICATION 2.7 in., CA area, fairly common. Male cerci of wedge-type. Lateral thoracic stripes narrow, straight, black-edged, white below shading to blue above. Abdominal spots intense dark sky blue, the posterior spots of each segment fused, the midlateral spots vestigial on S7 and lacking on S8, and S10 black. Face with black cross-line. **Blue Form** female has blue abdominal spots, **Green Form** has yellowish olive-green spots.

SIMILAR SPECIES Males of the other 5 Mosaic Darners within the range of Walker's have the midlateral spots well developed on S7 and present on S8. Only the Blue-Eyed is likely in the same habitat and season, but males have pure blue eyes. Male Paddle-Tailed of higher elevations has lateral thoracic stripes often yellow below, posterior abdominal spots not fused on all segments, S10 with pale spots, and S1 with a vertical pale streak. Shadow Darner has lower halves of lateral thoracic stripes yellow. Females are usually inseparable from other Mosaic Darners, but Green Form has lateral thoracic stripes white below, whereas these stripes are yellow below in Green Form of other far western species.

HABITAT Foothill streams in chaparral and oak woodland, up to the pine zone.

SEASON Mid-June to mid-Nov.

COMMENTS Named for Edmund Walker, Canadian entomologist. Hunts along sunny slopes in late afternoon. Males fly along a stream, examining the steepest sides and any crannies, from midmorning to midafternoon, often in shade. It ranges into Baja California, and on Santa Cruz Island.

Persephone's Darner *Aeshna persephone* Plate 4

IDENTIFICATION 3.0 in., AZ area, uncommon. Male cerci of wedge-type. Note wide, nearly straight yellow lateral thoracic stripes, and dark abdomen. Abdomen appears dark due to S4–S6 having only anterodorsal and posterodorsal spots well developed, and S7–S9 having only posterodorsal spots well developed. Black facial cross-line present. Abdominal spots sky blue in males, pale yellow-green in females.

VARIATION The Chiricahua and Huachuca Mountains populations in AZ have the widest lateral thoracic stripes.

SIMILAR SPECIES Males of other Mosaic Darners in its range have at least the upper halves of the lateral thoracic stripes blue, and midlateral spots present on S6–S8. The only other Mosaic Darner in its range with wedge-type cerci is the Paddle-Tailed Darner of higher elevations. Female Persephones can usually be identified by their wide yellow lateral thoracic stripes and dark abdomens.

HABITAT Mountain streams edged with grass in the oak or pine zone, up to about 6000 ft.

SEASON Early Aug. to late Oct.

COMMENTS Named for Persephone, daughter of Zeus, kept in the underworld but allowed in the upper world occasionally. Similarly, the dragonfly moves between shady canyons and sunny slopes. Feeds at treetop height on sunny slopes, and at dusk with a fast erratic flight over streams. Males fly up and down the canyon several feet high, dropping down to closely inspect the banks of grass-edged pools before moving on. It ranges south to Nayarit, Mexico.

Blue-Eyed Darner *Aeshna multicolor* Plate 5

IDENTIFICATION 2.7 in., the most common lowland western Darner. Thoracic stripes straight and narrow. Males have eyes, face, and abdominal spots sky blue (latter darkens at cool temperatures), lateral thoracic stripes whitish blue, and frontal stripes blue and usually well developed. S2 has a wide blue band half as long as the segment. Forked male cerci as seen in side view are diagnostic in the west. **Blue Form** females have thoracic stripes and abdominal spots blue, **Green Form** females have yellow thoracic stripes and yellow-green abdominal spots. Female wings often tinted yellow anteriorly between nodus and stigma.

SIMILAR SPECIES The male Arroyo Darner of the southwest is identical except that its cerci are not forked, and the anterior lateral thoracic stripe has a dorsal posterior extension. The male California Darner is a smaller spring species with a black facial cross-line, small frontal thoracic spots, paler blue abdominal spots, and teardrop-shaped anterior lateral thoracic stripe. The male Variable Darner of high latitudes or elevations has a grayer face with a black cross-line, and small or absent frontal thoracic spots. The female Blue-Eyed cannot normally be separated from several other Mosaic Darners, but she has short frontal thoracic stripes, usually unicolored lateral thoracic stripes, and no black face-line.

HABITAT Lakes, ponds, and slow streams up to about 6300 ft., usually warm waters with emergent or floating plants, but tolerates alkaline water and acid bogs.

SEASON Late April to late Oct. Some stray to east TX in the fall.

COMMENTS Feeds over open fields from before sunrise to after sunset, hanging under trees and brush during hot midday hours. Males patrol large areas of water in an irregular pattern, spending most of their time flying slowly in or near tules or cattails, and hovering at places about 6 ft. apart. It ranges south to Baja California and Morelos, Mexico.

Arroyo Darner *Aeshna dugesi* **Plate 5**

IDENTIFICATION
2.8 in., southwestern, uncommon. Nearly identical to Blue-Eyed Darner, but male cerci not forked, anterior lateral thoracic stripe has a posterior extension at its upper end, thoracic stripes slightly wider, and abdominal spots slightly smaller. Rare **Blue Form** females have blue markings. **Green Form** females have green-yellow thoracic stripes and yellow-green abdominal spots. Intermediate females have yellow thoracic stripes, and yellowish gray-blue abdominal spots, notably so at base of S3.

SIMILAR SPECIES
Males of most other southwestern Mosaic Darners have thoracic stripes partly or wholly yellow. Female probably not separable from female Paddle-Tailed, Blue-Eyed, or Variable Darners. See also Similar Species under Blue-Eyed Darner.

HABITAT
Pools of mountain streams in oak and pine zones, and possibly nearby ponds. Usually higher toward headwaters of a stream than Blue-Eyed Darner, and where pools are edged with grass and trees rather than cattails (*Typha*).

SEASON
Late June to mid-Sept.

COMMENTS
Males patrol low along edges of stream pools, beginning in early morning. It ranges south to Baja California and Oaxaca, Mexico.

Spatterdock Darner *Aeshna mutata* **(see Plate 5)**

IDENTIFICATION
2.8 in., northeastern, local. Males the only eastern Darners with all-blue markings and eyes, and forked cerci. Nearly identical to Blue-Eyed Darner, but eastern with an early flight season. Rare **Blue Form** female has blue markings and eyes, scarce **Green Form** female has green abdominal spots, yellow thoracic stripes, and green-brown eyes. Intermediate females, most common, have green markings except for blue dorsal abdominal spots and eyes, the bright blue eyes being distinctive among female Mosaic Darners with green markings.

BODY FEATURES
Male cerci have distance from dorsal summit to tip in side view 1/3 length of cerci (more than 1/3 in Blue-Eyed Darner). Female has cerci narrow and more than 0.25 in. long, anterior lateral thoracic stripe with a narrow posterior extension, and pale spots of S10 vestigial or absent. Female Blue-Eyed has shorter cerci, no stripe extension, and spots on S10.

SIMILAR SPECIES   Springtime Darner is much smaller, with a brown spot at base of each wing.

HABITAT   Fishless ponds, usually with water lilies. Occasionally bog ponds.

SEASON   Mid-May to late Aug. About 7 weeks at each locale, the earliest eastern Mosaic Darner.

COMMENTS   Feeds over fields with a leisurely flight about 10–15 ft. up. Males patrol low over vegetation with a leisurely, erratic flight for 10–15 min. at a time, paying special attention to flowers of plants such as spatterdock (yellow water lily *Nuphar luteum*). Females usually perch on the flowers of spatterdock and water shield to lay eggs if they can reach the underwater part of the stem.

California Darner *Aeshna californica* Plate 5

IDENTIFICATION   A small Mosaic Darner, 2.5 in. Western, common. Lateral thoracic stripes straight and narrow, anterior one pointed dorsally. Face has black cross-line, thorax has small frontal spots. Male and **Blue Form** female have whitish-blue markings (darken when cool) and opalescent blue eyes. **Green Form** female has yellow thoracic stripes and pale yellow-green abdominal spots. Both forms seem equally common. Intermediate females have yellow thoracic stripes and blue abdominal spots.

SIMILAR SPECIES   Male Blue-Eyed and Arroyo Darners have frontal stripes, darker blue abdominal spots, and pure blue eyes. Male Variable Darner is larger, with darker blue markings, partly green eyes, and are found at higher altitudes in summer. Other male Mosaic Darners have yellow thoracic stripes or wedge-type cerci, or both. Female Californias can perhaps be identified by a combination of small size, small frontal spots, teardrop-shaped anterior lateral thoracic stripe, and black facial line.

HABITAT   Small lakes, ponds, stream pools, and marshes, including alkaline waters, below about 4500 ft.

SEASON   Late March to late Aug., primarily spring, often the first dragonfly of spring.

COMMENTS   Feeds over roads and clearings. Males patrol without a definite beat low along shore and among emergent plants. It ranges into Baja California.

Variable Darner *Aeshna interrupta* Plate 5

IDENTIFICATION   2.9 in., northern, plus western mountains, common. Thorax has reduced pale markings, including short or absent frontal stripes, and face has black cross-line. Male eyes blue anteriorly, dark glassy green posteriorly. **Blue Form** females have blue abdominal spots, **Green Form** females have yellow thoracic stripes and green abdominal spots, **Yellow Form** females have all markings yellow, and wings often tinted orange-brown from base to stigma. Intermediate females have blue lateral abdominal spots and green or yellow dorsal spots.

VARIATION   The **Spotted Form**, eastern and west coast, has lateral thoracic stripes divided into 4 spots, which may be all blue, or ventral ones may be yellow. **Striped Form** of Great Plains, Rocky Mountains, and western Canada has thin straight lateral thoracic stripes.

SIMILAR SPECIES   Both sexes of Spotted Form easily identified by 4 lateral thoracic spots. Spotted Darners have only 2 such spots. Striped Form resembles California Darner, a lower-elevation early-season species, which is smaller and lacks yellow on thorax of males. Males of other similar Darners have long frontal stripes and wider lateral thoracic stripes. Thorax of Variable appears dark olive green at a distance, rather like a Common Green Darner, but latter has a striped abdomen. Female Striped Form Variable Darners cannot be separated from several other western Mosaic Darners, particularly Paddle-Tailed and Blue-Eyed Darners.

HABITAT   Marshy or boggy ponds, lakes, fen pools, and slow streams, usually acid, and including saline waters. They like prairie ponds and habitats dominated by sedges or cattails.

SEASON   Late May to late Oct., earliest on Great Plains, peak numbers July and Aug.

COMMENTS   The most common Mosaic Darner in northern prairie regions. Feeds, often in swarms, with a light and graceful flight in the open and along roads until dark, often only a few inches above ground. In cool weather they may hang in weeds or bask on the ground, tree trunks, or rocks. Patrolling males fly along shore over or through emergent vegetation, or fly an erratic beat about 15 yards in diameter. Tandem pairs fly for some distance with the male abdomen curled downward, not so gracefully as the Common Green Darner.

Black-Tipped Darner *Aeshna tuberculifera* Plate 5

IDENTIFICATION   3.0 in., southern Canada/northern U.S., absent Great Plains? Uncommon. Lateral thoracic stripes broad, straight, and yellow-white to pale blue. Frontal thoracic stripes long but narrow. S10 is black. Female abdomen long and slender, notably constricted at S3, with a large ovipositor. **Blue Form** female has blue abdominal spots, rare **Yellow Form** has yellow abdominal spots. No face line.

SIMILAR SPECIES Nearly all other male Mosaic Darners with straight lateral thoracic stripes have pale spots on S10, and some have wedge-type cerci or a black face line. Female Lance-Tipped Darners have posterior lateral thoracic stripe widened dorsally, S9 longer than S8, pale spots of S9 wrapped ventrally, and some have wings tinted orange-brown from base to stigma. Other female Mosaic Darners with straight lateral thoracic stripes have a thick, nearly cylindrical abdomen and small ovipositor, most have pale spots on S10, some have a black face line, and some have short or absent frontal stripes.

HABITAT Ponds and lakes, especially acid ones with boggy edges; in the east, commonly ponds edged by cattails. Also vegetated streams.

SEASON Late June to late Oct.

COMMENTS Feeds along forest lanes and edges, hanging occasionally on trunks of saplings. May join feeding swarms. Males patrol both shores and open water. Blue Form Females act like males, thus avoiding unnecessary male attention. Females usually lay eggs late afternoon and evening in green emergent plants from below the waterline to a yard above it, even in cattail leaves waving in the breeze, but also in the grass or mud of dry ponds.

Sedge Darner *Aeshna juncea* Plate 5

IDENTIFICATION 2.7 in., Canada, and high western U.S. mountains; common. Lateral thoracic stripes wide and straight, the anterior tapered above and greenish yellow below. Male and **Blue Form** female have lateral thoracic stripes blue above, lateral spots of S1–S2 yellow to green, spots posterior to S3 pale blue. **Green Form** female has green markings, **Yellow Form** female has yellow markings. This species does not darken when cool. Face has a black cross-line, and thorax has full-length frontal stripes.

SIMILAR SPECIES Anterior lateral thoracic stripe diagnostic. In similar Darners stripe is narrow, bent, notched, or widened above, and often grass green or all blue. Subarctic Darner has that stripe bent forward in upper half. Black-Tipped Darner has S10 black and lacks a face line. Males of California Darner and Striped Form of Variable Darner have short frontal thoracic stripes and blue lateral spots on S1–S2.

HABITAT Prefers ponds and marshes with sedges. Also peaty ponds and large pools with emergent plants, including semitemporary ponds, as well as small lakes, marshy bays, mossy fens, ditches, rock pools, and slow parts of streams.

SEASON   Mid-June to early Oct., peaking in late July.

COMMENTS   The most common Mosaic Darner in forested areas of the far north. They sometimes hunt along tree trunks or until dark. Males patrol territories of about 3 × 10 yards (smaller than that of Subarctic Darner) with a slow, even flight from 7 A.M. to 8 P.M., each male making several short visits to the habitat each day. It is circumboreal, ranging through northern Europe to Japan.

Subarctic Darner *Aeshna subarctica* **Plate 5**

IDENTIFICATION   2.8 in., Canada/northernmost U.S., uncommon. Coloration pastel. Thoracic pattern unique, the lateral stripes bent forward in their upper halves, yellow below and pale blue above. Male abdominal spots pale blue, sometimes pale green, and often yellow laterally on basal segments. **Blue Form** female colored like male, **Green Form** female has green abdominal spots, **Yellow Form** female shows yellow thoracic and abdominal markings, and its wings are often tinted brown. Face has black cross-line. It does not darken when cool.

SIMILAR SPECIES   Compare with closely related Sedge Darner. Shadow Darner has narrow straight lateral thoracic stripes, wedge-type male cerci, and no face line.

HABITAT   Mossy bog ponds and deep fens with well-defined edges, and northern swamps.

SEASON   Early June to early Oct.

COMMENTS   Feeds in the open until evening, often capturing tandem pairs of Meadowhawks. Males defend a territory only at low population densities, and do not fly a constant route. They fly over the open bog, hover less, and spend less time in one place than the Sedge Darner. It is circumboreal, occurring through central and northern Europe to Japan.

Canada Darner *Aeshna canadensis* **Plate 6**

IDENTIFICATION   2.8 in., Southern Canada/northern U.S., common. Anterior lateral thoracic stripe sharply notched on front edge, narrowed in upper half, and with a narrow posterior offshoot from top. Males usually have this stripe green below, blue above, but sometimes it is all blue or all green. Those with green lateral thoracic stripes cannot be told from the Green-Striped Darner. Face pale green, unstriped. The rare **Blue Form** female is colored like male, **Green Form** females have green markings, and wings often tinted brown, especially in the north. Intermediate females are most common, usually with green lateral thoracic stripes and dorsal abdominal spots, and blue lateral abdominal spots. This species darkens when cool.

BODY FEATURES   Males have a row of tiny teeth along dorsal edges of cerci that can be felt with the finger; these teeth are absent in the Green-Striped Darner. Anterior ends of wedge-shaped anterior hamules point toward thorax in male Canada, toward midline in bracket-shaped [] hamules of Green-Striped. Female cerci less than 0.25 in. long in Canada, longer in Green-Striped. Side of ovipositor sheath bounded by high, sharp ridges (carinae) ventrally and posteriorly in female Green-Striped; these ridges are low in female Canada.

SIMILAR SPECIES   Anterior lateral thoracic stripe usually differs from that of closely related Green-Striped Darner in being blue above, with corner of anterior notch nearly square instead of obtusely angled, posterior upper extension narrower, and posterior edge not notched (latter sometimes notched in Green-Striped). Posterior lateral thoracic stripe usually all blue in male and Blue Form female Canadas, green below in Green-Striped Darner. Flight season of Green-Striped starts later, and it has a more limited range. The larger Lake Darner has a black facial cross-line, and its anterior lateral thoracic stripe is constricted at middle. Female Lance-Tipped Darner has anterior lateral thoracic stripe only slightly notched, and broad pointed leaflike cerci (cerci narrow and rounded at tips in female Canada).

HABITAT   Marshy and boggy lakes, ponds, fens, and sluggish creeks. They like ponds with grassy or peaty margins, and floating vegetation or logs, such as beaver ponds.

SEASON   Mid-June to mid-Oct.

COMMENTS   Feeds until nightfall along forest edges, in small clearings, or even within forest, and may join swarms. Males patrol a fairly definite beat of about 20 yards along the water's edge, either several feet up or low and close to shore. They hover often, but not so often as the Variable Darner.

Green-Striped Darner *Aeshna verticalis* **Plate 6**

IDENTIFICATION   3.0 in., northeastern, uncommon. Like Canada Darner, but anterior lateral thoracic stripe entirely green, obtusely notched on front edge, with a broad posterior offshoot from its top. Posterior lateral thoracic stripe green below, blue above.

Females have green abdominal spots, except some have blue lateral spots.

SIMILAR SPECIES Compare with Canada Darner.

HABITAT Spring-fed ponds and marshy meadows, and marshy or swampy lakes, ponds, and slow streams, especially those bordered by sedges.

SEASON Mid-June to late Oct.

COMMENTS Feeds along forest edges or in small clearings until dusk, periodically hanging under branches or on tree trunks. It may join feeding swarms, and some migrate along the Atlantic Coast. Males patrol especially along sedges bordering open water.

Lake Darner *Aeshna eremita* **Plate 6**

IDENTIFICATION Our largest Mosaic Darner, 3.1 in. Canada, northernmost U.S., high western U.S. mountains; common. Anterior lateral thoracic stripe is constricted at middle by a rounded anterior notch. Face has black cross-line. Male and uncommon **Blue Form** female have lateral thoracic stripes green below and blue above, or all blue. **Green Form** females have all markings yellow-green. Intermediate females usually have blue lateral and green dorsal abdominal spots. This species darkens when cool.

SIMILAR SPECIES Canada Darner is smaller, with anterior lateral thoracic stripe narrowed in upper half. Canada and Green-Striped Darners lack a face line. These species have 2 large green spots anterior to base of each FW; Lake Darner has 1 such spot.

HABITAT Marshy lakes, ponds, deep fens, bogs, and slow streams, especially sparsely vegetated or wooded lakes.

SEASON Mid-June to late Oct., primarily July and Aug., one of earliest dragonflies to mature in far north.

COMMENTS Feeds along forest edges, often perching on tree trunks or, rarely, on the ground. They can fly at 50°F, and in light rain. In the far north they may fly virtually all day (and all night under the midnight sun). Males are not territorial and patrol with a slightly arched abdomen, closely inspecting anything in the water.

Zigzag Darner *Aeshna sitchensis* **Plate 6**

IDENTIFICATION A small Mosaic Darner, 2.4 in. Canada/northernmost U.S., common. Anterior lateral thoracic stripe narrow and zigzag, colored white, yellow, or pale blue. Face usually pale yellow, with black cross-line. Abdomen has large pale spots, and S9–S10 are mostly pale. Abdomen of male has spots pale blue and lacks yellow spots. **Blue Form** females have markings pale gray-blue, but often appear dull olive-green in the field. **Green Form** females have yellow-green markings. Eyes relatively small, the seam between them not much longer than the triangular occiput. Black T-spot on forehead has a distinctive crescent-shaped base next to eyes.

SIMILAR SPECIES   Azure Darner is smaller, with larger abdominal spots generally forming irregular stripes.

HABITAT   Prefers bog pools of 10 square yards or less, usually without emergent plants, including pools that dry in summer. Also shallow, evenly vegetated sedge/moss fens with puddles.

SEASON   Early June to late Sept., beginning about 2 weeks later than Azure Darner's at each locale.

COMMENTS   Unusually for a Darner, usually perches low, often on the ground. Apparently does not feed in dusk swarms. Males patrol slowly without a definite beat along pool edges.

Azure Darner *Aeshna septentrionalis* **Plate 6**

IDENTIFICATION   2.2 in., Canada, common. Similar to Zigzag Darner, but abdominal spots larger and usually fused into irregular stripes, and face is blue to green. Male abdomen appears pale blue, with an irregular brown dorsal stripe and a lateral brown spot on each segment. Female abdomen has spots joined into at least lateral stripes. **Blue Form** female has blue abdominal spots, **Green Form** female has yellow-green spots.

SIMILAR SPECIES   Abdomen of male Zigzag Darner looks brown with blue spots. Abdomen of female Zigzag has separated spots.

HABITAT   Mossy fens and bogs, with or without emergent plants such as sedges and horsetails, especially with pools 10–15 yards long with sloping edges.

SEASON   Mid-June to mid-Sept.

COMMENTS   The most common Mosaic Darner near the arctic tree line, ranging farther north than any of our other dragonflies. Males fly low, patrolling mats of moss and pond edges, perching frequently flat on moss.

Mottled Darner *Aeshna clepsydra* **Plate 6**

IDENTIFICATION   2.7 in., northeastern, locally common. Pastel mottling of thorax in blue, yellow, and green, along with large size, are diagnostic. Face has a brown cross-line. Scarce **Blue Form** female has blue abdominal spots, **Green Form** female has pale yellow-green spots.

SIMILAR SPECIES   Pygmy Darners are much smaller spring species.

HABITAT	Small lakes, or bays of large lakes, with marshy or boggy edges, and usually water lilies and clear, soft water.
SEASON	Mid-June to mid-Oct., primarily Aug. and Sept.
COMMENTS	Feeds in open woods and clearings, faster and higher than most other Mosaic Darners, and perches on tree trunks. In the evening they may feed over streams or join feeding swarms. Males patrol closely and slowly along shores from midmorning to late afternoon.

Turquoise-Tipped Darner *Aeshna psilus* **Plate 6**

IDENTIFICATION	A small atypical Mosaic Darner, 2.4 in. Southeastern AZ and southern TX, rare in U.S. Male our only dragonfly with underside of S9–S10 pale blue. Thorax has bold yellow-green frontal and lateral stripes, the anterior lateral stripe slightly zigzag. Both male and female have small green abdominal spots, except male has blue spots on S2. Juveniles have thoracic stripes and dorsal abdominal spots white, the lateral abdominal spots pale blue. Female has wings yellow in basal 1/6, and very long cerci, as long as S8–S10. No face stripe; face of male pale blue.
SIMILAR SPECIES	Female Blue-Eyed and Arroyo Darners are larger, with small frontal thoracic spots, straight lateral thoracic stripes, and larger abdominal spots. Springtime Darner has straight lateral thoracic stripes and a brown spot at base of each wing.
HABITAT	Ponds, ditches, and sluggish streams, including temporary ones.
SEASON	All year.
COMMENTS	Forages low in open areas. Males patrol close to shore from about 11 A.M. to 5 P.M., often in shade, periodically briefly hovering facing the bank. Females may lay eggs in dry pond bottoms. It ranges south into the Greater Antilles and Peru.

Riffle Darner
(genus *Oplonaeschna*)

Only 1 species of this genus, which looks like a Mosaic Darner, is found north of Mexico. Another species, *O. magna*, occurs in central Mexico.

Riffle Darner *Oplonaeschna armata* **Plate 6**

| IDENTIFICATION | 2.6 in., southwestern, fairly common. Coloration brown with 2 lateral thoracic stripes that are blue above and yellow below, |

upper 1/3 of anterior stripe nearly separated from lower 2/3. Male abdomen has small blue spots, decreasing in size and shading to yellow posterior to S4 or S5. Male cerci similar to those of Mosaic Darners with wedge-type cerci, and S10 with a dorsal fingerlike projection. Female cerci as long as S9 + S10 but break off during egg laying, and female abdomen notably short and stout. **Blue Form** female has blue abdominal spots, **Green Form** has green spots, **Yellow Form** has yellow spots. Males and Blue Form females have deep-blue eyes, Green Form and Yellow Form females have yellow-green to dark brown eyes.

SIMILAR SPECIES Mosaic Darners within its range have larger abdominal spots, and a nonsegmented (usually straight) anterior lateral thoracic stripe.

HABITAT Rocky streams in mountain oak woodland and pine forest, which vary seasonally from trickles to torrents.

SEASON Early June to late Aug., about a month at each locale.

COMMENTS Feeds around the lower halves of trees in open forest on mountain slopes. Patrolling males are unwary and fly slowly along a semi-shaded long or short portion of a stream. They fly all day, but are more active in the morning. It ranges south to Guatemala.

Clubtails
(family Gomphidae)

Very distinctive, most species with S7–S9 enlarged and clublike, usually seen perching horizontally and on flat surfaces. Males usually have a larger club than females and commonly raise and display it like a flag. Clubtails generally have a camouflage pattern, usually brown or black marked with yellow in juveniles, the yellow becoming green after a few days. They have separated eyes as in the Petaltails, but females have a notched or split subgenital plate on the underside of S8 instead of an ovipositor with blades. Males have a forked epiproct, while females of some species have hornlike spines on the top or back of the head. None of our species has bright red markings, blue markings are rare (Blue-Faced Ringtail), and the maximum wing marking is a small brown spot at each wing base (some Sanddragons). Clubtails do not soar, feed in swarms, or lay eggs in tandem. Many species are uncommon, wary, have short flight seasons or restricted ranges, perch mostly in the trees, or all of the above. These factors, combined with the similarity of many species, make Clubtails a difficult challenge to locate and identify in the field. Our species perch to mate for 10 minutes or more, and in some (most notably the Dragonhunter), the male abdominal appendages punch holes in the female head, damage that is unexplained.

Some other dragonflies have clubbed abdomens, notably some male Cruisers, male Clubskimmers, and female Baskettails carrying egg balls. Pondhawks commonly perch like Clubtails, but have the eyes in contact on top of the head.

Most Clubtails breed in flowing water, where they are quite susceptible to pollution, particularly because their (known) life cycles are 2-plus years. Most of our 98 species are eastern, and at least 1000 species occur worldwide.

Dragonhunter
(genus *Hagenius*)

Only 1 species is usually classified in this genus.

Dragonhunter *Hagenius brevistylus* **Plate 6**

IDENTIFICATION	Our largest Clubtail, Darner sized, 3.3 in. Eastern, common. Mostly black with 2 wide bright yellow lateral thoracic stripes. Head small with bright green eyes and yellow face, legs long and black, wings long and narrow. Male abdomen vertically compressed on S3–S6, enlarged from S7 to S10, widest at S10. Female abdomen cylindrical with small lateral flange on S9. Male easily recognized by Valkyrie-like flight with end of abdomen bent downward in a J shape, and periodic short glides.
VARIATION	New England individuals are smaller, 2.7–3.1 in. Central TX populations have larger yellow markings, often with a basal yellow ring on S8.
SIMILAR SPECIES	Huge size unique among our Clubtails. Widely separated green eyes and horizontal perching distinguish it from all our other large dragonflies. Arrowhead Spiketail has eyes in contact on top of head, short legs, and perches vertically or obliquely. River Cruisers have only one yellow lateral thoracic stripe.
HABITAT	Forested streams and rivers with a moderate to fast current, sometimes lake channels or bays.
SEASON	Mid-April to early Nov. in FL, late June to mid-Sept. in NJ.

COMMENTS Eats other dragonflies up to the size of Cyrano Darners, and large butterflies. Away from water it is wary and furtive, skulking near cover on the ground, on tree limbs or twigs, or flying like an accipiter hawk along a forest edge. At water they perch on rocks, twigs, or leaves with a commanding view in sun or shade. Egg-laying females may swoop rhythmically to the water near the bank, splash eggs from the water onto the bank, fly over open water while tapping the abdomen to the surface, or hover near the bank and "bomb" the water with eggs.

Common Clubtails
(genus Gomphus)

"Common" applies to many species in this group, but some are scarce, and only 4 occur west of the Rocky Mountains. None of the species has any of the following characteristics: bright grass green coloration, orange club (but Sulphur-Tipped Clubtail is close), pale abdominal rings, exceptionally long or short legs, or basal brown wing spots. The cerci are rarely pale, and in males are bonded to S10. A dark midfrontal thoracic stripe is always present, usually producing a pair of pale frontal stripes shaped like upside-down 7s. The spines on the hindlegs are much larger in females, which fits them for capturing larger prey than males. Most Common Clubtails have an early-spring or early-summer flight season. The classification of this genus is controversial, but our 38 species are divided here into 4 Subgenera. About 7 other species occur in Europe and north Africa.

Phanogomphus Group
(genus *Gomphus*,
subgenus *Phanogomphus*)

The commonest of the Common Clubtails, principally because some species can breed in ponds. Medium in size and proportions of head, thorax, and legs. The club has yellow edges on S8–S9, and is small to moderately developed in males, barely present in females. Females have S10 square to elongate-rectangular, interrupted pale lateral abdominal stripes, and a pale epiproct. Some species when flushed fly in a fast vertical UUUU pattern, which makes them difficult to keep in sight. These dragonflies are diverse, and some look like species in other groups of Clubtails, notably the Stenogomphurus Group (Rapids, Harpoon, and Beaverpond Clubtails), and the Plains Clubtail of the Gomphurus Group (Pronghorn Clubtail).

Males have straight cerci in side view, each with a lateral keel that extends onto the basal half. Either or both the lateral keel and a median ventral keel have an angle or tooth (except in Lancet Clubtail). Among the males of our 17 species, 5 have a lateral tooth on each of the cerci, 8 have a lateral angle, and 4 have the outer edges of the cerci straight. In a direct dorsal view, the epiproct spreads well beyond the cerci in 4 species, slightly beyond in 9, and to the same width in 4. The female subgenital plate is usually very short, but may be up to half the length of S9. Mating usually occurs not far from water on the ground or low plants for 15–20 min. In North America 17 species occur, only 4 in the west, with only the Pacific and Pronghorn Clubtails west of the Rockies. In Europe and north Africa, 5 other species occur.

Pacific Clubtail *Gomphus kurilis* **Plate 7**

IDENTIFICATION 2.1 in., far western U.S., common. Only Clubtail in its range with combination of all-black legs and one black stripe on pale gray-green side of thorax, and only Phanogomphus lacking an anterior lateral thoracic dark stripe. Amount of pale yellow on S9 variable, from none to spotted to ringed. S10 black in males, usually yellow dorsally in females.

SIMILAR SPECIES Pronghorn Clubtail has an anterior lateral thoracic black stripe and pale shins. Columbia Clubtail has a wide black lateral thoracic band. Gray Sanddragon has side of thorax gray, short legs, and a pale ring on S7.

HABITAT Lakes, ponds, and silt-bottomed stream and river pools up to 4500 ft. elevation.

SEASON Late April to late July.

COMMENTS Formerly incorrectly named *G. confraternus*. Away from water perches on bare ground. Males at water perch on the shore or low plants. They make occasional irregular short patrols over the water with spurts of wing beats, but begin to leave the water about 4:30 P.M.

Pronghorn Clubtail *Gomphus graslinellus* **Plate 7**

IDENTIFICATION 2.0 in., TX to southern BC and Ontario, common. Relatively robust and brightly colored. S8–S9 bright yellow laterally, S8 with a small yellow dorsal spot, S9 all yellow dorsally. Shins pale. Anterior and posterior dark lateral thoracic stripes often somewhat fused. Male hind thigh black, streaked with green in female. Male epiproct spreads only slightly beyond cerci.

BODY FEATURES Male cerci each has a lateral tooth, thus shaped like a horn of the Pronghorn (Antelope), and with a small tooth under tip. Female occiput straight-edged; subgenital plate thick, 1/6 as long as S9, V-notched for half its length.

SIMILAR SPECIES More likely confused with certain species of Gomphurus Group than Phanogomphus Group, but Pronghorn does not hover over riffles. In the northwest, Columbia Clubtail is larger, with a black lower rear thoracic stripe, and all-black lower legs. Pacific Clubtail lacks an anterior lateral black thoracic stripe, and has all-black legs.

In midcontinent, the Plains Clubtail cannot always be separated from the Pronghorn, though the Plains is larger. The male Plains patrols flowing parts of rivers, lacks lateral teeth on cerci, and has epiproct spreading beyond cerci. Midland Clubtail has an interrupted anterior lateral thoracic black stripe, black lower legs, and dorsal yellow on S9 is often absent. Handsome Clubtail is larger, usually has an interrupted anterior lateral black thoracic stripe, black lower legs, and female usually has black thighs. Ozark Clubtails have black lower legs and S9 either black dorsally or with only a narrow dorsal yellow stripe. Sulphur-Tipped Clubtail of Great Plains is paler, with dorsal and lateral yellow spots of S9 only narrowly separated, and S7 yellow laterally (mostly black in Pronghorn). The male Sulphur-Tipped has pale streaks on hind thighs and pale genitalia on S2 (both black in Pronghorn). Tennessee Clubtail is very like Pronghorn, but has an isolated TN range.

HABITAT Ponds, lakes, and slow streams, up to 2200 ft.

SEASON Mid-March to mid-Aug.

COMMENTS Usually perches on open ground or low herbs, but sometimes forages in forest or perches in trees. When disturbed often flies a vertical pattern of UUUUs 15–20 ft. high. Males perch at the water's edge, and at a stream prefer the bare shores of the largest pools. Sometimes they fly slowly or hover along vegetation bordering open water.

Tennessee Clubtail *Gomphus sandrius* (see Plate 7)

IDENTIFICATION 2.0 in., south-central TN, local. Identical to Pronghorn Clubtail, but ranges do not overlap. Thorax deep gray-green, yellower in female. Female hind thigh mostly green, mostly black in Pronghorn. Eyes aqua-blue, grayer in female.

BODY FEATURES Male cerci each has a lateral angle, and a prominent rounded ventral keel. Crest of female occiput concave.

SIMILAR SPECIES Handsome Clubtail has black lower legs, mostly black female thighs, and anterior lateral thoracic black stripe is usually interrupted.

HABITAT Slow streams with bare bedrock shores.

SEASON Mid-May to late June.

COMMENTS Away from water perches on ground or low plants. Males prefer the widest parts of a stream where they warily perch on bedrock shores, but not on rocks in the water, from 9 A.M. to late P.M. Occasionally they fly leisurely patrols over the pools.

Sulphur-Tipped Clubtail *Gomphus militaris* Plate 7

IDENTIFICATION 2.0 in., southern Great Plains, common. Our palest Phanogomphus. Thorax yellow-green, including a well-developed pale shoulder stripe. Anterior lateral thoracic black stripe may be incomplete, and area between lateral thoracic stripes may be gray. Abdomen with full-length dorsal yellow stripe, and S7–S9 deep yellow on sides. Dorsal and lateral yellow of S9 only narrowly separated by brown. Male club well developed, with a rusty tinge at maturity. Female has sides of S1–S2 yellow. Thighs and shins mostly pale in both sexes.

BODY FEATURES Male has a very large rounded yellow penis hood that has a bumpy surface (smooth in other dragonflies). Female subgenital plate 1/10 as long as S9 and shallowly notched.

SIMILAR SPECIES Pronghorn and Plains Clubtails are blacker, with pale shoulder stripe very narrow or absent, dorsal and lateral yellow of S9 well separated, S7 mostly black laterally, and males have black thighs and S2 genitalia. Oklahoma Clubtail differs in the same ways and is much smaller. Flag-Tailed Spinyleg is larger, with long legs, pale basal rings on middle abdominal segments, a vertically flattened club, and black lower legs.

HABITAT Mud-bottomed ponds, lakes, and slow parts of streams and rivers.

SEASON   Early April to mid-Aug.

COMMENTS   Perches on the ground or weeds, and males patrol over water away from the bank. The larger Flag-Tailed Spinyleg may keep them from water in the morning, and the Common Sanddragon may restrict them to parts of streams with vegetation on both banks. It ranges south into Nuevo León, Mexico.

Clearlake Clubtail *Gomphus australis* **Plate 7**

IDENTIFICATION   2.1 in., southeastern Coastal Plain, uncommon. S9 proportionately the longest in the Phanogomphus Group, much longer than either S8 or S7. Abdomen mostly black with a very slender club narrowly edged with bright yellow on S8–S9. Face with a narrow brown cross-line, and legs all black. S9–S10 usually black above, rarely with yellow spots or stripes. Head exceptionally broad, and body is hairy.

SIMILAR SPECIES   Diminutive and Westfall's Clubtails are much smaller with pale shins, and have S9 shorter than S7.

HABITAT   Sand-bottomed lakes.

SEASON   Mid-March to early May.

COMMENTS   Males carry their abdomens slightly arched. They perch on lily pads where available, or else shoreline sand and vegetation, or on the bulging bases of bald cypress trees.

Diminutive Clubtail *Gomphus diminutus* **Plate 7**

IDENTIFICATION   1.7 in., Carolinas area, uncommon. Similar to Clearlake Clubtail but much smaller, with area between lateral thoracic stripes darkened, S9 longer than S8 but shorter than S7, and shins pale. S9 usually black dorsally, but occasionally with a dorsal yellow stripe.

BODY FEATURES   Male cerci each have a lateral angle, and a large ventral spine at 1/2 length. Spine lacking in Westfall's Clubtail, which might be a subspecies of Diminutive, although no connecting populations are known.

SIMILAR SPECIES   Clearlake Clubtail is much larger. Other small southeastern Clubtails have S9 no longer than S8 (except Westfall's of FL). Hodges' is a stream species with no face line and more extensive green on thighs. Lancet, Cypress, and Sandhill Clubtails have a full-length yellow dorsal stripe on S8–S10. Rapids Clubtail, primarily a mountain stream species, has black lower legs. Species of the Gomphus Group have stubby abdomens with wider clubs.

HABITAT   Boggy trickles, slow small streams, and lakes, all with part sand, part silt, bottoms, and sphagnum moss margins.

SEASON Early April to late May.

COMMENTS Away from water perches on grass or on the ground near vegetation. Males at water perch inconspicuously on low plants or sticks near shores of muck-bottomed pools, making occasional sorties over the water.

Westfall's Clubtail *Gomphus westfalli* (see Plate 7)

IDENTIFICATION 1.7 in., western FL Panhandle, local. Identical to Diminutive Clubtail, except pale between the dark lateral thoracic stripes.

SIMILAR SPECIES As for Diminutive Clubtail.

HABITAT Boggy streams and seepages with muck-bottomed pools.

SEASON Mid-March to late April.

COMMENTS Named for Minter J. Westfall, Jr., American odonatist. Forages from the ground or low plants in small grassy clearings. Males perch on shore, occasionally flying a fast, low, irregular patrol.

Rapids Clubtail *Gomphus quadricolor* Plate 7

IDENTIFICATION A small Phanogomphus, 1.7 in. Eastern south to GA, uncommon. Legs all black, abdomen slender and black dorsally on S8–S10 (rarely small yellow spot on S8 or S10). Area between the black lateral thoracic stripes sometimes darkened.

BODY FEATURES Male anterior hamule has distinctive sickle shape. Female subgenital plate thick, 1/7 as long as S9 and V-notched nearly to base.

SIMILAR SPECIES Other small Phanogomphus in its range have a yellow dorsal stripe on S9. Harpoon, Beaverpond, and Dusky Clubtails are notably larger and less brightly colored, and Beaverpond has a narrower brown midfrontal stripe. Females of the 3 latter species have a pale lateral stripe on S7, where female Rapids have only a pale basal spot. Female Harpoon and Dusky usually have pale hind thighs and a pale dorsal stripe on S10. Both sexes of the Dusky have pale shins and a dorsal yellow spot on S8. Species of the Gomphus Group, such as Spine-Crowned Clubtail, appear stockier with wider clubs, and have S9 shorter than S8 (equal in Rapids).

HABITAT Large streams, and rivers, with gravel in rocky riffles or rapids, but also recorded from sluggish mud-bottomed rivers.

SEASON Early May to mid-July.

COMMENTS Away from water perches on the ground, or on low plants, including both broad leaves and grass. When disturbed they may fly a series of vertical UUUUs. Males at water perch on rocks or tips of vegetation in or near rapids or riffles.

Harpoon Clubtail *Gomphus descriptus* **Plate 7**

IDENTIFICATION 2.0 in., northeastern and Appalachian, uncommon. Abdomen slender and hardly clubbed, S8–S10 black dorsally (some females with dorsal yellow stripe on S10). Legs black, except hind thigh of female streaked with green. Anterior lateral thoracic black stripe sometimes interrupted. Eyes dark gray-green.

BODY FEATURES Male penis hood distinctive, narrow, black, and notably taller than wide. Male cerci barbed like a harpoon head, each with a lateral angle, and a large medial tooth at 1/3 length; epiproct spreads widely beyond cerci. Female occiput tall, erect, and shallowly notched. Subgenital plate black, 1/3 as long as S9, V-notched for half its length. Rapids Clubtail is like a miniature Harpoon Clubtail, but its penis hood is short and rounded, and female occiput and subgenital plate are short.

SIMILAR SPECIES Beaverpond Clubtail has gray-blue eyes, a narrow midfrontal brown thoracic stripe, and female has all-black legs. Dusky Clubtail has pale shins, and a yellow dorsal spot on S8. Rapids Clubtail is smaller, the female with black thighs and just a pale basal lateral spot on S7 (stripe in female Harpoon). Sable Clubtail has black facial stripes and a black occiput (green in Harpoon). Cherokee Clubtail has a narrow black facial cross-line, abdomen more clubbed, and female has black hind thighs and more yellow on sides of S8–S9. Some females of the Gomphurus Group are similar, but most are larger, with notable clubs, black hind thighs, or dorsal yellow spots on S8 or S9.

HABITAT Clear, rapid, rocky streams and rivers with silt-bottomed pools. In eastern Canada, sand-bottomed streams.

SEASON Early May to late July.

COMMENTS Forages in clearings and along forest edges, perching on the ground, sometimes on tree leaves. Males at water fly low over the current, then perch on rocks or sunny overhanging tree leaves. Females sometimes perch briefly on a rock with the abdomen curved upward slightly while accumulating a cluster of eggs.

Beaverpond Clubtail *Gomphus borealis* **Plate 7**

IDENTIFICATION 1.9 in., northeastern, uncommon. Front of thorax mostly green due to exceptionally narrow midfrontal brown stripe. Legs black. Abdomen only slightly clubbed and mostly black, sometimes with a yellow dorsal spot on S8, and in female usually with a dorsal yellow stripe on S10. Eyes greenish to silvery gray-blue.

SIMILAR SPECIES Harpoon Clubtail has dark gray-green eyes, a wide midfrontal brown stripe, and female has partly green hind thighs. Dusky Clubtail has a wide brown midfrontal stripe, and pale shins. Rapids Clubtail is smaller, with a wide black midfrontal stripe. Lilypad, Horned, and Unicorn Clubtails are larger, with lateral dark thoracic stripes absent or nearly so, both sexes with a pale dorsal spot on S10, and rusty orange edges on S9. Horned and Lilypad have bright blue eyes, while the Unicorn has pale shins. Some females of the Gomphurus Group are similar but have wider midfrontal brown stripes and wider clubs, and some have green streaks on the hind thighs.

HABITAT Mud-bottomed ponds, slow streams, and lakes.

SEASON Late May to late July.

COMMENTS Away from water perches in meadows on low vegetation or rocks. Males at water perch unwarily near shore. On beaver ponds they systematically patrol along the edge; on streams they fly short patrols over both riffles and pools.

Ashy Clubtail *Gomphus lividus* **Plate 8**

IDENTIFICATION 2.0 in., eastern, common. Not usually separable from Dusky Clubtail in the northeast. Dully colored, the thorax brown (black in northern part of range) with 2 pale lateral stripes. Abdomen slender and scarcely clubbed; S8 nearly always has a dorsal yellow basal spot, S9 is brown or dull yellow dorsally, and S10 is pale dorsally in females and some males. Hind thighs pale to dark, but usually pale brown. Shins pale. Face occasionally with dark cross-lines. Female eyes ventrally pale gray to brown or deep violet.

VARIATION Markings brighter in west TN area, resembling a large Lancet Clubtail.

BODY FEATURES Male cerci each with a lateral angle, but no ventral tooth or keel; epiproct as wide as cerci. Female occiput convex, occasionally straight-edged. Subgenital plate about 1/9 length of S9 and shallowly notched.

SIMILAR SPECIES Note lack of contrasting markings, medium size, and slender form. Dusky Clubtail of WV and northward is barely if at all distinguishable, but is generally blacker, the male epiproct extends widely beyond the cerci, and females do not have violet eyes. Other species of Phanogomphus of similar size and form are the Harpoon and Beaverpond Clubtails, which have sides of thorax mostly green, and black lower legs.

HABITAT Gently flowing water from trickles to rivers, but sometimes trout streams or lakes.

SEASON Mid-March to late Aug.

COMMENTS Forages from the ground, or occasionally tree leaves, in open woodland or clearings. When disturbed they often fly a series of vertical UUUUs. Males perch on shore, less often tree leaves. They ignore the smaller Lancet Clubtail, and patrol until after 7 P.M., even in shade, with alternating flits and sails.

Dusky Clubtail *Gomphus spicatus* Plate 8

IDENTIFICATION 2.0 in., northeastern, common. An obscurely patterned brownish-black species, not usually separable from Ashy Clubtail. S9 and S10 variably patterned, S9 black in nearly all females and most males but dull yellow in some, S10 with a pale dorsal stripe in females and some males. Hind thighs usually brown in male but pale in female, shins pale in both sexes. Male eyes gray to blue-gray, female eyes gray above, dark gray to brown below.

BODY FEATURES Male cerci each have a lateral tooth and a spikelike ventral tooth at midlength; epiproct spreads widely beyond cerci. Female occiput convex at its middle, concave on each side; subgenital plate 3/8 as long as S9, V-notched 1/2–2/3 toward its base, forming 2 pointed lobes.

SIMILAR SPECIES Ashy Clubtail is often paler brown, and female usually has lower part of eyes violet. Male Ashy lacks lateral teeth of cerci, and epiproct is not wider than cerci. Harpoon and Beaverpond Clubtails have separate lateral black thoracic stripes, and black lower legs. The Beaverpond has a narrow midfrontal brown thoracic stripe, while the Harpoon lacks a dorsal yellow spot on S8. Lancet Clubtail is considerably smaller. Certain females of the Gomphurus Group are similar, but are more robust, more sharply patterned, have noticeable clubs, lack a lower rear thoracic brown stripe, and most have black hind thighs.

HABITAT Boggy or marshy ponds, lakes, and slow streams, often sandy.

SEASON Mid-April to late July.

COMMENTS Forages from the ground or low vegetation in clearings or open woods, females sometimes in trees. It sometimes flies a series of fast vertical UUUUs. Males perch on shore or lily pads.

Lancet Clubtail *Gomphus exilis* Plate 8

IDENTIFICATION 1.7 in., eastern, commonest eastern Clubtail. Thorax has fused lateral brown stripes and a brown lower rear stripe. Abdomen with a full-length dorsal yellow stripe, and yellow sides on S8–S9. Male club small. Thighs usually brown in males, mostly green in females; shins pale in both sexes. Eyes grayish aqua-blue in males, dark gray to gray-green in females.

BODY FEATURES Male cerci lancet-shaped, with a triangular ventral blade, but without a lateral angle or tooth. Female subgenital plate 1/5–1/4 as long as S9, V-notched halfway to its base.

VARIATION Over most of range a dully colored, mostly brown species, but sometimes appears to be marked with black. In southernmost part of range it is more sharply patterned, with bright yellow abdominal markings and sometimes dark green eyes. Dorsal yellow on S9 varies from a narrow stripe, especially in the north, to almost the whole segment yellow in the south.

SIMILAR SPECIES Oklahoma Clubtail is nearly identical but does not range east of western AR/LA. Other similar Phanogomphus, all southeastern, lack a brown lower rear thoracic stripe, the lateral brown thoracic stripes are not fused, and some have S9 black dorsally or have brown face lines. Ashy and Dusky Clubtails are considerably larger. Pronghorn and Tennessee Clubtails are larger and more brightly colored, with well-developed male clubs. Eastern species of the Gomphurus Group with fused lateral thoracic dark stripes are larger, have wide male clubs, no dark lower rear thoracic stripe, and S9 is generally black dorsally (yellow in Plains Clubtail).

HABITAT Slow streams, lakes, and ponds, but especially marsh-bordered ponds in the open, and sand-bottomed lakes.

SEASON Early March to mid-Sept.

COMMENTS Settles unwarily on the ground or low plants. When disturbed they may fly a series of UUUUs 10 ft. high. Males perch on the shore or on low vegetation.

Oklahoma Clubtail *Gomphus oklahomensis* **Plate 8**

IDENTIFICATION 1.9 in., OK/LA area, common. Like Lancet Clubtail, but with a more western range.

BODY FEATURES Male cerci each with a lateral tooth, and a ventral keel in the posterior 1/4. Female has a small pit between each lateral simple eye and the compound eye (female Lancet has a small bump or spine there). Subgenital plate 1/8–1/6 as long as S9, V-notched for more than 1/2 its length.

SIMILAR SPECIES Pronghorn Clubtail is larger and more brightly colored, with a large club in the male. In LA check Hodges' Clubtail, which has only a narrow yellow dorsal line on S9, no dark area between the brown lateral thoracic stripes, and S10 is all black dorsally.

HABITAT Mud-bottomed ponds, lakes, slow streams, and rivers.

SEASON Late March to mid-July.

COMMENTS Perches on the ground or low vegetation. Males perch on the shore or leaves near the water's edge.

Hodges' Clubtail *Gomphus hodgesi* **Plate 8**

IDENTIFICATION 1.7 in., central Gulf Coast, uncommon. Abdomen slender and mostly black, S8–S9 (and S10 of female) with narrow yellow dorsal streaks. Lower half of thigh and shin green.

BODY FEATURES Male cerci uniquely shaped, like a pair of cow horns in dorsal view.

SIMILAR SPECIES Diminutive and Westfall's Clubtails have S9 longer than S8, a brown facial cross-line, and blacker thighs. Lancet, Oklahoma, Cypress, and Sandhill Clubtails have wide yellow dorsal stripes on S8 or S9, male abdomen more clubbed, and S10 of male has a yellow dorsal spot. Species of the Gomphus Group have stubbier, more widely clubbed abdomens, no dorsal yellow on S8–S10, and black lower legs.

HABITAT Clean sand-bottomed streams and rivers.

SEASON Early March to late May.

COMMENTS Named for Robert S. Hodges, American odonatist. Perches on the ground. Males do not visit water until they are old, thus most mating occurs away from water.

Cypress Clubtail *Gomphus minutus* **Plate 8**

IDENTIFICATION 1.8 in., far southeastern, common. Dully colored. Abdomen has a full-length dorsal yellow stripe, yellow sides on S7–S9, and male club moderately developed. Shins pale, thighs with or without pale streaks. Young juveniles may have upper face and dorsal S9 brown.

BODY FEATURES Male cerci like those of Lancet Clubtail, but each has a basal tooth on ventral blade. Female occiput distinctly concave in Cypress, straight-edged in Lancet.

VARIATION FL Panhandle individuals are larger and blacker than others.

SIMILAR SPECIES Only similar species in the FL Peninsula is Sandhill Clubtail, a sand-bottomed lake species that is usually smaller, has a brown facial cross-line, and males have lateral teeth on the cerci. Elsewhere, Lancet Clubtail has fused lateral thoracic brown stripes and a brown lower rear thoracic stripe. Hodges' Clubtail has only narrow yellow dorsal streaks on S8–S9, and male has a narrow club with S10 black dorsally. Westfall's Clubtail has S9 longer than S8, S8–S10 mostly black dorsally, and male club is slender.

HABITAT Slow streams and rivers, including small forest trickles, sometimes lakes, and occasionally ponds.

SEASON   Late Feb. to early June.

COMMENTS   Perches on the ground or low plants. When flushed it may fly a series of fast vertical UUUUs. Males at water perch in the afternoon on shore, sometimes on floating or emergent vegetation, less often on overhanging leaves. They fly fast smooth patrols over the water with the abdomen raised 40° but with the tip bent downward. In flight over land they may appear reddish brown, while over water they appear pale green. Males do not return to water until late in their lives, so most mating occurs in fields.

Sandhill Clubtail *Gomphus cavillaris* Plate 8

IDENTIFICATION   1.7 in., far southeastern, common FL. Note dark facial cross-line, pale shins, and yellow sides on S7–S9. Abdomen has a dorsal yellow stripe on S1–S8, and usually also on S9–S10 (on S10 especially in females). Male club moderately developed.

BODY FEATURES   Male cerci each have a lateral tooth and small ventral tooth. Female occiput straight-edged.

VARIATION   The **Brown Form** of the FL Peninsula is marked with brown and dull yellow, with rusty brown thighs. **Black Form** (*G. c. brimleyi*) of Carolinas and FL Panhandle is marked with black and bright yellow, with thighs pale ventrally. S9–S10 usually brown dorsally in NC.

SIMILAR SPECIES   Cypress Clubtail very similar, but usually larger and without a face line, and males lack lateral teeth on cerci. Cypress is only similar species in the FL Peninsula, and is not found in NC. Lancet Clubtail is brown, with fused lateral thoracic dark stripes and no face line. Hodges' Clubtail, a stream species of the FL Panhandle, has only narrow dorsal yellow streaks on S8–S9, no face line, and male abdomen is only slightly clubbed. Clearlake, Diminutive, and Westfall's Clubtails have S9 longer than S8, S8–S10 mostly black dorsally, slender male clubs, and the Clearlake is larger. The Gomphus Group contains stream species with short abdomens, wider clubs, black legs, and S8–S10 black dorsally.

HABITAT   Sand-bottomed lakes.

SEASON   Late Jan. to late May.

COMMENTS   Forages from the ground or low horizontal stems in open woodland, settling more quickly and directly than the Cypress Clubtail. Males are present at water from about 10:30 A.M. to 5 P.M., and perch on shore, floating objects, the bases of bald cypress trees, or waterside vegetation. They fly patrols lasting up to about 30 seconds close to shore.

Gomphus Group
(genus *Gomphus*, subgenus *Gomphus*)

Recognized by small size, chunky shape, black legs, and mostly black abdomen. The abdomen has a compact oval club due to having S7–S10 each successively shorter posteriorly, especially in females. S8–S10 are black dorsally, with at most a yellow dorsal dot on S8 or S10. They occupy clean streams and rivers, where males can be seen hovering over moving water. Both sexes usually squat unwarily flat on a sunny leaf. This group was formerly classified with a now-unused subgenus (*Hylogomphus*).

The male cerci are characteristic—thick, straight, and with a ventral tooth near the tip, but no lateral keel or tooth. Cerci and epiproct are divergent to the same degree. Females have long subgenital plates, 1/3 as long to as long as S9. They use these plates to accumulate egg balls between egg-laying bouts as they perch on the bank with abdomen curved upward. Females of most species have a pair of small spines on top of the head. While 6 species occur in eastern North America, 2 others are European.

Mustached Clubtail *Gomphus adelphus* Plate 9

IDENTIFICATION 1.7 in., northeastern and Appalachian, common. Recognized by chunky build, gray-green thorax with a narrow black posterior lateral stripe (anterior stripe usually incomplete), black abdomen, and black face stripes. Our only member of the Gomphus Group with more than 1 black facial stripe. Male abdomen beyond S4 almost all black, but female club edged with yellow.

SIMILAR SPECIES Green-Faced Clubtail lacks black facial markings and lateral thoracic stripes, and male has pale lateral spots on S5–S7. Other northern species of Gomphus Group lack black face stripes and have large lateral yellow spots on S8–S9. Pygmy Clubtails are smaller, blacker, and more slender, and males do not hover over water. Female Rapids Clubtails lack black facial markings, and S9 is as long as S8 (S9 shorter in Mustached).

HABITAT Mostly rapid clear rocky streams and rivers, sometimes lakes with exposed shores.

SEASON Early May to late Aug., about 1 month at each locale.

COMMENTS Formerly named *G. brevis*. Away from water perches on leaves of trees and bushes, sometimes in shade. Males hover over water at heads of riffles with abdomen raised and slightly arched, and

Green-Faced Clubtail *Gomphus viridifrons* **Plate 9**

perch on shore, rocks in the water, or tree leaves.

IDENTIFICATION | 1.8 in., northeastern and Appalachian, scarce. Robust, face and side of thorax clear gray-green, and abdomen mostly black (male has pale lateral spots on S5–S7, female has side of club pale yellow). Female markings may be yellow-green, especially face. Eyes dark green.

BODY FEATURES | Male penis hood distinctive, in side view a narrow triangle as tall as posterior hamule. Female subgenital plate black and as long as S9.

VARIATION | AL populations have a complete posterior lateral black thoracic stripe, and yellow sides on club in both sexes.

SIMILAR SPECIES | Mustached Clubtail has black facial markings, and males lack pale spots on S5–S7. Can be told from rest of Gomphus Group (except in AL) in that other males have sides of club yellow, and other females usually have black lateral thoracic stripes. Rapids Clubtail (Phanogomphus Group) has 2 black lateral thoracic stripes.

HABITAT | Clear rocky rivers and streams with a mixture of gravelly sand and silt among rocks. Generally larger streams than for Mustached Clubtail.

SEASON | Late April to late July.

COMMENTS | Away from water squats on leaves of weeds or trees, in sun or shade. Males often more active in late afternoon, especially in shade or when a cloud covers the sun. They hover with raised abdomen and extended hindlegs over riffles or rapids, perching occasionally on rocks in the water or shoreside bushes.

Twin-Striped Clubtail *Gomphus geminatus* **Plate 9**

IDENTIFICATION | 1.6 in., FL Panhandle area, common. Chunky, with a black facial cross-line, and 2 complete black lateral thoracic stripes. Eyes aqua-blue, becoming green when old. It has the most prominent black lateral thoracic stripes and bluest eyes in the Gomphus Group.

BODY FEATURES | Male penis hood is an equilateral triangle in side view. Male has each branch of epiproct narrower in ventral view than male Piedmont Clubtail. Female has only vestigial spines on top of head, and cross-ridge behind simple eyes extends to compound eyes. Female Piedmont has a short but stout spine between each end of cross-ridge and compound eyes. Subgenital plate of Twin-

Striped 3/4 as long as S9, split for 2/5 length with pointed tips of lobes turned laterally. Plate of Piedmont about 8/9 as long as S9, split for 1/3 length and shallowly V-notched at tip to form 2 bluntly pointed lobes.

VARIATION   Individuals east of the Apalachicola River in FL are larger (1.7–1.9 in.).

SIMILAR SPECIES   Only member of Gomphus Group in its range, but Piedmont Clubtail just to the north in central AL and central GA looks identical.

HABITAT   Clean, sand-bottomed streams.

SEASON   Early March to mid-June.

COMMENTS   Away from water perches from the ground to in the trees. Males at water may be wary, usually perching on overhanging leaves, but sometimes on the bank.

Piedmont Clubtail *Gomphus parvidens* Plate 9

IDENTIFICATION   1.7 in., southeastern Piedmont, uncommon. Chunky, without a black face-line (except in AL and GA), but with a well-developed club that has bright yellow sides. Eyes gray, becoming dark green to blue-gray in males, duller in females.

VARIATION   Posterior lateral black thoracic stripe complete, but anterior stripe variable, incomplete from MD to Carolinas and in GA females. In AL and GA face has a dark cross-line.

SIMILAR SPECIES   Twin-Striped Clubtail of southern AL and southern GA looks identical, but ranges not known to overlap. Spine-Crowned Clubtail may sometimes be impossible to distinguish, but has: (1) area between lateral black thoracic stripes usually darkened, (2) male occiput convex (straight in Piedmont), and (3) female usually has a dorsal yellow spot on S10, in addition to pale epiproct. Banner Clubtail has: (1) area between lateral thoracic stripes usually darkened, (2) face grayer or browner, and (3) male club wider and held higher when hovering over water. The female Rapids Clubtail (Phanogomphus Group) has S9 as long as S8 (S9 shorter in Gomphus Group).

HABITAT   Clean streams and rivers with sand or rock bottoms and silt deposits.

SEASON   Early April to late June.

COMMENTS   Called *G. carolinus* by some authors. Away from water perches on leaves from near ground to in the trees in semi-shaded humid areas that may be very localized. Males at water perch on low sunny overhanging leaves, or occasionally on the bank. They usually hover over water only under cool conditions.

Spine-Crowned Clubtail *Gomphus abbreviatus*
Plate 9

IDENTIFICATION 1.5 in., New England and Appalachian, uncommon. Chunky, with a yellow face, and a well-developed club with bright yellow sides. Side of thorax with 2 narrow black stripes, the anterior incomplete, the area between them usually gray. Female S10 normally with a dorsal yellow spot (in addition to epiproct).

BODY FEATURES Male genitalia differ from others in Gomphus Group in that posterior hamule is bladelike rather than pointed, and penis hood in side view is wider at base than tall. Female subgenital plate shorter than others of Gomphus Group, 2/5 as long as S9, 1/2 or more in others. Female has a thin spine behind each lateral simple eye.

SIMILAR SPECIES S10 all black in other females of Gomphus Group. See Similar Species under Piedmont Clubtail, and compare range with Piedmont and Banner Clubtails.

HABITAT Clean streams and rivers, either sand- or rock-bottomed, but with muck deposits.

SEASON Mid-April to early July.

COMMENTS Away from water perches on leaves of weeds or trees, often on hilltops. Males hover facing upstream at heads of riffles, and perch on rocks in the stream or on shoreline leaves. They are most active in late afternoon, but may begin patrolling in midmorning.

Banner Clubtail *Gomphus apomyius* Plate 9

IDENTIFICATION 1.5 in., Southeastern to NJ, scarce. Chunky, with a particularly wide male club that is yellow-sided. Area between the 2 black lateral thoracic stripes often clouded with brown, and face dull brownish green.

BODY FEATURES Male penis hood convex posteriorly in side view (concave to straight in others of Gomphus Group). Ventral tooth of male cerci is a knife-edged ridge. Female very like female Piedmont Clubtail, but spines on top of head often absent. Subgenital plate of Banner more deeply V-notched, forming divergent pointed lobes (bluntly pointed in Piedmont).

SIMILAR SPECIES Only member of Gomphus Group found west of Mississippi, and with the widest male club. Piedmont Clubtail does not have area between lateral black thoracic stripes darkened, anterior lateral stripe is often incomplete, face is green, and male occiput is straight (convex in Banner). The female Spine-Crowned Clubtail normally has a dorsal yellow spot on S10. See Similar species under Piedmont Clubtail.

HABITAT	Clean sand/gravel-bottomed streams and rivers, but can tolerate some silt.
SEASON	Mid-March to late June.
COMMENTS	Forages along forest edges from 5 ft. up into the canopy, mostly in morning and late afternoon. Males hover, most often when cool, at heads of riffles with the abdomen raised almost straight up with the club widely flared, bannerlike, but from about 6 to 7:30 P.M. the abdomen is raised less. They perch on the leaves of overhanging bushes, emergent rocks, or the bank.

Stenogomphurus Group
(genus *Gomphus*, subgenus *Stenogomphurus*)

The 2 mostly black species in this group are Appalachian and seldom seen. The club is slender in males, barely present in females, and all black dorsally on S8–S10. The thorax is small, and the HW are scarcely widened basally, suggesting that these species fly little, and that they evolved in a forest habitat protected from high winds.

Cherokee Clubtail *Gomphus consanguis* Plate 9

IDENTIFICATION	1.9 in., Southern Appalachians, rare. Slender and mostly black, with 2 narrow lateral black thoracic stripes. Thorax green-gray in male, yellow-green in female. Abdomen with a narrow interrupted pale dorsal line on S1–S7, the club small and equally undeveloped in both sexes. Face with a very narrow upper black cross-line. Dorsal surface of occiput pale, male eyes aqua-green, female eyes dull green. Legs black.
SIMILAR SPECIES	Sable Clubtail has a widely interrupted anterior lateral black thoracic stripe, 2 black face stripes, and a black occiput. The male Harpoon Clubtail practically lacks a club and has a green thorax, while the female has pale streaks on hind thighs, a pale epiproct, and sometimes dorsal pale spots on S8 or S10. Rapids Clubtail is much smaller, with brighter yellow on sides of S8–S9. Species of Gomphurus Group differ by one or more of the following: wide club, yellow dorsal spots on S8 or S9, S8 black posterolaterally (yellow in Stenogomphurus), lack of one or both lateral black thoracic stripes, larger size, and pale markings less gray than

male Cherokee. Similar species of Hanging Clubtails have narrow isolated pale frontal thoracic stripes, pale dorsal spots on S8 or S9, more yellow on sides of S8–S9; some have pale thighs, and males have a green thorax. Similar Pond Clubtails have a pale dorsal spot on S10, narrow black midfrontal thoracic stripe, and some have pale leg stripes.

HABITAT Spring-fed moderately flowing forest streams, especially where they drain small ponds.

SEASON Mid-May to early July.

COMMENTS Forages from low perches on leaves at semi-shaded forest edges. Males perch unwarily on streamside vegetation, launching slow patrols over the stream about a yard up, hovering occasionally.

Sable Clubtail *Gomphus rogersi* **Plate 9**

IDENTIFICATION 2.0 in., Appalachian, common but secretive. Slender, mostly black, with the anterior lateral black thoracic stripe widely interrupted. Thorax of male pale gray-green, green-yellow in female. Club equally undeveloped in both sexes, face with 2 black cross-stripes, legs black. Black dorsal surface of occiput diagnostic, but crest bent so far forward, especially in females, that pale rear surface shows in a perpendicular dorsal view. Eyes bright green in males, duller in females.

SIMILAR SPECIES No similar species has a black occiput. Cherokee Clubtail has anterior lateral black thoracic stripe complete though narrow, and one inconspicuous face line. Most similar Clubtails lack black facial stripes and have a complete anterior lateral black thoracic stripe. See Similar Species under Cherokee Clubtail.

HABITAT Clear, moderately flowing forest streams, usually rocky with some silt and sand, especially below a logjam or other obstruction.

SEASON Mid-April to late July.

COMMENTS Forages from semi-shaded leaves at forest edges, often well above ground. Males perch on rocks, overhanging grass, or floating plants. They are at water from midmorning to late afternoon, hovering briefly during occasional patrols. Compared with Cherokee Clubtail, Sable stays more in shade, is less nervous, and flight is slower.

Gomphurus Group
(genus *Gomphus*, subgenus *Gomphurus*)

Most members of this group are striking large insects with a characteristic shape, given by the wide club, large thorax, and small head. Many species are both scarce and wary. Males are usually seen patrolling far out over rivers with a bouncy flight and raised club. S8 and S9 each have yellow or green lateral and dorsal spots, the relative sizes of which are useful in field identification.

The common and pollution-resistant Black-Shouldered Spinyleg behaves like a Gomphurus, but is more slender with less yellow on the club, and when perched its unique thoracic pattern and extra-long hindlegs can be seen. The Zebra Clubtail looks more like a Gomphurus than like other Hanging Clubtails. Gomphurus with a dorsal yellow marking on S9 do not occur in the southeast or east of the Appalachians, making separation from the Phanogomphus Group easier in those areas.

The male epiproct spreads as wide as the cerci in 5 of our Gomphurus, slightly wider in 7, and considerably wider in the Plains Clubtail. The female subgenital plate is usually narrow and straplike, about half as long as S9. Females of most species have a pair of small spines on top of the head. Of the 11 species seen mating, about half mate in trees and half on the ground or low plants, not necessarily correlated with habitat. All 13 species of this group live in North America, but only 2 range into the west: the Plains and Columbia Clubtails.

Skillet Clubtail *Gomphus ventricosus* Plate 10

IDENTIFICATION   Smallest Gomphurus, 1.9 in. Northeastern, rare. Recognized by very wide yellow-striped club and lack of black lateral thoracic stripes. It has the proportionately widest club of any of our Clubtails, wider than the thorax. S8–S9 bear large yellow lateral spots that are usually joined into stripes, and S8–S10 are black dorsally (rarely S8 or S10 with tiny dorsal yellow spot). Legs black (rarely female hind thigh with pale streak).

SIMILAR SPECIES   The larger Handsome and Midland Clubtails have a yellow dorsal spot on S8, and widely separated lateral yellow spots on S8–S9. All our other Clubtails with wide clubs have dark lateral thoracic stripes.

HABITAT   Small to large turbid rivers with at least a partly mud bottom but good water quality. Sometimes clean lakes with sand or sand-marl (calcium-rich) bottoms.

SEASON   Mid-May to late July.

COMMENTS A jewel of a dragonfly named for its skillet- or frying-pan-shaped abdomen. Away from water perches on weeds or the ground, often in shade. Males perch on leaves or the bank, often inconspicuously down among plants. They make short patrols consisting of a few loops with a bouncy flight over the water, gradually working toward shore, then suddenly fly to a perch.

Cobra Clubtail *Gomphus vastus* **Plate 10**

IDENTIFICATION   2.1 in., eastern, fairly common. **Black Form** found in most of range recognized by wide club with yellow lateral spot of S8 much smaller than that of S9, and wide black face stripes. Spot of S8 does not reach lateral edge of its segment, but spot of S9 does. In most of the east, it is the only Gomphurus with black face stripes. Lateral thoracic dark stripes usually complete, S8–S10 black dorsally, and legs black. Basal 1/4 of wings tinted yellow. Eyes usually dark green.

BODY FEATURES   Penis hood of male uniquely square-tipped in side view. Female occipital crest concave, and in side view subgenital plate is bent dorsally at middle into a wide V profile. Plate 1/2 as long as S9, split for 1/2 length into 2 narrow pointed parallel lobes, the sides convergent to tips of lobes. Female Blackwater Clubtail has occipital crest straight, and subgenital plate nearly parallel-sided in ventral view, straight in profile.

VARIATION   Primarily in the Great Lakes/New England area, anterior lateral dark thoracic stripe may be incomplete, and posterior stripe may be nearly lacking. Facial stripes may be reduced or absent in Mississippi River and TX individuals. The **Brown Form**, found Southwest of AR, has brown markings and may have a pale basal ring on S7. TX individuals have dull yellow-green eyes, and S8 may have a dorsal yellow spot.

SIMILAR SPECIES   Blackwater Clubtail of the southeast is larger, with smaller pale lateral spots on both S8 and S9, the spot of S9 often not reaching the lateral edge of the segment. Gulf Coast Clubtail has a narrow facial line, and conspicuous lateral yellow spots on both S8 and S9. Other somewhat similar Clubtails have narrower clubs.

HABITAT   Mostly large rivers with a moderate to rapid current, but sometimes large streams or large lakes.

SEASON   Early April to mid-Sept.

COMMENTS   Named for wide club, shaped like the hood of a cobra snake. Ranges up to 1/2 mile from water, where it perches on weeds or in trees. Males perch on overhanging leaves, sometimes on shore, and fly long reconnaissance patrols over pools. At a distance they look dark, with only the yellow spot of S9 conspicuous. Females may accumulate a large mass of eggs before leaving a perch on shore.

Blackwater Clubtail *Gomphus dilatatus* **Plate 10**

IDENTIFICATION   Largest Gomphurus, 2.7 in. Southeastern, common. The only Gomphurus in the FL Peninsula. Identified by wide club with only small green to yellow lateral spots on S8–S9, and mostly black face. Spot of S8 does not reach edge of segment, and it is the only Gomphurus in which spot of S9 may not reach edge of its segment. S8–S10 black dorsally, and legs black. Thorax has both lateral black stripes; these are occasionally narrowed, rarely interrupted. Wings tinted yellow in basal 1/3. Rarely, S7 has a pale basal ring.

SIMILAR SPECIES   Cobra Clubtail has a bright yellow lateral spot on S9. Gulf Coast Clubtail has a narrow black facial line, and large yellow lateral spots on both S8 and S9. Other similar Clubtails have narrower clubs.

HABITAT   Usually moderately flowing, clean, blackwater (tannin-stained), silt-bottomed rivers and streams, but sometimes muddy rivers.

SEASON   Early March to late Aug., most common in late spring.

COMMENTS   Away from water this impressive insect is wary and perches on both ground and leaves. Males usually perch on overhanging leaves, but may squat on the bank, flying periodic patrols about 100 ft. long. They arrive at water when the morning becomes warm and leave about 3 P.M., with peak numbers 10 A.M. to 12 P.M.

Gulf Coast Clubtail *Gomphus modestus* **Plate 10**

IDENTIFICATION   2.4 in., central Gulf Coast area, scarce. Identified by its wide club with conspicuous yellow lateral spots on both S8 and S9, and a black facial cross-line. Lateral spot of S8 does not reach edge of segment. S8–S10 black dorsally (S8 occasionally has small basal pale spot). Thorax has both black lateral stripes; legs black.

BODY FEATURES   Female occipital crest straight to slightly concave, and subgenital plate has bluntly rounded lobes (only other Gomphurus with rounded lobes is Splendid Clubtail).

SIMILAR SPECIES   Blackwater Clubtail has a mostly black face, and inconspicuous lateral pale spots on S8–S9. Cobra Clubtail usually has wide black facial stripes, and a small lateral spot on S8. Splendid Clubtail has a small club with lateral spot of S8 reaching edge of segment, and a narrow, almost parallel-sided midfrontal black thoracic stripe (stripe widens downward in Gulf Coast).

HABITAT Clean rivers and streams, with silty sand or rocky bottoms.

SEASON Mid-April to late June.

COMMENTS Apparently spends most of its time in trees, and males seem not to come down to small streams where females will lay eggs. Males in late morning perch warily on the sunny bank, at midday much less warily on sunny overhanging leaves, and in midafternoon on shaded sticks and leaves. They spend little time patrolling, leaving the water about 3 P.M., but may fly over water at dusk. Females apparently visit riffles for mating when they are still soft juveniles.

Splendid Clubtail *Gomphus lineatifrons* **Plate 10**

IDENTIFICATION 2.6 in., eastern U.S., uncommon. Club relatively small for a Gomphurus, compressed to form vertical sides, with large yellow lateral spots on S8–S9 that reach edges of segments, and S8–S10 black dorsally (rarely small yellow basal spot on S8). It has an interrupted black anterior lateral thoracic stripe, a narrow black facial cross-line, and black legs. Midfrontal black thoracic stripe usually parallel-sided and narrower than green stripe on either side of it. Eyes bright green.

SIMILAR SPECIES Cobra, Blackwater, and Gulf Coast Clubtails have wide, horizontally flattened clubs with lateral spot of S8 not reaching edge of segment, and a wide, black midfrontal thoracic stripe. Black face stripes of Cobra and Blackwater Clubtails are much wider, and pale lateral spot of S8 is small. Midland, Handsome, and Plains Clubtails are smaller and lack a face line; latter 2 also normally have a yellow dorsal stripe on S9.

HABITAT Clear, rapidly flowing, usually rocky rivers, with sandy gravel and silt among the rocks.

SEASON Early May to late July.

COMMENTS Forages from the ground or weeds. Males perch on shore or overhanging leaves near riffles until dusk. A little clumsy for a dragonfly, they often turn on their legs to face a different direction, like an airplane taxiing for takeoff. Since they are heavy bodied, they hover over water only when temperature conditions are exactly right, raising and flaring out their clubs to present a striking figure.

Midland Clubtail *Gomphus fraternus* **Plate 10**

IDENTIFICATION 2.2 in., northeastern, uncommon. Cannot always be told from Handsome Clubtail, as discussed below. S8–S9 have large lateral yellow spots, and S8 has a dorsal yellow spot, while in most of range S9 is black dorsally. Anterior lateral black thoracic stripe interrupted, posterior stripe varies from well developed to absent. Legs black, except hind thigh of female normally has a pale lateral stripe. Eyes gray-green, becoming aqua-blue at cool temperatures.

BODY FEATURES Males lack a lateral tooth on the cerci that is present in the Handsome Clubtail. Male epiproct spreads beyond cerci; as wide as cerci in Handsome. Female is only Gomphurus with a unicorn-like upright point at middle of occipital crest.

VARIATION **Pale Form** (*G. f. manitobanus*) has more extensive yellow markings. In southeastern Manitoba they have yellow dorsal stripes on S9–S10, and yellow shins. Some individuals, especially females, from SD and Indiana also have one or more of these yellow markings.

SIMILAR SPECIES Some Handsome Clubtails look like Midland, but: (1) Handsome has smaller range, (2) Midland lacks a dorsal yellow spot on S9 (except from Indiana westward) that is nearly always present in Handsome, and (3) female Midland nearly always has a pale lateral stripe on hind thigh that is usually lacking in Handsome. Male Handsome Clubtails at water appear larger and darker, with eyes aqua-blue rather than gray-green, and patrol with the club held higher, 45° instead of 30°. Ozark, Plains, Pronghorn, Tennessee, and Sulphur-Tipped Clubtails have 2 complete lateral black thoracic stripes, which are often fused (anterior stripe incomplete dorsally in Tennessee Clubtail), the last 3 species are smaller, and all but Ozark have pale shins. Splendid Clubtail is larger, normally black dorsally on S8–S9, and has a narrow black facial cross-line.

HABITAT Moderately to rapidly flowing rivers and large streams with clay or fine sand bottoms. Also large lakes with emergent vegetation.

SEASON Early April to early Aug.

COMMENTS Away from water squats on ground or low plants in fields or open woods. At rivers most males are at riffles, but some patrol quiet water. They perch on the bank or rocks, seldom on gravel bars or leaves, and launch long, fast, sweeping patrols with some hovering, often far out over open water.

Handsome Clubtail *Gomphus crassus* **Plate 10**

IDENTIFICATION 2.2 in., AL to OH, uncommon. Not always distinguishable from Midland Clubtail, as discussed below. Thorax of male deep gray-green, yellow-green in female. S8–S9 with large yellow lateral spots, and nearly always a wide dorsal yellow stripe on S9. Anterior lateral black thoracic stripe usually interrupted, and black posterior stripe often obscure or absent. Legs black, hind thigh of female occasionally with pale stripe. Eyes aqua-gray-blue in males, green in females.

SIMILAR SPECIES   Compared with Midland Clubtail, patrolling males appear larger and darker, with eyes aqua-blue rather than gray-green, and they raise the club higher, 45° instead of 30°. See Identification and Similar Species under Midland Clubtail.

HABITAT   Clean small to medium-size rivers with a rapid current and gravel bottom.

SEASON   Early May to late July.

COMMENTS   Away from water perches on the ground or weeds near forest edges in shade or sunlight, and may make extended hunting flights over low vegetation. Males hover over riffles, and usually fly to the trees when leaving the water, but occasionally perch on the shore.

Septima's Clubtail *Gomphus septima* **Plate 11**

IDENTIFICATION   2.3 in., AL to NY, mostly NC, rare. Markings dark brown, lateral dark thoracic stripes nearly absent (anterior widely interrupted, posterior obscure or absent). Dark shoulder stripes wide and fused dorsally. Club small, with small pale lateral spots on S8–S9, and S8–S10 brown dorsally (tiny basal pale spot on S8 in some). Legs dark brown with pale streaks on hind thighs of some, especially females.

BODY FEATURES   Crest of female occiput wavy, concave in a wide V at middle and convex toward the ends.

VARIATION   NC males are smaller (2.2 in.) than AL ones (2.5 in.). NY individuals are blacker.

SIMILAR SPECIES   Splendid, Midland, and Handsome Clubtails are more brightly colored, with sharply defined black markings and bright yellow lateral spots on S8–S9. Splendid is much larger, while Handsome usually has a yellow dorsal stripe on S9. Black-Shouldered Spinyleg has only narrow green frontal thoracic lines (wide green stripes in Septima's), and usually has dorsal pale spots on S8–S10.

HABITAT   Clean rocky rivers.

SEASON   Early May to early June.

COMMENTS   Named for Septima Smith, American entomologist. Away from water perches mostly on the ground or flat on low leaves in fields or sunny spots in forest, but sometimes in trees. Males perch warily on rocks in or near riffles from about 11 A.M. to 6 P.M. They make wide sorties over the water, occasionally hovering for a few seconds.

Ozark Clubtail *Gomphus ozarkensis* **Plate 11**

IDENTIFICATION 2.0 in., Ozark area, fairly common. Black shoulder stripes essentially fused with each other, as are the black lateral thoracic stripes (gray between lateral stripes in juveniles), thus forming 2 broad bands. S8–S9 have large yellow lateral spots, S8 is normally black dorsally. S9–S10 black, or may have narrow dorsal yellow stripes. Legs black.

SIMILAR SPECIES Plains Clubtail has wide yellow dorsal spots or stripes on S8–S10. Cocoa Clubtail is smaller and dull brown, with lateral yellow spot of S8 inconspicuous and nearly isolated from lateral edge of segment. Pronghorn Clubtail is smaller with a wide yellow dorsal stripe on S9.

HABITAT Clear moderately flowing rivers and streams.

SEASON Late April to late June, about a month at each locale.

COMMENTS Forages from about 10 A.M. to 7:30 P.M., perching on the ground or low tree leaves. Males patrol in the afternoon with a bouncy flight over a wide area, hovering occasionally.

Plains Clubtail *Gomphus externus* **Plate 11**

IDENTIFICATION 2.1 in., Great Plains area and UT, fairly common. Cannot always be separated from Pronghorn Clubtail as discussed below. Body black, extensively marked with bright yellow, including a dorsal spot or stripe on all abdominal segments, large lateral spots on S8–S9 that reach the edges of the segments, and the shins. All dark thoracic stripes complete, shoulder stripes usually fused dorsally, lateral stripes often joined by gray or brown. Thighs black in males, often pale dorsally in females. Male epiproct spreads well beyond cerci.

BODY FEATURES Male cerci straight in side view and without a lateral tooth (epiproct a little wider than cerci and tooth present in Pronghorn Clubtail). Female subgenital plate 3/5 as long as S9 (1/6 in Pronghorn). Female has a slender, yellow, laterally slanting spine on top of head next to each compound eye (spines absent in Tamaulipan Clubtail).

VARIATION In NM and west TX looks like Tamaulipan Clubtail, with paler coloration, narrow brown thoracic stripes, and mostly yellow S8–S9.

SIMILAR SPECIES Pronghorn Clubtail of Phanogomphus Group very similar but smaller, the male epiproct barely spreads beyond cerci, and males are not likely to patrol flowing parts of rivers. Sulphur-Tipped Clubtail is smaller, has a pale shoulder stripe, yellow thighs in both sexes, and more yellow on club. Midland and Handsome Clubtails have narrow black lateral thoracic stripes that are never fused, the anterior usually interrupted, the yellow lateral spot of S8 often not reaching the edge of its segment, and black legs (except Pale Form of Midland).

HABITAT   Moderately flowing rivers and large streams with muddy bottoms, occasionally lakes.

SEASON   Early April to mid-Aug., most common in spring.

COMMENTS   Away from water perches on ground or weed tips. Males at water are wary and alert, perching on the shore or rocks in the water, or, if other perches are lacking, on overhanging vegetation. They reconnoiter with occasional long sweeping patrols over open water, then commonly fly over shore vegetation to perch on open ground.

Tamaulipan Clubtail *Gomphus gonzalezi* **Plate 11**

IDENTIFICATION   1.9 in., southernmost TX, local. Very similar to Plains Clubtail, but smaller, and brown marked with pale yellow, with a brown lower rear thoracic stripe, yellow bands on S8–S9, and all-brown lower legs. Male epiproct barely wider than cerci.

SIMILAR SPECIES   The only Gomphurus found on Rio Grande in south TX, although Plains Clubtail occurs farther upstream in west TX.

HABITAT   Rivers, either clear and rocky, or muddy.

SEASON   Mid-April to late June.

COMMENTS   Away from water perches on the ground or low vegetation. Males perch on rocks in the water, or on overhanging vegetation. It ranges south through Tamaulipas to San Luis Potosí, Mexico.

Columbia Clubtail *Gomphus lynnae* **Plate 11**

IDENTIFICATION   2.3 in., WA/OR, local. Only Clubtail in its range with a dark lower rear thoracic stripe. Also our most pruinose Clubtail; with thorax and S1–S2 covered with translucent blue-gray wax at maturity. Black shoulder stripes nearly fused with each other, as are the black lateral thoracic stripes, forming 2 wide bands. Abdomen mostly black with pale dorsal and lateral spots on S8 and S9. Legs black.

SIMILAR SPECIES   Pacific and Pronghorn Clubtails are smaller and not pruinose.

HABITAT   Open rivers with mud and gravel among rocks.

SEASON   Late May to late Aug.

COMMENTS	Wanders up to 200 yards from water, perching on the ground or low vegetation. Males at water perch on the bank.

Cocoa Clubtail *Gomphus hybridus* Plate 11

IDENTIFICATION	2.0 in., southeastern, fairly common. Smaller, browner, and more dully colored than most Gomphurus. Brown lateral thoracic stripes complete, the area between them tinted brown. S8 has small dorsal and lateral pale spots, with the lateral spot isolated or nearly so from the edge, while S9 is widely yellow laterally. Legs brown with pale streaks on shins.
BODY FEATURES	Occiput of both sexes like a thick ax blade with a very convex crest.
SIMILAR SPECIES	Ozark Clubtail is larger and blacker, with a larger yellow lateral spot on S8, and thoracic stripes more completely fused. Brown Form of Cobra Clubtail is larger, with separate brown lateral thoracic stripes. Plains Clubtail has a yellow dorsal stripe on S9, and large lateral yellow spots on S8–S9 which reach edges of segments. Other similar Clubtails such as Ashy Clubtail have longer more slender abdomens with narrow clubs.
HABITAT	Medium to large rivers with silt/sand bottoms.
SEASON	Late March to early June.
COMMENTS	A cryptic species that does not advertise itself. Away from water usually perches on the ground in semi-shaded areas, sometimes in small areas down among weeds, but as rain approaches they perch in trees near the trunk. They also perch on weeds and tree leaves, and are not too wary but fly fast. Males perch on the bank in semi-shade and spend little time patrolling.

Hanging Clubtails
(genus *Stylurus*)

These medium-size Clubtails fly primarily in late summer and autumn, and inhabit rivers and streams, occasionally lakes. Males commonly patrol over water for long periods, then perch on top of leaves, which their weight often bends downward until they are hanging nearly vertically. The abdomen is long and slender, moderately clubbed in males (wide club in Zebra Clubtail) but little clubbed in females. The front of the thorax is dark with 2 isolated pale stripes that are divergent downward (not isolated in Olive and Brimstone Clubtails). The legs are short. The male cerci, which are fused to S10, lack teeth, and have at most a lateral angle. The branches of the epiproct diverge at the same angle as the cerci, and the anterior hamule is reduced and rodlike without teeth. The female occiput is similar and straight-edged in our 11 species, but 6 have spines on top of the head. The subgenital plate is short, less than 2/5 the length of S9.

The Zebra Clubtail looks like a member of the Gomphurus Group, while the Russet-Tipped Clubtail resembles the Southeastern Spinyleg, although the latter has long legs. The Black-Shouldered Spinyleg looks like a Hanging Clubtail over the water, but it often perches on the bank or on rocks, and then its long hindlegs can be seen.

Of our 11 species, only 3 occur in the west (Olive, Brimstone, and Russet-Tipped). About 20 others are Eurasian.

Zebra Clubtail *Stylurus scudderi* Plate 12

IDENTIFICATION 2.3 in., northeastern and Appalachian, fairly common. Most robust of our Hanging Clubtails, resembling a Gomphurus. The only eastern Clubtail (except Least) which is mostly black with pale green rings on S3–S7. Also note 2 black facial stripes, wide and partly fused black lateral thoracic stripes, and black legs. Male abdomen widely clubbed, female abdomen very stout and not clubbed. Female yellower than male, with porthole-like lateral spots on S2–S9.

SIMILAR SPECIES This exotic-looking species, with alternating pale and black markings for the whole length of the body, looks like no other within its range. Female could be mistaken for Tiger Spiketail.

HABITAT Clear forest streams and small rivers with riffles, a slow to rapid current, and a sand/muck bottom, including trout streams.

SEASON Mid-June to early Oct.

COMMENTS Forages along forest edges and in clearings. Males perch on sand or logs, as well as on leaves of bushes, from where they make occasional swift but short patrols over riffles. They are wary and are most active late in the day.

Arrow Clubtail *Stylurus spiniceps* Plate 12

IDENTIFICATION Our largest and most elongate Hanging Clubtail, 2.5 in. Eastern, fairly common. Our only Hanging Clubtail with S9 notably longer than S8. Black marked with whitish green, the black lateral thoracic stripes wide and often fused, and face and legs black. S9 and sometimes S8 with lower sides pale yellow to green, S9–S10 black dorsally.

SIMILAR SPECIES   Laura's and Elusive Clubtails are smaller, with narrow black lateral thoracic stripes, large yellow lateral spots on S8–S9, and a shorter S9.

HABITAT   Large rivers, rarely streams or lakes, usually with sandy bottoms. Seems most common in the Piedmont.

SEASON   Mid-June to mid-Oct.

COMMENTS   Away from water perches in grass, brush, and apparently in treetops. The wary males patrol with their abdomen only slightly raised, most actively from late afternoon to dark, but sometimes at midday. They fly long straight sweeps over midstream, only occasionally perching on tree leaves.

Olive Clubtail *Stylurus olivaceus* Plate 12

IDENTIFICATION   2.2 in., western, scattered populations. Thorax gray-green with wide parentheses or ()-shaped pale frontal stripes, and sides without dark stripes. Thighs with pale stripes, lower legs black. Some individuals have a narrow dark line across face.

VARIATION   **Pale Form** (*S. o. nevadensis*) ranging east of Sierra Nevada Mountains has pale markings yellower and dark markings browner than **Dark Form** from west of those mountains. Pale Form has S3–S7, and often S8–S9, with pale basal rings, and S10 brown to yellow dorsally. In Dark Form, rings are most likely on S6–S7 of females, and S10 is black in males, either black or yellow in females.

SIMILAR SPECIES   Brimstone Clubtail is smaller and yellow-green. Pacific Clubtail has a black posterior lateral thoracic stripe. Snaketails have much narrower dark midfrontal and shoulder stripes.

HABITAT   Mud- or sand-bottomed rivers and streams up to 1000 ft.

SEASON   Mid-June to mid-Oct.

COMMENTS   Roosts in trees, from which they descend to lower branches, or even the ground, about 10 A.M., the females lower than males. Males move to the leaves of weeds and trees along the river at midday. They make patrols lasting several minutes, flying slowly and smoothly with occasional sudden darts for a few yards. They prefer patrolling over rippling but deep water, and are wary when patrolling.

Brimstone Clubtail *Stylurus intricatus* Plate 12

IDENTIFICATION   1.9 in., central Great Plains, and western, scattered populations. Our palest Hanging Clubtail, and the only one with pale shins. Mostly yellow-green, including thighs and basal rings on S3–S7. Front of thorax more pale than dark, anterior dark shoulder stripe nearly isolated, and lateral dark thoracic stripes faint to absent. S8–S10 sulfur-yellow laterally and sometimes dorsally. Stigmas tan.

SIMILAR SPECIES   Olive and Russet-Tipped Clubtails are larger and gray-green, with front of thorax and the abdomen more dark than pale. Eastern Ringtail is brighter green, with an orange club and black stigmas. Flag-Tailed Spinyleg has a vertically flattened rusty orange club and long legs. Snaketails lack abdominal rings and S8–S9 have black stripes.

HABITAT   Rivers in open country, including muddy, warm, sluggish, and sand-bottomed ones.

SEASON   Early June to mid-Oct.

COMMENTS   Feeds from tips of low vegetation in open fields, retiring to bushes under windy conditions. Males at water perch on driftwood or bushes, seldom on the ground, and fly wide-ranging patrols.

Russet-Tipped Clubtail *Stylurus plagiatus* **Plate 12**

IDENTIFICATION   2.4 in., eastern and southwestern, common southeastern Coastal Plain, scarce northward. Patrolling **Eastern Form** males readily recognized by gray-green thorax and rusty orange club. Female abdomen very elongate and practically clubless. Both lateral thoracic dark stripes present and complete, and thighs pale green to brown.

VARIATION   Eastern Form has green eyes and russet club, and is largest and darkest in the southeast, where markings are black, frontal pale stripes are isolated, and the face is brown. In the Great Plains states, green frontal stripes are often connected to form a W-shaped marking, posterior lateral thoracic brown stripe may be faint, and the face is green. **Western Form** has brown markings, blue eyes, and the club is yellow and brown or black; S8–S9 have dorsal and lateral yellow spots, which in males may be connected diffusely or conspicuously to form basal bands. South TX populations are intermediate, like the Eastern Form but with blue eyes.

SIMILAR SPECIES   Shining Clubtail of the southeast is much paler, with a yellow-green thorax and pale orange club. Southeastern Spinyleg is larger, with long black legs, and males do not patrol extensively over open water. Two-Striped and Narrow-Striped Forceptails have sides of thorax more brown than green.

HABITAT   Rivers, streams, and lakes, often with silty sand bottoms.

SEASON   Late April to early Dec. in FL, late June to late Sept. in NJ.

COMMENTS   Forages from leaves along forest edges and in treetops, often perching facing the vegetation. Males patrol areas of 40-plus yards diameter over deep water from 9 A.M. until dark, occasionally perching on tree leaves. Periodically they hover for up to 30 seconds or more, facing two or three directions, then make off to a new location at high speed. It ranges south into Nuevo León and Sonora, Mexico.

Shining Clubtail *Stylurus ivae* Plate 12

IDENTIFICATION   2.2 in., southeastern, uncommon. Palest eastern Hanging Clubtail, with sides of thorax yellow-green and club mostly pale orange. Brown lateral thoracic stripes narrow and often incomplete. Stigmas brown.

SIMILAR SPECIES   Russet-Tipped Clubtail has a gray-green thorax and rusty orange club. Eastern Ringtail is much smaller, with black stigmas and front of thorax mostly pale. Southeastern Spinyleg is larger, with a gray-green thorax, well-developed black lateral thoracic stripes, and long legs. Flag-Tailed Spinyleg has a prominent green shoulder stripe (narrow to absent in Shining), small head, long legs, and male has a vertically flattened club.

HABITAT   Clean, sand-bottomed streams and rivers.

SEASON   Mid-Aug. to mid-Nov., beginning later than any other southeastern dragonfly.

COMMENTS   Forages in sunny clearings and along forest edges, perching on leaves of weeds or trees. Males may be at water for only the mid-day hours, perching on overhanging leaves or on sticks in the water. Patrolling males cover about 30 yards of stream, and at a distance may appear to be two shining spots moving together, the thorax and the club. They hover more, and shift positions less often and more slowly, than do male Russet-Tipped Clubtails.

Yellow-Sided Clubtail *Stylurus potulentus* Plate 12

IDENTIFICATION   2.0 in., central Gulf Coast, rare. Body very slender, mostly black with sides of thorax and club yellow. Also note dark blue eyes and brown face. Rounded wingtips, and parallel-sided HW mark this as a forest species, not adapted for flying in the open.

SIMILAR SPECIES   Similar species have green eyes. Townes' Clubtail has a yellow-green thorax and wider club. Laura's Clubtail is larger, with a green thorax bearing brown lateral stripes. Shining Clubtail is larger, with a pale orange club and a later flight season. Juvenile Black-Shouldered Spinylegs have long black legs, and reduced pale lateral markings on club.

HABITAT   Pristine, sand-bottomed forest streams and rivers.

SEASON	Mid-May to early Aug.
COMMENTS	During the day rests on leaves along shady thicket edges, usually low under overhanging branches. Beginning about 6 P.M. males patrol beats 5 yards long over open water, flying with extended lower hindlegs.

Laura's Clubtail *Stylurus laurae* **Plate 13**

IDENTIFICATION	2.3 in., eastern U.S., uncommon. Eyes green, face dark brown, abdomen elongate with S8–S9 yellow laterally, and S8 developing a black edge in mature males. Males have green thoracic markings and brown legs, females yellow thoracic markings and thighs. In juveniles narrow pale shoulder stripe and area between lateral thoracic stripes are brown, these areas becoming paler at maturity, but latter area remaining darkened.
SIMILAR SPECIES	Riverine and Townes' Clubtails are smaller, without the wide diffuse lateral brown thoracic stripe, and Riverine has wide nearly parallel green frontal thoracic stripes. Townes' has S9–S10 mostly black dorsally, and side of S2 black. (In Laura's S9–S10 tend to be red-brown dorsally, while side of S2 is pale.) Elusive Clubtail has separate lateral thoracic stripes, blue eyes, and black legs.
HABITAT	Clean streams with sand-mud bottoms.
SEASON	Late May to early Oct.
COMMENTS	Named for Laura Ditzler, member of the expedition that first found the species. Forages from leaves along forest edges. Males perch mostly on leaves overhanging water, but also briefly on rocks and logs. They arrive at water about 10 A.M. but are most active after 6 P.M.

Riverine Clubtail *Stylurus amnicola* **Plate 13**

IDENTIFICATION	2.1 in., eastern, uncommon. Frontal thoracic pale markings composed of a 3-pointed star, and a pair of wide stripes slightly divergent downward. Green shoulder stripe very narrow or absent, and lateral black thoracic stripes variably present. Face variably mottled black, eyes dark green, hind thighs yellow. Male club notably wide for a Hanging Clubtail, with large yellow lateral spots on S8–S9. Female yellower than male, and S8 and usually S9 have black lateral edges.
SIMILAR SPECIES	Townes' Clubtail of the southeast has narrow, strongly divergent green frontal thoracic stripes and a poorly developed frontal star; female has yellow lateral edge on S8. Elusive Clubtail has widely divergent frontal green stripes, no frontal star,

blue eyes, 2 complete lateral black thoracic stripes, and black legs. Laura's Clubtail has narrow, widely divergent frontal stripes, and area between the lateral thoracic stripes clouded with brown. Yellow-Sided Clubtail of the far south is very slender, with a narrow club, narrow frontal stripes, and blue eyes. Black-Shouldered Spinyleg has a similar frontal thoracic pattern, but has long black legs and reduced pale lateral spots on S8–S9.

HABITAT Medium to large rivers with a rapid current and sand, gravel, or mud bottom.

SEASON Early May to early Sept.

COMMENTS Feeds from leaves of forest undergrowth in sun or shade, and is unwary. In the Midwest, reported to forage in thick grass and brush. Males patrol from midmorning to late afternoon, with a fast flight over midstream.

Townes' Clubtail *Stylurus townesi* **Plate 13**

IDENTIFICATION 2.0 in., southeastern, scarce. Extremely similar to Riverine Clubtail, differing primarily in having green frontal thoracic stripes narrow and strongly divergent downward. In females S8–S9 have yellow lateral edges. *Some* Townes' also differ in having face all green, a wider green shoulder stripe, brown occiput, brown hind thigh, and female middle thigh yellow (occiput pale, hind thigh yellow, and middle thigh dark in Riverine Clubtail).

VARIATION Palest in Mississippi, where face is green, and posterior lateral black thoracic stripe is usually absent. Darkest in FL, where males usually have a black face and well-developed black lateral thoracic stripes. NC males have upper part of face black.

SIMILAR SPECIES Elusive Clubtail has 2 black lateral thoracic stripes, blue eyes, and black legs. Laura's Clubtail has area between lateral thoracic stripes clouded with brown. Yellow-Sided Clubtail is very slender with a narrow club, and blue eyes. Black-Shouldered Spinyleg has long black legs and reduced pale lateral pale spots on S8–S9.

HABITAT Clean sand-bottomed forest streams and rivers.

SEASON Early June to late Sept.

COMMENTS Named for Henry K. Townes, Jr., American entomologist. Perches on leaves and twigs of streamside trees from 1 to 20 ft. high. They hunt gnats by hovering near overhanging branches. Behavior unusual in that males seldom patrol, and females stay near water even when not mating or egg laying. They are active at dawn and in cloudy weather, but become more active in the evening until dark.

Elusive Clubtail *Stylurus notatus* Plate 13

IDENTIFICATION   2.4 in., eastern, scarce. Slender, mostly black, with 2 complete lateral black thoracic stripes, and blue eyes. S8–S9 bear large pale green to yellow lateral spots. Legs black, except basal half of hind thigh pale in female. Male has upper face black.

SIMILAR SPECIES   Similar species have green eyes. Riverine Clubtail has yellow hind thighs, less divergent green frontal thoracic stripes, and a pale frontal thoracic star. Townes' Clubtail of the southeast has yellow hind thighs, and may have a pale face, or lateral dark thoracic stripes may be absent. Laura's Clubtail has S8–S9 usually brown instead of black dorsally, and area between lateral thoracic stripes darkened. Arrow Clubtail is larger and very elongate, with S9 much longer than S8 and lateral black thoracic stripes partly fused. Only Riverine and Arrow Clubtails would likely join Elusive Clubtails in patrolling open water of big rivers. Black-Shouldered Spinyleg has long legs, green face, a pale dorsal spot on S10, and only small lateral pale spots on S8–S9.

HABITAT   Rivers (usually large) and large lakes, often with sandy bottoms, sometimes also with silt and gravel.

SEASON   Late May to mid-Oct.

COMMENTS   This frustrating species almost never perches even within binocular range. They live in treetops on sides of valleys, from where males launch sweeping extended patrols far out over the water, and from where females descend to lay eggs. In nonforested areas they are reported to forage in grass and brush. Most males patrol from 12 to 3 P.M.

Spinylegs
(genus *Dromogomphus*)

The long comblike hind thigh, unique among our dragonflies, bears 4 to 11 long ventral spines and extends to the base of S3. Otherwise these dragonflies are like the Common Clubtails, though the head is proportionately small. All 3 species are eastern North American.

Black-Shouldered Spinyleg *Dromogomphus spinosus* Plate 13

IDENTIFICATION   2.5 in., eastern, common. Recognized by combination of wide black shoulder bands, mostly black abdomen with reduced pale lateral spots on slender club, and long black legs. Most of front and side of thorax shiny yellow in juveniles, pale green at maturity, with lateral dark stripes variably developed but usually absent. S8–S9 usually marked with short yellow dorsal triangles, but triangles may be full length or absent; S10 yellow dorsally. Female abdomen barely clubbed. Eyes green.

VARIATION In FL the face usually has a wide black cross-stripe, or may be almost completely black.

SIMILAR SPECIES Most Common Clubtails have 2 black lateral thoracic stripes, and many have large yellow lateral spots on club. The long black legs of the Black-Shouldered Spinyleg when folded up under the thorax in flight make the insect seem bigger than it is, and patrolling males look like males of the Gomphurus Group until the long legs, thoracic pattern, and narrower, blacker club can be seen.

HABITAT Clear to muddy streams and rivers, sometimes lakes or oxygenated ponds, preferably with rocky shores. Larvae tolerate some pollution but are intolerant of acid waters.

SEASON Mid-April to mid-Nov. in FL, early June to mid-Sept. in Ontario.

COMMENTS Forages along forest edges or in fairly dense forest, often flying through cover and perching in shade. It perches on the leaves of trees or bushes, or on the ground. Males settle gently onto leaves over the water or the bare shore, beginning in midmorning. They make large irregular patrols over the water with a fast, smooth flight, hovering occasionally.

Southeastern Spinyleg *Dromogomphus armatus* Plate 13

IDENTIFICATION 2.6 in., southeastern, scarce. Note long legs, green eyes, brown facial cross-line, 2 black lateral thoracic stripes, and striped middle abdominal segments. Male club slender, but compressed vertically and bright rusty orange, while female club is undeveloped and marked with pale green to rusty brown.

SIMILAR SPECIES Flag-Tailed Spinyleg is smaller and paler, with pale rings on middle abdominal segments, blue eyes, no face line, and male has a deeper club. Russet-Tipped Clubtail has short legs, and male has a horizontally flattened club. Two-Striped Forceptail has thorax more brown than green, blue eyes, short legs, and a laterally flanged club.

HABITAT Shallow clear water flowing over deep liquid muck in forest. Usually small spring-fed streams, but occasionally larger streams where current is slowed by sparse emergent plants.

SEASON Early June to late Nov., most common in late summer.

COMMENTS Away from water this premier species is often very wary and skulks within cover, perching on the ground or tree leaves. Males at water are less wary, and perch on sticks, logs, or leaves. If no perches overhang the water, they rest on bushes back from the shore. When disturbed they fly wildly over a wide area before selecting another perch.

Flag-Tailed Spinyleg *Dromogomphus spoliatus*
Plate 13

IDENTIFICATION 2.3 in. Broadly TX to Ontario, common southwestward. Male club vertically flattened, its sides pale yellow to rusty orange, female club slender and yellowish to rusty brown. S4–S6 have pale basal rings, while S7–S9 each have a rounded lobe on lower posterior margin. Legs long, eyes blue.

SIMILAR SPECIES Southeastern Spinyleg is larger and darker, without pale abdominal rings, but with green eyes and a brown facial cross-line, and males have a shallower club. Other similar Clubtails have shorter legs, and smaller or horizontally flattened clubs, such as Russet-Tipped Clubtail, Sulphur-Tipped Clubtail, Forceptails, Leaftails, and Ringtails.

HABITAT Rivers with at least the pools mud-bottomed, possessing heavily to sparsely forested banks. Also mud-bottomed lakes and ponds with clear to muddy water.

SEASON Late May to early Oct. in the south, early July to mid-Sept. in IN.

COMMENTS Males perch on shore, less often on vegetation, obelisking vertically on hot days. They fly missions over open water and along shore, often hovering for long periods at points a few to 20 ft. apart. It ranges south to San Luis Potosí, Mexico.

Pond Clubtails
(genus *Arigomphus*)

These have a rather distinct appearance, given by the robust gray-green thorax, large head, and slender club. The face lacks dark cross-lines, and S10 and usually the cerci are pale. Both frontal and lateral thoracic dark stripes are poorly developed. These are some of the few Clubtails capable of breeding in still water, and they are usually very wary when perched in the open. Females are our only Clubtails with an ovipositor, developed as a spout 1/3–1/2 as long as S9, used while females hover or fly slowly forward. The male cerci, fused to S10, are forked in dorsal view, each with a needlelike inner branch. All 7 species are eastern North American.

Lilypad Clubtail *Arigomphus furcifer* Plate 14

IDENTIFICATION 2.0 in., northeastern, uncommon. Thorax mostly pale gray-green, with black midfrontal and shoulder stripes. Abdomen mostly black, with a pale dorsal stripe on S1–S7 and S10 (sometimes short streak on S8), and bright rusty brown lower edges on S8–S9. Male abdomen nearly unclubbed but widest at S8; female abdomen tapers from S7 to a very narrow S10. Eyes bright aqua-blue, legs black.

BODY FEATURES Occiput of both sexes straight-edged or slightly convex.

SIMILAR SPECIES Unicorn Clubtail usually has green eyes, and has pale shins, S8 nearly all black, longer wings, male abdomen thicker and more clubbed, and female abdomen much less tapered. Horned Clubtail has a pale dorsal stripe on S8, male abdomen widens to S10, and female occiput projects well above eyes. Black-Shouldered Spinyleg has wide black shoulder bands. Snaketails are usually brighter green, and have a large pale dorsal spot on S9.

HABITAT Ponds, lakes, and slow streams with floating vegetation, often with submergent vegetation and low brushy shores, including small bog lakes.

SEASON Mid-May to mid-Aug.

COMMENTS Feeds along forest edges, perching on the ground or small trees. Males perch on lily pads, other floating objects, or sometimes on shore.

Horned Clubtail *Arigomphus cornutus* Plate 14

IDENTIFICATION 2.2 in., MT to Quebec, uncommon. Males the only medium-size Clubtails in their range with abdomen widest at S10, and females have the tallest and most conspicuous occiput of any of our Clubtails. Thorax gray-green with both black shoulder stripes well developed. Abdomen black with a pale dorsal stripe on S1–S8 and S10, and rusty orange lower edges on S8–S9. Abdomen hardly clubbed, and tapering from S6 to S10 in female. Eyes blue, legs black, except female thighs pale on sides.

BODY FEATURES Occiput of both sexes high, convex, and platelike. Male epiproct cow-horn-shaped, and twice as wide as S9. Female has a prominent hornlike spine near each compound eye.

SIMILAR SPECIES Male Lilypad Clubtails have S8 wider than S10, while females have a normal occiput and narrow S10. Unicorn Clubtails usually have green eyes and lack a distinct orange edge on S8. Black-Shouldered Spinyleg has wide black shoulder bands. Snaketails are usually brighter green and have a large dorsal pale spot on S9.

HABITAT	Ponds, and sluggish streams and rivers, permanent and often with marshy or boggy edges.
SEASON	Late May to late July.
COMMENTS	Forages from sticks and low leaves in meadows and open woods, flying into trees when disturbed. Males perch on lily pads or other floating objects 2–3 yards from shore, or sometimes on shore.

Unicorn Clubtail *Arigomphus villosipes* Plate 14

IDENTIFICATION	2.0 in., northeastern, common. Thorax gray-green with black midfrontal, shoulder, and occasionally lateral stripes. Abdomen black, with a pale dorsal stripe on S1–S7, S9 rusty brown laterally, and S10 yellow. Legs mostly black, with pale streaks on shins, and sometimes on thighs. Eyes gray-green to bright green.
BODY FEATURES	Occiput of both sexes has a hornlike projection at middle of crest, pointed in males but tooth-edged and often square-tipped in females.
VARIATION	A few individuals in Kentucky and Indiana have pale rings on the middle abdominal segments, which gives them a very different overall appearance. Central PA populations have aqua-blue eyes.
SIMILAR SPECIES	See Similar Species under Lilypad Clubtail.
HABITAT	Ponds, lakes, and slow streams, with muddy bottoms and little submerged vegetation. At lakes, prefers the inlet.
SEASON	Early May to late Aug.
COMMENTS	Males perch on shore, less often on logs, algae mats, or low vegetation, and fly with the abdomen raised but with S10 bent downward.

Stillwater Clubtail *Arigomphus lentulus* Plate 14

IDENTIFICATION	2.1 in., TX to IN, uncommon. Thorax mostly grayish yellow-green with both brown shoulder stripes equally developed. Abdomen has yellow-green rings on S3–S6, except in some females. S7–S9 brown, S8 usually darkest, and S10 pale. Eyes gray-blue, thighs and shins pale.
BODY FEATURES	Male epiproct longer than cerci. Occiput of both sexes convex; crest in female blackened, roughened, and notched at middle.
SIMILAR SPECIES	Jade Clubtail is gray-green, with S7–S9 equally dark, and with posterior brown shoulder stripe narrow. Bayou Clubtail is smaller, with a gray-green thorax bearing better-developed dark midfrontal and lateral stripes, and S7–S9 equally dark.
HABITAT	Ponds, lakes, and ditches.

SEASON   Late March to mid-July.

COMMENTS   Forages in fields, perching on low plants. Males perch on open shores, floating vegetation, or on emergent sticks or plants.

Jade Clubtail *Arigomphus submedianus* Plate 14

IDENTIFICATION   2.1 in., eastern Great Plains area of U.S., uncommon. Thorax grayish jade green with only the anterior brown shoulder stripe well developed. Abdomen brown with gray-green rings on S3–S6, S7–S9 dark rusty brown, and S10 pale. Eyes green, thighs and shins pale.

BODY FEATURES   Male epiproct wider than cerci, and male occiput convex. Female occiput straight-edged or slightly notched at middle of crest, its edge not blackened or roughened.

SIMILAR SPECIES   Stillwater Clubtail is grayish yellow-green, with both brown shoulder stripes well developed, and S8 usually darker than S7 and S9. Bayou Clubtail is smaller, with more thoracic stripes, yellow-green rings on abdomen, and S7–S9 brown, not rusty.

HABITAT   Permanent mud-bottomed ponds, sloughs, and lakes.

SEASON   Late April to early Aug.

COMMENTS   Forages along forest edges and in swampy woods. Males perch on shore, floating objects, or projecting sticks, usually near cover.

Bayou Clubtail *Arigomphus maxwelli* Plate 14

IDENTIFICATION   1.9 in., TX to IL and AL, uncommon. Thorax gray-green with dark brown, sharply defined, and well-separated midfrontal and shoulder stripes. Lateral thoracic stripes often incomplete. Abdomen dark brown, with yellow-green rings on S3–S6, and S10 yellow. Eyes dark green, thighs mostly pale, shins pale.

SIMILAR SPECIES   Like Stillwater and Jade Clubtails but differs by smaller size, contrast between gray-green thorax and yellow-green abdominal rings, separated placement of brown anterior shoulder stripe, and dark brown S7–S9.

HABITAT   Ponds, and slow streams, including swampy bayous, often flowing more than for other Pond Clubtails.

SEASON   Early May to late July.

COMMENTS   Away from water perches either in trees or on the ground. Males are present at water primarily from 9 A.M. to 1:30 P.M. They perch in semi-shaded places on the bank, floating mats of vegetation, or low leaves, but may be driven away from water by the larger Jade Clubtail. In places with a tree canopy they perch in the trees, visiting sunny spots on the shore only for periods of about 1–5 min.

Gray-Green Clubtail *Arigomphus pallidus* **Plate 14**

IDENTIFICATION
2.3 in., far southeastern, common FL Peninsula, rare elsewhere. The only Clubtail in its range virtually lacking dark thoracic stripes. Body robust, thorax dark gray-green with faint brown stripes. Abdomen mostly gray-green with S8–S9 brown and S10 pale. S4–S6 in males each have a green and a brown ring, whereas females have dorsolateral brown stripes. Eyes green, legs stout and strong, shins pale.

SIMILAR SPECIES
No other Pond Clubtail has been found in its range.

HABITAT
Permanent, usually fertile, ponds, lakes, and stream backwaters with muck bottoms.

SEASON
Early March to mid-Oct. Two peaks of emergence, a major one in spring, a minor one in late summer, scarce from late June through July.

COMMENTS
Away from water this bulldog-like hunter perches on the ground or low vegetation, or sometimes in trees. Females in particular hover and skulk through heavy vegetation, on cloudy days coming into the open like the males. Males arrive at water after the morning coolness to perch on shore or low plants near cover, with the abdomen bent down at the tip, making occasional short sallies over water.

Least Clubtails
(genus *Stylogomphus*)

This genus has 1 species in North America and 8 others in Asia.

Least Clubtail *Stylogomphus albistylus* **Plate 15**

IDENTIFICATION
Very small, 1.5 in. Eastern, fairly common. Size and white cerci are diagnostic. Thorax mostly pale green in males, greenish yellow in females. Pale basal spots on S4–S7 are often joined into narrow basal rings. Body slender, legs black, face and thorax variably striped with black.

SIMILAR SPECIES
Pygmy Clubtails have black cerci.

HABITAT
Rocky riffles, preferably wide gravelly ones, of clear streams, warm or cold.

SEASON
Mid-May to early Sept.

COMMENTS
Forages from tree leaves. Males perch on sunny stones in riffles, making occasional sorties without hovering, and obelisking vertically on hot days. Usually invisible in flight over rippling water,

they are the gremlins of the riffles, magically appearing and disappearing from the rocks. When disturbed they fly straight up to a high tree leaf.

Pygmy Clubtails
(genus *Lanthus*)

Along with the Least Clubtail, our smallest Clubtails. They are mostly black, including black facial stripes, legs, and male cerci. They sometimes can be located by their silhouette as they perch on a sunny tree leaf near good habitats, which are indicated by native Brook Trout populations. Our 2 species are eastern, while 1 other (*L. fujiacus*) occurs in Japan.

Northern Pygmy Clubtail *Lanthus parvulus* Plate 15

IDENTIFICATION — Very small, 1.5 in., northeastern, scarce. Size in combination with 2 black lateral thoracic stripes and black cerci are diagnostic. Pale thoracic markings dull whitish green, abdomen almost entirely black posterior to S3.

SIMILAR SPECIES — Southern Pygmy Clubtail lacks the anterior lateral black thoracic stripe. Least Clubtail has white cerci, and usually pale rings on middle abdominal segments.

HABITAT — Small rocky and pristine spring-fed brooks in or near forest, and rivers in the north.

SEASON — Mid-April to mid-Aug.

COMMENTS — Away from water perches on tree leaves in sun or shade. Males perch unwarily on sunny rocks in riffles.

Southern Pygmy Clubtail *Lanthus vernalis* Plate 15

IDENTIFICATION — 1.4 in., New England and Appalachian, uncommon. Similar to Northern Pygmy Clubtail, but thorax whitish yellow with only 1 black lateral thoracic stripe (the posterior).

SIMILAR SPECIES — As for Northern Pygmy Clubtail.

HABITAT — Clear undisturbed spring brooks, streams, and rivers in forest, often with a mud bottom, and shadier than for Northern Pygmy.

SEASON — Mid-May to late July.

COMMENTS — Forages in clearings, perching in both sun and shade, males on high tree leaves, females near the ground. Males perch unwarily on leaves up to 12 ft. above riffles, or on rocks, sometimes in shade.

Grappletail
(genus *Octogomphus*)

Only 1 unusual species occupies this genus.

Grappletail *Octogomphus specularis* **Plate 15**

IDENTIFICATION
Medium, 2.0 in. Far western, fairly common. Thoracic pattern diagnostic—all yellow to pale green with wide black shoulder stripes (a thin black posterior lateral stripe may be present). Male is only Clubtail west of Rocky Mountains with abdomen widest at S10. Female abdomen cylindrical. Abdomen posterior to S2 mostly black, but S10 has a yellow dorsal spot, and cerci are yellow. Legs black.

SIMILAR SPECIES
Other Clubtails of the Pacific Coast have a dark midfrontal thoracic stripe, dark lateral thoracic stripes, and/or large pale abdominal spots.

HABITAT
Partially shaded headwaters of rapid clear mountain streams, except those fed largely by melted snow.

SEASON
Early April to late Sept.

COMMENTS
Away from water perches on twigs in trees. Males perch unwarily on stones in riffles, or on nearby leaves up to 4 ft. high from about 12 to 3 P.M. They usually perch in sunny spots, but often fly patrols through shade. It ranges into Baja California.

Sanddragons
(genus *Progomphus*)

Trim, medium-size dragonflies with mostly brown coloration, short legs, and yellow cerci. The abdomen is narrowly clubbed in males, practically clubless in females. They are our only Clubtails with wing markings, an inconspicuous brown spot at each wing base. Our species lack the green body markings so prevalent in other Clubtails. The alert and wary males are usually seen perched on sandy shores. Mating takes 10–20 min. as the pair perches low. Females usually tap eggs to the water in swift low flight, but all our species also spray their dry round eggs while hovering with a slightly downcurved abdomen 6–12 in. over water.

Our Sanddragons have a small fingerlike ventral projection from S1, which in males presumably helps position females for mating. Males are unique among all dragonflies in that the epiproct is divided into 2 movable halves, which allow them to adjust their grip on the heads of females. We have 4 species, 3 eastern and 1 western, while at least 63 other species are tropical American.

Gray Sanddragon *Progomphus borealis* Plate 15

IDENTIFICATION 2.3 in., western U.S., common southward. Only western Clubtail with gray sides on thorax. One brown lateral thoracic stripe present, the posterior. Long and slender dark brown abdomen only slightly clubbed, but brightly patterned with pale yellow dorsal triangles on S2–S6, a pale basal band on S7, and small pale lateral spots on S8–S9. Eyes gray, sometimes tinged with olive green.

SIMILAR SPECIES Common Sanddragon is smaller, with 2 brown lateral thoracic stripes, larger basal brown wing spots, yellower markings, and greener eyes. Other somewhat similar western Clubtails have pale dorsal spots on S8–S9 and green sides on thorax.

HABITAT Sand-bottomed streams in arid country. Occurs with Common Sanddragon in the TX Panhandle.

SEASON Mid-April to early Nov.

COMMENTS Away from water perches on twig tips. Males usually perch on sandy shores near riffles. It ranges south into Baja California and Morelos, Mexico.

Common Sanddragon *Progomphus obscurus* Plate 15

IDENTIFICATION 2.0 in., southern Great Plains, and eastern, common. Each wing has a brown spot at base. Slender brown abdomen has dorsal yellow triangles on S2–S7, and obscure or small lateral pale spots on S8–S10. The 2 lateral brown thoracic stripes are usually partly joined. Eyes olive green-yellow in males, brown in females. Near western edge of range thorax has a yellow cast that looks green in the field.

SIMILAR SPECIES Our other Sanddragons are generally larger. Gray Sanddragon of the west lacks an anterior brown lateral thoracic stripe. Belle's Sanddragon of the far southeast has sharply defined yellow lateral spots on S8–S9. Tawny Sanddragon of the FL Peninsula has large yellow lateral blotches on S8, and is usually found on sandy lakeshores.

HABITAT Sand-bottomed streams and rivers, and, in the north, sand-bottomed lakes.

SEASON Early April to mid-Sept.

COMMENTS Away from water perches on the ground, or on weed or twig tips up to the treetops, and females may skulk inside bushes. Males, most active from 10:30 A.M. to 4 P.M., preferably perch on sand near water, obelisking vertically in hot weather. They make occasional swift brief patrols over the water, but over rivers may make sustained patrols of flutters and short glides, including hovering in midstream.

Belle's Sanddragon *Progomphus bellei* Plate 15

IDENTIFICATION 2.3 in., far southeastern, local. Similar to Common Sanddragon, but larger, with 2 squared yellow lateral spots on S8.

BODY FEATURES Closely related to Tawny Sanddragon of the FL Peninsula, but has a separate range. Female subgenital plate 1/5 as long as S9, with a deep V-notch, U-notched in Tawny. Common Sanddragon has male cerci as long as S9, longer in Belle's and Tawny. Female Belle's has small pale spots on S10 at bases of cerci, these absent in female Common.

SIMILAR SPECIES Common Sanddragon is smaller, with reduced or diffuse yellow lateral spots on S8. The female usually has a shorter dorsal yellow spot on S7, 1/3 length versus 1/2 length in Belle's. Common normally engages in reproductive activity at streams or rivers, while Belle's prefers either trickles or lakes.

HABITAT Sand-bottomed lakes, or open sandy spring-fed trickles.

SEASON Early May to mid-Aug.

COMMENTS Named for Mr. Jean Belle, Dutch entomologist. Both sexes forage together in sunny clearings, up to 1/2 mile from water. Males prefer to perch on sand near water, but otherwise perch on tips of nearby weeds.

Tawny Sanddragon *Progomphus alachuensis* Plate 15

IDENTIFICATION 2.2 in., FL Peninsula, fairly common. Like Common Sanddragon but larger, and with S7–S9 mottled with yellow laterally. Female Tawny has orange rather than yellow dorsal triangles on S2–S6. Eyes olive tan.

SIMILAR SPECIES Common Sanddragon is a stream species in FL, and has the yellow lateral spots on S8 small or absent. The female Common usually has dorsal yellow spot of S7 1/3 length, compared to 2/3 length and more orange in female Tawny.

HABITAT	Sand-bottomed lakes. Also sandy rivers in south FL, where Common Sanddragon does not occur.
SEASON	Early April to late Aug.
COMMENTS	Away from water perches or obelisks on weed tips or the ground. At water males usually perch on sandy shores from 10 A.M. to 4 P.M. Their flight is a little higher, slower, and smoother than that of the Common Sanddragon.

Snaketails
(genus *Ophiogomphus*)

The "trout" among dragonflies, as beautiful as the trout who share their clear stream habitats. Their thorax is generally brighter green than in other Clubtails, and the abdomen has a repeating serpentlike pattern of white lateral spots and yellow dorsal spots. When perched in vegetation they are difficult to see because the thorax blends with the leaves, while the abdomen resembles a stem. The legs are short. Females of most species have a long subgenital plate, about 3/4 length of S9 and split for 2/3 length, and some have 1 or 2 pairs of hornlike spines on the head. Since the larvae burrow shallowly in streams and rivers, they are very vulnerable to flood scouring, such as occurs when humans deforest the land.

Unfortunately for Snaketail seekers, the common Eastern and Western Pondhawks look and act much like Snaketails. The Pondhawks differ in having the eyes in contact on top of the head, a projecting ovipositor, no dorsal yellow abdominal spots, and no black markings on S2.

Of the 18 species discussed in this book, 12 occur in the east, 5 in the west, and 1 (Boreal Snaketail) is transcontinental. At least 6 species may occur in the same river. About 7 other species are Eurasian.

Boreal Snaketail *Ophiogomphus colubrinus* Plate 16

IDENTIFICATION	1.9 in., Canada, and adjacent northeastern U.S., fairly common. Note black facial cross-stripes, one brown lateral thoracic stripe (the posterior), narrow green dorsal spots on dark brown abdomen, mostly pale thighs, and mostly black lower legs.
BODY FEATURES	Female has a pair of postocular horns that are stout, blunt, black, and crumpled. About 10% also have a slender backward-slanting occipital horn on either side of midline.
SIMILAR SPECIES	Our only other Snaketail with black facial stripes is the Extra-Striped, which has 2 lateral black thoracic stripes, and black legs.

Other similar Snaketails have blacker markings and wider yellow dorsal abdominal spots. Rapids Clubtail is smaller and more extensively black, including all-black legs.

HABITAT   Clear rapid streams and rivers with gravel bottoms. Ranges farther north than any other of our Clubtails.

SEASON   Early May to mid-Sept.

COMMENTS   Away from water perches on the ground or low plants in open woods, or sometimes on small branches within the canopy of trees. Males perch on the ground or bushes. They patrol with a bouncy flight over a wide area of rippling water, hovering periodically.

Extra-Striped Snaketail *Ophiogomphus anomalus* Plate 16

IDENTIFICATION   1.7 in., WI to Nova Scotia, scarce. Our only Snaketail with anterior and posterior black lateral stripes forming an (interrupted) N-shaped marking on the thorax, which is bright green. Face with narrow black cross-stripes, eyes green, legs black.

BODY FEATURES   Female has a pair of black upright occipital horns, one horn-diameter apart on either side of midline, and may also have a pair of microscopic black postocular horns.

SIMILAR SPECIES   Other Snaketails in its range lack at least the upper part of the anterior lateral black thoracic stripe. Only other Snaketail with black facial stripes is the Boreal, which is larger with mostly pale thighs. Rapids Clubtail has a gray-green thorax, and reduced or absent yellow lateral spots on S8–S9. Northern Pygmy Clubtail is very small, and has front of thorax mostly black.

HABITAT   Clear, rapid, medium to large rivers.

SEASON   Late May to early Aug.

COMMENTS   Apparently spends most of its time in treetops far from water, but can be found perched on bushes near the tree line bordering riffles. It rarely perches on rocks, and is unwary.

Bison Snaketail *Ophiogomphus bison* Plate 16

IDENTIFICATION   2.1 in., CA area, uncommon. Thorax bright yellow-green, with the brown shoulder stripes essentially fused into a broad, straight band. The only Snaketail in its range with black shins. Brown posterior lateral thoracic stripe is a narrow line. Eyes gray becoming gray-blue, thighs partly pale, S10 and cerci dull yellow.

BODY FEATURES   Female has a pair of long occipital horns, a little closer to each other than to compound eyes, reminiscent of the horns of a bison (buffalo), but no postocular horns.

SIMILAR SPECIES   Pacific Clubtail has a pale green thorax, all-black legs, and S10 and cerci mostly black. Grappletail has a nearly all-black abdomen. Olive Clubtail has a gray-green thorax and small dorsal pale spots on S4–S7 (nearly full-length spots in Bison).

HABITAT   Generally small permanent lowland streams without much snow meltwater, sometimes clear rivers up to 6800 ft. elevation.

SEASON   Mid-May to mid-Aug.

COMMENTS   Forages from the ground. Males perch warily on shore, and patrol over both slow and fast water.

Arizona Snaketail *Ophiogomphus arizonicus*
Plate 16

IDENTIFICATION   2.1 in., AZ/NM, local. Thorax unmarked gray green (grass green in juveniles) except for black shoulder stripes. Anterior shoulder stripe is an elongate spot, posterior is a thin black line. Eyes aqua-blue, thighs pale on sides, shins pale.

BODY FEATURES   Closely related to Pale Snaketail, but male epiproct only half length of cerci (75%–85% length in Pale). Female without postocular horns, and occipital horns present or absent; when present stout and blunt, separated by a large semicircular notch. Dorsal surface of occiput usually crushed by male epiproct during mating. Females without horns are identical to Pale Snaketails, except that latter has a V-shaped undulation in ridge behind median simple eye.

SIMILAR SPECIES   Pale Snaketail is identical but has a separate range. Dashed Ringtail has pale abdominal rings. Western Pondhawk has a short abdomen with a black dorsal stripe. Great Pondhawk has S1–S3 bulbous and all green, S4–S7 banded, and S8–S10 all black.

HABITAT   Mountain streams with rocks and silt-bottomed pools, constantly flowing but not torrential.

SEASON   Early June to early Sept.

COMMENTS   Forages from the ground or low twigs. Males perch on sunny rocks, from where they launch rapid circling patrols. They prefer the wider, shallow, and silted pools.

Pale Snaketail *Ophiogomphus severus* Plate 16

IDENTIFICATION   2.0 in., western, common. Told from other Snaketails in most parts of its range by the absent or isolated black anterior shoulder stripe. Other black thoracic stripes may be present or absent. Within the range of the Great Basin Snaketail cannot be separated unless the midfrontal black thoracic stripe is absent. Eyes gray-blue, shins pale.

BODY FEATURES   Male cerci straight and pointed. Male epiproct 3/4–6/7 as long as cerci, its forks convergent to tips, in side view with a dorsal shoulder at 1/4 length. Female lacks both occipital and postocular horns, and male epiproct routinely punches a hole in top of female head during mating. Compare females with nearly identical Arizona and Great Basin Snaketails.

VARIATION   Mountain populations usually have more extensive black thoracic markings, particularly the addition of a midfrontal thoracic stripe. Some individuals have reduced black markings on abdomen, especially on club of males.

SIMILAR SPECIES   The only Snaketail found in the U.S. Rocky Mountains north of AZ, and on the Great Plains. Arizona Snaketail is identical but has a separate range. Great Basin Snaketail always has a dark midfrontal thoracic stripe, and often a complete anterior shoulder stripe. Horned Clubtail has a complete anterior black shoulder stripe and black legs. Western and Eastern Pondhawks have eyes in contact on top of head, Western has a black dorsal abdominal stripe, and Eastern has S1–S3 all green.

HABITAT   Rivers and streams with a moderate current, and large lakes, with mud, sand, or gravel bottoms.

SEASON   Mid-May to mid-Sept.

COMMENTS   Forages from the ground or occasionally from bushes. Males are unwary and prefer to perch with the tip of the abdomen curled downward on large stones at the heads of riffles, but also perch on gravel bars and vegetation. They are present from about 12 noon to 7 P.M. At cool times they make long patrols, but in the heat of the day they fly less, obelisk high, and may perch in shade.

Sinuous Snaketail *Ophiogomphus occidentis*
Plate 16

IDENTIFICATION   2.0 in., northwestern, common. Thorax gray-yellow-green with narrow black shoulder stripes, the anterior sinuous or wavy and only slightly separated from the posterior. Anterior black lateral thoracic stripe absent, black posterior lateral stripe present or absent. Eyes dark gray, thighs mostly pale, shins and S10 yellow.

BODY FEATURES   Male cerci narrow, blunt, and nearly straight. Female has a pair of divergent occipital horns, nearer the compound eyes than to each other, and a pair of large yellow or black divergent postocular horns.

VARIATION   The **Pale Form** (*O. o. californicus*), found in the northern Central

Valley of CA, is marked with yellow and brown instead of green and black.

SIMILAR SPECIES   Great Basin Snaketail has grayer thorax, including between wing bases, usually blue eyes, and greener dorsal abdominal spots. Anterior dark shoulder stripe of Great Basin is wider, straighter, and well separated from dark posterior shoulder stripe, and the male has stout cerci. Boreal Snaketail has black facial stripes and narrow green dorsal abdominal spots (wide yellow spots in Sinuous). Bison Snaketail has brighter green thorax and black shins. Pronghorn Clubtail has 2 prominent black lateral thoracic stripes. Also see Similar Species under Bison Snaketail.

HABITAT   Large streams and rivers, and sometimes lakes, with rock and gravel bottoms. Usually at low elevations in mountains, in oak and conifer zones.

SEASON   Late May to early Oct.

COMMENTS   Perches on nearly anything, usually weed tips but seldom sand. Males make long patrols, after which they often fly far from water. When approached by a male over water, females with egg balls raise the whole body vertically and fly slowly upward (backward) for several feet until the male desists.

Great Basin Snaketail *Ophiogomphus morrisoni* Plate 16

IDENTIFICATION   2.0 in., far western U.S., fairly common. Thorax yellow-gray-green with straight, black, well-separated shoulder stripes. Shins pale, eyes pale gray-aqua. Some individuals cannot be distinguished from the Pale Snaketail.

BODY FEATURES   Male cerci stout and inflated. Female has no postocular horns, but some, especially where the range overlaps that of Pale Snaketail, have a thick, square-topped, occipital horn adjacent to each compound eye (horns lacking in female Pale). Otherwise, proportions of top of head are best way to separate these females: Ratio of length in midline between ridge behind simple eyes and anterior margin of occiput to closest distance between compound eyes is 51%–58% in Great Basin Snaketail, 32%–49% in Pale.

VARIATION   The lower-elevation **Pale Form** (*O. m. nevadensis*) is larger and paler, with narrower dark thoracic stripes and grayer green markings. Some individuals have isolated or incomplete anterior dark shoulder stripes.

SIMILAR SPECIES   Sinuous Snaketail has yellower thorax, including between wing

bases, dark gray eyes, and yellower dorsal abdominal spots.
Anterior dark shoulder stripe of Sinuous is narrow, wavy, and
only slightly separated from dark posterior shoulder stripe, and
male Sinuous has slender cerci. Those Pale Snaketails with an
isolated anterior shoulder stripe cannot be differentiated unless
they lack a dark midfrontal thoracic stripe. Bison Snaketail has a
yellow-green thorax. See also Similar Species under Bison
Snaketail.

HABITAT   Rivers, sometimes lakes (even alkaline ones), with mostly gravel and rock bottoms in arid areas.

SEASON   Mid-June to late Aug.

COMMENTS   Males perch on stones or bushes near flowing water.

Pygmy Snaketail *Ophiogomphus howei* Plate 16

IDENTIFICATION   Very small, 1.3 in. Appalachian area, and northeastern, scarce.
Easily recognized by its size, chunky shape, and yellow HW
bases (basal 1/2 in males, 2/3 in females). Eyes green, legs black.

SIMILAR SPECIES   None.

HABITAT   Big, clear, strongly flowing, clean rivers with gravel/sand bottoms, rarely small rivers. Apparently cannot breed in conditions
found below dams.

SEASON   Late April to late June.

COMMENTS   This little jewel of a dragonfly is difficult to see against rippling
water. They forage primarily in treetops on sides of river valleys,
but occasionally in riverside trees, or even on low plants in nearby fields. Males patrol with a bouncy flight over rippling water,
but not over pools or rapids. They are active in late morning and
early afternoon, with peak activity from 2:30 to 3:30 p.m.
Females are easier to see than males because they display their
tinted HW by holding them vertically much of the time during
flight.

Rusty Snaketail *Ophiogomphus rupinsulensis* Plate 17

IDENTIFICATION   2.0 in., northeastern, fairly common. Thorax is a beautiful glow-
ing green with 2 brown shoulder stripes but only vestigial brown
midfrontal and lateral stripes. Abdomen mostly rusty brown,
with black V-markings or blotches on S7–S9. Eyes yellow-green
to blue-green, browner in female.

BODY FEATURES   Male cerci blunt-tipped and nearly straight. Male epiproct in
side view curved upward with a sharp dorsal angle at 4/5 length;
in dorsal view forks separated by a deep V-notch, each fork ter-

minating in a flat, triangular, dorsal surface. Female has a pair of large brown postocular horns, and about 40% also have small occipital horns that are a little closer to each other than to compound eyes. Subgenital plate 3/4 to as long as S9. Hybridization with Riffle Snaketail is known.

SIMILAR SPECIES Acuminate Snaketail of central TN area has blue eyes, and abdomen not rusty and with (usually) reduced black markings. Westfall's Snaketail has only 1 dark shoulder stripe. Stillwater and Jade Clubtails have a gray-green thorax and slender clubs. Eastern Pondhawk has eyes in contact on top of head, no shoulder stripes, and a shorter abdomen.

HABITAT Rapid large streams and rivers.

SEASON Early May to late Sept.

COMMENTS Away from water feeds in fields, often on hilltops. They perch on the ground at cool times, on twig tips during warmer times, sometimes in shade. Males fly over deep water in late afternoon, becoming more active over riffles from 6 to 8 P.M. They fly swiftly and erratically, perching occasionally on the bank, rocks in the water, or in shoreline trees.

Acuminate Snaketail *Ophiogomphus acuminatus* Plate 17

IDENTIFICATION 2.0 in., west-central TN area, uncommon. Like Rusty Snaketail but has blue eyes (gray in female), and abdomen not rusty.

BODY FEATURES Male cerci sharply pointed (acuminate), versus blunt-tipped in Rusty Snaketail. Male epiproct in side view with a dorsal angle at 1/2 length; in dorsal view median cleft is narrow. Female has short occipital horns (rarely, lacking) a little closer to compound eyes than to each other, but no postocular horns. Female subgenital plate longer than S9 (75%–100% of S9 in Rusty).

VARIATION In north-central TN, abdomen may be mostly black on S1– S8. Elsewhere, abdomen mostly tan with black markings reduced or absent.

SIMILAR SPECIES Rusty Snaketail, which has green eyes (browner in female) and a rusty brown abdomen, has not been found at same streams as Acuminate. Rusty also has obscure pale basal rings on S4–S6, and shins are pale full length (no rings and only knee area of shin pale in Acuminate). Jade Clubtail has a gray-green thorax, wide green bands on S4–S6, and club lacks pale sides. Eastern Pondhawk has eyes in contact on top of head, no shoulder stripes, and a shorter abdomen.

HABITAT Clear, mostly shaded streams with sandy gravel bottoms.

SEASON   Mid-May to late June.

COMMENTS   Males are unwary and perch on rocks or plants from about 9 A.M. to 6 P.M., usually at heads of riffles, and often in shade. They fly occasional patrols with a diameter of about 20 ft., in a series of bouncy spurts with the abdomen raised but S10 decurved.

Westfall's Snaketail *Ophiogomphus westfalli*
Plate 17

IDENTIFICATION   2.0 in., Ozark area, fairly common. Like Rusty Snaketail, but the only Clubtail in its range with a bright grass-green and nearly unmarked thorax. Thorax has 1 brown shoulder spot or stripe (the posterior), and abdomen has brown to black dorsolateral dark stripes. Male eyes greenish pale blue, female eyes greenish gray.

BODY FEATURES   Male cerci straight and tapered. Male epiproct flat on underside, with a large lateral pointed tooth at 7/10 length, in dorsal view with a V- to U-shaped median cleft. Female has occipital horns that are close together, and vestigial bumplike postocular "horns." Subgenital plate 5/6 as long as S9.

SIMILAR SPECIES   Rusty Snaketail has 2 dark shoulder stripes. Eastern Ringtail has a dark midfrontal thoracic stripe, 2 shoulder stripes, and pale abdominal rings. Pond Clubtails have a gray-green thorax, 2 dark shoulder stripes, slender male clubs, and usually pale abdominal rings. Eastern Pondhawk has eyes in contact on top of head and a short abdomen.

HABITAT   Clear rocky rivers.

SEASON   Early May to late July.

COMMENTS   Away from water perches on low plants. Males frequent riffles in the middle of the day, where they perch on gravel bars or emergent plants. Occasionally they fly short, low patrols.

Appalachian Snaketail *Ophiogomphus incurvatus*
Plate 17

IDENTIFICATION   A small Snaketail, 1.7 in. Southeastern Piedmont, uncommon. Note vestigial or absent dark lateral thoracic stripes, and mostly pale thighs. Midfrontal and shoulder stripes brown, sides of club and S10 deep yellow to orange. Male eyes grayish aqua-blue, female eyes gray.

BODY FEATURES   Male cerci arched upward in side view, arched outward, parentheses or ()-shaped in dorsal view. Male epiproct longer than cerci, in side view with a dorsal angle at 3/5 length, in dorsal view with forks closely parallel. Female has occipital horns a little closer to compound eyes than to each other, but no postocular horns.

VARIATION The status of populations west of the Allegheny Mountains has not been satisfactorily resolved. There they are larger (2.0 in.) and have a narrow brown posterior lateral thoracic stripe. They are sometimes considered a subspecies, *O. i. alleghaniensis*, but seem more closely related to the Maine Snaketail. Male epiproct in side view has a large dorsal tooth rather than an angle.

SIMILAR SPECIES Similar Snaketails in its range are larger and striped with black, including 1 or 2 lateral thoracic stripes, their clubs are marked with yellow-green, and most have S10 partly black. Eastern Ringtail is larger and has pale rings on S4–S7. Eastern Pondhawk lacks dark thoracic stripes, and S8–S9 are all black.

HABITAT Clear streams at low elevations in the open, with sandy or gravelly riffles.

SEASON Early April to early June.

COMMENTS Formerly named *O. carolinus.* Away from water it is wary and perches on tips of twigs, sometimes several feet up or in shade. Males perch near riffles on overhanging vegetation or gravel bars. They are usually active at midday, but on hot days may not appear at the stream until evening. They make short patrols with a slightly bouncy flight low over riffles, hovering occasionally.

Southern Snaketail *Ophiogomphus australis*
Plate 17

IDENTIFICATION A small Snaketail, 1.7 in. MS/LA, local. The only Snaketail in its tiny range. Two black lateral thoracic stripes present, eyes blue.

BODY FEATURES Closely related to Appalachian Snaketail, of which it might be a subspecies. Female has vestigial postocular horns, in addition to occipital horns like those of Appalachian.

SIMILAR SPECIES Eastern Ringtail has pale rings on S4–S7. Eastern Pondhawk has no thoracic stripes, eyes in contact on top of head, and S8–S9 all black.

HABITAT Gravel-bottomed streams.

SEASON Early to late April.

COMMENTS Males perch on shore near riffles from 10 A.M. to 3 P.M. On hot days both sexes come to water primarily at dusk.

Edmund's Snaketail *Ophiogomphus edmundo* Plate 17

IDENTIFICATION 1.8 in., southern Appalachian area, local. The only Snaketail in its range with 2 black lateral thoracic stripes (anterior often broken at middle). Eyes green-blue to blue-green in males, green-brown in females, legs black, cerci tan.

BODY FEATURES Our only Snaketail with male epiproct usually bent downward at midlength. Females may have postocular horns but lack occipital horns; subgenital plate is as long as S9 with lobes abruptly convergent at tips.

SIMILAR SPECIES Maine Snaketail has green eyes and only one black lateral thoracic stripe. Rapids Clubtail has a grayer green thorax and black cerci; in males the club is slender with the top of S9 all black. Eastern Pondhawk has eyes in contact on top of head and S8–S9 all black.

HABITAT Clear, moderately flowing mountain streams and rivers.

SEASON Mid-April to early June.

COMMENTS Named for Edmund, grandson of James Needham, who described the species. Spends most of its time in trees. Males are unwary and perch on rocks in riffles from about 10 A.M. to 7:30 P.M., from where they launch short patrols without hovering.

Maine Snaketail *Ophiogomphus mainensis* Plate 17

IDENTIFICATION 1.8 in., Appalachian and northeast, fairly common. Black posterior lateral thoracic stripe present, legs black. Abdomen bears narrow dorsal pale streaks on S1–S7, sometimes on S8, least often on S9. Male has side of club and the cerci yellow. Eyes green.

BODY FEATURES Female has a pair of large occipital horns with swollen bases close together at midline. Postocular horns usually absent. Male epiproct nearly as long as cerci, in side view with a large upcurved lateral tooth at 2/3 length. In *O. m. fastigiatus* of central PA and eastern WV, males have lateral tooth of epiproct short and set at 1/2 length, so that epiproct looks wedge-shaped in ventral view.

SIMILAR SPECIES Riffle and Brook Snaketails have wider pale dorsal spots on all abdominal segments, including S8 and S9, and their clubs are less yellow. The Brook and sometimes the Riffle have green-sided thighs, and the Riffle's thorax is usually paler green. Boreal Snaketail has black facial stripes and green-sided thighs.

CLUBTAILS

HABITAT	Clear, moderately rapid rocky streams and rivers in forest, often where they drain lakes or swamps.
SEASON	Mid-May to early Aug.
COMMENTS	Feeds in fields. Males during the day perch on rocks in gentle rapids and are somewhat wary. About 7–8 P.M. they become unwary and very active in the shade, perching on rocks and overhanging leaves.

Riffle Snaketail *Ophiogomphus carolus* Plate 17

IDENTIFICATION	1.7 in., northeastern, fairly common. Thorax whitish green over most of its range, and a black posterior lateral thoracic stripe is present. Legs usually black, sometimes with green sides on thighs. Abdominal dorsal pale spots are wide triangles on S2–S7, a lengthwise rectangle on S8, and a crosswise basal rectangle on S9. Eyes vary from green to pale blue.
BODY FEATURES	Male cerci pointed and slightly arched but not inflated. Female with or without a pair of occipital horns, when present closer to each other than to compound eyes. Subgenital plate about as long as S9.
VARIATION	In eastern Canada the thorax is bright green.
SIMILAR SPECIES	Maine, Brook, and Sand Snaketails have a grass green thorax and a pointed, triangular dorsal yellow spot on S8, or Maine may have S8 black dorsally. Maine also has narrow dorsal abdominal markings and males have a brighter yellow club. Boreal Snaketail has black facial stripes.
HABITAT	Clear, rapid, sandy or rocky streams and rivers.
SEASON	Early May to late Aug.
COMMENTS	Away from water perches on weed tips, broad leaves in clearings or in tree crowns, or, if the air is cool, on the ground. Males at water are warier when perched on the ground than on overhanging leaves. They sometimes select an inconspicuous, hidden perch, or may perch in trees.

Brook Snaketail *Ophiogomphus aspersus* Plate 18

IDENTIFICATION	1.9 in., Appalachian and northeastern, uncommon. Thorax grass green with black posterior lateral thoracic stripe present, and thighs have green sides. S2–S8 have wide pale dorsal triangles, while pale dorsal spot of S9 may be triangular, square, or rounded. Eyes dark green.
BODY FEATURES	Male cerci bulbous and inflated. Female has small to large postocular horns but no occipital horns. Subgenital plate about 2/3 as long as S9.

SIMILAR SPECIES   In central WI, see Sand Snaketail. Riffle Snaketail has a whitish-green thorax, a rectangular dorsal pale spot on S8, and often all-black legs. Maine Snaketail has narrow dorsal abdominal markings, with S8–S9 often black dorsally, all-black legs, and males have a yellower club. Boreal Snaketail has black facial stripes.

HABITAT   Clear streams in the open, with brushy banks and sandy, gravelly, or rocky riffles.

SEASON   Late April to late Aug.

COMMENTS   Forages in fields and along trails through forest at midday, and at water. Males descend from streamside trees primarily between 8 and 11 A.M., and especially about 7 to 8 P.M. They perch in or near riffles on sandbars or rocks, or on twigs, grass, and leaves, in that order of preference.

Sand Snaketail *Ophiogomphus sp.* **Plate 18**

IDENTIFICATION   1.8 in., IA/WI, local. Nearly identical to Brook Snaketail, but dorsal pale spot of S9 full length (half length in Brook). Shins and posterolateral parts of S8–S9 generally more extensively pale than in Brook. Eyes blue-gray.

BODY FEATURES   Not scientifically named at time of this writing. Male cerci and epiproct like those of Brook Snaketail, but anterior hamule with hook as wide as gap, gap much wider than hook in Brook. Female has small occipital horns close to eyes (these horns lacking in Brook), and small postocular horns. Female subgenital plate 1/2 length of S9, 2/3 length in Brook.

SIMILAR SPECIES   See Similar Species under Brook Snaketail, which has a separate range.

HABITAT   Sand-bottomed rivers and streams.

SEASON   Late May to late July.

COMMENTS   Perches on sand, shifting to sticks if the sand becomes too hot. Males fly without hovering over rippling water, then perch on the bank or well back from it.

Wisconsin Snaketail *Ophiogomphus susbehcha* **Plate 18**

IDENTIFICATION   2.0 in., MN/WI, local. Thorax bluish green with a black posterior lateral stripe. S2–S7 have wide pale dorsal triangles, S8 has a triangular to rectangular spot, S9 bears a rounded spot, and S10 is yellow. S8–S9 of female often black dorsally. Eyes gray-blue, legs black except at base.

BODY FEATURES   Male cerci pointed, bulging ventrally in posterior 3/5 of length.

Male epiproct longer than cerci, in side view with a dorsal tooth at 1/2 length. Epiproct has a pair of dorsal bulges near its base, hard to see but distinctive. Female has small black postocular horns but no occipital horns.

SIMILAR SPECIES Riffle, Brook, and Sand Snaketails have some black on S10, and may have green eyes and green sides on thighs. Boreal Snaketail has black facial stripes, narrow green dorsal streaks on middle abdominal segments, and mostly green thighs. None of these 4 species is normally found in the same places as the Wisconsin Snaketail, which is usually only associated with the quite different Pygmy and Rusty Snaketails.

HABITAT Medium-size, clear, fast-flowing rivers with mixed gravel, sand, and rock bottoms.

SEASON Late May to late June.

COMMENTS Forages in fields and along forest edges, perching on weeds, twigs of small trees, or logs, but rarely on the ground. Males, which seem very short-lived, perch in the fields between patrols over the river.

Ringtails
(genus *Erpetogomphus*)

These are some of our most colorful Clubtails, with prominent white rings on S3–S7, orange clubs, pale faces, and short legs. Males have S10 at least as long as S9, while females lack clubs. The male cerci of our species resemble two nearly parallel fingers, nearly straight (2 species), or slightly bent downward with dorsal "knuckles" at midlength and tapering tips (4 species). Our 6 species inhabit southwestern streams and rivers, with only the Eastern Ringtail ranging into the east. At least 17 other species are tropical American.

Eastern Ringtail *Erpetogomphus designatus*
Plate 18

IDENTIFICATION 2.0 in., U.S., common TX, scattered northward to MT. The only Ringtail found east of TX. Thorax bright yellow-green with an isolated brown anterior shoulder stripe, and poorly developed anterior lateral brown stripe, but with posterior shoulder and posterior lateral stripes well developed. S1–S2 yellow dorsally, extreme wing bases tinted strongly amber, and eyes gray, becoming blue to purple. Abdominal rings white to pale green. Legs short, with pale thighs.

BODY FEATURES   Our only Clubtail with a prominent domed bulge on dorsal surface of occiput. Male cerci of bent type.

SIMILAR SPECIES   Dashed and Yellow-Legged Ringtails of the southwest have vestigial dark posterior shoulder and posterior lateral thoracic stripes, S1–S2 green dorsally, and males have dark stripes on S8 (lacking on Eastern Ringtail in the southwest). Flag-Tailed Spinyleg is larger with a proportionately larger club in both sexes, and long black legs. Leaftails are much larger with wide-flanged clubs and prominent dark thoracic stripes. The green Pondhawks lack brown thoracic stripes, and their eyes touch on top of the head.

HABITAT   Rivers and streams, usually with riffles, and often with sandy gravel among rocks.

SEASON   Mid-April to mid-Oct.

COMMENTS   Away from water perches on tips of weed stems, or sometimes on barbed-wire fences, often below the level of surrounding brush. Males perch on the bank or twigs, in hot weather obelisking nearly vertically. Males hover on patrol, darting periodically to new stations. It ranges south to Durango, Mexico.

Dashed Ringtail *Erpetogomphus heterodon*
Plate 18

IDENTIFICATION   2.0 in., NM and west TX, local. Thorax pale green to bright yellow-green with poorly developed dark stripes, the lateral stripes vestigial or absent, the anterior shoulder stripe often reduced to an elongate spot or dash. S1–S2 green dorsally, black dorsolaterally, and S8 (sometimes S7–S10) black dorsolaterally. Eyes gray, lower legs black.

SIMILAR SPECIES   Yellow-Legged Ringtail lacks dark markings on thorax and S1, and has yellow shins. Eastern Ringtail has better-developed dark thoracic stripes, S1–S2 yellow dorsally, S8 without dark stripes, and amber wing bases. Arizona Snaketail lacks abdominal rings. Great Pondhawk has S1–S3 bulbous and all green.

HABITAT   Clear mountain streams with rocks.

SEASON   Early Aug. to late Sept.

COMMENTS   Away from water perches on the ground or weed tips. Males are unwary and perch on the bank or stones in riffles, flying occasional sorties. Ranges south into Chihuahua, Mexico.

Yellow-Legged Ringtail *Erpetogomphus crotalinus*
Plate 18

IDENTIFICATION	2.0 in., southeastern AZ and southern NM, local. Our only Ringtail which practically lacks dark thoracic markings, and has pale shin stripes. Pale basal rings of middle abdominal segments may be incomplete, especially in females. S1 all pale, and S8 black dorsolaterally. Eyes gray.
BODY FEATURES	Male cerci of bent type. Crest of occiput black, versus yellow in Dashed Ringtail.
SIMILAR SPECIES	Dashed Ringtail has an anterior dark shoulder spot, black lower legs, and a black dorsolateral spot on S1. Arizona Snaketail has partial dark shoulder stripes and dark spots on S1. See also Similar Species under Dashed Ringtail.
HABITAT	Streams in arid country, up to at least 7000 ft.
SEASON	Early July to late Aug. in Mexico.
COMMENTS	Males perch on rocks in streams. It ranges south to Morelos, Mexico.

White-Belted Ringtail *Erpetogomphus compositus*
Plate 18

IDENTIFICATION	2.0 in., western U.S., uncommon. Our only Clubtail with white markings on front of thorax, and with the most definite (grayish) white midlateral thoracic stripe or belt. Most of thorax yellow-green, face off-white, eyes gray. S8, and often S7 or S9, dark brown dorsally, and wings sometimes amber near bases.
BODY FEATURES	Male cerci of straight type. Female occiput about 1/2 as long as vertex behind median eye, rear edge of occiput little if any darkened or raised, and usually wavy like a shallow M in dorsal view. (Occiput of female Serpent Ringtail is as long as vertex, with a straight raised darkened rim.)
SIMILAR SPECIES	Gray Form of Serpent Ringtail (CA) has gray and brown thoracic markings. Sulphur-Tipped and Plains Clubtails lack complete abdominal rings.
HABITAT	Streams and rivers.
SEASON	Mid-April to late Sept.
COMMENTS	Away from water perches on twig tips from low to the treetops. Males perch on the bank, rocks in the water, or on bushes. Their patrols are swift and bouncy, covering a wide area. It ranges south into Baja California and Sonora, Mexico.

Serpent Ringtail *Erpetogomphus lampropeltis*
Plate 18

IDENTIFICATION
2.0 in., southwestern, uncommon. Thorax pale green or gray with a complete set of brown stripes. S8–S9 usually dark brown dorsally, eyes blue.

BODY FEATURES
Male cerci of bent type. Compare female with White-Belted Ringtail.

VARIATION
Gray Form of CA has a gray thorax, with brown shoulder stripes nearly fused, brown lateral stripes nearly fused, and thighs brown dorsally. **Green Form** (*E. l. natrix*), found east of CA, has a pale green thorax with narrow brown stripes, and mostly pale thighs.

SIMILAR SPECIES
Eastern Ringtail has a bright yellow-green thorax with anterior brown shoulder stripe incomplete at lower end.

HABITAT
Streams and rivers.

SEASON
Early July to mid-Oct.

COMMENTS
Away from water perches on tips of tall weeds. Males are remarkably unwary, perching on rocks in riffles during the day, and flying fast over heads of riffles at dusk. It ranges through Mexico to Guatemala, including Baja California.

Blue-Faced Ringtail *Erpetogomphus eutainia*
Plate 19

IDENTIFICATION
Small, 1.7 in. Central TX, local. Our only Clubtail with blue markings, and the smallest Clubtail in its range. Face, top of head, and dorsal markings on S1–S7 tinted aqua-blue. Thorax blue-green on front, yellow-green on sides, with a complete set of brown stripes. White abdominal rings are around *middle* of each segment on S3–S7. Male has S7–S9 dark rusty brown and S10 orange, in female S8–S10 are dark brown. Eyes blue.

SIMILAR SPECIES
Other Ringtails, and most other Clubtails with pale abdominal rings, have rings around the *bases* of the segments.

HABITAT
Spring-fed rivers.

SEASON
Late June to mid-Sept.

COMMENTS
Formerly incorrectly named *E. diadophis*. This nifty dragonfly seems very particular about its feeding habitat, usually being found in localized areas of partially shaded grass. Males hover over heads of riffles, usually facing downstream. It ranges south to Costa Rica.

Leaftails
(genus *Phyllogomphoides*)

Eye-catching large Clubtails with leaflike lateral flanges on S8–S9. They have short legs and faces with brown cross-stripes. Cerci of males are pincerlike, with a dorsal tooth near the middle, while those of females are long, longer than S10. Our species were formerly classified in the genus *Gomphoides*, now known to be a strictly South American group. Our 2 species are southwestern, but at least 44 others are tropical American.

Four-Striped Leaftail *Phyllogomphoides stigmatus*
Plate 19

IDENTIFICATION 2.7 in., NM/TX/OK, fairly common. Thorax mostly yellow-green, without a brown lower rear stripe. Seen from side thorax appears to have 4 complete brown stripes. Also note prominent pale rings on bases of S3–S8, black stigmas, yellow cerci, and short legs. In male S8–S9 are marked rufous and have wide lateral flanges, but female lacks the rufous and has flanges only half as wide. Eyes pale gray.

SIMILAR SPECIES Five-Striped Leaftail bears a dark brown lower rear thoracic stripe on its gray-green thorax. Forceptails also have brown lower rear thoracic stripes, and their abdomens are more obscurely ringed and narrowly flanged. Ringtails are considerably smaller, without flanged abdomens. Flag-Tailed Spinyleg is smaller, and has long hindlegs and a vertically flattened club.

HABITAT Lakes, ponds, and slow parts of rivers and streams. Generally prefers slower water than Five-Striped Leaftail.

SEASON Late May to mid-Sept.

COMMENTS Often ranges miles from water, where it perches on twig tips or barbed-wire fences. Males fly with abdomens arched, cruising for long distances over water or emergent plants with alternate spurts of wing beats and short glides. They perch warily on twigs or rocks. Females may drop eggs from above the water surface while hovering. It ranges south to Nuevo León, Mexico.

Five-Striped Leaftail *Phyllogomphoides albrighti*
Plate 19

IDENTIFICATION 2.5 in., NM/TX, fairly common. Similar to Four-Striped Leaftail, but with a gray-green thorax bearing a brown lower rear stripe.

Also, Five-Striped lacks a pale ring on S8, female has flanges of S8–S9 nearly as wide as in male, and eyes are blue-gray.

SIMILAR SPECIES Forceptails have abdomen obscurely ringed and more narrowly flanged, and have tan rather than black stigmas.

HABITAT Rivers and streams.

SEASON Late May to late Sept.

COMMENTS Away from water perches on weed tips, barbed-wire fences, twigs in tree crowns or, in cloudy weather, on the ground. Males perch on sticks over the current, and spend more time patrolling than the Four-Striped Leaftail. It ranges south to San Luis Potosí, Mexico.

Forceptails
(genus *Aphylla*)

Large, slender, short-legged Clubtails with flanged clubs. In our species, the thorax appears brown with pale stripes, and the stigmas are tan. They also have dark legs, brown facial markings, and yellow costal veins. Males differ from all our other dragonflies in having a vestigial epiproct that takes no part in gripping females' heads. Instead, the lower posterior corners of S10 are prolonged to catch on the occipital crest of the female during mating. Male cerci of our species are forcepslike without teeth or spines. Our 3 Forceptails are southeastern and Texan, while at least 21 other species are tropical American.

Two-Striped Forceptail *Aphylla williamsoni* **Plate 19**

IDENTIFICATION 2.8 in., southeastern Coastal Plain, common FL. Distinguished by large size, mostly brown thorax, and rufous end of abdomen. Pattern on dark brown thorax distinctive, with a yellow W on front, 2 greenish-yellow lateral stripes, but no pale shoulder stripes. Some individuals, usually females, have a narrow third pale lateral stripe between the other two. Other features are rufous S8–S10, short dark legs, pale tan stigmas, and yellow face with brown cross-stripes. S8 has a wide yellow to orange flange in males, a narrow flange in females. Eyes tinted green in juveniles but blue-gray at maturity.

SIMILAR SPECIES Broad-Striped Forceptail is smaller, with a narrow pale shoulder stripe, and narrow flange on S8 in both sexes.

HABITAT Muck-bottomed lakes, permanent ponds, and slow streams.

SEASON   Early April to early Nov.

COMMENTS   Forages mostly in treetops, but sometimes in brushy fields or on the ground among woodland shrubs. Males perch warily on low waterside plants, or occasionally on the bank, making periodic patrols about 60 ft. in diameter over open water near shore. Their flight is fast and smooth, with the abdomen raised about 30° but with the club decurved, and they are active until sundown. Females lay eggs most often about 8:00–8:30 P.M. They may hover near vegetation and swoop rhythmically to the water at 2-second intervals, fly a rapid irregular pattern over open water while tapping the surface at points 2–3 yards apart, or drop eggs while hovering over the water near vegetation.

Broad-Striped Forceptail *Aphylla angustifolia* Plate 19

IDENTIFICATION   2.5 in., coastal TX to MS, uncommon. Similar to Two-Striped Forceptail, but with a third narrow yellow to green lateral thoracic stripe between anterior and posterior stripes. Broad-Striped also has narrow pale shoulder stripes (often connected dorsally with W-shaped frontal marking), and abdomen has more extensive pale green markings (rusty orange in juveniles). Lateral flanges of S8–S9 very narrow in both sexes. Eyes gray-green in males, dark blue in females.

SIMILAR SPECIES   Two-Striped Forceptail lacks pale shoulder stripe, and male has a wide flange on S8. Narrow-Striped Forceptail has the 3 lateral pale thoracic stripes all equally narrow, and a wide flange on S8.

HABITAT   Muck-bottomed ponds, slow rivers, and pools of intermittent streams. May occur with Two-Striped Forceptail.

SEASON   Late May to mid-Sept., reported in April in Mexico.

COMMENTS   Forages in weedy fields and open woodland, perching on weeds. Males at water perch warily on twigs, or sometimes rocks. It ranges through eastern Mexico to Guatemala.

Narrow-Striped Forceptail *Aphylla protracta* Plate 19

IDENTIFICATION   2.6 in., south TX, local. Similar to Broad-Striped Forceptail, but with the 3 lateral pale thoracic stripes all equally narrow, less extensive pale markings on abdomen, and wide flanges on S8 of both sexes. S7–S10 are rusty orange, with S7–S9 black dorsally in females. Eyes gray.

SIMILAR SPECIES   Broad-Striped Forceptail has anterior and posterior pale lateral thoracic stripes wider than middle stripe, and a narrow flange on S8.

HABITAT	Muck-bottomed lakes.
SEASON	Late April to mid-Nov.
COMMENTS	Away from water perches on vegetation 1–2 ft. up, often in small spaces among dense brush. Males at water perch on sticks, often on shore and facing away from water, and do not make regular patrols. It ranges south to Costa Rica.

Spiketails
(family Cordulegastridae, genus *Cordulegaster*)

These fascinating dragonflies are large black or brown insects with contrasting yellow markings, but are not commonly seen except at just the right time and place. The thorax bears 2 (occasionally 3) lateral pale stripes, and the legs are short. They are easily distinguished from other families by the green or blue eyes, which meet at one point on top of the head, and the spikelike ovipositor of the female. Females hover over shallow water and lay eggs by driving the ovipositor vertically into the bottom in a sewing machine–like manner. S9–S10 of the female are soft and can accordion up when the ovipositor enters the bottom. Mating pairs of most species hang in trees for 50 min. to over 5 hours. During mating the ovipositor fits into a deep pocket in the base of the male's abdomen and thorax. Three species (Say's, Delta-Spotted, Brown) with slightly separated eyes are classified in the Subgenus (*Zoraena*), sometimes used as a genus.

Spiketails inhabit seepages, trickles, and forest streams. They feed mostly in fields, where they generally perch on vertical twigs and stems at an oblique angle to the ground. They do not feed in swarms. Males of stream species patrol great distances along the stream. The estimated life cycle of European species is 2–5 years, and juveniles mature in about 10 days.

Spiketails are not readily confused with other dragonflies, but note that Cruisers have only one pale lateral thoracic stripe and very long legs. The Dragonhunter Clubtail has separated eyes, long hindlegs, and a clubbed abdomen.

Of our 8 species, 4 eastern species and their subspecies show an amazing parallel variation, in which the northern form is black with bright yellow markings and green eyes, while the southern form is brown with pale yellow markings and (usually) blue eyes. About 25 other species are Eurasian.

Pacific Spiketail *Cordulegaster dorsalis* Plate 20

IDENTIFICATION 3.1 in., western, fairly common. Only western Spiketail with a spotted abdomen. Thorax has 2 wide yellow lateral stripes, abdomen has saddlelike yellow dorsal spots, and forehead is yellow. Female ovipositor projects at least length of S10 beyond abdomen. Eyes aqua-blue (red-brown in juveniles).

VARIATION **Great Basin Form** (*C. dorsalis deserticola*) is more extensively yellow, including a third yellow lateral thoracic stripe between the other two, posterior yellow spots on S3–S6 or S8, and a yellow ring on S7.

SIMILAR SPECIES None.

HABITAT Clear, usually shady, foothill and mountain streams with occasional muck-bottomed pools, up to 6300 ft. elevation. Great Basin Form lives in desert spring runs, which often lack tree cover.

SEASON Mid-May to mid-Sept.

COMMENTS Forages along forest edges, hanging under twigs of bushes and trees, or occasionally perching on vertical rock surfaces. Males patrol at a smooth, even medium speed for long distances, even through shade and tangles of branches. It ranges into Baja California.

Apache Spiketail *Cordulegaster diadema* Plate 20

IDENTIFICATION 3.3 in., AZ area, local. Only western Spiketail with a banded abdomen. Male abdomen widened at S6–S8, female ovipositor extends length of S10 beyond abdomen. Eyes aqua-blue, yellow-green in juveniles. Rear of head behind eyes yellow to brown.

SIMILAR SPECIES None.

HABITAT Small clear mountain streams with silt-bottomed pools, possibly including intermittent ones.

SEASON Late June to early Nov.

COMMENTS This magnificent insect, resembling a giant wasp, hangs from twigs at a height of 2–3 yards, and makes extended feeding flights at the same level. Males patrol streams in sunny weather from about 8:30 A.M. to 4 P.M. It ranges south to Morelos, Mexico, and then as the blacker subspecies *C. d. godmani* to Costa Rica.

Tiger Spiketail *Cordulegaster erronea* Plate 20

IDENTIFICATION 2.9 in., eastern U.S., local. Only Spiketail in its range with a banded abdomen. Thorax has 2 wide yellow lateral stripes.

Female ovipositor extends length of S10 beyond abdomen. Upper face black, eyes pale metallic green. Rear of head behind eyes black.

SIMILAR SPECIES Say's Spiketail has a magenta stripe between 2 white lateral thoracic stripes, and a yellow upper face.

HABITAT Small spring trickles, too small for fish, in partial shade, sometimes gravelly without silt.

SEASON Early June to early Sept.

COMMENTS At least males forage in fields, swamps, and along trails late in the day until dusk. Males fly slowly along a trickle from about 10 A.M. to as late as 7 P.M., peaking about 6 P.M., hovering occasionally. When encountering emergent grass, they do not reverse direction but fly off through the forest, seeking other trickles. Periodically they perch obliquely on twigs from near the ground to 15 ft. up.

Say's Spiketail *Cordulegaster sayi* Plate 20

IDENTIFICATION 2.6 in., northern FL to central GA, local. Only Spiketail in its range with a banded abdomen. Thorax bears a magenta stripe between 2 white lateral stripes; also dull magenta are most of front and dorsal area between wings. Female ovipositor barely extends beyond abdomen. Upper face yellow, eyes pale gray-green. Rear of head behind eyes white.

SIMILAR SPECIES Tiger Spiketail lacks magenta on thorax, and has greener eyes and a black upper face.

HABITAT Trickling hillside seepages in deciduous forest near weedy fields.

SEASON Late Feb. to late April.

COMMENTS Named for Thomas Say, American entomologist. As beautiful as it is rare, this species perches on weed stems while foraging along forest edges. They may defend feeding perches for at least 30 min., and sturdy perches seem necessary to exploit grassy areas. Males patrol over seepage areas during the middle of the day, hovering and perching often. They may grab and drop small flying insects just to get them out of their space.

Twin-Spotted Spiketail *Cordulegaster maculata* Plate 20

IDENTIFICATION 2.8 in., eastern, the most common eastern Spiketail. Recognized by pairs of short yellow dorsal spots on abdomen. Male abdomen slightly clubbed, female ovipositor extends length of S9 + S10 beyond abdomen. Forehead brown; upper face yellow in males, brown in females.

VARIATION	**Northern Form**, north of VA, has body black marked with bright yellow, and sea-green eyes. **Southern Form** has body brown marked with pale yellow, and aqua-blue eyes.
SIMILAR SPECIES	Delta-Spotted and Brown Spiketails are smaller, have short ovipositors, and have larger triangular abdominal spots forming a stripe on at least S2. Some female Mosaic Darners have yellow abdominal spots, but have eyes in wide contact.
HABITAT	Clear forest streams and small rivers, including trout streams.
SEASON	Late Feb. to late April in FL, mid-May to early Aug. in NH.
COMMENTS	Warily forages along forest edges, perching on weed stems and twigs, sometimes miles from the larval habitat. Males patrol long lengths of stream from about 9 A.M. to dusk, commonly peaking about 6 P.M.

Delta-Spotted Spiketail *Cordulegaster diastatops* Plate 20

IDENTIFICATION	2.4 in., northeastern, fairly common. Body black, with at least S6–S8 bearing pairs of long pointed triangular yellow spots. At least S2 has a pair of yellow stripes. Thorax usually has 3 lateral yellow stripes, the middle one narrowest, posterior one widest. Male abdomen slightly clubbed, female ovipositor extends length of S10 beyond abdomen. Forehead yellow, eyes sea green.
BODY FEATURES	Male cerci said to be 1.3X longer than epiproct, these equal in Brown Spiketail, which may be a subspecies of Delta-Spotted.
SIMILAR SPECIES	Brown Spiketail has a brown body with blunt triangular abdominal spots, and 2 equally narrow lateral thoracic stripes. Twin-Spotted Spiketail is larger, with smaller, more closely paired abdominal spots, no stripes on S2, and a long ovipositor. Some female Mosaic Darners have yellow abdominal spots, but have eyes in wide contact.
HABITAT	Sunny seepages and small streams, usually spring runs, including boggy ones.
SEASON	Mid-May to late Aug.
COMMENTS	Feeds in forest clearings, perching on weed stems or twigs. Male patrols are sometimes only a few yards long. Females may lay eggs above the waterline in moss.

Brown Spiketail *Cordulegaster bilineata* Plate 20

IDENTIFICATION	2.5 in., eastern U.S., uncommon. Similar to Delta-Spotted Spiketail but body brown, with bluntly triangular abdominal spots, and 2 equally narrow yellow lateral thoracic stripes.

Abdominal spots form stripes on S2–S3. Eyes whitish green (rarely pale blue).

SIMILAR SPECIES	See Similar Species under Delta-Spotted Spiketail.
HABITAT	Trickles, often sandy or boggy, and usually sunny.
SEASON	Late March to early Aug.
COMMENTS	Males patrol sunlit trickles at cool times of day, hovering periodically and perching occasionally.

Arrowhead Spiketail *Cordulegaster obliqua* Plate 20

IDENTIFICATION	2.7–3.5 in., eastern, local. Dorsal arrowhead markings on abdomen are diagnostic. Female ovipositor projects about length of S10 beyond abdomen.
VARIATION	**Southern Form**, of the southeastern Coastal Plain, (form or subspecies *fasciata*) is larger, 3.3 in., with blue eyes and paler yellow markings, compared with **Northern Form**, 3.1 in., and green-eyed.
SIMILAR SPECIES	None, but see genus discussion.
HABITAT	Spring-fed muck-bottomed forest rivulets, sometimes with rocks.
SEASON	Mid-April to late Aug.
COMMENTS	A wonderful dragonfly that perches from low on weed stems to high on twigs along forest edges. When alarmed it shoots up over trees like an arrow. Males patrol rivulets during the middle of the day. If they reach the end of water they reverse direction and return.

Cruisers
(family Macromiidae)

Medium- to large-size dragonflies, brown or black with yellow markings, that cruise long distances looking for mates and prey on stiff narrow wings built for sustained speed. A yellow belt around the thorax forms a single stripe on each side, and the middle abdominal segments each have only one spot or one pair of spots. The eyes, brilliant green in several species, are in contact on top of the head, and each bears a posterior lateral bump. The face is dark with 2 yellow cross-stripes, while the HW exhibit a rounded anal loop. The legs are very long and bear forked claws. The abdomen is clubbed in males, except for the Royal River Cruiser, but cylindrical in females. Males have ventral rubbery keels on the lower leg of the fore- and hind legs, and of variable length according to species on the middle leg. Females lack ovipositors, and lay their green eggs by touching the tip of the abdomen to the water surface at high speed, usually near a high or overhanging bank. The female subgenital plate is short and V-notched.

Cruisers are usually absent from bedrock streams. Most of the 150-plus species live in the Northern Hemisphere, of which North America claims 9.

Brown Cruisers
(genus *Didymops*)

This genus contains only 2 species, both found in eastern North America, which are brown with pale yellow markings and green eyes. They are similar to River Cruisers but differ by: short dorsal eye seam with occiput bulging rearward, abdomen tends to be ringed on S4–S6, early-spring flight season, perch and mate low, and hover while hunting. River Cruisers have larger eyes, spotted abdomens, fly primarily in the summer, typically fly higher, with singles and mating pairs hanging in trees, and rarely hover.

Stream Cruiser *Didymops transversa* Plate 21

IDENTIFICATION 2.2 in., eastern, common. Usually recognizable by combination of spring flight season, brown coloration, and male cruising behavior along shores of streams. Thorax brown with one pale yellow lateral stripe. Each wing has a small brown basal spot, and costal vein is pale brown at maturity. Male abdomen conspicuously clubbed, bearing yellow cerci. Eyes brown in juveniles, changing slowly to glassy green, most slowly in females. Rear of head yellow-brown, and no yellow lower rear thoracic stripe present.

SIMILAR SPECIES Florida Cruiser is grayer and a little larger, and males cruise edges of sand-bottomed lakes. It lacks basal wing spots, and costal veins are pale yellow. Males of both species resemble a Clubtail in flight, but hang rather than squat on a perch, and eyes are in contact on top of head. Bronzed River Cruiser of TX is larger, with yellow frontal thoracic stripes and no wing spots.

HABITAT Streams, rivers, and lakes (but rarely lakes in FL), often forested with a sandy bottom and slow current.

SEASON Late Jan. to mid-May in FL, early May to mid-Sept. in the north, primarily early spring.

COMMENTS Feeds by flying low over fields, or sometimes by hovering in spaces among weeds or forest undergrowth. It perches oblique-

ly on weed stems or hangs beneath twigs. Males fly patrols up to *131*
100 yards long near shore. Before their eyes change to green,
both sexes can mate, and females can lay eggs.

Florida Cruiser *Didymops floridensis* **Plate 21**

IDENTIFICATION   2.6 in., FL and adjacent AL, common. Similar to Stream Cruiser but larger, gray-brown, with yellow costal veins but no brown basal wing spots. Identified by brown coloration, and male habit of cruising along shores of sand-bottomed lakes in early spring. Rear of head pale yellow, and lower rear edge of thorax has a narrow pale yellow stripe.

SIMILAR SPECIES   Compare with Stream Cruiser.

HABITAT   Sand-bottomed lakes edged with grass or bald cypress.

SEASON   Mid-Jan. to early May.

COMMENTS   In spite of its subdued coloration, a dragonfly with class. Forages by flying for long distances through woodlands and weedy clearings, occasionally perching obliquely on weed stems or hovering among bushes. Males fly fast long patrols along the outer edge of lakeshore vegetation. Females fly at breakneck speed, touching the tip of the abdomen to the water to wash off eggs, sometimes selecting a cypress tree and circling its base many times. When finished egg laying, they often grab a damselfly and carry it away to be eaten.

River Cruisers
(genus *Macromia*)

Like the Brown Cruisers, but larger and more resplendent, with dark green or blue iridescent reflections on the head and thorax. The wings often show traces of brown at the base, more pronounced in females. Even the most different species of River Cruisers sometimes hybridize. To identify River Cruisers, pay special attention to the presence or absence of yellow frontal thoracic markings, and to whether the yellow rings around S2 and S7 are complete or interrupted. Known life cycles are 2 years.

River Cruisers should not be confused with other dragonflies, but note that Spiketails have 2 or 3 pale lateral thoracic stripes, shorter legs, and eyes touching at only one point. The Dragonhunter Clubtail has 2 pale lateral thoracic stripes, a yellow face, a striped abdomen, and separated eyes.

North America has 7 River Cruisers, but 130-plus other species occur in the Old World, including a few whose bodies are metallic green.

Western River Cruiser *Macromia magnifica* **Plate 21**

IDENTIFICATION 2.8 in., western, fairly common. The only Cruiser west of the Rocky Mountains. Body brown, thorax with 1 lateral yellow stripe, half-length yellow frontal stripes, and covered by thin white pruinescence. S2–S8 have large pale yellow dorsal spots, brightest on S8, abdomen clubbed in male. Eyes opalescent brown, costal vein yellow. Yellow ring of S2 may be interrupted dorsally and laterally.

BODY FEATURES Male our only River Cruiser without a keel on middle leg.

VARIATION The **Northern Form**, of the British Columbia area (subspecies or form *rickeri*), has reduced yellow spots on S2–S6.

SIMILAR SPECIES Bronzed River Cruiser very similar but range not known to overlap. Spiketails have 2 pale lateral thoracic stripes.

HABITAT Clean, often sand-bottomed, lowland and foothill rivers and streams up to 1000 ft.

SEASON Mid-May to early Sept.

COMMENTS Forages mostly from afternoon until late twilight at any height over open fields. Males fly long beats over stream pools, mostly 7–10 A.M., with a fast bouncy flight, often swinging out over land for the return part of a patrol. It ranges south to Hidalgo, Mexico.

Bronzed River Cruiser *Macromia annulata* **Plate 21**

IDENTIFICATION 2.8 in., NM/TX, fairly common. Identified by bronzy brown coloration with a single lateral yellow thoracic stripe, combined with nearly full-length frontal yellow stripes. Thorax thinly white pruinose, and male abdomen slightly clubbed. In females yellow band of S2 abruptly narrowed to half width in upper half, and juvenile females have outer halves of wings tinted orange. Eyes gray to opalescent blue-green, costa vein yellow. Rear of head and side of S1 yellow, these areas dark in our other River Cruisers (except Gilded). Yellow ring of S2 may be interrupted dorsally.

BODY FEATURES Male cerci in dorsal view widen to blunt tips, these taper to pointed tips in our other River Cruisers. Keel of male middle leg 40%–44% length of lower leg. Hybrids with Royal River Cruiser are known.

SIMILAR SPECIES Stream Cruiser is a smaller spring species that lacks yellow frontal thoracic stripes.

HABITAT Streams and rivers in dry country.

SEASON Late May to late Aug.

Males fly over water well out from the bank. It ranges south to 133
San Luis Potosí, Mexico.

Gilded River Cruiser *Macromia pacifica* **Plate 21**

IDENTIFICATION 2.8 in., TX to OH, local. Told from other River Cruisers by its nearly half yellow coloration, like bright yellow paint on a dark brown body. Thorax has parallel-sided full-length yellow frontal stripes, S3–S8 each have half-length yellow spots, and male abdomen is slightly clubbed. Eyes brilliant blue-green, costal vein yellow. In females yellow ring of S2 is wide, and yellow markings of S2–S6 are interrupted dorsally, while juvenile females have amber-tinted wings.

BODY FEATURES Keel of male middle leg 33%–43% length of lower leg. Apparent hybrids with the Royal River Cruiser have been called *M. wabashensis.*

SIMILAR SPECIES Other River Cruisers are less yellow. The female Bronzed River Cruiser has much paler overall coloration, with yellow band of S2 narrowed abruptly in its upper half, and spots of S2–S6 connected across midline.

HABITAT Streams and rivers.

SEASON Mid-April to late Aug.

COMMENTS Feeds over fields. Males have a beat of about one pool, and usually fly level and straight along the bank, occasionally hanging on a twig.

Illinois River Cruiser *Macromia illinoiensis* **Plate 21**

IDENTIFICATION 2.8 in., eastern, common. Mostly black with a single yellow lateral thoracic stripe. Abdomen of male clubbed. Juveniles often have yellow-tinted wings. Eyes brilliant green.

VARIATION The **Southern Form** (*M. i. georgina*) of the southeast has half-length yellow frontal thoracic stripes, a complete yellow band on S2, and conspicuous yellow spots on S3–S8. In females wings become tinged brown with age, beginning at tips. **Northern Form** has no frontal thoracic stripes, band of S2 is interrupted both dorsally and laterally, and the only conspicuous abdominal spot is on S7; some females have orange-brown wingtips.

BODY FEATURES Males of Northern Form are our only River Cruisers with black auricles. Males of Southern Form have each hamule with a long slender tip beyond the end barb, tip short in our other River Cruisers. Keel of male middle leg 25%–50% length of lower leg (14%–20% in Allegheny River Cruiser, 50%–58% in Mountain River Cruiser).

SIMILAR SPECIES   Allegheny River Cruiser resembles Northern Form, but yellow ring of S2 is complete laterally, and males have a complete yellow band on S7 (yellow spots of S7 occasionally more or less also joined into a band in Illinois River Cruiser). Thorax of Allegheny usually brown, contrasting with black abdomen. In the southern Appalachian area, the Illinois, Allegheny, and Mountain River Cruisers are too alike to tell apart. Royal River Cruiser is considerably larger than these, S7 usually bears a pair of yellow spots, and male abdomen is not clubbed.

HABITAT   Streams to large rivers, and lakes, the latter more often in the north.

SEASON   Early March to early Nov. in FL, early June to early Sept. in Canada.

COMMENTS   Forages by flying long distances along roads and through open forest, sometimes methodically up and down rows of corn, until sunset. It sometimes soars high among swarms of other dragonflies. Males fly patrols 50-plus yards long, mostly near the bank, and primarily in the morning. At cool temperatures they have one of the fastest sustained cruising speeds of any of our dragonflies, but at warm temperatures they fly by alternate flits and sails on raised wings.

Allegheny River Cruiser *Macromia alleghaniensis* Plate 21

IDENTIFICATION   2.8 in., eastern U.S., uncommon. Thorax lacks frontal stripes, and is usually browner than abdomen. Abdomen has yellow ring of S2 interrupted dorsally, in males clubbed and with a complete yellow basal band on S7. Eyes brilliant green.

BODY FEATURES   Legs a little longer than in Illinois River Cruiser, but keel of male middle leg shorter, 14%–20% length of lower leg. FW triangle usually 1-celled, and 2 cells border FW subtriangle posterobasally.

SIMILAR SPECIES   See Similar Species under Illinois River Cruiser.

HABITAT   Streams and rivers.

SEASON   Early June to mid-Sept., beginning about 2 weeks earlier than for Illinois River Cruiser.

COMMENTS   Behavior like Illinois River Cruiser, but patrolling males fly higher and slower, from 8 A.M. to 5 P.M.

Mountain River Cruiser *Macromia margarita* (see Plate 21)

IDENTIFICATION   2.9 in., southern Appalachians, local. Although a little larger, male cannot be distinguished from male Allegheny River Cruiser, nor can female be told from female Illinois River Cruiser.

BODY FEATURES FW triangle generally 2-celled, and 3 cells border FW subtriangle posterobasally. Keel of male middle leg 50%–58% length of lower leg. Female has yellow ring of S2 interrupted in side view, and formed as in female Illinois River Cruiser, a transverse streak posteriorly plus a square spot in the anterior ventral corner.

SIMILAR SPECIES See Similar Species under Illinois River Cruiser.

HABITAT Clean mountain or Piedmont streams and rivers.

SEASON Early June to late Aug.

COMMENTS Males patrol long stretches of river, 100-plus yards, as fast as the Illinois River Cruiser.

Royal River Cruiser *Macromia taeniolata* Plate 21

IDENTIFICATION Our largest Cruiser, Darner sized, 3.3 in. Eastern, common southward, scarce northward. Our only Cruiser with male abdomen not clubbed, although it widens posteriorly. Thorax bears half-length frontal yellow stripes, yellow ring of S2 is interrupted dorsally, and abdomen has small yellow spots, including usually a pair of spots on S7. Female wings often tinted yellow, becoming browner with age. Eyes brilliant green, costa vein partly to entirely yellow.

BODY FEATURES Keel of male middle leg short but variable, usually about 9% length of lower leg, but ranging from 5% to 33%.

SIMILAR SPECIES A single yellow spot is present on S7 in similar Cruisers. See Similar Species under Illinois River Cruiser.

HABITAT Clean rivers, streams, and lakes.

SEASON Mid-April to late Nov. in FL, mid-June to early Sept. in IN.

COMMENTS The ceaseless male patrol flights of this magnificent dragonfly are higher and slower, about 4 mph, than for most River Cruisers, usually along the bank, and beginning in early morning in warm weather.

Emeralds
(family Corduliidae)

Although most species are plain brown, many are elegantly symmetrical and display emerald green jewel-like eyes (red-brown in juveniles). Some also have green or bronze metallic iridescence on the body. The eyes are in contact on top of the head, and females either lack an ovipositor or have a spout-shaped one. Males often have a spindle-shaped abdomen, narrowed toward both ends. The HW anal loop is distinctively club-shaped, each eye has a posterior lateral bump, and males have ventral rubbery keels on their lower legs.

Like their namesake gems, Emeralds are generally scarce and difficult to find. Many species breed in rare types of aquatic habitats (especially bogs), are secretive, have a short flight season, or fly for only a short time each day. The Baskettails are exceptional in that they are dully colored and are often common inhabitants of ordinary ponds and lakes. Emeralds are flyer dragonflies, seldom perching during feeding, and often hovering during male sexual patrols. When they do perch, they hang vertically or obliquely from stems. Note that some Skimmers are brown and look superficially like Emeralds, especially the Evening Skimmer of the far south. Known life cycles of Emeralds are 1 year, up to 2–3 years. Emeralds are primarily northern in distribution, and of the 200-plus species worldwide, 49 are North American.

Common Emeralds
(genus *Cordulia*)

This group contains 1 species in North America and a second very similar species, the Downy Emerald (*C. aenea*), in Eurasia. Little Emeralds and Striped Emeralds exhibit some differences in wing venation, but they all could perhaps be classified in one genus.

American Emerald *Cordulia shurtleffii* Plate 22

IDENTIFICATION   Medium, 1.9 in. Canada and northern U.S. (except Great Plains), common. Thorax hairy, metallic green and bronze, without pale markings. Abdomen has brown spots on S1–S3, a narrow pale ring between S2/S3, and is black beyond S4. Male abdomen slender at S3 but gradually widens to S8, and cerci are slightly divergent. Female abdomen cylindrical with a white spot along lower edge of S3, and cerci as long as S9 + S10. Eyes brilliant green, forehead metallic green, face dark.

BODY FEATURES   Male epiproct nearly as long as cerci, forked with each branch notched at its tip. Male lower leg keels 1/2 length on foreleg, 1/3 length on middle leg, full length on hindleg. Female subgenital plate 1/4–1/3 as long as S9, V-notched 1/2 length to form 2 blunt lobes.

SIMILAR SPECIES Little Emeralds of the northeast are smaller, with a basal brown-orange spot on S3; in the American Emerald paler areas of S3 are on lower edge, small and usually obscure brown or white in males, a white crescent-shaped spot in females. Uhler's Sundragon has a yellow face, dark brown markings at wing bases, brown lateral spots on posterior abdominal segments, and males patrol streams. Striped Emeralds usually are larger, more slender, have longer cerci, and have pale lateral thoracic stripes or spots; some have pale lateral spots or rings on abdomen beyond S4, or dorsal basal pale spots on S3.

HABITAT Ponds and lakes, usually in bogs or with boggy edges. Also sedge marshes, fens, and forest ponds.

SEASON Late April to mid-Sept. Primarily in spring, for 2 months at each locale, one of the earliest spring dragonflies.

COMMENTS Forages along edges of woods, often flying in a limited area and into shade. Sometimes basks flat on leaves. Males patrolling near shore hover, then dart a few yards to hover again. They have brief moving territories, patrolling about 10–25 yards of shore for a few minutes, then patrolling elsewhere.

Little Emeralds
(genus *Dorocordulia*)

This group includes only 2 small species, both found in northeastern North America, with luminous green eyes. The keels on the lower legs of males are 1/3 length on forelegs, vestigial on middle legs, and full length on hind legs.

Racket-Tailed Emerald *Dorocordulia libera* Plate 22

IDENTIFICATION 1.6 in., northeastern, fairly common. Males have the most widely clubbed abdomen among our Emeralds, expanded to a wide flat club on S7–S9, but female abdomen is only slightly clubbed. Thorax is unmarked metallic green and bronze, S3 has an orange base, and abdomen is all black beyond S4. Eyes brilliant green, face mostly dark metallic green.

BODY FEATURES Rear of occiput black. Male cerci converge toward tips. Female subgenital plate 1/2 as long as S9, narrowly slotted for 1/2 length. Petite Emerald has rear of occiput yellow, parallel male cerci, and U- to V-notched subgenital plate with rounded lobes.

SIMILAR SPECIES   Petite Emerald has abdomen barely clubbed in males, not clubbed in females, and female has orange lateral spots at bases of S4–S7. American Emerald is larger, and lacks lateral basal orange spot on S3. See also Similar Species under American Emerald. Abdomen of Racket-Tailed Emerald is flattened horizontally; in Striped Emeralds it tends to be flattened vertically.

HABITAT   Ponds, lake coves, and slow streams, with boggy or marshy borders and acid water.

SEASON   Early May to late Aug., primarily midsummer.

COMMENTS   Feeds along forest edges, but sometimes hunts in shade. Rests by hanging under twigs, sometimes high in trees, or it may bask flat on a leaf. Males generally patrol with the abdomen slightly arched and tilted upward. Compared with American Emerald, male patrols are higher and slower with less hovering, and are less regular and more wandering over open water or marsh. Patrolling males occasionally perch on twigs or pitcher plant flowers.

Petite Emerald *Dorocordulia lepida* **Plate 22**

IDENTIFICATION   1.5 in., New England/Maritimes, uncommon. Body slender with an unmarked metallic green and bronze thorax. Male abdomen slightly widened beyond S3, and usually black beyond S4, but sometimes has tiny lateral pale spots. Female abdomen cylindrical with orange-brown lateral basal spots on S4–S7 or S8. Eyes brilliant green, but female eyes ruby red when seen from certain angles such as from the rear. Face mostly dark metallic green.

SIMILAR SPECIES   Racket-Tailed Emerald has abdomen clubbed in both sexes, and black beyond S4. American Emerald is larger, without an orange lateral basal spot on S3. See also Similar Species under American Emerald.

HABITAT   Marshes, bog lakes and ponds, and streams in cedar swamps, sometimes coexisting with Racket-Tailed Emerald.

SEASON   Late May to late Aug., primarily July in Canada.

COMMENTS   Feeds in grassy clearings 2 ft. up, occasionally abruptly perching on a twig or flat on a leaf. Males patrol along edges of emergent vegetation 2 to 3 ft. up, primarily in the afternoon and along channels, but also over adjacent low vegetation. They are more active, and hover less, than male Racket-Tailed Emeralds.

Boghaunters
(genus *Williamsonia*)

Both species of this genus are North American, and are our smallest Emeralds, with minimal metallic coloration. They are rare and local charismatic inhabitants of northeastern bogs.

Ringed Boghaunter *Williamsonia lintneri* **Plate 22**

IDENTIFICATION
1.3 in., coastal New England, and MI/WI, local. Unmistakable due to small size, orange-brown face, and orange bands on posterior ends of S2–S9. Thorax all brown, eyes gray-blue to aqua.

SIMILAR SPECIES
Ebony Boghaunter has a dark brown face, and black abdomen posterior to S5. The female Elfin Skimmer is even smaller, and has partial yellow bands on *bases* of S2–S6 or S7, and yellow markings on thorax. Hudsonian Whiteface has a white face and spotted abdomen.

HABITAT
Shallow bog pools and acid fens, often with wiry or three-way sedges (*Dulicium*), not overgrown with bushes, but near Atlantic white cedar, black spruce, larch, or other forests. Larvae can survive some drying, but often absent from small bogs.

SEASON
Late April to early July, primarily early spring, the earliest non-migratory dragonfly in its range.

COMMENTS
Usually seen in forest basking on the ground or tree trunks up to 500 yards from breeding sites. Males are not territorial.

Ebony Boghaunter *Williamsonia fletcheri* **Plate 22**

IDENTIFICATION
1.3 in., MN to Nova Scotia, local. Body dark brown to black with white bands on posterior ends of S2–S4. Face dark brown, male eyes bright green, female eyes gray.

SIMILAR SPECIES
Ringed Boghaunter has an orange-brown face, and orange bands on S2–S9. Black Meadowhawk is either all black, or has yellow spots on S2–S4 plus other yellow markings. Petite Emerald is larger, more metallic, and lacks abdominal rings. Whitefaces have white faces, and most have abdominal spots.

HABITAT
Bog pools and fens in forest. Only occasionally found at same locales as Ringed Boghaunter.

SEASON
Mid-May to early July.

COMMENTS
Away from water perches in forest at sunny spots on low leaves

or the ground, or on tree trunks at any height. Males patrol small bog pools, resting on moss or dead branches.

Sundragons
(genus *Helocordulia*)

The 2 species of this genus are native to eastern North America.

Selys' Sundragon *Helocordulia selysii* Plate 22

IDENTIFICATION   Medium, 1.7 in. Southeastern, uncommon. Body dark brown, with a nearly complete orange basal ring on S3, and small orange lateral spots at bases of S4–S7 or S8. Male abdomen slightly clubbed, widest at S8. Each wing bears a brown spot at base, followed by brown dots along front edge to nodus (often beyond nodus in females). Face yellow, eyes pale green.

BODY FEATURES   Male cerci each have a lateral and a medial tooth, and are parallel in their posterior halves. Female subgenital plate orange, 1/4–1/2 as long as S9, widely V-notched to base, forming 2 pointed lobes, lateral edges of lobes divergent.

SIMILAR SPECIES   Uhler's Sundragon, whose range barely overlaps, has a small amber spot next to the brown spot at each wing base. Baskettails have yellow sides on abdomen. Shadowdragons lack orange ring of S3.

HABITAT   Clean, usually sand-bottomed, streams and small rivers in forest.

SEASON   Mid-March to mid-May.

COMMENTS   Named for M. E. DeSelys-Longchamps, Belgian odonatist. Forages along forest edges, perching obliquely on weed stems near the ground. Males patrol a short stretch of stream bank, often hovering briefly, mostly in sunshine from mid-A.M. to mid-P.M.

Uhler's Sundragon *Helocordulia uhleri* Plate 22

IDENTIFICATION   1.6 in., eastern, but only highlands southward, uncommon. Nearly identical to Selys' Sundragon except that a small amber spot lies adjacent to brown spot at each wing base, and in females abdominal spots are larger. Eyes gray in juveniles.

BODY FEATURES   Male cerci lack a medial tooth and are bowed laterally, becoming parallel only near their tips. Female subgenital plate orange, 1/3–1/2 as long as S9, narrowly V-notched for 1/2–2/3 length, the lobes with convergent lateral edges.

SIMILAR SPECIES   Boghaunters are smaller, bog species, with either a dark face or

conspicuous orange bands on the abdomen. Also see Similar
Species under Selys' Sundragon.

HABITAT   Clean forested rivers and streams where the flow has been
slowed, and occasionally lakes, with water that is not too acid.

SEASON   Mid-March to early Aug., primarily spring.

COMMENTS   Named for Philip R. Uhler, American entomologist. Feeds in
clearings, perching on weed stems, bushes, or even on the
ground. Males patrol close to shore, in sun or shade, and until
dusk. They fly swiftly with frequent brief hovering, but may
bask on rocks.

Baskettails
(genus *Epitheca*)

These exceptionally agile flyers have a brown body, less metallic than most
Emeralds, with lateral yellow abdominal stripes, a yellow lateral dot on the
thorax, and a yellow to brown face. Males have a spindle-shaped abdomen,
widest at S6. The female subgenital plate is flat, flexible, and forked from its
base, with the 2 lobes extending to the posterior end of S9 or beyond. Females
use their subgenital plate like a forklift to carry their yellow to orange eggs,
resembling a miniature sea plane with their cargo of eggs "in one basket."
They also resemble Clubtails at this time. Males apparently do not attempt to
mate while the females are carrying egg balls. Females deposit the egg mass
with a quick double dip on a nearly submerged plant, where it unravels into a
gelatinous rope more than 6 in. long containing several hundred eggs. By this
means the female is exposed only briefly to aquatic predators, and the eggs are
held near the water surface where higher temperatures and oxygen content
speed development. These advantages are counteracted when many females
select the same place, forming large masses of egg ropes that prevent the
development of eggs nearest the center. The egg ropes sometimes become
infiltrated with algae, which provide an additional source of oxygen through
photosynthesis in the daytime. Mating pairs fly in the wheel position for long
distances before perching in a shrub or tree to complete mating for about 10
min., although the Common Baskettail apparently does not perch during its 5
min. mating flight.

    Our Baskettails include the large and distinctive Prince Baskettail, and 8
small species, the "sparrows of the dragonflies," which are very difficult to
identify. The Prince is now classified in the subgenus *Epicordulia*, our small
species in the subgenus *Tetragoneuria*. Of our 9 species, only 2 range into the
west, while 3 additional species, all in the subgenus *Epitheca*, are Eurasian.

Prince Baskettail *Epitheca princeps* **Plate 23**

IDENTIFICATION
Medium to large, 2.2–3.2 in. Eastern, common. Our only Emerald with extensively brown wingtips. In most of its range it also has brown nodal and basal wing spots. Eyes of juveniles red-brown, of male bright green, of female bronzy brown. Forehead lacks a black T-spot, and female cerci are longer than S9 + S10. With aging the yellow body markings become obscured. Wings notably stiff and brittle.

VARIATION
Southeastern individuals, form or subspecies *regina*, are Darner sized and have large dark brown wing spots. The spot at the tip extends along the rear edge of the wing past the stigma. In most of the east, it is the size of a King Skimmer and has smaller wing spots; that at the tip is generally cut off at the outer end of the stigma. Sometimes the wing spots are greatly reduced, especially northward. Nodal spots may be missing, and the basal spot of the FW nearly so. There may be great variation at a single locale.

SIMILAR SPECIES
Certain King Skimmers, notably female Twelve-Spotted Skimmers and Common Whitetails, have a similar wing pattern, but abdomen of Prince is more slender and as long as a wing, males have green eyes, and it is a flyer rather than a percher. Lake Emerald of the north lacks wing spots, and males do not patrol a definite beat. Note that no Darner in North America has large brown wing spots.

HABITAT
Permanent ponds, lakes, and slow streams and rivers, with clear to muddy water.

SEASON
Mid-March to early Dec. in FL, early June to late Aug. in Canada.

COMMENTS
This elegant dragonfly usually flies over the trees when foraging, but may form feeding swarms at any level in the evening. It perches by hanging under twigs, often with wings partly elevated. Males on their large patrols leisurely fly with alternate flits and sails on slightly raised wings about 6 ft. up for hours anytime from dawn to dusk. Females lay eggs mostly in the evening, carrying an orange egg ball poised on the end of the abdomen, which is curled vertically upward. The egg rope is about 1.5 ft. long after it is draped over a stem awash at the water surface.

Common Baskettail *Epitheca cynosura* **Plate 23**

IDENTIFICATION
Medium, 1.6 in. Eastern, common. Body dark brown with yellow lateral abdominal stripes. Some individuals have a triangular brown basal spot in HW; spot does not reach rear margin

and seldom reaches nodus. Individuals without such markings cannot usually be differentiated from other clear-winged Baskettails. Abdomen usually rather stout, and female cerci are short.

VARIATION Brown basal HW spot varies from tiny to a large triangle even at a single locale. Forehead T-spot may be well developed or absent. Eyes may be red-brown, glassy green, or blue.

BODY FEATURES Male cerci have a ventral angle in side view, with a ventral keel extending posteriorly from it. There is also a lateral keel on each cercus, with lateral area between keels flat (but this area bulging in individuals from eastern edge of Great Plains). Male Florida Baskettails also have flat-sided cerci, but lack the ventral angle.

SIMILAR SPECIES Mantled Baskettail in the Carolinas has HW spot extending to rear edge of HW, and S3 of males is less narrowed. Shadowdragons lack lateral yellow stripes on abdomen, or have amber markings at wing bases. Marl Pennants are either all black or have the abdomen mostly yellow. Clear-winged Common Baskettails are identified, if at all, by elimination; if the individual in question is not any of the other Baskettails in the area, then it must be a Common.

HABITAT Lakes, ponds, marshes, swamps, and slow streams and rivers.

SEASON Early Jan. to mid-Aug. in U.S., plus early Oct. to early Dec. in north FL. Early May to early Aug. in Canada. Primarily in spring for about 5 weeks at each locale, beginning about 2 weeks after Spiny Baskettail.

COMMENTS These ace stunt fliers feed with a fast erratic flight, often in swarms of both sexes on prey such as winged termites, or over water in the evening with Shadowdragons. They perch obliquely on weed stems or twigs. Males continuously patrol about 3–10 yards of shoreline, often hovering in one spot for minutes at a time, favoring a patch of submerged vegetation. They may patrol most of the day, but attain peak activity in late afternoon.

Mantled Baskettail *Epitheca semiaquea* Plate 23

IDENTIFICATION 1.3 in., eastern U.S. Coast, and OK/TX, local. Generally distinguished from other Baskettails by brown basal half of HW, in which the brown spot reaches both nodus and rear edge of wing.

BODY FEATURES Sides of male cerci swollen; compare with Common Baskettail. These two species were confused in the literature until at least 1973.

VARIATION Basal half of HW normally brown in the Carolinas, but some individuals there and elsewhere have a reduced spot and cannot be separated from Common Baskettail.

SIMILAR SPECIES In the slightly larger Common Baskettail, HW spot does not reach rear edge of wing and seldom reaches nodus, and abdomen of male is often more narrowed at S3.

HABITAT Lakes, ponds, and ditches with clear water, including grassy or swampy beaver ponds, and often with a sandy bottom.

SEASON Late March to mid-May in the Carolinas, mid-April to late June in NJ.

COMMENTS Forages in clearings with a rapid bouncy flight which resembles that of a skipper butterfly. Perches obliquely on weed stems and twigs of bushes. Males may patrol in shade or at dusk.

Stripe-Winged Baskettail *Epitheca costalis* Plate 23

IDENTIFICATION 1.7 in., eastern U.S. and southern Great Plains, fairly common. The brown stripe along the front edge of each wing of **Stripe-Winged Form** females is diagnostic (but such females only in southeast and less than 10% of population). **Clear-Winged Form** females can be identified with care by their long cerci, as long as S9 + S10. Males have a slender abdomen, and in most of range have 2 small brown basal spots in HW. Eyes have a metallic-green horizontal band, or are all green.

BODY FEATURES In the southeast males have long cerci without a ventral keel, but with the sides swollen behind the ventral angle which projects downward and inward. The male Common Baskettail has sides of cerci flattened, except along the eastern edge of the Great Plains, where the slender abdomen of the Stripe-Winged is the distinguishing feature. The female Florida Baskettail cannot be differentiated with certainty from clear-winged females of the Stripe-Winged.

VARIATION In the TX area, the distinctive **Dot-Winged Form** *petechialis* has a row of small brown dots (larger in females) along the front of each wing.

SIMILAR SPECIES Males cannot ordinarily be separated from other clear-winged Baskettails, except in the TX area and westward where the only other small Baskettail is the Common, which has a stouter abdomen. Sundragons have an orange ring on S3. Shadowdragons lack bright green eyes, and either lack lateral yellow abdominal stripes or have amber markings at wing bases.

HABITAT In the southeast, mostly sand-bottomed lakes. Elsewhere, other kinds of ponds and lakes, and pools of clean streams and rivers, usually with sparser vegetation than for Common Baskettail.

SEASON	Mid-Jan. to mid-July, primarily in spring.
COMMENTS	Forages along forest edges, sometimes in shade, occasionally perching on twigs of trees. Males patrol and hover along a stretch of shore longer than that used by male Common Baskettails.

Florida Baskettail *Epitheca stella* (see Plate 23)

IDENTIFICATION	1.8 in., FL Peninsula, common. Cannot normally be distinguished from other clear-winged small Baskettails except by range. It has only touches of brown at base of HW (none in some females), and no brown in FW. Abdomen long, slender, and parallel-sided. Eyes red-brown to metallic green.
BODY FEATURES	Male cerci flat on sides, but without a ventral angle in direct side view. Females cannot be distinguished with certainty from Clear-Winged Form female Stripe-Winged Baskettails.
SIMILAR SPECIES	Stripe-Winged Baskettail has not been found south of Orlando FL, so a slender-bodied Baskettail south of there should be the Florida. For more certainty, look south of Lake Okeechobee, where the only other small Baskettail is the Sepia.
HABITAT	Almost any type of pond in south FL, but in north FL it prefers semifertile lakes edged with sawgrass. It has also been found at slow streams.
SEASON	Early Jan. to late April.
COMMENTS	Often feeds in swarms. Males patrol short stretches of shore from about 9 A.M. to 3 P.M.

Spiny Baskettail *Epitheca spinigera* (see Plate 23)

IDENTIFICATION	1.9 in., southern Canada/northern U.S., common. Similar to Clear-Winged Form of Stripe-Winged Baskettail but with a more northerly range. Body dark brown, HW has 2 or 3 short brown basal streaks, and forehead has a black T-spot. Male abdomen notably spindle-shaped. Female cerci long, as long as S9 + S10. Male eyes iridescent blue, female eyes green.
BODY FEATURES	Male cerci each have a diagnostic sharp ventral spine at 1/3 length (rarely, spine absent).
VARIATION	Largest in northern part of range. A few individuals have brown dots along front of wings, and a few females have a brown smudge in the outer halves of the wings.
SIMILAR SPECIES	Males cannot be distinguished from clear-winged Common Baskettails, but females can be separated with care by their long cerci. Beaverpond Baskettail lacks forehead T-spot, and has cerci bent downward at tips in males, short in females. Uhler's Sundragon has an orange ring on S3.

HABITAT Marshy lakes, ponds, and slow streams, acidic and infertile with some water motion.

SEASON Early May to early Sept. Primarily early spring, beginning about 10 days after Beaverpond Baskettail, lasting about 5 weeks at each locale.

COMMENTS Feeds along forest edges, or over water, sometimes in swarms. Males patrol about 50 ft. of shore, with a faster flight than male Common Baskettails, hovering often.

Sepia Baskettail *Epitheca sepia* (see Plate 23)

IDENTIFICATION 1.6 in., far southeastern, common FL. No visible brown spot at base of HW, and no green in eyes even when mature. Thorax olive yellow, paler than in our other Baskettails, and yellow sides of abdomen more prominent. Male abdomen appears stubby and tapered. Eyes bright red-brown, female cerci short. Males usually patrol in late afternoon, when they appear reddish brown. Also note long flight season, thus the only small Baskettail likely to be seen in the southeast in summer.

BODY FEATURES Male epiproct long, at least 78% as long as cerci, 74% or less in other southeastern Baskettails (except Robust). Female subgenital plate has straight lobes.

SIMILAR SPECIES Perched individuals can be separated from similar Baskettails by the entirely clear wings, except for female Florida Baskettail, which has a longer, more slender abdomen. The Sepia sometimes flies with Shadowdragons at dusk, and probably cannot be distinguished from them in flight.

HABITAT Lakes and slow streams, with sand or mud bottoms.

SEASON Early March to late Nov., most common in spring.

COMMENTS Commonly feeds with a fast erratic flight at dusk, often high, and perches on tree twigs. Males patrol about 10 yards of shore from late afternoon to dusk, hovering occasionally.

Robust Baskettail *Epitheca spinosa* (see Plate 23)

IDENTIFICATION 1.8 in., southeastern to NJ, local. Abdomen notably wide, and thorax bears a coat of long white hair. Forehead lacks a dark T-spot, while HW each have 2 small brown spots at base. Male eyes metallic aqua-green, female eyes milky dark red.

BODY FEATURES Male cerci are bent downward and outward near tips, with a pointed dorsal spine at the bend. Male cerci of Beaverpond Baskettail similar, but spine is blunt. A few hybrid males have been found between Robust and Common Baskettails; they had an intermediate flight season.

SIMILAR SPECIES Robust Baskettail is larger and has a wider abdomen than other small Baskettails, and its thorax appears paler due to its coat of longer white hair. Male is only southern Baskettail with cerci bent downward at tips. Compared with male Common Baskettails, Robust has brighter green eyes, a steadier, less bouncing flight, and more prolonged hovering.

HABITAT Swamps with some water movement, such as those bordering lakes or rivers. Occasionally boggy ponds or lakes.

SEASON Mid-March to early June, the earliest dragonfly within its range.

COMMENTS Forages along forest edges, usually perching high under slanted twigs. Males patrol small sunny channels among the trees of swamps.

Beaverpond Baskettail *Epitheca canis* (see Plate 23)

IDENTIFICATION 1.8 in., southern Canada/northern U.S., common. Mature females have wings tinted brown from base to stigma, and are easily identified seen against sky or water. Male abdomen in side view appears clubbed at S8–S9, but males can usually be identified only if the downturned tips of the cerci can be seen. Males have 2 small brown basal spots in HW, juvenile females have 1 small spot. Female cerci shorter than S9 + S10. Thorax has a thin covering of brown hair, and forehead lacks a dark T-spot. Eyes metallic green to blue. Rear of head tan.

BODY FEATURES Male cerci like those of Robust Baskettail, but with a blunt dorsal spine and a ventral bump at 2/5 length. Lobes of female subgenital plate straight, wide, and blunt.

SIMILAR SPECIES Robust Baskettail has a wider abdomen, paler thorax, and more distinct yellow edgings on abdomen. Spiny Baskettails have a black T-spot on forehead, and female cerci are as long as S9 + S10. Some Common Baskettails are indistinguishable unless the black back of the head or the straight male cerci can be seen.

HABITAT Boggy or marshy ponds, lakes, and slow streams, with acid infertile water.

SEASON Late April to early Aug., about 6 weeks at each locale, the earliest dragonfly within its range.

COMMENTS Feeds in sunny openings, sometimes in swarms, perching on twigs. Occasionally it may bask flat on a leaf, or hunt above the trees if it is not too windy. Males patrol territories about 3–4 yards in diameter, hovering periodically. Females over water display their tinted wings by holding them upward much of the time.

Striped Emeralds
(genus *Somatochlora*)

This group of slender, graceful, mostly medium-size dragonflies includes more than half of our species of Emeralds. Most are intriguing rare to uncommon denizens of wild forests, difficult to encounter because many are secretive or fly high when feeding. Most of our species are dark brown with 1 or 2 pale lateral stripes or spots on the thorax, and brilliant green eyes (dark red in juveniles). In most species the thorax is coated with metallic green wax. All of our species are pale dorsally between the wings and have a pale ring between S2 and S3.

Of our 26 species, the female subgenital plate projects as an ovipositor in 20; a horizontal trough in 9, perpendicular and spoutlike in 6, and slanting obliquely rearward in 5. Male cerci are of 5 fundamental shapes: (1) Ski Type, straight with an upturned tip in 6 species; (2) Straight Type, with a ventral spine near tip in 2 species; (3) Bent Type, bent downward at half-length in 6 species; (4) Pincer Type in 5 species; and (5) Bent-Curled Type, bent inward at 2/3 length with tips upcurled in 7 species.

Some Striped Emeralds apparently gather on hilltops for mating purposes; at least mating pairs are often seen far from water. Mating takes from 1 min. to 1 hr. as the pair hangs from a bush or tree, sometimes on the trunk of a tree. Striped Emeralds occur only in the Northern Hemisphere. Of about 40 species, 26 occur in North America, including 10 widespread across Canada, 13 restricted to the east, and only 3 basically western. They are absent from southwestern lowlands.

Whitehouse's Emerald *Somatochlora whitehousei*
Plate 23

IDENTIFICATION 1.9 in., Canada, uncommon. HW has small brown spot at base (in addition to membranule). Thorax dark brassy green with an indistinct anterior stripe, but no posterior stripe. Abdomen widest at S7 in males, S6 in females, and S3 of female with much larger orange anterior basal spot than male. Females have an oblique spoutlike ovipositor 3/4 as long as S9, and cerci longer than S9 + S10. Upper face black.

BODY FEATURES Male cerci of bent-curled type, each with a ventral spine at 1/3 length, and a lateral angle at 3/5–2/3 length. Male cerci of Muskeg Emerald similar but with spine at 2/5 length and angle at 1/3 length. Cerci of our other Striped Emeralds lack ventral spines.

SIMILAR SPECIES Only 2 other Striped Emeralds have a brown spot at base of HW (spot not normally visible in flight), the similar Muskeg and the quite different Delicate. Male Whitehouse's and Muskeg Emeralds cannot be differentiated, but the female Muskeg lacks an ovipositor. Most Striped Emeralds in the range of Whitehouse's have either 2 lateral thoracic pale markings, or white abdominal rings posterior to S3. Kennedy's Emerald has a more slender abdomen and a yellow upper face.

HABITAT Mossy sedge fens and small bog pools.

SEASON Mid-June to early Sept.

COMMENTS Named for Mr. Francis Whitehouse, Canadian entomologist. Males slowly patrol with an arched abdomen over bog pools in no definite sequence. The female taps eggs on both water and moss at edges of bog pools.

Muskeg Emerald *Somatochlora septentrionalis* (see Plate 23)

IDENTIFICATION 1.8 in., Canada, uncommon. Male identical to Whitehouse's Emerald. Female like Whitehouse's but lacks an ovipositor, and has abdomen widest at S5 rather than S6.

BODY FEATURES Female subgenital plate is 1/4–1/3 length of S9 and deeply notched.

SIMILAR SPECIES Treeline Emerald of Yukon area lacks HW spots and thoracic stripes, and abdomen of male is widest at S6 instead of S7. See Similar Species under Whitehouse's Emerald.

HABITAT Open mossy muskeg and fen pools about 8–20 yards in diameter, with gently sloping mucky edges and scattered sedges. Male Mosaic Darners apparently chase them from pools with firm edges.

SEASON Mid-June to late Aug.

COMMENTS Perches out of the wind in grass-rimmed potholes. Males patrol an irregular course about 1 ft. up with an arched abdomen, usually one at a time over a pool, mostly over mucky edges but also over open water and seldom hovering.

Treeline Emerald *Somatochlora sahlbergi* Plate 23

IDENTIFICATION 2.0 in., Alaska to Northwest Territories, uncommon? Body appears all black (tiny orange anterior lateral thoracic spot in some). Male abdomen stout, widest at S6. Female has slender cerci as long as S9 + S10, but lacks an ovipositor.

BODY FEATURES Male cerci of bent-curled type, but lack angular projections or spines. Female subgenital plate 1/2 as long as S9, with a deep V-

EMERALDS

notch. Hybridizes with Ringed and Hudsonian Emeralds in the northern Yukon area.

SIMILAR SPECIES — Whitehouse's and Muskeg Emeralds have a small brown spot at base of HW, male abdomen is widest at S7, and female Whitehouse's has an ovipositor. Ringed and Hudsonian Emeralds have white rings posterior to S3.

HABITAT — Deep, cold, mossy ponds and pools in bogs and fens at the edge of the Arctic tundra. In Siberia, recorded from slowly moving water. Its range is within 60 miles of the latitudinal tree line, and within 200 yards of the altitudinal tree line.

SEASON — Early June to early Aug.

COMMENTS — Males fly slowly and are unwary as they crisscross over the open water of small ponds, occasionally perching on bushes. It ranges across northern Eurasia.

Ringed Emerald *Somatochlora albicincta* Plate 23

IDENTIFICATION — 1.9 in., Canada and northernmost U.S., common. Thorax brassy green with one (anterior) lateral thoracic stripe, which is short, white, and diamond-shaped. Narrow white rings are present between all abdominal segments, and S10 has pale spots at junctions with cerci. Females have no ovipositor, cerci a little longer than S9 + S10, and a pale epiproct.

BODY FEATURES — Male cerci of bent-curled type, with a basal and a midlength angle on the lateral edge. Male epiproct triangular in ventral view (rectangular and forked in Lake Emerald). Female subgenital plate 1/2 or less as long as S9, deeply V-notched.

VARIATION — On the Pacific slope below about 5100 ft. it is darker and about 0.2 in. longer, with less distinct abdominal rings. Females as large as Lake Emeralds have been found on the Queen Charlotte Islands (*S. a. massettensis*).

SIMILAR SPECIES — Quebec Emerald nearly lacks abdominal rings on S3–S7, and has S10 black. Hudsonian Emerald, found west from Hudson Bay, is usually larger with a more obscure thoracic stripe, larger pale spots anterior to bases of FW, and no pale spots on S10. The female Hudsonian has an ovipositor, more contrasting orange-tan lateral basal spots on S2–S4, and a black epiproct. Lake Emerald virtually lacks thoracic stripes, has thorax more brown than green, and is active over water far from shore.

HABITAT — Slow streams, ponds, and lakes, at up to 2200 ft., with some water movement, and often with shallow boggy shores and sparse vegetation such as scattered sedges. Also mossy fen ponds.

SEASON   Mid-June to early Oct.

COMMENTS   Perches on twigs of trees but does not usually fly high for feeding. Males fly slowly close to shore, in shade or sunlight, hovering briefly every 1–3 yards. They prefer to patrol a water/land interface, second choice a grass/water interface, last choice a barren or brushy bank.

Hudsonian Emerald *Somatochlora hudsonica*
Plate 23

IDENTIFICATION   2.1 in., common Alaska to Hudson Bay, local Rocky Mountains to CO. Almost identical to Ringed Emerald, but female has a short, oblique ovipositor 2/3 as long as S9.

BODY FEATURES   Male cerci of bent-curled type, with a large pointed ventral angle at midlength. Ringed Emerald has a lateral angle, Quebec Emerald lacks midlength angles.

SIMILAR SPECIES   See Similar Species under Ringed Emerald. Note that Ringed and Lake Emeralds lack ovipositors.

HABITAT   Deep, sedge-bordered lakes and ponds. Also ponds with firm boggy edges, lake inlets, sedge marshes, and boggy slow streams, including ditches and sloughs. Often found with Ringed Emerald.

SEASON   Early June to late Sept.

COMMENTS   Males patrol near the bank.

Quebec Emerald *Somatochlora brevicincta*
(see Plate 23)

IDENTIFICATION   1.9 in., ME and eastern Canada, scarce. Looks like Ringed Emerald except that white abdominal rings are lacking or widely interrupted dorsally on S3–S7, and S10 is usually all dark. Male abdomen widest at S5. Female wings often tint brown with age.

BODY FEATURES   Male cerci each have a sharp lateral angle near base that is visible in direct dorsal view. Male cerci of Ringed Emerald have 2 small lateral angles, neither visible in dorsal view. Male hamule a smoothly curved arc in Quebec Emerald, bent posteriorly in Ringed. Female subgenital plate nearly as long as S9 and not notched in Quebec Emerald, 1/2 as long as S9 and notched in Ringed.

SIMILAR SPECIES   See Similar Species under Ringed Emerald.

HABITAT   Poor fens, which are films of slowly moving water through pools in sedge marshes, and acid fens. Also grassy bogs with deep loose sphagnum moss.

SEASON   Late June to mid-Sept.

COMMENTS   Feeds about 6 ft. up in forest openings. Males patrol and hover over sparse sedges and along grassy edges 1–2 ft. up, in an even flight lower and slower than that of Muskeg Emeralds.

Lake Emerald *Somatochlora cingulata* Plate 24

IDENTIFICATION   A large Striped Emerald, 2.5 in. Southern Canada and northernmost eastern U.S., uncommon. Thorax unmarked brown (some have a very obscure pale brown anterior lateral stripe), and abdomen with narrow white rings between all segments. Female lacks an ovipositor, but has cerci much longer than S9 + S10.

BODY FEATURES   Male epiproct in ventral view rectangular and shallowly forked (triangular and not forked in other Striped Emeralds, doubly forked in American Emerald). Male cerci of bent-curled type, each with a lateral basal spine. Female subgenital plate 1/3 as long as S9, only shallowly notched. Compare with Ringed Emerald.

SIMILAR SPECIES   Unlike our other Striped Emeralds, the male Lake Emerald flies far and wide over open water. Other northern Striped Emeralds with white abdominal rings have a brassy green thorax bearing a white anterior lateral stripe. Prince Baskettail of the east has brown wingtips, usually also brown spots at nodus and base, and males are territorial.

HABITAT   Lakes, boggy or not, occasionally large rivers.
SEASON   Mid-June to early Sept.
COMMENTS   Feeds high. Males fly over open water without hovering, seldom come near shore, and are not territorial.

Mocha Emerald *Somatochlora linearis* Plate 24

IDENTIFICATION   Our largest Striped Emerald, 2.6 in. Eastern U.S., uncommon. Slender and elegant, with brown-tinted wings and unmarked thorax. Females have a slender, perpendicular spoutlike ovipositor as long as S9 and about half as long as the cerci, which are longer than S9 + S10. With maturity, wings become browner, the face shifts from yellow-brown to brown, a white lateral spot on S2 fades, and orange-brown laterobasal spots on S3–S8 fade.

BODY FEATURES   Male cerci of Straight Type, with a ventral spine at tip. Cerci of Plains Emerald similar, but it has yellow thoracic stripes.

SIMILAR SPECIES   In spite of being plain brown, the Mocha Emerald can be recognized by its large size, brown wings, elegant shape, and forest stream habitat. Male Clamp-Tipped Emeralds have a circular gap between the terminal abdominal appendages in side view. Male Williamson's Emeralds are smaller and darker brown, and often patrol open sunlit shores. Female Clamp-Tipped and Williamson's Emeralds have ovipositors much longer than S9. Twilight Darner of the far southeast is larger and paler brown, and has broad wings.

HABITAT Small forest streams about 1–3 yards wide, including those that partially dry in summer.

SEASON Mid-May to early Oct.

COMMENTS Usually feeds high over clearings, but sometimes hunts by hovering in forest undergrowth. On occasion, two will fly in unison, one a yard above the other. It is most active in early morning beginning at dawn, and from late afternoon to dusk. It hangs from a twig, or sometimes a tree trunk, in forest shade most of the day. When traveling it often flies with rapid, 3 ft. up-and-down and side-to-side undulations, but at other times its flight is leisurely with considerable gliding. Males patrol about 20–30 yards of stream, frequently hovering. Females lay eggs while flying just above the shore in a limited area. With rapid taps of the abdomen, they poke eggs into mud from near the waterline to several feet up the shore.

Fine-Lined Emerald *Somatochlora filosa* **Plate 24**

IDENTIFICATION A large Striped Emerald, 2.4 in. Southeastern to NJ, common in FL. Thorax dark green with 2 narrow white lateral stripes, the anterior stripe narrowest and slightly concave anteriorly (occasionally reduced or absent), while the posterior stripes meet under the thorax. Abdomen mostly black, often with narrow white rings between S8–S10. Face brownish white. Female usually noticeably larger than male, with a skidlike horizontal ovipositor that extends almost to tip of S10. Juvenile females have wings tinted orange in stigma area, but orange is lost as the wings become tinted brown with age. Abdomen of juvenile females flattened vertically from S6 to S8, but becomes cylindrical as it fills with eggs. Female cerci longer than S9 + S10.

BODY FEATURES Male cerci nearly straight but with tips curled down and inward. Female ovipositor thin and thornlike in either ventral or lateral view.

SIMILAR SPECIES Juvenile females flying overhead, with their orange wingtips, are distinctive. Thoracic pattern and ovipositor also distinctive, but difficult to see. Other southeastern Striped Emeralds have wide straight thoracic stripes, or no stripes, and males often have cerci of the bent type.

HABITAT Breeding habitat unknown. Probably either boggy forest trickles or sheet-flow swamp thickets.

SEASON Late June to late Dec.

COMMENTS Feeds in forest clearings, or sometimes in dense shade, from near the ground to treetops, perching on tree twigs. Males of this mysterious dragonfly may patrol and hover in areas of a few square yards about 3 ft. up over dry ground at the edges of swamps, and over slow acidic streams with emergent vegetation.

Treetop Emerald *Somatochlora provocans* (see Plate 24)

IDENTIFICATION 2.0 in., southeastern to NJ, scarce. Thorax has 2 conspicuous yellow to white lateral thoracic stripes, and face is yellow. The posterior stripes meet under the thorax. Narrow white rings are present between S8 to S10, especially in males, and S10 is all brown. Female ovipositor is a horizontal narrow trough that extends to tip of S10, and female cerci are usually shorter than S9 + S10.

BODY FEATURES Compare with very similar Texas, Ozark, and Calvert's Emeralds. All have similar male cerci, bent downward at half-length and convergent to vertically flattened tips. Male cerci of Treetop bent 30°, in dorsal view divergent in basal halves, each with a midlength pointed lateral angle. Metallic blue of forehead ends above uppermost facial groove, and forehead lacks pale spots.

SIMILAR SPECIES Calvert's Emerald males have white rings between middle abdominal segments, and a white dorsal spot on S10, while females have a brown stripe from nodus to stigma in all wings.

HABITAT Forest seepages and trickles, often boggy ones.

SEASON Early June to early Sept.

COMMENTS Feeds intermittently from dawn to dusk, flying along forest edges at treetop height and perching on high twigs. Males patrol boggy seepages at a height of 6 ft.

Texas Emerald *Somatochlora margarita* Plate 24

IDENTIFICATION 2.1 in., east TX to central LA, local. Identical to Treetop Emerald but with a separate range.

BODY FEATURES Male cerci bent downward at 35°, without a lateral bump at the angle, but with a lateral ridge from base to vertically flattened tip (ridge ends at angle in related species). Female ovipositor narrow and troughlike, only slightly convex ventrally. Female often has a pair of small yellow spots on forehead.

SIMILAR SPECIES   Treetop, Ozark, and Calvert's Emeralds have not been found in Texas Emerald's range.

HABITAT   Breeding habitat unknown. Probably forest seepages.

SEASON   Late May to late July.

COMMENTS   Feeds over roads through forest at cool times of day. Usually flies near treetops, females lower than males, but also low over fields at dusk. When feeding high usually flies in a smooth, steady, rectangular pattern of straight lines, except when pursuing prey.

Ozark Emerald *Somatochlora ozarkensis* (see Plate 24)

IDENTIFICATION   2.1 in., Ozark area, uncommon. Identical to Treetop and Texas Emeralds, but with reduced white abdominal rings and a separate range. Females have short brown streaks at wing bases, and cerci shorter than S9 + S10.

BODY FEATURES   Male cerci bent downward 40° at midlength, each with a lateral bump at the angle. Female ovipositor wider, more convex ventrally, and more scooplike than in related species, such as Texas Emerald. A pair of small yellow spots is usually present on the metallic green forehead.

SIMILAR SPECIES   Fine-Lined Emerald has narrow white thoracic stripes, the male with straight cerci, the female with cerci longer than S9 + S10 and a thin, thornlike ovipositor.

HABITAT   Highland forest streams.

SEASON   Early June to early Aug.

COMMENTS   Feeds in early morning or late afternoon over fields or hilltops, occasionally hanging on tree twigs.

Calvert's Emerald *Somatochlora calverti* Plate 24

IDENTIFICATION   2.1 in., far southeastern, uncommon. Male similar to Treetop Emerald but with more extensive white markings, including usually a white dorsal spot on S10, and 4–6 intersegmental white abdominal rings (starting at S4, S5, or S6). Female our only Striped Emerald with a brown stripe in each wing from nodus to stigma. Female ovipositor is a narrow, horizontal trough extending to tip of S10, female cerci are usually a little longer than S9 + S10.

BODY FEATURES   Male cerci bent downward 50° at midlength, each with a posterior brush of hairs at the angle, and a small lateral bump just before the vertically flattened tip. Blue of forehead lacks yellow spots and extends to upper facial groove at least at midline; blue ends above groove in related species.

SIMILAR SPECIES Fine-Lined Emerald has narrow white thoracic stripes, straight male cerci, and in juvenile females, orange wingtips.

HABITAT Larval habitat unknown. Probably boggy forest seepages.

SEASON Mid-June to late Aug.

COMMENTS Named for Philip Calvert, American odonatist. Feeds morning or evening with a rapid bouncy flight about 6 ft. up over roads through forest, flying long distances in one direction, but also forages high in open spaces between tree crowns. Singles and mating pairs hang on dead twigs.

Clamp-Tipped Emerald *Somatochlora tenebrosa* Plate 24

IDENTIFICATION 2.3 in., eastern, fairly common. In males, the circular gap seen in side view between the bent-down cerci and upcurved epiproct is diagnostic. The 2 yellow lateral thoracic stripes fade with age, the anterior stripe first. Abdomen usually all brown posterior to S3 (obscure anterior lateral pale spots may be present, most often on S6–S8 of female). Face varies from yellow to brown, except upper lip varies from orange to black. In females the FW and outer 3/4 of HW become tinted brown with age. Female ovipositor is a slender triangular spout longer than S9 and slanting slightly posteriorly. Female cerci longer than S9 + S10.

BODY FEATURES Male cerci of bent type, in dorsal view shaped like human arms with the palms pressed together. Male epiproct is curled perpendicularly in its posterior 1/3. Female Williamson's Emerald has ovipositor perpendicular and more tapered, and cerci are cylindrical (cerci taper rapidly in posterior 1/3–1/2 in Clamp-Tipped).

SIMILAR SPECIES Male Williamson's and Ski-Tailed Emeralds have nearly straight cerci. The female Williamson's normally cannot be differentiated, but usually has yellow-tinted wings, pale lateral spots on S4–S8, more distinct thoracic markings, dorsal area between wing bases yellow-brown (yellow in Clamp-Tipped), and upper lip black. The female Ski-Tailed has a wide conical ovipositor. Hine's Emerald has bright yellow thoracic stripes, the male cerci enclose an oval space and have their tips hooked forward in side view (tips slant rearward in Clamp-Tipped), and the female ovipositor is thick and oblique.

HABITAT Shady forest streams from trickles to about 2 yards wide, often partly dry, and occasionally boggy or swampy.

SEASON Late May to mid-Oct. in U.S., late June to early Sept. in Canada.

COMMENTS Feeds along forest edges, mostly in early morning or in late evening until 30 min. after sunset. It usually perches in shade on tree twigs, but sometimes on weeds and bushes. Males patrol in shade, sometimes down among grass or brush, with intermittent hovering. Compared to Mocha Emerald, males hover more often, leave the creek more often, and hang up higher and farther from the stream. Females hover low to tap eggs to water among vegetation or rocks, or into wet moss or mud.

Williamson's Emerald *Somatochlora williamsoni* Plate 25

IDENTIFICATION 2.3 in., Appalachian and northeastern, fairly common. A dark, elongate Striped Emerald with indistinct pale markings at maturity. Thorax has an orange to yellow-brown anterior lateral stripe and posterior oval spot. Small dull yellow anterior lateral spots occur on S5–S8 of male and S3–S8 of female. Abdomen longer than a wing, and widest at S5 in male. Female wings often tinted yellow, particularly near bases and tips. Ovipositor a slender perpendicular spout, longer than S9, and female cerci longer than S9 + S10.

BODY FEATURES Male cerci of ski type, with small lateral spines at base and 2/5 length, but no definite ventral angle. Compare female with Clamp-Tipped Emerald.

SIMILAR SPECIES Kennedy's Emerald has 1 (obscure) lateral thoracic stripe, male abdomen is widest at S6, and female has a horizontal ovipositor. Also see Similar Species under Clamp-Tipped Emerald; female Clamp-Tipped cannot normally be separated.

HABITAT Slow streams and lakes, with or without shade or emergent plants, usually with clear water. Occasionally bog lakes.

SEASON Mid-June to mid-Sept.

COMMENTS Named for Edward B. Williamson, American odonatist. Feeds high in forest clearings, often within an area of only a few square yards, occasionally in mixed-species feeding swarms. Males patrol near shore with frequent hovering. They fly higher in sun than in shade, sometimes hovering under overhanging banks. Egg-laying females are very secretive, often hovering under bushes where there is scarcely any flying room. They lay eggs in the surface of the mud a few inches from the waterline, sometimes clearing the ovipositor with a tap to the water for each 7–8 taps to the mud.

Ski-Tailed Emerald *Somatochlora elongata* Plate 25

IDENTIFICATION 2.3 in., Appalachian and northeastern, common. Elongate, with bright yellow lateral thoracic markings, the anterior a stripe, the posterior an oval spot. Abdomen black posterior to S3, and proportionately longer in females. Female ovipositor widest of the perpendicular type among our Striped Emeralds, a conical scoop as long as S9, in side view nearly an equilateral triangle. Female cerci short, as long as S9 + S10. Face yellow to brown.

BODY FEATURES   Male cerci of ski type, with a lateral basal spine, and in side view a sharp ventral angle.

SIMILAR SPECIES   In Clamp-Tipped and Williamson's Emeralds the thoracic markings quickly fade with age. Williamson's has small lateral spots on S5–S8, while male Clamp-Tips have a circular gap between their abdominal appendages in side view. Females of both have narrow ovipositors. Plains Emerald has a brighter yellow face, and female has a narrow ovipositor and very short cerci.

HABITAT   Slow to moderately flowing streams, including shady and boggy ones. Also marshy beaver ponds and lake inlets or outlets.

SEASON   Late May to late Sept.

COMMENTS   Feeds high, sometimes in shade. Males patrol shorelines, hovering every 1–3 yards, occasionally perching on nearby twigs or grass. Egg-laying females hover near mossy banks, striking the bank and water alternately in an irregular rhythm, or lay eggs in small seepage pools.

Ocellated Emerald *Somatochlora minor* Plate 25

IDENTIFICATION   A small Striped Emerald, 1.8 in. Canada/northern U.S., uncommon. Readily recognized by its size, 2 oval yellow lateral thoracic spots, and short abdomen. Face black (with yellow spot on side). Male abdomen as long as a wing, thin at S3, widest at S5, and without pale markings posterior to S3. Female ovipositor is a large yellow-brown perpendicular spout as long as S8. Female has wings tinted brown, and cerci longer than S9 + S10.

BODY FEATURES   Male cerci of ski type, and convergent to tips.

VARIATION   Pacific slope individuals are about 0.2 in. longer.

SIMILAR SPECIES   Brush-Tipped Emerald is similar in size and shape, but differs by: anterior lateral thoracic marking is a stripe, face may be yellow, small yellow lateral spots are present on S5–S7, male cerci appear enlarged at the tips, and female ovipositor is oblique. Ski-Tailed Emerald is larger and more elongate, and has an anterior lateral thoracic stripe, while the female ovipositor is short and wide. Forcipate Emerald has pale lateral spots on middle abdominal segments, and female has a horizontal ovipositor. Mountain Emerald of the west has a more elongate abdomen, a more metallic green thorax, and female lacks an ovipositor. Uhler's Sundragon has a yellow face and no thoracic markings.

HABITAT Clear, quietly flowing, partly sunny forest streams without emergent vegetation. They are partial to narrow, rocky, shady, trickling streams. In Washington State reported from slow streams in open sedge meadows at up to 3300 ft.

SEASON Early June to late Sept.

COMMENTS Feeds while flying about 6 ft. up in shady forest glades or along forest edges. Sometimes perches in grass. Patrolling males fly smoothly and rapidly forward a few yards, then hover for up to 30 seconds, to as late as 7:30 P.M. Females hover near the bank or among rocks, commonly tapping eggs to the moss above the waterline once for each 2–3 taps to the water.

Brush-Tipped Emerald *Somatochlora walshii*
Plate 25

IDENTIFICATION A small Striped Emerald, 1.9 in. Southern Canada/northern U.S., uncommon. Thorax has a yellow anterior stripe and posterior spot. Abdomen is short, in male as long as a wing, thin at S3, widest at S5, with a dull yellow spot at tip of S10, and cerci have expanded blunt tips. In both sexes, small anterior lateral yellow spots are present on S5–S7 (sometimes also S4 or S8). Face all yellow or with an upper yellow cross-stripe. Female's ovipositor is a dark oblique triangular scoop longer than S9, and female cerci are much longer than S9 + S10. Juvenile females have orange-tinted wingtips, amber-tinted wing bases, and a tan ovipositor.

BODY FEATURES Male cerci of ski type; the dense brush of copper-brown hairs covering the posterior 1/3 is unique in North American dragonflies.

SIMILAR SPECIES Ocellated Emerald is similar in size and shape, but lateral thoracic markings are rounded spots, ovipositor is yellow-brown and perpendicular, face is blacker, and no pale spots are present posterior to S3. Clamp-Tipped and Ski-Tailed Emeralds are larger with more elongate abdomens, usually have no pale spots posterior to S3, and female Ski-Tailed has a perpendicular ovipositor. Forcipate Emerald has a more elongate abdomen and oval thoracic spots, while the female has a large pale spot on S4 and a horizontal ovipositor.

HABITAT Small, clear, very slow streams running through open bogs, fens, marshes, or swamps, especially lake or pond outlets. In the west often associated with open western red cedar swamps up to 2500 ft.

SEASON Early June to mid-Sept.

COMMENTS Feeds with some hovering from low to high along forest edges, occasionally in mixed-species feeding swarms and flying until dusk. Males patrol about a yard over streams with the abdomen slightly arched, hovering frequently and darting from place to place. Sometimes they patrol over marsh grass with little visible water.

Plains Emerald *Somatochlora ensigera* **Plate 25**

IDENTIFICATION 2.0 in., northern Great Plains, scarce. Face yellow, 2 bright yellow lateral thoracic stripes. Male abdomen lacks pale markings posterior to S3 (except pale rings between S8 to S10), but female has wide yellow lateral stripes on S2–S6. Female ovipositor is a slender perpendicular spout as long as S8. Female cerci very short, shorter than either ovipositor or S9 + S10. Costa vein yellow.

BODY FEATURES Male cerci of straight type, with a ventral spine near tip.

SIMILAR SPECIES Hine's Emerald is larger, the male with bent cerci, the female without yellow abdominal stripes and with an oblique ovipositor. Other Striped Emeralds with bright yellow thoracic markings within the range of the Plains Emerald have dark faces.

HABITAT Streams and ditches, with or without trees.

SEASON Mid-June to mid-Aug.

COMMENTS Feeds high in sunny openings over or near creeks. Males hover periodically as they patrol along grassy banks until evening. Singles and mated pairs perch on slender streamside stems. Females tap eggs into mud shores above the waterline, or hover under overhanging grass and dip eggs into shallow water.

Hine's Emerald *Somatochlora hineana* **Plate 25**

IDENTIFICATION A large Striped Emerald, 2.4 in. Primarily west shore Lake Michigan, local. Thorax has 2 bright yellow lateral stripes, the posterior shortest and broadest. Face yellow. Male cerci and epiproct in side view enclose a narrow oval space. Female ovipositor is an oblique trough, longer than S9. Females have wings tinted brown (clear in about 15% of females), and cerci longer than S9 + S10.

BODY FEATURES Male cerci are bent ventrally at a right angle near the tip, the tips hooked forward.

SIMILAR SPECIES Plains Emerald has straight male cerci, short female cerci, and a circular gap between their abdominal appendages, while females have a nearly perpendicular ovipositor. Mature Clamp-Tips have obscure yellow markings.

HABITAT Seasonally dry marshy fens, with sheets of water seeping through plants, especially spring-fed seepages over limestone bedrock, often shown by marl (calcium carbonate) deposits. Narrow-leaved cattails or sedges and stonewort algae often present.

SEASON Late May to early Sept.

COMMENTS Named for James Hine, American entomologist. Feeds over meadows or at forest edges, by 7 A.M. on hot days, but most active from 9:30 A.M. to 1:30 P.M., occasionally hanging from twigs. Sometimes they feed in swarms during the day or near sunset. Males patrol territories of 2–5 yards over rivulets, darting between hovering points where they pivot in different directions. Females with the rear half of the abdomen muddy look two-toned, and their flickering brown wings are visible at some distance. Unfortunately, currently listed as a federally endangered species.

Forcipate Emerald *Somatochlora forcipata* Plate 26

IDENTIFICATION 2.0 in., Canada and northeastern U.S., uncommon. Thorax has 2 pale yellow oval lateral spots, and abdomen is slender. Male abdomen 1/4 longer than a wing and widest at S5–S6, female abdomen 1/8 longer than a wing. Small dull yellow anterior lateral spots present on S5–S8 of male, S3–S7 of female. Female ovipositor is a horizontal yellow scoop longer than S9. Female cerci slightly longer than S9 + S10.

BODY FEATURES Male cerci forcepslike, arched in side view, with a ventral bump just beyond midlength. Male cerci of Incurvate Emerald are not arched and lack a ventral bump in direct side view. Ovipositor of female Incurvate is slightly longer than Forcipate's.

SIMILAR SPECIES Incurvate Emerald is larger with a proportionately longer abdomen, a stripelike (usually obscure) anterior lateral thoracic spot, and male has a pale lateral spot on S4. Kennedy's Emerald is more robust, lacks the posterior lateral thoracic spot, and lacks pale spots posterior to S3. Delicate Emerald has brown basal HW spots. Mountain Emerald of the west has a more metallic-green thorax, larger yellow thoracic spots, and lacks abdominal spots posterior to S3.

HABITAT Small, often boggy, spring-fed streams, and alder swamps.

SEASON Late May to late Aug.

COMMENTS Usually feeds in forest glades, from low to high, generally perching on high twigs. Males patrol streams at a height of 3 ft.

Incurvate Emerald *Somatochlora incurvata* Plate 26

IDENTIFICATION 2.4 in., northeastern, local. Nearly identical to Forcipate Emerald, but larger and more elongate. Male abdomen 1/3 longer than a wing, female abdomen 1/4 longer than a wing, widest at S5 in both sexes, with dull yellow anterior lateral spots on S3–S8. Lateral thoracic pale markings obscure, the anterior an elongate spot, the posterior an oval spot. In females the ovipositor is a horizontal yellow scoop extending to half the length of S10, and cerci are slightly longer than S9 + S10. Juvenile females have orange wingtips.

SIMILAR SPECIES Forcipate Emerald is smaller, less elongate, with oval thoracic spots that are usually distinct, and males lack a pale spot on S4. Kennedy's Emerald lacks the posterior lateral thoracic spot. The smaller Delicate Emerald has brown basal HW spots, and males have a proportionately even longer abdomen.

HABITAT Bog pools.

SEASON Early June to mid-Oct.

COMMENTS Feeds high in clearings until after sundown, sometimes in swarms of other species. Males are not territorial and fly widely over the bog about a yard up, occasionally hovering low over small pools, or perching obliquely on a bare twig.

Kennedy's Emerald *Somatochlora kennedyi* Plate 26

IDENTIFICATION 2.1 in., Canada and northeastern U.S., uncommon. This nondescript species has an obscure anterior lateral thoracic stripe, no posterior stripe, and no (or tiny) pale spots posterior to S3 on the elongate abdomen. Abdomen 1/4–1/3 longer than a wing, widest at S6–S7 in male. Females have a large dorsolateral pale basal spot on S3, a yellow horizontal scooplike ovipositor as long as S9, and cerci as long as or longer than S9 + S10.

BODY FEATURES Male cerci of pincer type, similar to those of Forcipate Emerald, but with 2 ventral bumps in direct side view, at 1/3 and 1/2 length.

SIMILAR SPECIES Forcipate and Incurvate Emeralds have a posterior lateral thoracic spot, and pale spots on the middle abdominal segments. Delicate Emerald is smaller and even more elongate, and has brown basal HW spots.

HABITAT Slow open streams in bogs or marshes, and cold or shady bog ponds. Also boreal swamps, and in the far north, usually sedge fens with mossy puddles.

SEASON Late May to early Aug., early for a Striped Emerald.

COMMENTS Named for Clarence Kennedy, American entomologist. Feeds over roads and streams. Males often patrol in shade, frequently hovering and pivoting. They perch often, usually on low bushes.

Mountain Emerald *Somatochlora semicircularis*
Plate 26

IDENTIFICATION 2.0 in., western, common. Thorax shiny metallic green with 2 large ovoid pale yellow lateral spots, and a yellow cross-bar anterior to the FW bases. Abdomen about 1/4 longer than a wing, widest at S6 in males. Small dull yellow anterior lateral spots may be present on S4 or S5 to S8. Face dark with an upper yellow cross-line (may be incomplete). Females have a large orange-brown dorsolateral basal spot on S3, and cerci longer than S9 + S10, but no ovipositor. Juvenile females have brown-tinted wings, amber at the bases.

BODY FEATURES Male cerci of pincer type, resembling those of Incurvate Emerald. Female subgenital plate 1/2 length of S9, shallowly to deeply notched.

SIMILAR SPECIES Thoracic pattern brighter than associated Striped Emeralds, except for Plains Emerald, which has a yellow face and projecting ovipositor.

HABITAT Ponds, marshes, bogs, fens, and swamps, with emergent grassy plants, including ponds that go dry part of the year, to over 10,000 ft.

SEASON Early June to mid-Oct.

COMMENTS Feeds from low to high in sunny clearings. Males patrol low over emergent vegetation such as tall grass.

Delicate Emerald *Somatochlora franklini* **Plate 26**

IDENTIFICATION A small Striped Emerald, 2.0 in. Canada/northernmost U.S., scarce. Recognized by very slender build, elongate abdomen, and small brown basal spot in HW. Thorax bears a pale anterior lateral stripe (often obscure), but no posterior stripe. Abdomen very long and slender, 1/2 longer than a wing and widest at S9 in males, 1/5–1/3 longer than a wing in females. Female wings often tinted smoky or amber, especially in basal halves. Female ovipositor is a horizontal scoop as long as S9, and female cerci are slightly longer than S9 + S10. Female eyes brown, apparently taking a long time to turn green. Upper face black.

SIMILAR SPECIES   Whitehouse's and Muskeg Emeralds have shorter abdomens, widest at S7 in males. Forcipate, Incurvate, and Kennedy's Emeralds lack wing spots, and have the upper face yellow to orange. Forcipate and Incurvate have 2 lateral thoracic spots, and pale spots on middle abdominal segments.

HABITAT   Shallow mossy spring-fed bogs and fens, sometimes trickles, covered by a carpet of short sedges or horsetails (*Equisetum*). From a distance usually no open water is visible.

SEASON   Late May to late Aug.

COMMENTS   Feeds from low to high, sometimes in mixed-species swarms, and perches on tree twigs. Males patrol in sunshine about a yard above the bog in an irregular beat. They hover more, and pivot more often, than Kennedy's Emerald. Females hover low among plants, swinging the abdomen forward past vertical to lay eggs onto moss, mostly just above the waterline.

Coppery Emerald *Somatochlora georgiana* **Plate 26**

IDENTIFICATION   1.9 in., coastal states TX to NH, rare. Differs from all of our other Striped Emeralds by its brown-orange body, and in having the eyes remain red-brown at maturity. It is slender, with 2 prominent white lateral thoracic stripes. Female ovipositor is a triangular perpendicular spout as long as S9, and female cerci are much shorter than S9 + S10. HW is notably broad.

SIMILAR SPECIES   Resembles a Shadowdragon or Baskettail, but easily differentiated by the thoracic stripes.

HABITAT   Small, sand-bottomed forest streams.

SEASON   Mid-June to late Aug.

COMMENTS   Secretive, usually seen feeding over clearings up to treetop high, in early morning or late afternoon, sometimes in mixed-species swarms. It also hunts by closely inspecting ends of tree branches. Males sporadically patrol a few circuits over a section of stream during the middle of the day, but patrol more extensively in an undulating and zigzag flight in the evening.

Shadowdragons
(genus *Neurocordulia*)

Medium-size orange to brown, elusive and furtive dragonflies that hang from twigs in forest shadows by day, but become hyperactive for short periods over the water at dawn and dusk. The ample abdomen is about as long as a wing, giving them a somewhat stubby shape. The thorax has a yellow lateral dot, and the wings usually have a series of small amber to brown dots along the front edges, more extensive in females. The eyes are never metallic green, and the forehead lacks a dark T-spot. Lower legs of males all bear rubbery ventral keels. All 7 species are eastern North American.

Baskettails are similar but can be differentiated (except from Stygian and Broad-Tailed) by the yellow lateral abdominal stripes of the Baskettails. Baskettails also have no amber wing markings, and some have a black T-spot on the forehead. Sundragons have orange rings or spots on S2 and S3 that are lacking in Shadowdragons.

Alabama Shadowdragon *Neurocordulia alabamensis*
Plate 27

IDENTIFICATION 1.7 in., southeastern, common but seldom seen. Recognized by row of small amber dots along full length of front edge of each wing, and brownish-orange body with pale waxy white to yellow sides on thorax (latter may be indistinctly striped). Eyes red-brown with a yellowish sheen.

BODY FEATURES Males have only a trace of a keel on lower foreleg, and keels only 4% of lower-leg length on middle and hindlegs. Female subgenital plate short, with a shallowly concave rear margin.

SIMILAR SPECIES Cinnamon and Smoky Shadowdragons lack dots between nodus and stigma, and have sides of thorax more brown than yellow. Coppery Emerald has clear wings, slender abdomen, and 2 white lateral thoracic stripes.

HABITAT Small, clear, slowly flowing, forest streams, usually sand-bottomed.

SEASON Early May to early Aug.

COMMENTS One of the world's most elusive dragonflies, it flies over water for only 10–20 min. at dusk, commencing about 40 min. before total darkness.

Cinnamon Shadowdragon *Neurocordulia virginiensis*
Plate 27

IDENTIFICATION 1.8 in., southeastern, common. Wings clear except for a few amber dots along front edges near base (to nodus in some females). Males have a pale orange-brown body, and most of larger wing veins pale, thus appearing pale orange at dusk, while females appear browner. Eyes orange-brown. A touch of yellow is placed on side of thorax at base of HW.

BODY FEATURES Male keels are 7%–10%, 10%–11%, and 8%–14% length of lower leg on the fore-, mid-, and hind legs. Female subgenital plate short, deeply and squarely notched.

SIMILAR SPECIES See Similar Species under Alabama Shadowdragon.

HABITAT Clean rivers, especially rock-bottomed ones with riffles.

SEASON Mid-March to mid-Aug.

COMMENTS Hunts along branches in forest understory and over water. The two-part dusk flight over water may start before sunset in shady areas, and usually lasts for the 45–90 minutes preceding darkness. At first, they fly 1–2 yards above the water, wild, erratic, and wary. After a lull of a few minutes, they fly about 6 inches up for the last 30 min. before total darkness.

Smoky Shadowdragon *Neurocordulia molesta*
Plate 27

IDENTIFICATION 1.9 in., eastern U.S., uncommon. At maturity, brown bodied with smoky gray wings and olive-green eyes. Each wing has a short row of small dark dots at base (to nodus in some females). Yellow blotches are present on side of thorax near dorsal edge.

BODY FEATURES Male can be differentiated from any other dragonfly by the presence of a blunt projection tipped with several black spines on the inside base of the middle leg (but projection absent in FL males). The larger wing dots have dark edges that look like extra cross-veins. Male keels 10%–13%, 11%–14%, and 10%–14% length of lower leg on fore-, mid-, and hind legs. Female subgenital plate short, with a wide shallow rectangular to rounded notch.

SIMILAR SPECIES Smoky wings and olive-green eyes distinguish this species from other Shadowdragons.

HABITAT Clean large rivers, sometimes large streams.

SEASON Early April to early Aug.

COMMENTS Flies over water during the last hour before darkness, most intensely in the last half hour. Males are unwary and generally patrol small areas a few yards from the bank with a rapid bouncy flight.

Umber Shadowdragon *Neurocordulia obsoleta*
Plate 27

IDENTIFICATION 1.8 in., eastern U.S., uncommon. Wings have a prominent brown spot at base and nodus, connected by a row of small brown dots. Body brown, stigmas pale orange, eyes red-brown or yellow-brown.

SIMILAR SPECIES   Stygian Shadowdragon has amber in basal HW spot, lacks the other wing spots, and has yellow lateral stripes on S4–S8. Common Baskettail has prominent yellow lateral stripes on abdomen.

HABITAT   Clean streams, rivers, and lakes.

SEASON   Early April to late Oct. in the south, late June to late July in NH.

COMMENTS   Flies over riffles of rivers and near lakeshores from about 7 to 7:45 P.M.

Stygian Shadowdragon *Neurocordulia yamaskanensis* **Plate 27**

IDENTIFICATION   2.0 in., eastern, fairly common. Wings have few if any definite dots along front edges, but HW has a large amber spot at base enclosing a network of brown-edged veins. Body brown, with yellow lateral stripes on S4–S8. Front of thorax darker than sides, costa veins may be pale. Eyes glassy brownish green.

SIMILAR SPECIES   Stygian's wing pattern diagnostic, and it is larger than other Shadowdragons except the Orange, and darker brown than most. Broad-Tailed Shadowdragon of the far northeast is smaller and stouter, lacks a brown spot at base of HW, and has yellower eyes. Common Baskettail is smaller and has no amber in wings.

HABITAT   Clean lakes and large rivers, where the water is in motion and not too acid.

SEASON   Mid-May to early Aug.

COMMENTS   Occasionally active on overcast days, but usually fly over water for about 30 min., from soon after sunset to nearly moonlight. Males may or may not fly beats along shore.

Broad-Tailed Shadowdragon *Neurocordulia sp.* **Plate 27**

IDENTIFICATION   1.6 in., ME and New Brunswick, uncommon. Differs from other Shadowdragons by its wider abdomen with more yellow on sides, yellower eyes, and more distinct mid-dorsal pale stripe on thorax and abdomen. Abdomen notably inflated toward base, especially in females, and bearing a wide, interrupted lateral yellow stripe on S2–S8 or S9. Eyes yellow-green, red-brown in juveniles. Veins near wing bases outlined by amber, in females forming a series of dots along front edge of wing to nodus.

VARIATION	Individuals from ME are darker and more slender than those from NB.
BODY FEATURES	Not scientifically named at time of this writing. Male cerci each have a ventral spine in side view.
SIMILAR SPECIES	Stygian Shadowdragon is larger and more slender, with a brown basal triangle in HW, and browner eyes. Baskettails have any wing markings dark brown, greener eyes, and some have a black T-spot on forehead.
HABITAT	Clean medium to large forested rivers.
SEASON	Late May to late Aug.
COMMENTS	Flies over rivers for less than 40 minutes after sundown, feeding on mayflies but avoiding stoneflies. Males fly 2 yards or higher above water.

Orange Shadowdragon *Neurocordulia xanthosoma*
Plate 27

IDENTIFICATION	2.0 in., southern Great Plains/Ozark area, common. Basal 1/4 of male wings orange, while female has large brown spots at base, 1/4 length, and nodus of each wing. Each wing also has a row of amber dots along the full length of the front edge, and wings become pale brown at maturity. Body of male brownish orange, female browner. Eyes vary from golden brown to tan or gray.
SIMILAR SPECIES	Wing patterns separate both sexes from other Shadowdragons.
HABITAT	Small streams to large rivers with mud bottomed pools. Also lakes with clear to muddy water and wooded banks.
SEASON	Mid-May to early Aug.
COMMENTS	During the day, hangs in shady undergrowth, grass, and weeds. They fly over land or water from dawn to shortly after sunrise, and from after sunset for about the last 40 minutes of light. Sometimes they hunt in beats of 10 yards or less during overcast days or in the shade. Males may fly over wide areas of open water, or fly beats only 2 yards long next to the bank.

Skimmers
(family Libellulidae)

Skimmers are by far the most common dragonflies at still waters, and relatively few breed in running water. They are the most showy dragonflies, exhibiting a full spectrum of colors, which, however, are seldom metallic. Many species have a conspicuous wing pattern. Lacking in other North American dragonfly families, but found in some of our Skimmers, are: abdomen flattened from the base; abdomen of a solid color, including red or white; stigmas red, orange, green, or white; white wing spots; dark wing bands; orange or red wing veins; and male hover-guarding. Rare in other families, but more common in Skimmers, are: very small size; pruinosity; brown wing spots; striped abdomen; and complete mating in midair.

Nearly all Skimmers possess a characteristic foot-shaped anal loop, complete with knee, heel, and toe. This loop helps support the base of the HW, and is particularly large in the widened wings of gliding species. Males lack auricles on S2, as well as the correlated angle at the HW base, so that the shape of the HW is similar in males and females. As in most dragonflies, the eyes of Skimmers are in contact on top of the head, but the posterior bump on each eye present in Emeralds has been lost. In about 10% of our Skimmers, the female subgenital plate is developed into a spoutlike ovipositor (Scarlet Skimmer, Filigree Skimmer, 4 Pondhawks, and 4 Dragonlets). In about 25% of our Skimmers, the females have lateral flanges on S8 used to splash eggs onto the bank (Roseate Skimmer, Narrow-Winged Skimmer, and 22 King Skimmers).

Most Skimmers are perchers that cling horizontally to tips of stems or obliquely on sides of stems. Other Skimmers are gliders with widened HW that stay aloft for hours at a time. Many Skimmers lay eggs in tandem, but our only other dragonfly that does this is the Common Green Darner.

Known life cycles are usually 1 year, but vary from 1/3 year in some tropical species to 3 years in some northern species. Of the 1000-plus species worldwide, 103 occur in North America.

Evening Skimmers
(genus *Tholymis*)

The 2 species of this genus, including *T. tillarga* of the Old World tropics, look and act like Shadowdragons of the Emerald Family. The upside-down ovipositor of the female, not developed from the subgenital plate, is elaborated from the underside of S9 but extends under S10. It is troughlike, the trough facing downward and divided lengthwise by a median ridge into 2 grooves. A cage of hairs extending from the sides holds eggs in the grooves.

Evening Skimmer *Tholymis citrina* Plate 28

IDENTIFICATION   1.9 in., southernmost TX and FL Keys, rare in U.S. Plain brown, but readily identified by large amber spot at nodus of HW. FW may also have a small amber nodal spot. Abdomen tapered, and

HW wide. Wings tint brown with age, eyes grayish olive-green. Males darker than females, becoming black on forehead and front of thorax. Female cerci divergent laterally.

SIMILAR SPECIES No Shadowdragons have been found as far south as its range.

HABITAT Vegetated lakes, ponds, and ditches, including brackish waters.

SEASON All year.

COMMENTS Hangs vertically from twigs in deep shade during the day, and flies fast, low, and erratically over low vegetation at dusk. Males patrol an irregular beat over water at dusk, hovering occasionally. It ranges to Paraguay and Chile, including the Greater Antilles and Trinidad.

King Skimmers
(genus *Libellula*)

The dominant dragonflies at most ponds, the quintessential dragonflies. They are strong-flying; the author has seen males of several species that have matured, even defended territories, flying on 3 wings. Some species are our only dragonflies with white markings on the wings (other than the stigma), or all-white abdomens. The abdomen is shorter than a wing, tapered in males, parallel-sided in females (except Four-Spotted Skimmer), with lateral splash-flaps on S8.

In this book groups of species considered subgenera are called genera by some taxonomists. The subgenera are: (1) (*Belonia*) the Flame and Neon Skimmers, medium-large robust western species with red males; (2) (*Ladona*) the Chalk-Fronted, White, and Blue Corporals, small ground-perching spring species; (3) (*Plathemis*) or (*Platetrum*) the Common and Desert Whitetails, medium-size low-perching, chunky species in which males have pruinose white abdomens; and (4) (*Libellula*) the remaining 16 of our species, medium-large with black, yellow, orange, or blue abdomens, and which usually perch near the tops of tall stems.

Most species mate while hovering for 3–30 sec., but some in the subgenus *Libellula* perch for 15–60 sec. to complete mating. Males usually hover-guard egg-laying females, nearly all of which splash eggs onto the bank. Of the 23 species in North America, 11 occur only in the east, 7 only in the west, while 5 are transcontinental. In tropical America and Eurasia live 8 other species.

Widow Skimmer *Libellula luctuosa* **Plate 28**

IDENTIFICATION 1.8 in., U.S. and southeastern Canada, except Great Basin area and FL, common. The black and white bands on each wing of mature male are diagnostic. Female also easily identified by broad black basal wing band in combination with lateral yellow abdominal stripe. Basal 1/3–1/2 of all wings black, in mature male followed by a wide white nodal band. Females have black wingtips, and in both sexes HW are broader than in our other King Skimmers. In juveniles thorax has front brown with a mid-dorsal pale stripe, and side yellow with a brown stripe, while the abdomen is brown with a yellow lateral stripe. Female thorax becomes brown; male body becomes black with a thin whitish-blue pruinosity on abdomen and front of thorax. Females have a lateral flange on S8.

VARIATION From Great Plains westward, dark wing bands are paler basally. Also westward, and particularly from southern CA to central AZ, males become more pruinose and females become thinly pruinose. The smallest individuals, especially females, occur in northernmost part of range. Rarely, females have only dark smudges and streaks at wing bases.

SIMILAR SPECIES Most other dragonflies with black wing bases have the band only in the HW.

HABITAT Permanent ponds, lakes, marshes, and occasionally streams.

SEASON Early April to mid-Oct. in U.S., late June to early Aug. in Canada.

COMMENTS Formerly incorrectly named *L. odiosa*. Forages from weed tips in fields. At low density each male defends his own territory of about 250 square yards, but does not return to it on successive days. Males at high density defend group territories with a peck order in which the dominant male is most likely to mate. It ranges south to Durango, Mexico.

Common Whitetail *Libellula lydia* Plate 28

IDENTIFICATION 1.7 in., U.S. and southernmost Canada, abundant. Note chunky, biplane-like shape, and rapid smooth flight. In each wing, males have a brown stripe at the base and a wide brown band between nodus and stigma, while females have markings at base, nodus, and tip. Abdomen in juveniles brown with a zigzag white interrupted lateral stripe. In mature males the abdomen and a small spot at HW base become pruinose white. Thorax bears 2 narrow lateral stripes, which are yellow ventrally, white dorsally. Face brown. Female has lateral flange on S8 well developed. A few males have brown wingtips or a touch of white at FW base. A few female hybrids with the Desert Whitetail have been found.

SIMILAR SPECIES Female Twelve-Spotted Skimmer resembles female, but former is larger with dorsolateral straight yellow abdominal stripes. Eight-Spotted Skimmer of the west is similar to male, but has brown nodal bands not reaching stigma, straight yellow abdominal stripes, and often a white band at the stigma. Male Desert Whitetails have nodal brown wing band paler at its middle, and basal halves of wings mostly white. Band-Winged Dragonlet and Four-Spotted Pennant of the south are much more slender, and lack basal wing spots. Prince Baskettail is larger and more slender, with abdomen as long as a wing and bearing straight lateral yellow stripes, no white markings, and, in the male, green eyes.

HABITAT Nearly any still or slowly moving shallow water with a muddy bottom, including marshes, stream pools, trickles, and, rarely, bogs. Adults are attracted to the brown color of mud, and larvae are fairly tolerant of organic pollution and low oxygen. When found (seldom) with Desert Whitetail, Common prefers more pondlike areas.

SEASON Late Jan. to mid-Nov. in the south, mid-May to late Sept. in Canada.

COMMENTS Perches low, on the ground or weed stems. They defend territories of 20–180 square yards by raising their abdomens as a threat display; submissive males lower their abdomens. It ranges south into Nuevo León, Mexico.

Desert Whitetail *Libellula subornata* Plate 28

IDENTIFICATION 1.7 in., western, scattered populations. Shape like Common Whitetail, but flashy wing patterns of both sexes unique. Wings of females and juvenile males have a brown stripe at base, a brown crossband at nodus, and another at inner end of stigma. Abdomen has wide yellow dorsolateral stripes, while thorax has 2 wide yellow lateral stripes and a pair of yellow frontal stripes. In mature males area between wing bands fills with paler brown; and wing area between base and nodal crossband, abdomen, and sometimes front of thorax, become white pruinose. Face yellow. Female lateral flanges of S8 poorly developed. In females and juvenile males 2 yellow stripes are present on underside of abdomen.

SIMILAR SPECIES Mature male Common Whitetails have only a small white spot at HW base, while juvenile males have a white zigzag lateral abdominal stripe. Female Common Whitetails have brown wingtips, and lack brown band at stigma (rare exceptions). Eight-Spotted Skimmer is larger, lacks brown crossband at stig-

ma, and may have a white band at stigma. Band-Winged Dragonlet is slender and lacks dark markings at wing bases.

HABITAT Seepage springs, pools, and ponds, often marshy and sometimes
alkali.

SEASON Mid-April to mid-Oct.

COMMENTS Usually perches on weed tips, seldom on the ground. It ranges
south to Jalisco, Mexico.

Eight-Spotted Skimmer *Libellula forensis* Plate 28

IDENTIFICATION 1.9 in., western, common. Wing pattern consists of a dark
brown stripe at base and crossband at nodus of each. Males have
white areas around basal stripe and at stigma. Thorax brown
with 2 lateral yellow stripes, often broken into spots. Abdomen
brown with dorsolateral yellow stripes. In males front of thorax
and the abdomen become thinly gray-white pruinose. Forehead
black in males, yellow in females. Female with lateral flange on
S8.

VARIATION Females east of Sierra Nevada Mountains often have white wing
markings like males. Such females are our only female dragonflies with white wing markings.

SIMILAR SPECIES Twelve-Spotted Skimmer has brown wingtips, and in flight its
wings appear narrower with a smaller white spot at the stigma.
Male Whitetails are smaller and thicker-bodied, and the brown
nodal band reaches the stigma. Hoary Skimmer has a brown
spot rather than crossband at nodus.

HABITAT Ponds, lakes, spring runs, sloughs, and slow streams, often
brackish or alkali.

SEASON Late April to late Oct.

COMMENTS Perches on tips of weeds, and may raise abdomen to *gain* heat.
Males fly large sustained patrols, often not returning to their
previous perch.

Twelve-Spotted Skimmer *Libellula pulchella* Plate 29

IDENTIFICATION 2.0 in., U.S. and southernmost Canada, common. Wings
adorned with 3 large brown spots in each, at base, nodus, and tip.
In male, white spots develop between brown spots and at HW
base. Thorax has 2 lateral yellow stripes, abdomen has a yellow
lateral stripe. With age thoracic stripes fade, beginning at upper
ends, and abdomen of male becomes thinly white pruinose.
Female has a lateral flange on S8. Eyes red-brown.

SIMILAR SPECIES Eight-Spotted Skimmer of the west lacks brown wingtips. The
female Common Whitetail has a zigzag white lateral abdominal

stripe. Some Small Pennants have a similar wing pattern, but are much smaller, and usually have pale dorsal abdominal spots. Prince Baskettail has a slender abdomen as long as a wing, no thoracic stripes or white markings, and, in males, green eyes.

HABITAT Ponds, lakes, and slow streams, often eutrophic, shallow, or semipermanent. Occasionally marshes or bogs.

SEASON Late March to early Nov. in LA, late May to mid-Sept. in WI. Most abundant early, then decreasing, 2–3 months at each locale.

COMMENTS This species has been called the Ten-Spot, for the number of white spots in wings of male, rather than number of brown spots. Forages from tips of tall weeds in fields. Males prefer a sunny open area along the shore, with a bare tall perch close to shore that is surrounded by open shallow water; they avoid duckweed. To increase body temperature they may face the sun and raise the abdomen. During territorial disputes, the male that can fly vertical loops around his opponent wins. Migratory along Atlantic Coast.

Painted Skimmer *Libellula semifasciata* Plate 29

IDENTIFICATION 1.7 in., eastern, uncommon. Wing pattern diagnostic, amber at base and tip of each, with 1 or 2 brown streaks at base, a brown spot at nodus, and a brown band at stigma. Anterior lateral thoracic stripe white, posterior stripe yellow. Abdomen orange laterally, brightest posteriorly, with a black dorsal stripe on S6–S10. Face gray, becoming orange at maturity, and male wing veins become orange. Female has a small lateral flange on S8.

SIMILAR SPECIES Other King Skimmers with a similar wing pattern have brown wingtips. Small Pennants are smaller, have large brown areas at wing bases, and their slender abdomens are mostly black laterally.

HABITAT Marshy forest ponds, occasionally bogs or slow streams, most common coastal plain.

SEASON Late Feb. to early Oct. in U.S., late May to mid-July in Ontario. Most common spring, only stragglers later.

COMMENTS Rather wary, usually perching on tips of tall weeds. Migratory along Atlantic Coast.

Four-Spotted Skimmer *Libellula quadrimaculata* Plate 29

IDENTIFICATION 1.7 in., Canada, northern U.S., western mountains, abundant. Color pattern dull but unique. Wings have amber basal streaks, a small black nodal spot, and, in HW, a triangular black spot at base. Thorax gray-brown and hairy. Abdomen gray-brown on S1–S6, black on S7–S10, with a narrow lateral yellow stripe. Female abdomen shaped like male's, tapered and without flanges on S8. Rarely, a pale brown band is present near wingtips (form *praenubila*), probably caused by high water temperatures during larval development.

SIMILAR SPECIES   Distinctive at close range, but at a distance its gray coloration and intermediate size allow it to be mistaken for many other species. Hoary Skimmer of the west has a brown basal stripe in FW. The female Bleached Skimmer of the west has a low lateral flange on S8, pale-sided thorax, and dorsolateral yellow abdominal stripes.

HABITAT   Marshy or boggy lakes and ponds, as well as fens, slow streams, and borrow pits. It prefers acid waters of bog pools smaller than 10 square yards, but tolerates some salinity.

SEASON   Mid-April to mid-Oct., one of the earliest dragonflies.

COMMENTS   Should have been named the Six-Spotted Skimmer, but in deference to its scientific name, the 4 nodal spots are emphasized. Forages from weeds in the open, often far from water, but sometimes in sustained swarms over either land or water. It is circumboreal, ranging through Europe and northwestern Africa to Japan.

Hoary Skimmer *Libellula nodisticta* **Plate 29**

IDENTIFICATION   1.9 in., western U.S., scattered and rare. Wing pattern distinctive among western dragonflies, consisting of a brown stripe at base and a brown spot at nodus. In males wings become white pruinose around basal stripes. Thorax dark brown with 4 lateral yellow spots. Abdomen dark brown with dorsolateral interrupted yellow stripes. Both thorax and abdomen become pruinose hoary gray with age. Face yellow-gray, forehead black in males, yellow in females. Female has a lateral flange on S8.

SIMILAR SPECIES   Eight-Spotted Skimmer has a brown nodal crossband rather than a spot. Four-Spotted Skimmer lacks a basal brown stripe in FW. Bleached Skimmer has a white face, no thoracic spots, and mostly amber basal wing spots.

HABITAT   Streams, marshy beaver ponds, and springs.

SEASON   Mid-May to mid-Sept.

COMMENTS   Forages from weeds in the open. Males at water perch on emergent plants until nightfall. It ranges south to Michoacán, Mexico.

Chalk-Fronted Corporal *Libellula julia* **Plate 29**

IDENTIFICATION 1.6 in., southern Canada/northern U.S., often abundant. HW has a small triangular brown spot at base. Juveniles brown with a white shoulder stripe, and a wide black dorsal abdominal stripe. Males develop chalky white pruinosity on front of thorax and S2–S4 or S5, then posterior abdomen turns black. Females become nearly plain brown, with S2–S4 or S5 pruinose gray. They have a blunt abdomen about 1/3 shorter than a wing, with a flange on S8. Face brown, forehead gray in both sexes. The female Chalk-Fronted, one of our drabbest dragonflies, is recognized by her size, short abdomen, lack of any obvious field marks, and habit of perching on the ground. A few females become white-pruinose like the males.

SIMILAR SPECIES White Corporal and Blue Corporal are smaller. The male White lacks pruinosity on front of thorax, and has most of abdomen white. The male Blue Corporal has front of thorax and most of abdomen pruinose blue. Female White Corporals have a narrow black dorsal abdominal stripe, and usually a brown stripe at HW base. Female Blue Corporals have 2 brown streaks at HW base. Frosted Whiteface and the White Form of Red-Waisted Whiteface are smaller and more slender, with white faces. Brown female Meadowhawks are smaller and more slender, either without brown HW spots or with 2 lateral white thoracic spots.

HABITAT Boggy, marshy, or swampy ponds, lakes, and slow streams in forest, with acid water.

SEASON Mid-May to late Oct.

COMMENTS Corporal refers to the military-style shoulder stripes. Forages in open woods from the ground, or sometimes from bushes. Males perch on the bank or floating objects, and fly low and fast over the water with brief periods of hovering.

White Corporal *Libellula exusta* **Plate 30**

IDENTIFICATION Small, 1.4 in. Coastal northeast, common. Note brown basal stripe in each wing, and habit of perching on the ground. Thorax brown with a narrow white shoulder stripe. Abdomen brown with a narrow black dorsal stripe, becoming pruinose white in males. Face and forehead brown. Female with lateral flange on S8.

SIMILAR SPECIES Mature male Blue Corporal has abdomen and front of thorax pruinose blue. Female and juvenile male Blue Corporals have 2 basal streaks in each wing, and the black dorsal abdominal stripe is a chain of triangles. The larger Chalk-Fronted Corporal has a basal spot rather than stripe in the HW, a wider abdominal stripe, and mature male is white on front of thorax.

HABITAT Muck-bottomed ponds, lakes and bogs. Also gently flowing water such as lake inlets, particularly with emergent plants or lily pads.

SEASON Mid-April to early Sept.

COMMENTS Perches on the ground, tree trunks, or floating objects.

Blue Corporal *Libellula deplanata* **Plate 30**

IDENTIFICATION 1.4 in., eastern U.S., common. Similar to White Corporal, but differs by: (1) Mature males have both abdomen and front of thorax pruinose pale blue, (2) Each wing has 2 narrow brown basal streaks instead of 1 stripe, and (3) Dorsal black stripe of abdomen in females and juvenile males is a chain of triangles instead of a narrow line.

VARIATION Mature males from TX/OK to TN and LA are thinly pruinose dark blue.

SIMILAR SPECIES The larger Chalk-Fronted Corporal has a basal spot rather than streaks in HW, and mature male is white on front of thorax. The male Eastern Pondhawk has a green face, and side of thorax blue or green. Little Blue Dragonlet is much smaller, and lacks shoulder stripes and wing streaks.

HABITAT Ponds, lakes, and occasionally trickles or streams. Most common at infertile waters such as sand-bottomed lakes or new borrow pits. Breeds less in streams than White Corporal.

SEASON Early Jan. to early May in FL, late March to mid-July in NJ. Early spring, peaking 1–2 weeks earlier than White Corporal in NJ.

COMMENTS Forages mostly from the ground. Males patrol from the bank or floating objects with a fast wavering flight and some hovering. The female does not splash water as she lays eggs.

Spangled Skimmer *Libellula cyanea* **Plate 30**

IDENTIFICATION 1.7 in., eastern U.S., common. Only dragonfly east of the Mississippi River with a black and white stigma (basal half white). Wings have short dark basal streaks, an amber (sometimes brown in female) stripe along the front of each, and females have wingtips brown to the stigmas. Mature male dark pruinose gray-blue, with a black face. Female has a tan face, a yellow abdomen with a black dorsal stripe, and a lateral flange on S8. Side of thorax pale yellow with 1 brown stripe, with yellow area anterior to stripe diamond-shaped. Juvenile male like female but lacks brown wingtips. Eyes dark green in male, red-brown in female.

SIMILAR SPECIES   Yellow-Sided Skimmer has a yellow to brown stigma, with or without a black outer tip, and mature male is whitish blue. Juvenile Yellow-Sided has side of thorax bright yellow. Comanche Skimmer has a white face and no black basal wing streaks. Four-Spotted Pennant has all-white stigmas, and a slender abdomen.

HABITAT   Ponds, long-lasting puddles, lakes, and slow streams with abundant plants. Often associated with water lilies, cattails, and pond inlets or outlets.

SEASON   Late April to early Nov.

COMMENTS   Spangled refers to the flashy white stigmas. Both foragers in fields and territorial males perch on weed tips.

Comanche Skimmer *Libellula comanche* Plate 30

IDENTIFICATION   2.1 in., western U.S., fairly common. Stigma black and white like the Spangled Skimmer, but dark basal wing streaks are absent and face is white. Mature male gray-blue, not so dark as the Spangled Skimmer, and with a touch of white at HW base. Eyes gray-green in both sexes. Female wings have only narrow brown tips, and their stigmas are sometimes black and brown.

VARIATION   Southwestern desert individuals are smaller (1.9 in.), with reduced black in stigma. Such males are more pruinose on side of thorax, and females are lightly pruinose.

SIMILAR SPECIES   Only western dragonfly with basal half of stigmas white, but range abuts that of Spangled Skimmer in TX/OK. Mature male Spangled and Yellow-Sided Skimmers have black faces, and females have wingtips brown to the stigmas. Bleached Skimmer has black stigmas and white costal veins (costa black in Comanche). See also Similar Species under Spangled Skimmer.

HABITAT   Springs, and slow parts of streams and rivers.

SEASON   Late May to early Oct.

COMMENTS   Perches on tips of tall weeds. Males leisurely patrol a section of stream, resembling a Darner when seen at a distance. It ranges into Chihuahua and Sonora, Mexico.

Yellow-Sided Skimmer *Libellula flavida* Plate 31

IDENTIFICATION   1.9 in., eastern U.S., local. Females and juvenile males have sides of thorax butter yellow with 1 narrow brown stripe, face tan, and abdomen yellow with a black dorsal stripe. In mature males thorax and abdomen become pruinose whitish blue, last on side of thorax, and face turns black. Each wing has an amber stripe along front edge that often darkens into a streak at base, but stripe fades with age. Stigma yellow, usually with a black outer tip, turning brown with age. Thighs tan, becoming dark brown with age. Female has wingtips black to the stigma, and a lateral flange on S8.

SIMILAR SPECIES   Spangled Skimmer has black and white stigmas, and female has side of thorax pale yellow, with area anterior to its brown stripe reduced to a diamond shape. Comanche Skimmer of OK/TX has black and white stigmas, a white face, and females have narrow brown wingtips. Female Golden-Winged and Needham's Skimmers have sides of thorax tan, wingtips narrowly brown, and longer, more slender abdomens.

HABITAT   Mucky, sometimes boggy, spring seepages, at least partially sunny, most common on coastal plain.

SEASON   Mid-March to early Oct.

COMMENTS   Forages from stems in clearings. Males perch on a weed stem at the edge of a pool and periodically patrol over it.

Golden-Winged Skimmer *Libellula auripennis*
Plate 31

IDENTIFICATION   2.0 in., eastern U.S., common southeastward. Females and juvenile males have face and front of thorax brown, 2 diffuse pale lateral thoracic stripes, yellow stigmas, and a yellow abdomen with a black dorsal stripe. In mature males the face, front of thorax, wing veins, and abdomen become orange, while the stigma becomes red. Wing veins become orange from anterior to posterior in each wing. Note that lower hindleg is black, pale side of thorax stops at shoulder, and costa vein is pale. Female has a lateral flange on S8.

SIMILAR SPECIES   Yellow Form female Purple Skimmers of FL are identical. Male Needham's Skimmers have a redder face and body, brown lower hindlegs, and dark posterior wing veins. Female and juvenile male Needham's have side of thorax unstriped, but with a pale extension anterior to shoulder and above base of middle leg, plus their costal veins are dark from base to nodus. The female Yellow-Sided Skimmer has yellower side of thorax, shorter abdomen, and wingtips dark to stigmas.

HABITAT   Mostly grassy ponds and lakes, also ditches and slow streams.

SEASON   Late Feb. to late Nov. in FL, mid-May to late Aug. in NJ.

COMMENTS   Forages from weed stems in open fields, males usually from the tips, females from halfway down the stems. Males at water are active and wary, perching on weed tips at the water's edge, or flying and hovering about a yard above open water. It ranges south to Chiapas, Mexico.

Needham's Skimmer *Libellula needhami* Plate 31

IDENTIFICATION 2.1 in., Gulf and U.S. Atlantic Coast, common. Similar to Golden-Winged Skimmer but differs by: (1) Mature male redder, with front of thorax and abdomen vibrant red-orange, and face bright red; (2) Side of thorax not striped, and pale color extends forward of shoulder above base of middle leg; (3) Lower hindleg brown instead of black; (4) Females and juvenile males have costa vein black from base to nodus rather than all pale; and (5) Posterior veins of wings do not become orange. In males, side of thorax becomes dark brown, and basal half of costa vein becomes orange.

SIMILAR SPECIES Males are best separated from male Golden-Wings by redder face and body, along with brown lower hindlegs and less orange wings. Female and juvenile male Needham's best separated from Golden-Wings by lateral thoracic pattern, augmented by the two-toned costa.

HABITAT A more coastal species than the Golden-Winged Skimmer, and probably outcompeted by it in most habitats. Needham's usually breeds in brackish, mineralized, or fertilized waters, including marshes, lakes, ponds, tidal rivers, and canals.

SEASON Mid-Feb. to late Dec. in the south, late May to late Sept. in NJ.

COMMENTS Named for James Needham, American entomologist. Forages from weed stems or during sustained flights. Territorial males perch on weed tips along open shores. It ranges to Quintana Roo, Mexico, and in the FL Keys, Cuba, and the Bahamas.

Purple Skimmer *Libellula jesseana* Plate 31

IDENTIFICATION 2.1 in., FL, local. Similar to Golden-Winged Skimmer, but juvenile males have a dark brown face and body, while in mature males face and eyes become black and body becomes pruinose pale to dark blue. Wings clear in basal 1/4, but deep orange beyond, with orange stigmas. **Purple Form** females develop a lightly pruinose blue body, but most are **Yellow Form**, identical to female Golden-Winged Skimmers.

SIMILAR SPECIES The beautiful mature male is unmistakable.

HABITAT Clear-water, sand-bottomed lakes and ponds edged with maiden-cane grass and Saint-John's-wort bushes. It requires the most infertile lakes with the sparsest grass. Probably very susceptible to fertilization, eutrophication, and pollution of its native lakes, whereupon it would be replaced by the common Golden-Winged Skimmer.

SEASON Late April to mid-Sept.

COMMENTS Forages in scrub 100 yards from water. Males defend territories in sparse emergent grass, whereas the Golden-Winged Skimmer uses dense grass at the same lakes. Male Purples prefer to locate territories near cover, but are apparently not territorial at high population densities. They tend to perch on sides of stems, whereas male Golden-Winged usually perch on the tips and tend to fly lower and slower.

Flame Skimmer *Libellula saturata* Plate 32

IDENTIFICATION 2.1 in., western U.S., abundant southward. Very robust, with a large muscular brown thorax. In males basal halves of wings are orange, each with a basal brown streak (rarely absent). Face and abdomen tan in juvenile males, becoming orange-red with maturity. In females face and body remain tan, thorax has a white midfrontal stripe, and wings have an amber stripe along front edge, the stripe browner basally. Female abdomen very stout with narrow lateral flanges on S8.

SIMILAR SPECIES The male Neon Skimmer has face, front of thorax, and abdomen brilliant red, while wing bases are amber only in basal 1/4 and lack brown streaks. The female Neon has clear wings. Other similar species are less robust. Mayan Setwing is slender. The female Roseate Skimmer has white lateral stripes on thorax, and a rustier brown abdomen. Golden-Winged and Needham's Skimmers have a black dorsal abdominal stripe.

HABITAT Ponds, lakes, ditches, springs, and stream pools. Primarily hot springs in the north and at high altitudes.

SEASON Late April to late Oct. in the south, early June to mid-Sept. in MT.

COMMENTS Perches on tall weeds or twigs. At a stream they fly long stretches in early morning, then defend a perch at a pool in late morning. Skirmishing males fly an ascending "Red Baron" parallel flight for long distances and as long as 5 min. before the winner claims the perch. It ranges south to Baja California and Oaxaca, Mexico.

Neon Skimmer *Libellula croceipennis* Plate 32

IDENTIFICATION 2.2 in., southwestern, local. Robust, similar to Flame Skimmer but differs by: (1) Mature male becomes stunning brilliant red instead of orange-red on face and abdomen, as well as on front of thorax; (2) Male wings amber in basal 1/4 with a costal stripe to nodus, instead of amber in basal 1/2; (3) Male lacks brown streaks at wing bases; and (4) Female has clear wings. Lateral flange of S8 almost twice as wide in female Neon as in Flame.

BODY FEATURES Female has 0–2 (rarely 5) ankle cells in anal loop of HW, 2 cross-veins basal to HW triangle, and styles on underside of S9 black-tipped. Female Flame Skimmer has 5 or more ankle cells, 1 basal cross-vein, and all-brown styles.

SIMILAR SPECIES See Similar Species under Flame Skimmer.

HABITAT Small shaded spring-fed streams.

SEASON Early April to late Nov.

COMMENTS Hunts from weed tips or high "flagpole" perches at woodland edges. Males seem to glow as they perch in the shade several feet over a clear stream, and defend territories up to 50 yards long to about 3 P.M. Males exhibit a rudimentary courtship. When a female appears a male flies to an egg-laying site in his territory, waits until the female begins laying eggs, then approaches with his abdomen raised, repeatedly darting at her to cause her to fly up. If she does, they mate for about 20–30 seconds, before the female finishes egg laying. It ranges south to Colombia, including Baja California.

Bleached Skimmer *Libellula composita* Plate 32

IDENTIFICATION 1.8 in., western U.S., scattered and rare. Each wing has a white costal vein, a brown-amber spot at base, and often another brown-amber spot at nodus. In females thorax is white with a pair of wide brown frontal stripes, a narrow black shoulder stripe, and a narrow black posterior lateral stripe. The abdomen is black with an interrupted dorsolateral yellow stripe. In males thoracic stripes fade and abdomen turns black as body becomes pale pruinose blue, especially on front of thorax and S1–S3. Female has lateral flange on S8.

SIMILAR SPECIES The female Marl Pennant is smaller, has neither nodal spots nor pruinosity, and abdomen is mostly yellow. Four-Spotted Skimmer has S1–S6 brown dorsally, and the yellow abdominal stripes are lateral. Blue Dasher is smaller and has a black anterior lateral thoracic stripe.

HABITAT Spring-fed ponds and streams, sometimes alkaline ones, with emergent vegetation.

SEASON Mid-June to late Aug.

COMMENTS Males at water patrol much of the time, occasionally resting on reed tips. Pairs lay eggs in tandem, flying wildly between dips to the water.

Great Blue Skimmer *Libellula vibrans* Plate 32

IDENTIFICATION Largest North American Skimmer, 2.2 in. Eastern, common. Juveniles have face white, eyes red-brown, front of thorax brown with a white median stripe, side of thorax pale gray without brown markings, and abdomen yellow with a black dorsal stripe. Each wing is marked with black, including a streak at base, spot at nodus, black stigma, and black tip, which in females extends to the stigma. Some individuals have a black bar along front of wing near stigma. In mature females eyes become blue and abdomen becomes brown. In mature males eyes are blue, and front of thorax and then abdomen become pale pruinose blue. Female has lateral flange on S8.

SIMILAR SPECIES The male Bar-Winged Skimmer has a black face and a touch of white at HW base. Female and juvenile male Bar-Winged and Slaty Skimmers have brown or black faces, and a brown triangle on side of thorax at base of FW. Eyes are never blue in Bar-Winged and Slaty Skimmers, and male and some female Slaty Skimmers lack black wing markings. Comanche Skimmer has black and white stigmas, and no black wing markings. Spangled and Yellow-Sided Skimmers have a black and white or a yellow stigma, no nodal spots, and males have black faces.

HABITAT Swamp pools and slow forest streams, including temporary (?) ponds.

SEASON Early March to early Dec. in the south, early June to early Sept. in NJ.

COMMENTS This regal species is often tame, allowing a close approach as it perches on a shaded twig. A few migrate along the Atlantic Coast.

Slaty Skimmer *Libellula incesta* Plate 33

IDENTIFICATION 2.0 in., eastern, abundant. Juveniles similar to those of Great Blue Skimmer, but have face brown instead of white, and a brown triangular marking on side of thorax at base of FW. Pale pattern on side of thorax looks to some people like the head of a cartoon wolf, to others like a perched parrot. Males and some females lack black basal wing streaks, but sometimes have a dark bar between nodus and stigma. Other females have wing patterns identical to those of Great Blue Skimmer or Bar-Winged

Skimmer, and a few have a full-length brown stripe from base to stigma. Mature male Slaty Skimmers develop a black face and body, the side of the thorax last. In mature female Slatys the body becomes brown or lightly pruinose. Eyes red-brown, becoming dark brown in males.

BODY FEATURES   Male penis has a hooked projection visible in side view ahead of the hamules; this projection is straight in Great Blue Skimmer, lacking in Bar-Winged Skimmer.

SIMILAR SPECIES   The male Bar-Winged Skimmer has a touch of white at HW base, and front of thorax and base of abdomen are pale pruinose. The female Bar-Winged has a black face (usually pale around the edges), 1/5 length black basal wing streaks, black nodal spots, and a black bar between nodus and stigma; however, some female Slatys are identical. The female Great Blue Skimmer has a white face, blue eyes, and no brown triangle at base of FW. Great Blue always has black basal wing streaks and nodal spots. Other similar female King Skimmers have black and white, or yellow, stigmas, and most lack a brown marking on thorax at base of FW. Other dragonflies somewhat similar to female Slaty Skimmer lack lateral flange of S8. Regarding the black mature male Slaty, the male Black Setwing of the southwest is much smaller, and has a slender, slightly clubbed abdomen. The male Narrow-Winged Skimmer of south TX has a pale face and narrow HW bases. Other eastern black dragonflies are much smaller or have a black basal spot in HW.

HABITAT   Nearly any quiet water with a muck bottom, usually in or near forest, and sometimes rivers. In the north, even bog lakes.

SEASON   Late Feb. to early Nov. in FL, early June to early Sept. in Canada.

COMMENTS   Feeds from twigs along forest edges. The pugnacious males may be present at water from 7 A.M. to 6:30 P.M., but are most active in the morning, perching on shoreline stems. The female, even before her abdomen turns brown, can lay more than 2000 eggs in one bout.

Bar-Winged Skimmer *Libellula axilena* Plate 33

IDENTIFICATION   2.2 in., eastern U.S., fairly common southward. Females and juvenile males very similar to those of Slaty Skimmer, but have a darker face with contrasting pale lateral borders. Each wing marked with black, including a 1/5-length streak at base, small nodal spot, a bar or spot between nodus and stigma, and the tips. Maturing males quickly acquire a touch of white pruinosity at base of HW as body becomes black. In males gray-blue pruinosity is deposited first on front of thorax and between wings, then on S1–S3. Mature females become brown, the oldest lightly pruinose.

SIMILAR SPECIES   None of our dragonflies similar to the mature male has white at base of HW. The male Slaty Skimmer has an all-black body and lacks basal black wing streaks. The male Great Blue Skimmer has a white face, blue eyes, and an all-blue abdomen. The male Chalk-Fronted Skimmer of the north is much smaller, and lacks dark wing markings beyond bases. The female Slaty Skimmer may lack black streaks at wing bases, or, if streaks are present, they are often short, or shorter in HW than in FW. The female Slaty also has a browner face, usually lacks nodal black spots (especially in HW), and often has brown wingtips extending to inner end of stigma. However, a residue of female Slaty Skimmers is identical to the female Bar-Winged. The female Great Blue Skimmer has a white face, blue eyes, and no brown lateral thoracic triangle at base of FW. See also Similar Species under Slaty Skimmer.

HABITAT   Swampy forest pools and ditches, or sedgy woodland bogs, often more temporary than for the Great Blue Skimmer.

SEASON   Early March to mid-Oct. in the south, early June to late Sept. in New Jersey.

COMMENTS   Perches warily and high, from weed tips to treetops, and sometimes flies in sustained feeding flights. Males perch over swampy pools.

Tropical King Skimmers
(genus *Orthemis*)

These differ from King Skimmers in details of wing vein arrangement, but perform the same role in tropical America as the Kings do in North America. Only 1 species occurs in North America, while at least 17 others are tropical American.

Roseate Skimmer *Orthemis ferruginea* **Plate 33**

IDENTIFICATION   Medium-large, 2.0 in. Southern, common. Unusual in having 2 male color forms. The unmistakable **Pink Form** has a pale blue pruinose thorax and a pink to red-violet pruinose abdomen. The **Red Form**, primarily found in the FL Keys, is entirely bright red and not pruinose. Forehead metallic violet in the Pink Form, metallic red in the Red Form. Females and juvenile males have a brown thorax with lateral white stripes in an irregular *HIII* pattern, and a rusty brown abdomen. A median white stripe extends from neck over thorax to base of abdomen. Female has lateral flange on S8.

VARIATION   A few individuals of the species or form Orange-Bellied Skimmer (*O. discolor*) have been found in east-central TX. It seems to differ from Roseate by: face, forehead, and eyes red; side of thorax with *III* pattern of obscure white stripes or essentially unmarked; no black mark above base of middle leg or behind hindleg, and underside of thorax dull orange; wing veins darker; female flange of S8 wider and blacker; flight season shorter. Subgenital plate of female is usually black and shallowly V-notched, instead of brown and widely U-notched.

SIMILAR SPECIES   The lovely Pink Form male is our only dragonfly with a pink abdomen and clear wings. Red Form male is much larger than Scarlet Skimmer, which has an amber spot at HW base. Red-Tailed Pennant is smaller and has a brown thorax without pale lateral markings. Flame and Neon Skimmers of the southwest also lack pale lateral thoracic markings, and are thick-bodied. Straw-Colored Sylph of the southwest is smaller, with a slender abdomen that lacks a flange on S8.

HABITAT   Lakes, ponds, ditches, slow streams, and trickles, including brackish, muddy, and temporary waters.

SEASON   All year. Thought to have two emergence peaks in LA: spring and late summer.

COMMENTS   From 1875 to 1930 this species was known in North America only from the FL Keys. It forages from weed stems in fields. Males arrive at water within an hour of sunrise to patrol territories about 10 yards long, hovering often. It ranges south at least to Costa Rica, including Baja California. Closely related subspecies or species range throughout the West Indies, the Bahamas, and tropical America. It was accidentally introduced to Hawaii by 1976.

Filigree Skimmer
(genus *Pseudoleon*)

This genus includes only 1 ornate species.

Filigree Skimmer *Pseudoleon superbus* Plate 33

IDENTIFICATION Medium, 1.6 in., southwestern, uncommon. The intricate brown and black filigree pattern on both wings and body gives this dragonfly a unique persona. Dark brown markings of male FW include a wide band extending from nodus to outer end of stigma, and a spot near base. HW has an additional spot near base, and all these markings may be connected along rear edge of HW. The spaces between these spots in basal half of HW become filled with paler brown during maturation. Female wings have narrower bands and smaller spots, and HW base remains clear between spots. Inner half of stigma brown, outer half white. In females and juvenile males, thorax is brown mottled with tan, abdomen is mostly dark brown, with S2–S7 each marked by a pale V-shaped chevron, and eyes have alternating dark and pale brown vertical stripes. In males the eyes, stigma, and body rapidly darken to nearly black. Female has abdomen shorter than male, and a spoutlike ovipositor perpendicular to S9.

SIMILAR SPECIES Mature males look all black except for mostly clear basal halves of FW and wingtips, especially when perched on glaring surfaces of pale rocks. Black-Winged Dragonlet is more slender, and has outer edges of wing bands halfway between nodus and stigma. Band-Winged Dragonlet is slender-bodied, and has basal halves of both wings unmarked. Female and juvenile male Whitetails have white or yellow stripes on thorax and abdomen.

HABITAT Sunny, rocky, clear-water streams.

SEASON All year.

COMMENTS Usually perches on water-polished rocks, when the ventral posterior points on S3–S8 prevent backsliding. On hot days they obelisk, raising both abdomen and wings, and resemble an animated flower sprouting from a rock. Males may patrol long stretches of stream. It ranges south to Costa Rica, including Baja California.

Rock Skimmers
(genus *Paltothemis*)

This genus includes only 3 species, the red one described below, the Blue Rock Skimmer (*P. cyanosoma*) that lives in Mexico, and a gray Central American species. They present an enigmatic amalgam of structure and behavior, because although the HW is exceptionally broad at the base, they do not exhibit the behavior of the glider dragonflies.

Red Rock Skimmer *Paltothemis lineatipes* **Plate 34**

IDENTIFICATION
Medium-large, 2.0 in. Southwestern, common. Females and juvenile males have face pale gray, and thorax and abdomen gray mottled with black. Male face and abdomen change to dull red. In males basal 1/4 of each wing is orange, but in females wings are clear. Stigmas dark brown.

SIMILAR SPECIES
No similar species usually perches on rocks. Flame, Neon, and Roseate Skimmers, and Mayan Setwing, all lack black mottling on the abdomen. Spot-Winged Glider resembles female Red Rock in flight, but is more brown than gray, and has a brown basal HW spot. Variegated Meadowhawk is much smaller and has stigma yellow at both ends.

HABITAT
Small rocky hill or mountain streams in oak woodland, chaparral, pine forest, or desert, up to 6000 ft.

SEASON
Late April to early Oct.

COMMENTS
Usually perches on rocks, where females are very cryptic. Feeding flights take place over both water and land, becoming more localized, faster, and erratic at dusk. Males maintain territories from 1 to 20 yards long along gentle rapids in the morning, often beginning at dawn. It ranges south to Panama, including Baja California.

Scarlet Skimmers
(genus *Crocothemis*)

This Old World genus seems the same as the New World Dragonlets, and the relationship between them needs study. The 1 species of our fauna was accidentally introduced from Asia. About 6 other species occur in the Old World tropics, some of which are black, gray, or pruinose blue.

Scarlet Skimmer *Crocothemis servilia* Plate 34

IDENTIFICATION
Medium, 1.6 in. FL, common south half. Females and juvenile males pale yellow with a white shoulder stripe and white between wings, and a black dorsal abdominal stripe. Male becomes entirely bright red. Each HW has a small basal amber spot. Female has an oblique spoutlike ovipositor 3/4 as long as S9.

SIMILAR SPECIES
Red Form of Roseate Skimmer is much larger and lacks amber basal HW spot. Red-Tailed Pennant has S1–S3 swollen, thorax brown without shoulder stripes, and female lacks an ovipositor. Golden-Winged and Needham's Skimmers are much larger, males are orange or orange-red, and females lack shoulder stripes and ovipositors. Wandering and Garnet Gliders lack shoulder stripes and forage in sustained flight.

HABITAT
Lakes, ditches, canals, slow streams, and ponds, including temporary ones.

SEASON
All year.

COMMENTS
Discovered near Miami in 1975, it had spread to Orlando by 1986. It forages from low perches in fields. The dazzling males usually perch with wings cocked downward on low plants on the bank of their territories. They threaten each other by curling their abdomens upward, and may return to the same territory on different days. It now occurs in the FL Keys, Cuba, and Hawaii, and in the Old World ranges from the Middle East to Japan and Australia.

Meadowhawks
(genus *Sympetrum*)

Small to medium-size perky dragonflies, most species of which forage on small prey in grassy meadows. In all of our species except the Black Meadowhawk, mature males (and some females in 8 of 12 species) bear red markings. Most of our species are rather tame and have a late summer season. Mating in most lasts 5–30 min. while the pair perches on a weed, or sometimes on the ground. Some have large round eggs that are dropped in flight like tiny bombs onto the dry bottoms of temporary ponds. Such eggs have a dry surface that allows them to roll down through grass to the soil, where they hatch with the rains of the next spring.

To identify Meadowhawks, it is important to critically note the coloration of the face, legs, and wing veins, as well as the body. Male cerci of 5 of our species have a prominent ventral tooth, 8 lack the tooth. Female subgenital plates vary from short to long, with (8 species) or without (5 species) a median notch (shapes of cerci and subgenital plate not correlated). Three species (Cardinal, Variegated, Red-Veined) were formerly classified in the genus *Tarnetrum*, now considered a subgenus.

The 13 North American species include 7 transcontinental, 4 western, and 2 eastern. At least 44 other species live throughout the world except Australia. One Asiatic species (*S. gracile*) is blue, and females of some Old World species have spikelike ovipositors.

Black Meadowhawk *Sympetrum danae* Plate 34

IDENTIFICATION Small, 1.2 in. Canada, northern U.S., western mountains; common west, uncommon east. Our only Meadowhawk without red markings, the male our only one with a dark face. Females and juvenile males have a characteristic black chain- or ladder-like marking on yellow side of thorax that encloses 2 or 3 small yellow spots. Abdomen in juveniles yellow with a black lateral stripe. Rapidly (2–4 days) in males, more slowly and less completely in females, each segment blackens to produce rows of dorsolateral spots, which in males linger longest on S8. Costal vein yellow, darkening with age. Juvenile females have an amber stripe at nodus, but this fades, while a touch of amber develops at wing bases. Female has a yellow face and a short, spoutlike ovipositor. Legs and stigmas of both sexes black.

SIMILAR SPECIES The male Seaside Dragonlet is more slender and has a denser mesh of wing veins; females have black facial markings, an all-black S9, and a longer ovipositor. Double-Ringed Pennant has a small black basal HW spot. Ebony Boghaunter has pale rings on S2–S4, but no other pale markings. Elfin Skimmer is much smaller, Slaty Skimmer much larger.

HABITAT Bogs, fens, and marshes, sometimes associated with ponds or lakes, including semipermanent ones. Occasionally saline or moving water.

SEASON Mid-June to mid-Nov.

COMMENTS Forages from weeds in fields, sometimes hiding on the opposite side of a stem from an observer. Males tend to perch low, often on the ground, while females perch higher and in more over-grown areas. Males search for females in the fields in the morning where both sexes roosted, often 200 yards from water, and after mating the pair flies in tandem to water. Males at water are not territorial, and either wait for a female or fly a search pattern. Females lay eggs in tandem for about 2 minutes, mostly by tapping water or wet moss at the waterline, but they also drop eggs from the air into water, tap eggs to mud, or lay eggs while perched on mud. In Europe it occasionally hibernates as an adult, and has been seen migrating over the sea. It is circumboreal, ranging through Europe to Japan.

Blue-Faced Meadowhawk *Sympetrum ambiguum*
Plate 34

IDENTIFICATION Small, 1.4 in. Eastern, common. Our only Skimmer with a blue to green (nonmetallic) forehead. Also note white face, gray thorax, tan legs, slender form, and diffuse black bands on posterior ends of S4–S9. Abdomen brown, becoming mostly red in males and some females. Eyes red-brown, becoming aqua-gray. Blue of forehead may become green at cool temperatures (and disappears in dry specimens).

SIMILAR SPECIES If blue forehead not visible, combination of gray thorax, tan legs, and black-ringed abdomen is also distinctive. White-Faced Meadowhawk has black legs and a black lateral abdominal stripe.

HABITAT Usually temporary semi-shaded pools, such as overflow pools in river floodplains. Also marshes, permanent ponds, swamps, and woodland bogs.

SEASON Early May to early Dec.

COMMENTS   Often inconspicuous, due to perching on twig tips in forest shade above human eye level. Males typically perch on low vegetation in dry pond bottoms. Females drop eggs from a down-curved abdomen either while flying slowly above grass near water, or while perched over a dry pond bottom.

Cardinal Meadowhawk *Sympetrum illotum* **Plate 34**

IDENTIFICATION   Small, 1.4 in. Western, common. Readily recognized by 2 white lateral thoracic spots and short brown streaks at wing bases. White lateral thoracic spots are ventral ends of gray stripes in newly emerged individuals. Basal 1/4 of each wing amber, with a costal extension to the nodus. Females and juvenile males brown, becoming brilliant red (darkening when cool) on forehead, costa vein, and abdomen in males. Abdomen lacks black markings, in males parallel-sided, not narrowed at middle as in our other Meadowhawks. Female has spoutlike ovipositor.

SIMILAR SPECIES   Striped Meadowhawk has white lateral thoracic stripes, and virtually no amber in wings. Variegated Meadowhawk has black and white abdominal markings. Straw-Colored Sylph of the southwest is much more slender and lacks brown basal wing streaks.

HABITAT   Ponds, lakes, sloughs, marshes, and stream pools.

SEASON   Late March to early Nov. in U.S., late May to mid-Aug. in Canada. Most common in spring, but may have a second emergence in fall.

COMMENTS   Perches on tips of low plants, often with the wings cocked downward, and obelisks high on hot days. Pairs lay eggs in tandem near shore. It ranges to Costa Rica, including Baja California, and in the Greater Antilles. A similar species or subspecies (*S. gilvum*) occurs south to Argentina and Chile.

Variegated Meadowhawk *Sympetrum corruptum* **Plate 35**

IDENTIFICATION   Medium, 1.5 in. U.S. and southern Canada; abundant west, migratory east. Mostly gray with a characteristic but complex color pattern of pastel hues. Thorax bears 2 lateral white stripes that are yellow at their lower ends, but in mature males the stripes fade and only yellow spots remain. Abdomen has a black dorsal stripe on S8–S9 and a chain of white lateral spots on S2–S8 bordered dorsally by a black line. In females and juvenile males the face is tan, and S3–S7 are each outlined in orange dorsally and posteriorly. In mature males the face and orange abdominal markings become red. S2 is black dorsally in females, orange to red in males. In both sexes several anterior wing veins are orange, stigma is yellow at both ends, and legs are black with yellow lateral stripes.

SIMILAR SPECIES   Readily recognized at close range, but its mostly gray coloration and medium size allow it to be confused with many other dragonflies at a distance. One of its best field marks is the orange wing veins, but several western Meadowhawks have a resemblance. Red-Veined Meadowhawk has all-white thoracic stripes, all-black legs, and amber- or brown-tinted wings. Striped Meadowhawk lacks black dorsal stripes on S8–S9 as well as white lateral abdominal spots. Cardinal Meadowhawk has no black markings on abdomen.

HABITAT   Still water and slow streams, except bogs, but including temporary pools, trickles, and fertile or saline waters at up to 8500 ft. It seems most at home at sand-bottomed ponds in arid, barren country.

SEASON   All year in the south, mid-May to early Nov. in WA. In the north emergence peaks early and late; in the east migration peaks in spring and fall.

COMMENTS   Perches on the ground or twigs, and is active from shortly after dawn to dusk. It is the dragonfly most likely to be seen in the desert miles from water. Unlike most Meadowhawks, males compete with other dragonflies over open water. They are wary, and intermittently fly, hover, and perch on sparse emergent vegetation. Pairs lay eggs in tandem over wide areas in open shallow water or on algae. It has an unusual but weak migratory pattern, dispersing (sometimes in swarms) from the west toward the east coast and FL Keys in the fall, and northward in the spring. It ranges to Baja California and Morelos, Mexico, and in Siberia.

Striped Meadowhawk *Sympetrum pallipes*
Plate 35

IDENTIFICATION   Small, 1.4 in. Western, common. Thorax brown with 2 lateral white stripes. Abdomen of juveniles yellow-brown, and legs tan. During maturation abdomen becomes pale red, while legs turn black. Face brown, anterior wing veins pale. Generally little black on abdomen, and little amber at wing bases, but some northern individuals have a black lateral stripe on S4–S9, and a few juvenile females have as much as basal 1/5 of wings amber. Abdomen lacks a black dorsal stripe.

BODY FEATURES Each male cercus has a large ventral tooth. Each hamule has a small terminal notch, as in White-Faced Meadowhawk. Female subgenital plate 1/3 as long as S9, V-notched and grooved in midline, each half very convex in lateral view, like plate of Ruby Meadowhawk.

SIMILAR SPECIES In the Red-Veined Meadowhawk, juveniles have an amber costal wing stripe, females have a white lateral abdominal stripe, and mature males have a red face. Variegated Meadowhawk has yellow lower ends on lateral thoracic stripes, and white lateral abdominal spots. Cardinal Meadowhawk is more robust, and has dark streaks at wing bases.

HABITAT Permanent or semipermanent ponds, including bogs and fens, and vegetated streams. Occasionally lakes.

SEASON Late May to early Nov.

COMMENTS Typically perches on tips of low weeds. Egg-laying pairs are attracted to green grass near water, where the female drops eggs into the grass from the air.

Red-Veined Meadowhawk *Sympetrum madidum* Plate 35

IDENTIFICATION Medium, 1.6 in. Western, uncommon. In juveniles each wing is amber at the base, the color extending along the front as a costal stripe, and basal and anterior wing veins are yellow. With maturity costal stripe fades but whole wing becomes tinted brown, and in males the basal and anterior veins turn red. Females and juvenile males have a gray face, and a brown-gray body with 2 white lateral thoracic stripes. Abdomen has a white lateral stripe on S2–S8 that is bordered dorsally by a narrow black stripe; top of S2 pale in female. Body markings fade as face and body become red (duller when cool) in males, brown in females. Legs black.

BODY FEATURES Male cerci lack large ventral teeth. Characteristic male hamule is shaped like a baseball catcher's mitt. Female subgenital plate 1/3 as long as S9, V-notched into 2 short, thick, triangular lobes.

SIMILAR SPECIES Meadowhawks similar to mature male include Cherry-Faced, which has a prominent black lateral stripe on S4–S9, and Saffron-Winged, which has a brown face. Striped Meadowhawk is like juvenile male Red-Veined, but seldom has more than a touch of amber at wing bases, and may have partly pale legs. Cardinal Meadowhawk has white lateral thoracic spots and brown basal wing streaks. Variegated Meadowhawk has yellow lower ends on lateral thoracic stripes, and partly pale legs.

HABITAT   Marshy temporary ponds, including brackish ones.

SEASON   Mid-May to early Sept., often peaking both spring and fall.

COMMENTS   Perches on tips of low plants, or sometimes on the ground. The female lays eggs in water near plants, or in dry ponds.

Yellow-Legged Meadowhawk *Sympetrum vicinum* Plate 35

IDENTIFICATION   Small, 1.3 in. U.S. and southernmost Canada, common except scarce southwest. Our most slender and palest Meadowhawk, with minimal black markings. Wings have a touch of amber at bases. In females and juvenile males forehead tan, thorax yellow to gray, legs yellow, and abdomen brown. In males forehead, lower side of thorax, and abdomen become red, and legs become red-brown. Old females also develop a red abdomen. As temperature decreases, red becomes orange, then brown. Female subgenital plate flares into a trumpetlike cone.

BODY FEATURES   Male cerci lack large ventral teeth. Hamule in side view looks like 2 fingers held in a V. Cerci and hamule of Spot-Winged Meadowhawk are similar.

VARIATION   TX/NM individuals have a small brown basal HW spot.

SIMILAR SPECIES   Saffron-Winged Meadowhawk is larger, and has some black on legs. The female Plateau Dragonlet has a much stouter abdomen.

HABITAT   Marshes, ponds, bogs, lakes, and slow streams, usually wooded and permanent but sometimes temporary.

SEASON   Late May to late Dec., primarily late summer and fall. The last dragonfly to emerge in the north, it may not begin breeding until late Aug., and is often the last dragonfly seen each year.

COMMENTS   Maturation several weeks, mostly in woodland, where they can feed at temperatures below 50°F. At low temperatures they perch on the ground, switching to leaves, and then to stems as the temperature increases. Pairs often form tandems away from water, then fly to water where they make false egg-laying movements before mating and commencing real egg laying. The female often taps shallow water and the bank alternately, preferring bare shores, even if those are in shade, and pairs are attracted to other pairs.

Spot-Winged Meadowhawk *Sympetrum signiferum* Plate 35

IDENTIFICATION Medium, 1.5 in. Southeastern AZ, rare in U.S. Similar to Yellow-Legged Meadowhawk, but larger and with a triangular brown basal HW spot. Female subgenital plate very short, not trumpet-like.

SIMILAR SPECIES Cardinal Meadowhawk has white lateral thoracic spots. The female Plateau Dragonlet has a much stouter abdomen.

HABITAT Ponds, marshes, and vegetated stream pools, to 6000-plus ft. in Mexico.

SEASON Late Aug. to late Oct. in Mexico.

COMMENTS Ranges south to Nayarit, Mexico.

Saffron-Winged Meadowhawk *Sympetrum costiferum* Plate 35

IDENTIFICATION Medium, 1.4 in. Canada/northern U.S., common. Juveniles have an amber costal wing stripe that disappears in males, but persists longer in females. Anterior wing veins orange. Body with minimal black markings except on legs, which vary from mostly yellow to all black. Usually a thin black lateral abdominal line and dorsal stripe on S8–S9 are present. Females and juvenile males have a dull yellow face and abdomen, and a brown thorax. In males and at least some females, face and abdomen turn pale red.

BODY FEATURES Male cerci lack large ventral teeth. Female subgenital plate a very short trough, not notched.

SIMILAR SPECIES Yellow-Legged Meadowhawk is smaller and more slender, has amber only at extreme wing bases, and lacks black on legs. Red-Veined Meadowhawk of the west has brown-tinted wings and all-black legs. Other similar Meadowhawks have dark red males, brown females, black legs, and wide black lateral abdominal stripes. Other dragonflies with a similar color pattern are much larger.

HABITAT Ponds, especially marsh-bordered, barren sandy or gravelly ponds in the open, occasional at lakes or bogs. Tolerates saline, alkaline, and acid waters.

SEASON Early July to early Dec., one of the last dragonflies of autumn.

COMMENTS Warier and more active than most Meadowhawks. Forages from perches on tips of weed stems in clearings, or in cool weather

from the ground, but at times over half a mile from water on
telephone wires. Males perch on emergent vegetation near
shore, flying periodic sorties with occasional hovering. Pairs lay
eggs in tandem near shore with slow, deliberate taps to the
water.

Band-Winged Meadowhawk *Sympetrum semicinctum* **Plate 36**

IDENTIFICATION   Small, 1.3 in. Southernmost Canada and U.S. except south;
common west, local east. Separated from other Meadowhawks
in the east by the amber basal halves of the wings, and in the
west by the black W on the side of the thorax. Abdomen of juveniles brown with a black lateral stripe, becoming pale red in
males, and red mid-dorsally in **Red Form** females. The
abdomen of **Yellow Form** females becomes whitish yellow.
Face yellow to brown, legs black.

BODY FEATURES   The western forms have been classified as a species (*S. occidentale*), but are structurally identical to the **Eastern Form**. Male
cerci each have a row of small ventral teeth but no large tooth.
Female subgenital plate very short and widely U-notched.

VARIATION   The **Eastern Form** has HW amber to the nodus, with outer part
of this zone darkened to a brown nodal band in males and most
females. FW has basal 1/3 amber, and thorax is brown. The 3
western forms have narrow black lines, which often form an
irregular W, on the yellow to brown side of the thorax. **Great
Plains Form** (*S. s. fasciatum*) has all wings amber to nodus, and
brown nodal bands, or wings may be nearly clear except for the
brown bands, especially eastward. **Northwestern Form** (*S. s.
occidentale*) usually has basal halves of wings diffusely clouded
with amber-brown, but FW may be almost clear or wing color
may be pale. **Southwestern Form** (*S. s. californicum*) usually
has FW amber near base, and HW with basal half amber to
amber-brown, but wings may be almost entirely clear. All western forms ill-defined, and further study is needed to determine
their validity, if any.

SIMILAR SPECIES   On the Great Plains, from OH to the Rocky Mountains, it cannot
be certainly separated from some Cherry-Faced and Ruby
Meadowhawks. The female Cherry-Faced Meadowhawk west of
the Rockies sometimes has as much as the basal halves of the
wings amber, but lacks brown nodal bands and black lateral thoracic markings. The female Black Meadowhawk never has more

than a touch of amber at wing bases, or any red markings, but has more black on side of thorax and a projecting ovipositor.

In the east, the female Eastern Amberwing is smaller, and has a spindle-shaped abdomen and tan legs. Martha's and Amanda's Pennants have only the basal 1/4 of the HW amber, and S8–S10 all black.

In the west, the Cardinal Meadowhawk has 2 white lateral thoracic spots. The female Mexican Amberwing has an amber band between nodus and stigma. The female Slough Amberwing has the abdomen brown dorsally with only narrow pale mid-dorsal lines. The female Seaside Dragonlet has little amber in wing bases and a projecting ovipositor. The female Plateau Dragonlet has little amber in wing bases and no black lateral thoracic lines. The female Marl Pennant is larger with a brown basal HW spot.

HABITAT Primarily shallow marshy areas, sometimes in bogs or fens, usually with a slow current, spring-fed, and edged with sedges. It seems unable to compete well with other dragonflies and is susceptible to fish predation. Thus in the west, where there are fewer species of dragonflies, it is much more common, especially at newly created habitats such as river overflows or irrigated lands. It ranges up to an elevation of 6500 ft.

SEASON Late May to late Oct.

COMMENTS Males and females forage together, primarily in the morning, from tips of plants in open marshy areas. Western forms also perch on fences and telephone wires, and may feed in swarms like glider dragonflies, but with more hovering. Pairs lay eggs in tandem among emergent plants.

Cherry-Faced Meadowhawk *Sympetrum internum*
Plate 36

IDENTIFICATION Small, 1.3 in. Canada/northern U.S., common. Abdomen brown with a black lateral stripe, becoming dark red in both sexes at maturity. Legs black. **Eastern Form** cannot be distinguished from Ruby Meadowhawk except by range. It has black wing veins, a touch of amber at wing bases, and face of mature male is brown. There is no known way to separate females from juvenile female White-Faced Meadowhawks. **Western Form** (OH westward) has anterior wing veins orange, and the yellow to gray face becomes dark red in mature males. Some western females have basal halves of wings amber.

BODY FEATURES Male Cherry-Faced and Ruby Meadowhawks essentially must be identified under a 20X microscope. In Cherry-Faced, triangular medial shelf of hamule in ventral posterior view has its rear edge thickened (especially at blunt median and posterior lateral points), and oblique rear edge is straight or slightly concave. In Ruby, medial shelf is scooplike with a thin and smoothly convex edge. Hamule in side view in both species deeply V-notched (1/3 distance to kneelike bend). Hamule of White-Faced Meadowhawk has medial shelf like that of Cherry-Faced, but has a small V-notch (1/5 distance to knee bend) in side view. Males of all 3 species have a large ventral tooth on each cercus, and faces of dry specimens may appear nearly white in all 3.

Female subgenital plate about 40% as long as S9, deeply V-notched into 2 pointed lobes for 1/4 its length and split in midline for an additional 1/4 of its length, in side view convex but not humped. Plate of Eastern Form is essentially identical to that of White-Faced Meadowhawk, while plate of Western Form has the ventral longitudinal keel-like convexities of the lobes divergent, and has a basal wrinklelike fold. Plate of Ruby Meadowhawk 25%–33% as long as S9, shallowly V-notched into 2 short pointed lobes, and grooved but not split in the midline. In side view it is roundly convex and bulging.

In the northeast the Cherry-Faced and Ruby Meadowhawks, and to a lesser extent the White-Faced Meadowhawk, all hybridize. Intermediate appearing individuals may be hybrids or may be a separate species (Jane's Meadowhawk, *S. janae*). The taxonomic situation is still not resolved.

SIMILAR SPECIES In the east, Ruby and juvenile White-Faced Meadowhawks are not separable from the Cherry-Faced. White-Faced has a white face at maturity, and in the west has black wing veins. Saffron-Winged Meadowhawk usually has a narrower black lateral abdominal stripe and some yellow on legs, and red of male abdomen is pale. The male Red-Veined Meadowhawk of the west has an interrupted short black lateral abdominal stripe. Band-Winged Meadowhawk in the west has black lateral thoracic markings, while the Cherry-Faced has only a touch of amber in the wing bases in the east. Other similar dragonflies have S8–S9 almost entirely black.

HABITAT Ponds, lakes, marshes, bogs, and slow streams to 1000 ft.

SEASON Mid-June to late Oct. or even early Dec. Eastern Form emerges several weeks earlier than White-Faced Meadowhawk, Western Form emerges while White-Faced is mature.

COMMENTS Perches on low stems or rocks. Mating occurs near midday on hot sunny days, probably so that permanently moist ground can be distinguished from dew-wet grass. Pairs lay eggs in tandem while hovering, or while the male grasps a stem, to drop eggs from the air onto moist ground. Egg-laying pairs commonly group together, and often mistake watered lawns for appropriate habitat.

Ruby Meadowhawk *Sympetrum rubicundulum*
Plate 36

IDENTIFICATION 1.4 in., northern Great Plains eastward, common. Cannot be separated from Eastern Form of Cherry-Faced Meadowhawk. Both sexes have face yellow to brown, abdomen brown to dark red with a black lateral stripe, legs black, and wing veins dark. Abdomen of juvenile males becomes red in 13–16 days (probably longer in females). Some individuals from OH westward have as much as the basal halves of the wings amber. Compare with Cherry-Faced and White-Faced Meadowhawks.

SIMILAR SPECIES Inseparable from Cherry-Faced and White-Faced Meadowhawks, unless the latter is mature with a white face. Saffron-Winged Meadowhawk usually has a narrower black lateral abdominal stripe, orange anterior wing veins, some yellow on legs, and red of male abdomen is pale. Great Plains Form of Band-Winged Meadowhawk has brown nodal bands. Other similar dragonflies are either much larger with a black dorsal abdominal stripe, or have S8–S9 almost entirely black.

HABITAT Primarily temporary ponds, sometimes permanent ponds and marshes, occasionally lakes, swamps, bogs, and stream backwaters.

SEASON Mid-June to early Oct. in NY, also reported early May to mid-Nov.

COMMENTS Forages from weed stems in the open, and basks on the ground. Males establish territories of 3 ft. radius among grasslike emergent plants, preferably at the shoreward edge of the water, beginning about 11 A.M. The female lays eggs in tandem about 20% of the time, usually dropping eggs from the air into high grass on the bank within a yard of the water.

White-Faced Meadowhawk *Sympetrum obtrusum*
Plate 36

IDENTIFICATION Small, 1.3 in. Canada/northern U.S., common. Face yellow in juveniles, becoming white at maturity. Abdomen brown with a black lateral stripe, and sometimes a dorsal black line on S8–S9, becoming dark red in males and some females. Legs and wing veins black, wing bases with a touch of amber. Side of thorax yellow in newly emerged individuals, briefly tending to form 2 lateral pale stripes as thorax becomes brown during aging.

BODY FEATURES Compare with Cherry-Faced and Ruby Meadowhawks. There is no visual way to separate juvenile female White-Faced Meadowhawks from females of the Eastern Form of the Cherry-Faced Meadowhawk, even under a microscope.

SIMILAR SPECIES The white face separates this species from our other Meadowhawks, except the Blue-Faced, which has a blue forehead, brown legs, and black abdominal bands. Juvenile White-Faced cannot be separated from Cherry-Faced and Ruby Meadowhawks in the east, although the White-Faced is usually a little smaller and more delicately built. White-Faced apparently never has extensive amber in wing bases like some individuals of Ruby and Cherry-Faced. In the west the Cherry-Faced has orange anterior wing veins and mature males have red faces. Saffron-Winged Meadowhawk has orange anterior wing veins and may have pale legs. Black Meadowhawk and western forms of the Band-Winged Meadowhawk have black lateral thoracic markings. Other similar dragonflies have S8–S9 mostly black, and may have a dark basal HW spot.

HABITAT Temporary or permanent ponds, lakes, marshes, slow streams, and sometimes bogs. Tolerates acid water. More associated with forest than Cherry-Faced Meadowhawk.

SEASON Mid-June to early Nov.

COMMENTS Typically forages from tips of low weeds. At warm temperatures the male holds the female in tandem for egg laying, but at cool temperatures he releases her and hover-guards. The female, either perched or in flight, drops eggs onto mud among sparse shore grasses, or into water among emergent reeds.

Dragonlets
(genus *Erythrodiplax*)

These dragonflies in North America are black, blue, or brown, though some tropical species are red. Our species are southern, and include 2 of medium size, and 4 small or very small ones. About 46 other species live throughout tropical America and the Caribbean.

Band-Winged Dragonlet *Erythrodiplax umbrata*
Plate 36

IDENTIFICATION Medium, 1.7 in. Common TX and south FL, strays eastern U.S. Mature males easily recognized by slender black body, and a wide black band between nodus and stigma of each wing. The body becomes lightly pruinose, and cerci are pale. **Black Form** female is colored like male, except that wing bands often do not reach stigmas. Wing bands change from yellow to brown to black during maturation. Much more common **Brown Form** female is dull brown with brown wingtips and tan rectangular lateral spots on at least S5–S7. Juveniles of both sexes resemble Brown Form female, but have gray lateral abdominal spots. Some individuals have a spot at HW base, amber in Brown Form females, turning black in males and Black Form females. Intermediate females, with wing bands extending from the front partway across each wing, are known from the tropics.

BODY FEATURES A low, darkened, stripelike ridge on each side of the front of the thorax is absent or faint in other Dragonlets. Female subgenital plate spoutlike but only 1/4 as long as S9. Median planate of wings has 1 row of cells; 2 rows in Black-Winged Dragonlet.

SIMILAR SPECIES Rare Black-Winged Dragonlet of the southwest has wing bands usually extending to the base in the HW, and never reaching the stigmas. Brown Form females of Black-Winged have front of thorax darker than sides, and abdominal spots fade as abdomen blackens with age. Old and dull-colored females of these 2 species may be impossible to separate. Four-Spotted Pennant has black spots rather than bands between nodus and stigma, white stigmas, and a swollen abdominal base. Filigree

Skimmer of the southwest has basal part of HW black or with scattered black spots, and usually perches on rocks. Male Whitetails have a stout abdomen. Brown dragonflies similar to Brown Form female have some combination of clear wingtips, pale thoracic spots or stripes, or have the abdomen swollen at the base, tapered, unspotted, striped, or with a lateral flange on S8.

HABITAT   Temporary ponds and marshes. Accepts pools with taller shore vegetation than Black-Winged Dragonlet.

SEASON   All year.

COMMENTS   Perches on tips of stems, usually about 3 ft. up, but females often high in trees. They often hover a foot away from a perch for a few seconds to check for predators before settling on it. Males patrol small pools. Black Form females mimic males by confronting them face to face, thus avoiding unnecessary matings. It occurs in the FL Keys, Dry Tortugas, Bahamas and West Indies, and ranges south to Argentina.

Black-Winged Dragonlet *Erythrodiplax funerea*
Plate 36

IDENTIFICATION   Medium, 1.7 in. Stray to southwest. Mature male easily identified by slender black body and wide black wing bands that extend from near base, especially in HW, to halfway between nodus and stigma. Wingtips variably brown. **Banded Form** female like male but brown between wing bases. **Spotted Form** female like Banded Form but instead of wing bands has a round black basal HW spot. **Brown Form** female has a round amber basal HW spot, brown wingtips, and tan face. In Brown Form, thorax dark brown on front, tan on sides, abdomen brown with pale rectangular lateral spots on at least S5–S7, becoming uniform brown with age. Brown Form most common, Banded Form least common. In juveniles body brown and wing bands brownish yellow, darkening from outer edge toward base during maturation. A few females intermediate between Banded and Spotted Forms have been found, which have black bands extending various distances from base toward nodus. Compare with closely related Band-Winged Dragonlet.

SIMILAR SPECIES   Wing bands of Band-Winged Dragonlet not so basal, extending between nodus and stigma. Filigree Skimmer, which normally perches on rocks, has wing bands in male extending to stigma, while female has spotted or mottled wing bases, pale dorsal chevrons on abdomen, and a spoutlike ovipositor. Male White-tails have wing bands extending to stigma and a wide abdomen. The male Marl Pennant is similar to female Spotted Form, but has a more tapered abdomen and an open mesh of wing veins. Female Marl Pennants have a shorter abdomen with large brownish-yellow spots, and a brown W-shaped lateral thoracic marking. The male Black Setwing lacks wing markings. Spot-Winged Glider and Saddlebag Gliders have tapered abdomens, feed in sustained flight, and the dark basal HW spots differ in size, shape, or position from those of Black-Winged Dragonlet. Pin-Tailed Pondhawk has abdomen swollen at base. Brown Form female of Band-Winged Dragonlet has front and sides of thorax similar in color, but old females may look like Brown Form females of Black-Winged Dragonlet. Brown dragonflies similar to Brown Form female of Black-Winged have some combination of pale thoracic spots, clear wingtips, or have the abdomen thick, tapered, striped, or bearing flanges on S8.

HABITAT Temporary ponds in the open.

SEASON All year.

COMMENTS Males and mated pairs settle on tips of grass around pools. It ranges south to Peru.

Little Blue Dragonlet *Erythrodiplax minuscula*
Plate 37

IDENTIFICATION Very small, 1.0 in. Eastern U.S., common. Females and juvenile males have a tan face, and a tan thorax with diffuse brown shoulder stripes. Abdomen tan on S1–S6, with dorsal and interrupted lateral black stripes, and usually black S7–S9. In males face becomes black, and thorax and S1–S7 become pruinose pale blue. Thorax becomes pruinose beginning at front, while abdomen becomes pruinose from S7 forward. A small amber basal HW spot becomes black in males. Cerci usually white. Female ovipositor an oblique scoop as long as S9.

SIMILAR SPECIES Plateau and Red-Faced Dragonlets similar but ranges not known to overlap. In male Red-Faced of TX face becomes red but thorax remains brown. The male Elfin Skimmer, a bog species, is smaller and has a mostly white face. The male Blue Corporal is larger and has brown stripes in the wing bases. Brown female Meadowhawks lack a dorsal black abdominal stripe and have S7–S9 mostly brown.

HABITAT   Marshy ponds, lakes, and sometimes stream pools, at up to 5000 ft.

SEASON   All year.

COMMENTS   Perches on low stems in fields, often with wings cocked downward and abdomen elevated. Males defend territories about 3 yards in diameter. It ranges into the FL Keys.

Plateau Dragonlet *Erythrodiplax connata* **Plate 37**

IDENTIFICATION   Small, 1.3 in. Southwestern, local. Similar to Little Blue Dragonlet but mature males have a black thorax, an amber basal HW spot, and usually black cerci. HW spot is smaller in females, and may be absent in either sex. Females and juvenile males have a tan abdomen with an interrupted brown lateral stripe; dorsal brown abdominal stripe is variably present, more likely in males. Females identical to those of Red-Faced Dragonlet.

SIMILAR SPECIES   Mature male Red-Faced Dragonlet has a red face but thorax remains brown. Blue male Pondhawks are much larger and have a green face. Brown female Yellow-Legged, Spot-Winged, and Band-Winged Meadowhawks have more slender abdomens, and Band-Winged has black lateral thoracic markings.

HABITAT   Marshy ponds, lakes, and sometimes stream pools.

SEASON   All year.

COMMENTS   At streams, attracted to sections or pools containing green algae. Pairs may lay eggs in tandem. It ranges south to Baja California and Oaxaca, Mexico. This species(?) also occurs from Peru to Chile. If the latter populations are found to be a different species, ours will be named *E. basifusca*.

Red-Faced Dragonlet *Erythrodiplax fusca* **Plate 37**

IDENTIFICATION   Very small, 1.1 in. Central TX, local. Similar to Little Blue Dragonlet but mature males develop a red face, while thorax remains brown and basal HW spot becomes brown-amber. Thus males are our only dragonfly with a red face and a blue abdomen. Cerci brown. Females identical to those of Plateau Dragonlet. A red, nonpruinose male form is found in the tropics, and some females there develop a red-brown abdomen.

SIMILAR SPECIES   See Similar Species under Little Blue Dragonlet.

HABITAT   Marshy or swampy ponds, lakes, trickles, and stream pools.

SEASON   All year.

COMMENTS   Forages from weeds in fields, and males perch low on emergent plants. It ranges south to Argentina, and into the Lesser Antilles and Dutch Leeward Islands.

Seaside Dragonlet *Erythrodiplax berenice* **Plate 37**

IDENTIFICATION   Small, 1.3 in. Common Gulf and Atlantic Coasts, local southwest. Mature males all black with a slender abdomen. Females have a pointed spoutlike ovipositor as long as S8. Juveniles of both sexes mostly black, including forehead, with narrow yellow thoracic stripes, and S1–S7 orange-yellow dorsally. Males blacken very rapidly, with small yellow spots on S3–S7 disappearing last. Females blacken more slowly and in 3 different ways. In **Male-like Form**, thorax becomes black before abdomen, as in males. In **Unspotted Form**, abdomen becomes black before thorax. In **Spotted Form**, abdomen becomes black before thorax and each wing develops a large brown nodal spot. The Spotted Form seldom develops an all-black body. The oldest females finally become gray on the thorax.

BODY FEATURES   *E. b. naeva* with a slightly different wing venation ranges from FL Keys southward.

SIMILAR SPECIES   Similar dragonflies are seldom found in habitat of Seaside. Double-Ringed Pennant is a spring species with a small black basal HW spot. The male Black Meadowhawk of New England is a little huskier with a more open mesh of wing veins. Female Black Meadowhawks have the side of the thorax bearing a black chainlike marking, pale spots on S9, forehead pale, and ovipositor short. Whitefaces of the north have a white forehead and face. Elfin Skimmer is much smaller. Ebony Boghaunter of New England has pale rings on S2–S4. Blue Dasher is larger with a white face. Metallic Pennant of south FL has a dark brown thorax, an open mesh of wing veins, and female lacks an ovipositor. Black Setwing of the southwest is larger. Narrow-Winged Skimmer of TX is larger with narrow HW bases, and female has a lateral flap on S8. Pin-Tailed and Black Pondhawks of the far south are larger with a swollen abdominal base. Small Pennants lack ovipositors, and have a black and amber spot at base of HW, or a stripe-spot combination on side of thorax.

HABITAT   Salt marshes, mangrove swamps, and saline lakes. The only dragonfly in the Western Hemisphere that can breed in undiluted seawater.

SEASON   All year in FL, mid-May to mid-Sept. in NJ.

COMMENTS   Perches on stems or occasionally on the ground. Males perch near pools, in sunlight or shade, and defend about 5 yards of shore. Pairs lay eggs in tandem, usually into algae mats. It ranges south along the Atlantic Coast to Venezuela, and along the Pacific Coast from Baja California to Oaxaca, Mexico. It also lives in the FL Keys and Dry Tortugas, and some Caribbean Islands, including the Bahamas, Greater Antilles, and Antigua.

Elfin Skimmer
(genus *Nannothemis*)

The wing vein pattern of the only species in this genus is unique among North American dragonflies, in that the anal loop of the HW is incomplete (no toe present, loop opens on wing margin).

Elfin Skimmer *Nannothemis bella* Plate 38

IDENTIFICATION   Our smallest dragonfly, 0.8 in. Eastern, local. Tiny size is diagnostic. Juvenile males have thorax and abdomen black, becoming pruinose pale blue in 5–10 days. Male abdomen widens into a flat club at S8. In females thorax is black mottled with yellow, and abdomen is colored like a wasp's, black with transverse yellow basal spots on S2–S6 or S7, and with S10 yellow. Female wings orange in basal third. Face white on top and sides, black elsewhere, while eyes are silver, striped vertically with red-brown.

VARIATION   Females have reduced orange wing markings in the north, a brown streak at base of each wing in the south.

SIMILAR SPECIES   Male likely to be confused only with male Little Blue Dragonlet, which is larger, and has sides of thorax brown, abdomen not clubbed, cerci pale, and no white on face. The male Seaside Dragonlet is larger and has an all-black face and body. Whitefaces have elongate abdominal spots.

HABITAT   Bogs, sometimes calcareous fens with sedge meadows and marl deposits.

SEASON   Early March to early Sept. in U.S., late May to early Aug. in Canada. About 6 weeks at a locale.

COMMENTS   Perches with wings cocked downward on low stems. Males are on territories of 1/4 to 2 square yards from about 8 A.M. to 6 P.M. Pairs lay eggs in tandem.

Amberwings
(genus *Perithemis*)

Readily recognized by very small size, chunky build with a spindle-shaped abdomen, and in males, orange wings. Males and females resemble wasps of different species, enhanced by narrow pale yellow rings between the abdominal segments. Amberwings have the most complex courtships among North American dragonflies, after which pairs perch to mate for 20–30 sec., then males hover-guard egg-laying females. All 3 North American species occur in the southwest, but only 1 ranges into the east. At least 9 other species inhabit tropical America.

Eastern Amberwing *Perithemis tenera* Plate 38

IDENTIFICATION | Very small, 0.9 in. Eastern and central to AZ, common. Thorax mostly brown, with 2 wide greenish-yellow lateral stripes and a pair of narrow frontal stripes. The thick abdomen is either not striped or has narrow, zigzag, dorsolateral brown stripes. Male wings orange, with yellow veins and red stigma. Female wings variable, with a stained-glass effect, usually amber from base to between nodus and stigma, with a brown spot at 1/4 length of FW, and brown bands at 1/4 and 1/2 length of HW. Brown HW bands may be reduced to spots, or may be connected anteriorly, in which latter case amber coloration is lacking. Rarely, females have orange wings.

BODY FEATURES | Wing triangles, and FW subtriangle, seldom have cross-veins.

VARIATION | Brown in wings generally increases southward. Many males have brown spots at 1/4 length of wings, especially in HW. Some males in south FL have femalelike HW bands. Southern females often have amber or brown rear edges on wings from nodus to tip, particularly in HW. Many FL females have very wide brown bands, reaching stigma in FW.

SIMILAR SPECIES | Thoracic pattern of both sexes, and wing pattern of female, distinguishes it from our other Amberwings, which have thorax mostly pale.

HABITAT | Most permanent still or slowly moving waters such as ponds, lakes, ditches, and stream pools, including brackish water but not bogs.

SEASON | All year in FL, early June to mid-Sept. in NY.

COMMENTS | Perches on tips of weeds, often mimicking wasps by pulsing the narrow-waisted abdomen up and down while simultaneously waving the wings up and down. Females fly with the HW held mostly vertically while the abdomen is bent upward along the rear edge of the HW, causing the HW and abdomen together to look like the abdomen of a wasp. A male selects an egg-laying site that breaks the water surface, and defends a territory 3–6 yards in diameter around it. When a female appears, he courts her by leading her to his site and hovering above it with abdomen upcurved. If the female accepts, they mate and the female then plasters her eggs just above the waterline during a hovering flight. Females also lay eggs into pools on water lily leaves, and among emergent plants. It ranges south at least to Durango, Mexico.

Mexican Amberwing *Perithemis intensa* Plate 38

IDENTIFICATION   Very small, 1.1 in. Far southwest, common. Thorax and abdomen brownish yellow, usually without stripes. Thorax may have faint brown midfrontal and shoulder stripes, and abdomen may have narrow zigzag dorsolateral brown lines which are most distinct posteriorly and in females. Male wings orange with yellow veins and reddish-brown stigmas, often with a brown spot at 1/4 length. Female wings variable, usually with amber bands at 1/4 length and between nodus and stigma, and with brown spots at 1/4 length and nodus. The brown markings may be absent, expanded to bands, or replace amber bands. Occasionally female wings are orange with brown markings.

BODY FEATURES   Wing triangles usually have 1 cross-vein, FW subtriangle usually has 2 cross-veins.

SIMILAR SPECIES   The basically unstriped thorax differentiates this species from our other Amberwings. Slough Amberwing has definite straight brown stripes on abdomen, and female has brown HW tips.

HABITAT   Ponds, lakes, ditches, and river backwaters, often with green or muddy water.

SEASON   Mid-May to late Nov., all year in Mexico.

COMMENTS   Away from water, often perches several yards up on twigs. Other behavior like Eastern Amberwing. It ranges south to Baja California, Morelos, and Yucatán, Mexico.

Slough Amberwing *Perithemis domitia* Plate 38

IDENTIFICATION   Very small, 0.9 in. Mexican border, uncommon in U.S. Thorax greenish yellow with brown stripes, including a wide midfrontal, wide shoulder, and 1 or 2 lateral stripes. Abdomen dull yellow with wide, straight, full-length, dorsolateral brown stripes. Male wings orange with red veins and stigmas. Female wings amber in basal half, with brown spots at 1/4 length, 1 in FW and 2 in HW, plus a brown band at 1/2 length, and brown HW tips.

BODY FEATURES   Wing triangles lack cross-veins, FW subtriangle usually has 1 cross-vein.

VARIATION   Male wings rarely have small brown spots at 1/4 and 1/2 length, and female wings may have brown markings reduced or absent. These variants have not been seen yet in the U.S.

SIMILAR SPECIES   The straight brown abdominal stripes are distinctive among our Amberwings. Band-Winged Meadowhawk is larger, with a longer, more slender abdomen which has lateral black stripes instead of dorsolateral stripes.

HABITAT   Ponds, stream pools, and sloughs, often partly shaded.

SEASON   All year.

COMMENTS   Males are at water from about 8:30 A.M. to 5 P.M., where they defend territories about 2 yards in diameter, usually perching in shade. It ranges south to Brazil, including the Greater Antilles.

Blue Dasher
(genus *Pachydiplax*)

Only 1 species is classified in this genus.

Blue Dasher *Pachydiplax longipennis* **Plate 39**

IDENTIFICATION   Small to medium, 1.0–1.7, generally largest in spring. Southernmost Canada, U.S. except Great Basin area; abundant. Mature males easily recognized by combination of white face, metallic-green eyes, black and yellow striped thorax, and pale blue tapered abdomen. HW has 2 black streaks within an amber spot at base, and outer half of each wing is often tinted brown. Females have a short, blunt abdomen, with S10 very short, and no black streaks in HW. In juveniles, abdomen is black with dorsolateral, interrupted yellow stripes, and eyes are red-brown. During maturation the abdomen and dorsal area between the wings become pale pruinose blue, in about 9 days in males, slower in females.

BODY FEATURES   Only 1 cross-vein behind stigma is diagnostic.

VARIATION   S8–S10 of males usually remain black, but in southwestern arid areas whole abdomen plus dark markings on thorax become pruinose blue. Southwestern males may lack black basal HW streaks, and CA males usually lack amber at HW base.

SIMILAR SPECIES Our other blue dragonflies do not have a black and yellow striped thorax. Eastern and Western Pondhawks have a green face, and the Bleached Skimmer of the west has the costa vein white. The Tropical Dashers of the far south are like juvenile Blue Dashers, but their pale abdominal spots change from yellow to pale green at maturity, and spots of S7 are larger than more basal spots. Except in Three-Striped Dasher, the dark lateral thoracic stripes are forked.

HABITAT Most still waters, with or without fish, except bogs, including ponds, marshes, bays, ditches, and swamps. Sometimes flowing water, but uncommon there.

SEASON All year in FL, mid-June to early Sept. in Ontario.

COMMENTS Perches with lowered wings on tips of erect slender stems, from near ground to the treetops. Both sexes will defend a feeding perch for up to several days. A male defends a territory along the shore, preferably where vegetation is highest, confronting other males with abdomen raised. During territorial battles, each male tries to get under his opponent and force him up and away from the water with the whole upper surface of the body. It migrates along the Atlantic Coast in small numbers, and ranges south to Michoacán and Yucatán, Mexico, including Baja California, plus the FL Keys, Dry Tortugas, Bermuda, and the Bahamas.

Pondhawks
(genus *Erythemis*)

North American Pondhawks are colored green, blue, or black, but some tropical species are bright red. The green species are our only Skimmers with green faces. Pondhawks are voracious and commonly take prey as large as themselves, held by 3 large spines on each middle and hind thigh. We have 5 species, 4 medium and 1 medium-large, while 6 more are tropical American.

Eastern Pondhawk *Erythemis simplicicollis* **Plate 39**

IDENTIFICATION 1.7 in., eastern and central, abundant; also local southwest. Mature male pruinose pale blue with green face and white cerci, and abdomen slightly narrowed at S4–S5. Female and juvenile male grass green with black rectangular dorsal spots on S4–S6, and mostly black S8–S10. Female has spoutlike ovipositor. Eyes green, becoming blue in males. A few males have narrow black lines on thorax. Abdomen becomes blue first, beginning at S4–S5 (at 6–13 days of age), while thorax becomes blue beginning 2 days later on its front. The cartwheel contest described below usually identifies male Eastern Pondhawks as far as they can be seen.

SIMILAR SPECIES Mature male Western Pondhawks have black cerci, and a darker blue tapered abdomen. Females and juvenile males have a black dorsal abdominal stripe, and are pale on sides of S8–S9. Great Pondhawk of the far south is larger, with abdomen slender beyond its bulging base, and complete dark bands on S4–S7. Blue Dasher has white face and black and yellow striped thorax. Blue Corporal has dark streaks in wing bases, a brown face, and brown cerci. Snaketails and Ringtails have separated eyes.

HABITAT Most quiet waters, with or without fish, including slightly brackish water, but not bogs. Usually associated with mats of algae, duckweed, water lilies, or other flat floating plants.

SEASON All year in FL, early May to early Oct. in NJ.

COMMENTS One of our most ferocious dragonflies, attacking even each other. They hunt from the ground or low perches, often using a person or other large animal to flush game, and destroy great numbers of agricultural pests. A male territory encompasses about 5 square yards of algae mat or other floating plants. Males have unusual vertical circling contests in which one male which is following another flies under and up in front of the leading male, then the new follower repeats this maneuver, and so forth up to a dozen times. It is migratory in southern Canada, and ranges south to Costa Rica, including the FL Keys, Dry Tortugas, Bahamas, Cuba, Hispaniola, Jamaica, and Cayman Islands.

Western Pondhawk *Erythemis collocata* Plate 39

IDENTIFICATION 1.6 in., western, common. Male becomes pruinose gray-blue (last on sides of thorax) with black cerci on the robust tapered abdomen, and a green face. Female and juvenile male have face, thorax, and S1–S3 grass green. S4–S10 are tan-yellow, and a black mid-dorsal stripe extends from S2 to S9. Female has a spoutlike ovipositor. Eyes green, becoming pale blue in females, deep blue in males.

VARIATION A few individuals have 2 or 3 narrow black lateral stripes on thorax, and in western WY this is usual. Females in western WY have an abdominal pattern like that of Eastern Pondhawk, but have a pale dorsolateral spot on S8 (S8 all black in Eastern Pondhawk). Possibly hybridizes with Eastern Pondhawk, but these species are seldom found together.

SIMILAR SPECIES Male Eastern Pondhawks are paler blue with white cerci, and abdomen is slightly clubbed, narrowest and parallel-sided at S5. Female Eastern Pondhawks have a spotted abdomen. Great Pondhawk of the south is larger, with abdomen swollen at S1–S3, slender and parallel-sided on S4–S10, and banded with green and brown or black on S4–S7. Other similar blue western dragonflies have a white or a black face. The most similar green western dragonflies are Snaketails and Ringtails, which have separated eyes.

HABITAT Both quiet and flowing waters, including ponds, slow streams, marshes, and runoff from hot springs.

SEASON Late April to early Nov. in U.S., early June to early Sept. in British Columbia.

COMMENTS General behavior like that of Eastern Pondhawk, but seems warier, less ferocious, males have larger territories, and male vertical circling is rare. It ranges to Baja California and Chiapas, Mexico.

Great Pondhawk *Erythemis vesiculosa* Plate 39

IDENTIFICATION Medium-large, the largest Pondhawk, 2.4 in. Southern, commonest far south. Juveniles are our only dragonflies with green stigmas. Abdominal shape and pattern are distinctive; inflated at S1–S3 and slender beyond, banded with brown or black on S4–S7, cerci green. Both sexes are mostly green, but eyes green-gray in males and dark brown in females. Female ovipositor is an inconspicuous short spout.

SIMILAR SPECIES Eastern and Western Pondhawks smaller and mature males are blue. Those species have abdomen less inflated at base and either spotted or striped, and females have a projecting ovipositor. The Great Pondhawk can be mistaken for a Darner, such as the Blue-Faced Darner, but Darners do not perch much, and hang vertically when they do. Clubtails have separated eyes, and usually clubbed abdomens.

HABITAT Most quiet waters, including temporary ponds, and probably brackish waters.

SEASON All year.

COMMENTS   Sometimes classified in its own genus, *Lepthemis*. A wary species that hunts from the ground or low stems. In shaded areas, they may hover a yard up to survey for prey. Males patrol with their abdomen raised 30° over areas 10–20 yards in diameter, hovering often. It lives in the FL Keys and Dry Tortugas, and ranges south to Argentina and throughout the West Indies and Bahamas.

Pin-Tailed Pondhawk *Erythemis plebeja* Plate 40

IDENTIFICATION   1.8 in., south TX and south FL, uncommon. Beyond the swollen S1–S3, the abdomen of males is the most slender of any of our dragonflies. Each HW of both sexes has a small black spot at its base. Mature males all black except for tan cerci. Females and juvenile males dark brown, with forehead, front of thorax, S1–S3, and bands across S4–S7 tan. In males abdominal bands darken dorsally first, forming lateral spots before disappearing during maturation. Females have a spoutlike ovipositor. Eyes black in males, red-brown in females.

SIMILAR SPECIES   Other southern black dragonflies have a normally shaped abdomen, and usually perch on tips of stems. The male Black Pondhawk and male Marl Pennant have a much larger black basal HW spot. The female Black Pondhawk lacks tan front of thorax. The male Black Setwing and Narrow-Winged Skimmer of TX have little if any black at HW base, and a metallic-blue or violet forehead. Four-Spotted and Tawny Pennants lack black wing bases and a tan frontal thoracic stripe, and their abdomens appear striped. Female Band-Winged and Black-Winged Dragonlets have the abdomen not swollen basally, and thorax all tan, or darker on front than sides. Slaty Skimmer is larger, Metallic Pennant of FL much smaller.

HABITAT   Ponds, lakes, canals, and slow rivers.

SEASON   All year.

COMMENTS   A wary, active species that usually perches on sides of low stems. Males hover often as they patrol territories along weedy shores. It ranges south to Argentina, and in the Greater Antilles. It was first discovered in FL at Miami in 1971.

Black Pondhawk *Erythemis attala* Plate 40

IDENTIFICATION   1.6 in., stray? to AL. Juveniles dark brown with large brownish-white square spots on S4–S7. Males have a large black rounded spot at base of HW, this spot smaller, amber, or absent in females. Both sexes become entirely black except for tan cerci, with spots of S4, and finally S7, last to darken. Eyes red-brown, becoming black. Abdomen normally shaped, shorter than a wing, with a projecting spoutlike ovipositor in female.

SIMILAR SPECIES   Pin-Tailed Pondhawk has abdomen as long as a wing and very slender beyond its swollen base. In males HW spot is smaller, in females forehead and front of thorax are tan. The male Marl Pennant has black cerci, while female has a white face and gray thorax. Black Saddlebags have a wide black HW band, black cerci, and gliding flight. Most other similar dragonflies have little if any black at HW base, the abdomen as long as a wing, and dark cerci, or females lack a projecting ovipositor. Four-Spotted and Tawny Pennants have striped abdomens. Females of Band-Winged and Black-Winged Dragonlets have thorax all tan, or darker on front than sides.

HABITAT   Ponds, lakes, swamps, and slow streams.

SEASON   Probably all year in tropics, collected May 2, 1989, in AL.

COMMENTS   Active and wary, perching on low vegetation. Males defend small territories along the shore, preferably on algae mats. It ranges south to Argentina, and in the West Indies.

Rainpool Gliders
(genus *Pantala*)

The 2 species in this genus are widespread in North America. They are medium-size with a streamlined teardrop-shaped body that tapers from the large round head to the pointed tip of the abdomen. Their triangular HW are each longer than the abdomen, broad at the base and reaching halfway down the abdomen. They have a gray, unpatterned thorax, and allow the abdomen to droop on hot days to reduce the surface exposed to the sun. Pairs may lay eggs in tandem.

Wandering Glider *Pantala flavescens* Plate 40

IDENTIFICATION   1.9 in., U.S. to southern Canada; common south, migratory north. Easily identified by mostly yellow tapered abdomen, and sustained gliding flight on long broad wings. Face yellow, developing a red tint in males. Males also develop an orange tint dorsally on abdomen, and have brown wingtips.

SIMILAR SPECIES   Our other gliding dragonflies have dark spots or bands in HW base. Other yellow Skimmers, such as some female King Skimmers, and the female Scarlet Skimmer, have less broad HW, less tapered abdomens, and often perch near tops of plants.

HABITAT Primarily temporary ponds and puddles in the open with bare shores, including brackish ones. Rarely, slow moving water.

SEASON All year in U.S., mid-July to mid-Sept. in Canada, most common late summer.

COMMENTS The world's most evolved dragonfly, it drifts with the wind as it feeds on aerial plankton until an air mass of different temperature produces the rain pools in which it breeds. Over the ocean they fly day and night for thousands of miles. In North America they straggle north to breed, and the offspring migrate south in the fall. They may feed in swarms, often on small insects stirred up by large animals, and may "mob" or chase larger dragonflies attacking the swarm. They perch vertically down among the stems of low plants. Males patrol territories about 10–50 yards long at a height of 6 ft. for up to 30 min., hovering often. It is the only dragonfly found around the world, breeding on every continent except Europe. On many oceanic islands, such as Easter Island, it is the only dragonfly.

Spot-Winged Glider *Pantala hymenaea* **Plate 40**

IDENTIFICATION 1.9 in., U.S. to southern Canada; common southwest, mostly migratory elsewhere. Recognized by tapered mottled gray-brown abdomen and long broad wings. Round brown basal spot in HW diagnostic but sometimes difficult to see. Face yellow to orange, becoming red in mature males.

SIMILAR SPECIES Wandering Glider, female Red Rock Skimmer, and Variegated Meadowhawk lack HW markings. In addition, Wandering Glider has a yellow abdomen, female Red Rock Skimmer is grayer, and Variegated Meadowhawk is smaller. Red Rock Skimmer usually perches on rocks, while Variegated Meadowhawk usually perches on tips of stems. Saddlebag Gliders, Hyacinth Glider, and Pasture Gliders have a band, streak, or triangular dark spot at HW base, not a rounded spot. Female Saddlebag Gliders have the abdomen more uniformly brown, while Hyacinth and Pasture Gliders are smaller.

HABITAT Primarily temporary ponds and pools in the open, including brackish ones.

SEASON All year in U.S., mid-June to late Aug. in Canada. Tends to range northward earlier than Wandering Glider.

COMMENTS Feeds with a sustained flight from dawn to dark. The flight is more erratic with less hovering than that of the Wandering Glider, and seems more powerful, but apparently cannot be maintained for days like that of the Wandering Glider. It migrates in swarms along the Atlantic Coast, and can be seen in the desert 50 miles from any water. It perches vertically on twigs, higher than the Wandering Glider, and males patrol larger and more linear territories. It ranges south to Argentina and Chile, and on Bermuda, the Bahamas, the West Indies, and the Galápagos Islands.

Saddlebag Gliders (genus *Tramea*)

These red, brown, or black mostly medium-size dragonflies have a silhouette like the Rainpool Gliders, with a streamlined teardrop shape and long broad HW. Each HW has a dark band at the base reminiscent of the saddlebags on a horse's saddle, which make the body look larger than it really is. On hot days they allow the abdomen to droop into the shade of the wing bands. They have been called Dancing Gliders because during egg laying the male releases the female's head, the female dips to the water to release eggs, the male grasps his partner again, and then the couple repeats these steps. The female holds a mass of eggs between dips with a long, split subgenital plate. Saddlebags feed in a sustained gliding flight, occasionally perching horizontally on tips of stems or twigs. Mating is rarely seen, but takes 8–15 min. as the pair perches on a tall weed or tree near water. The stigma is longer on the anterior side, thus trapezoidal in shape, resulting in the name *Trapezostigma* which is occasionally used for this genus. Of our 7 species, the 3 widespread ones have wide HW bands, but the 4 generally restricted to the far south have narrow bands. About 17 other species are found worldwide except Europe.

Black Saddlebags *Tramea lacerata* Plate 40

IDENTIFICATION Medium-large, 2.1 in. U.S. and southernmost Canada, common. Easily identified in good light by its mostly black coloration, iridescent black band covering basal 1/4 of HW, and white dorsal abdominal spots. Females and juvenile males have a yellow-brown face and large white dorsal spots on S3–S7. In males the face becomes black, and abdominal spots darken, persisting longest on S7. In dorsal view the HW bands are shaped like theater comedy masks facing each other across the abdomen.

SKIMMERS

SIMILAR SPECIES None of our other Saddlebag Gliders has white abdominal spots, but red or brown species of Saddlebag Gliders can look black when silhouetted against the sky. Sooty Saddlebags has narrow HW bands. The female Widow Skimmer has yellow lateral abdominal stripes. The male Marl Pennant is smaller, and has a HW spot rather than band.

HABITAT Ponds, lakes, and ditches without fish, including temporary ponds.

SEASON All year in FL, mid-May to mid-Oct. in Ontario.

COMMENTS Some move north in spring to breed, then their offspring migrate south, often in swarms. This exceedingly agile flyer forages over wide areas several yards up. Males often patrol a whole pond, at a usual top speed of 17 mph, but normally leave by 2 P.M. It ranges south to Baja California and Quintana Roo, Mexico, and on Hawaii, the FL Keys, Bermuda, the Bahamas, and Cuba.

Carolina Saddlebags *Tramea carolina* **Plate 41**

IDENTIFICATION 2.0 in., eastern, common southward, migratory? northward. Basal 1/4 of each wing dark brown, thorax brown, and most of S8–S9 black. Females and juvenile males have abdomen and face brownish red, in males abdomen becomes bright red and face may become red. Forehead all metallic violet in males, basal half violet in females.

BODY FEATURES Male hamule usually projects little if any beyond genital lobe, compared to well beyond in Red Saddlebags. Female subgenital plate as long as S9, split for 1/2 length of side of S9, split for 3/4 length in Red Saddlebags.

SIMILAR SPECIES Red Saddlebags differs by some or all of the following: no violet on forehead, abdomen of mature male pale red, sides of S8–S9 pale, HW band covers basal 1/5 with a larger clear area next to the body and a clear streak parallel to the front edge of the wing, and HW band reaches to middle of anal loop instead of outer edge of loop.

HABITAT Ponds, lakes, swamps, and slow streams, including temporary ponds, but it avoids muddy water.

SEASON All year in FL, late May to late Aug. in Canada.

COMMENTS Feeds from dawn to dusk, often in swarms, at a height of about 2–8 yards. Shows some migratory movements. Perches on tips of stems, and may obelisk vertically on hot days. Males patrol large areas of water, hovering occasionally, mostly in the morning. It ranges into the FL Keys and Bermuda.

Red Saddlebags *Tramea onusta* Plate 41

IDENTIFICATION 1.8 in., common southwest, uncommon south FL, migrant through east. Like Carolina Saddlebags but has no violet on forehead, smaller HW band, S8–S9 pale-sided, and mature male has paler red abdomen. In Red Saddlebags, female HW band smaller than male's. Some males have a violet basal zone on forehead (hybrids with Carolina Saddlebags?).

SIMILAR SPECIES See Similar Species under Carolina Saddlebags.

HABITAT As for Carolina Saddlebags.

SEASON All year.

COMMENTS Males patrol territories about 10 × 30 yards, often flying faster and higher than Carolina Saddlebags. Migratory at least in Mexico, it ranges south to Venezuela, including Baja California, and in the FL Keys, Dry Tortugas, Bahamas, and West Indies.

Striped Saddlebags *Tramea calverti* Plate 41

IDENTIFICATION 1.9 in., south TX, stray northward, mostly along east coast. Our only Saddlebag Glider with a striped thorax. Thorax brown with 2 wide white to gray lateral stripes, HW has basal brown band edged with amber. Females and juvenile males have a yellow face and S1–S7 brown to rusty red, these areas becoming red in males. Posterior part of forehead violet, S8–S10 mostly black. Rarely, females have HW band reduced to a spot, or lack violet on forehead.

SIMILAR SPECIES Our only other gliding dragonfly with pale thoracic stripes is the Hyacinth Glider, which is much smaller and has a black dorsal abdominal stripe.

HABITAT Ponds and other quiet waters, including temporary and probably brackish ones.

SEASON All year. Strays seen mostly in autumn.

COMMENTS Formerly confused with *T. cophysa* of South America. Cruises steadily over wide areas while feeding at a height of about 6 ft. Males patrol loosely over water areas about 20 yards in diameter, or fly up and down shorelines. It ranges south to Argentina, including Baja California, and in the West Indies and Galápagos Islands.

Antillean Saddlebags *Tramea insularis* Plate 41

IDENTIFICATION 1.8 in., south TX and southernmost FL, uncommon in U.S. Thorax dark brown, HW with narrow brown basal band, which may be shortened to 2/3 width of wing in female. Abdomen red with S8–S9 black dorsally (sometimes S8–S10 all black). Face brown, becoming black in males. Forehead metallic violet posteriorly in females, all violet in males. Cerci very long, equal to S8–S10 in males, a little shorter in females. Females and juvenile males are not usually separable from those of Sooty or Vermilion Saddlebags.

BODY FEATURES Male hamule as long as genital lobe. Female subgenital plate nearly as long as S9, cleft or deeply U-notched for 3/5–2/3 its length, the lobes narrower toward tips and inflated, but not ridged.

SIMILAR SPECIES Female and juvenile male are identical to those of Sooty Saddlebags, but latter is a rare stray to U.S. Vermilion Saddlebags lacks violet on forehead, and mature males have a red face. Female Vermilions tend to have more red on S10 and a larger HW band. Garnet Glider is smaller, has only a small basal HW spot, and cerci shorter than S9 + S10.

HABITAT Ponds, lakes, and ditches.

SEASON All year.

COMMENTS Feeds with a rapid flight from low to about 15 ft. up over fields. Males patrol not far from shore, perching on tips of emergent plants. It ranges around the Caribbean area, including the FL Keys, Bahamas, Greater Antilles, and Campeche, Mexico.

Sooty Saddlebags *Tramea binotata* Plate 41

IDENTIFICATION 1.8 in., stray? to FL. Female and juvenile male identical to Antillean Saddlebags, but body of mature male becomes entirely black.

SIMILAR SPECIES Black Saddlebags has a wide basal HW band that is zigzag on the outer border; this band is much narrower and straight-edged in Sooty.

HABITAT As for Antillean Saddlebags.

SEASON All year.

COMMENTS No behavioral differences known from Antillean Saddlebags. Has been found in both FL Panhandle and Keys. Ranges south to Argentina, and in Greater Antilles.

Vermilion Saddlebags *Tramea abdominalis* Plate 41

IDENTIFICATION 1.9 in., fairly common southernmost FL, rare stray eastern U.S. Similar to Antillean Saddlebags, but lacks violet on forehead, and with a red face in mature males. Forehead brown, becoming red in males and yellow in females. Abdomen brown in juveniles, red at maturity, with a black dorsal stripe on S8–S10. Cerci longer than S9–S10, but shorter than S8–S10. Females are not normally separable from female Antillean or Sooty Saddlebags. Female HW band occasionally shortened to 2/3 width of wing.

BODY FEATURES   Male hamule almost 2X as tall as genital lobe. Female subgenital plate has lobes widest posteriorly, spatulalike; lobes parallel-sided or narrowed posteriorly in similar Saddlebags.

SIMILAR SPECIES   Antillean Saddlebags male has a violet forehead and black face. Garnet Glider is smaller, the male with a violet forehead, the female with cerci only a little longer than S10.

HABITAT   Ponds and stream pools.

SEASON   All year.

COMMENTS   Feeds in sustained flight about 6 ft. up, and often perches on topmost twigs of trees. Males in hot sun patrol leisurely with a hanging abdomen and no hovering, but near dusk fly fast and erratically, hovering occasionally. It ranges south to Argentina, and in the FL Keys, Bermuda, the Bahamas, West Indies, and has been accidentally introduced to Hawaii.

Hyacinth Gliders
(genus *Miathyria*)

The 2 species in this genus are associated with floating plants such as water hyacinths (*Eichornia*). Only 1 species has been found in North America, but the Lesser Hyacinth Glider (*M. simplex*) may turn up in FL or TX. It is small, with a rounded brown basal HW spot, and a bright red abdomen in males.

Hyacinth Glider *Miathyria marcella* **Plate 41**

IDENTIFICATION   Small-medium, 1.5 in. Southeastern, common coastally. Its size, gliding flight, and orange-brown abdomen make this species readily recognizable. Thorax brown with 2 oblique white lateral stripes. Wing veins orange-brown, and a brown band, wider in female, lies at base of HW. Face brown, and abdomen with a dorsal black stripe. In males the forehead is metallic violet, and the front and top of the thorax become pruinose hyacinth-violet.

SIMILAR SPECIES   Our only other gliding dragonfly with a striped thorax is the Striped Saddlebags, which is larger, with no black on the abdomen anterior to S8. Other somewhat similar dragonflies have a basal HW spot rather than band.

HABITAT   Quiet water with mats of water hyacinths or water lettuce (*Pistia*), among the hanging roots of which the larvae live. Adults are not attracted to duckweed or algae. It was first found in FL in 1934, after water hyacinth had been introduced from South America about 1890.

SEASON   All year.

COMMENTS Usually seen feeding leisurely about 6 ft. up over open ground in swarms containing both sexes. They seldom perch, but then obliquely on sides of stems. Migratory along TX coast. Males patrol territories about 10 yards long at edges of mats of floating plants, hovering often, sometimes curling the abdomen upward. Mating occurs in flight, then the pair in tandem makes a quick dash from a height of 3 to 6 ft. to place the eggs with a single tap near the base of floating plants. It ranges south to Argentina, and in the Greater Antilles.

Pasture Gliders
(genus *Tauriphila*)

Medium-size Gliders similar to Saddlebag Gliders, but smaller with shorter cerci, and the female subgenital plate is very short and U-notched. The female epiproct is notably large. While 2 species barely range into the U.S., 3 others are tropical American.

Garnet Glider *Tauriphila australis* Plate 42

IDENTIFICATION 1.7 in., south FL, rare in U.S. Face and body brown, with abdomen becoming bright red in males (sometimes with a row of small yellow dorsolateral spots on S3–S10). Abdomen has a full-length black dorsal line in females, a short stripe on S8–S9 in males. A small dark spot is placed at HW base, in females often merely an amber smudge. Males have a metallic violet or blue forehead, and the front of their thorax turns black. Cerci of both sexes much shorter than S9 + S10.

BODY FEATURES Male cerci nearly straight. A species found in Cuba, the Arch-Tipped Glider (*T. argo*), may turn up in FL. It lacks a black abdominal stripe, the male's face and thorax may be tinted red, and male cerci are arched in side view.

SIMILAR SPECIES Hyacinth Glider has pale lateral thoracic stripes, abdomen more orange-brown, and HW banded rather than spotted at base. Those Saddlebag Gliders with narrow HW bands are similar, but are larger, with more black on S8–S9, and cerci longer than S9 + S10. Spot-Winged Glider is larger, with a gray thorax and mottled abdomen. The female Red-Tailed Pennant is a percher with longer cerci.

HABITAT   Quiet water with mats of water hyacinth or water lettuce. First reported for FL in 1950.

SEASON   All year.

COMMENTS   Forages widely over open ground at a height of 6–10 ft. Males patrol territories over floating plants, hovering occasionally. It ranges south to Argentina, and in the Greater Antilles.

Aztec Glider *Tauriphila azteca* Plate 42

IDENTIFICATION   1.7 in., south TX, rare in U.S. Readily identified by combination of gliding flight and yellow-brown abdomen with diffuse dark bands at the joints. Also note black dorsal stripe on S8–S10, and dark brown basal spot in HW. Thorax and face brown, male with metallic-violet forehead.

SIMILAR SPECIES   Hyacinth Glider is smaller, with pale lateral thoracic stripes, and a full-length dorsal black abdominal stripe. Marl Pennant has a large round black basal HW spot, and more black on abdomen, at least a lateral black stripe.

HABITAT   Quiet waters with mats of floating plants such as water lettuce.

SEASON   Mid-April to late Aug.

COMMENTS   Perches obliquely on twigs. It ranges widely while feeding several yards above ground, and may be migratory. Males patrol territories over floating plants. It ranges south to Cuba and Costa Rica.

Marl Pennants
(genus *Macrodiplax*)

This genus includes 2 species, ours with black males in the Western Hemisphere, and 1 with red males (*M. cora*) in the Eastern Hemisphere.

Marl Pennant *Macrodiplax balteata* Plate 42

IDENTIFICATION   Medium, 1.6 in. Southern, common coastally, local southwest. HW has a large rounded black basal spot. Females and juvenile males have a white face, gray thorax marked laterally with an irregular brown W, S1–S7 dull yellow, and S8–S10 black. Males develop a black face and body. As S1–S7 darken, yellow spots are produced before the abdomen becomes all black.

SIMILAR SPECIES   Small Pennants of the east are much smaller and often have amber stripes through a dark HW spot. Pin-Tailed Pondhawk has a dark face in both sexes, and a very slender abdomen. Saddlebag Gliders have a basal HW band, not a spot. Spot-Winged Glider is larger, with basal HW spot placed posterior to junction with thorax. Widow Skimmer, and the Checkered Setwing of the southwest, have large dark markings at bases of both fore- and hind wings. Some female Black-Winged Dragonlets of the southwest have a basal HW spot, but have rounded brown wingtips (clear and pointed in Marl Pennant) and elongate abdomens.

HABITAT Ponds and lakes, usually brackish or mineralized. Often breeds in marl ponds, where calcium carbonate encrusts submerged vegetation such as stonewort algae (*Chara*).

SEASON All year.

COMMENTS Feeds from stem tips from near ground to the treetops. On hot days they obelisk by raising both wings and abdomen. Occasionally feeds in swarms with a sustained flight. The wary males usually perch far from shore on emergent stems, from where they fly extensive patrols with some hovering. Females deposit their green eggs in tandem. It ranges south to Argentina, including Baja California, and in the FL Keys, Dry Tortugas, Bahamas, Cayman Islands, and Greater Antilles.

Tropical Pennants
(genus *Brachymesia*)

These medium-size dragonflies perch on tips of stems or twigs, flaglike. All 3 species are found in the southern U.S. The Red-Tailed Pennant appears quite different from the other two slender black or brown species, but all have a plain dark thorax, the abdomen swollen at S2–S3, and a partial or complete black dorsal abdominal stripe.

Red-Tailed Pennant *Brachymesia furcata* Plate 42

IDENTIFICATION 1.7 in., southern southwest and southernmost FL, common. Females and juvenile males plain brown, with a narrow black dorsal stripe on S8–S9, and a small amber spot at HW base. Some individuals have a white dorsal stripe between the wings that extends onto the swollen base of the abdomen. In males face and abdomen become bright red, and some females also develop a red abdomen. Abdomen shorter and wider than in other Tropical Pennants, 1/5 shorter than a wing.

BODY FEATURES Male cerci curve upward to sharp, tapered tips and have a large ventral tooth at half length.

SIMILAR SPECIES Scarlet Skimmer of FL has a full-length dorsal black abdominal stripe. Female is yellower than female Red-Tailed Pennant, and has white shoulder stripes. Red Form male Roseate Skimmers are much larger and lack amber at wing bases. Female Roseates have white lateral thoracic stripes, and lateral flanges on S8. Flame and Neon Skimmers of the southwest are much larger and heavy-bodied, the males with at least basal 1/4 of HW amber. Mayan Setwing of TX has a longer abdomen, and basal 1/5 of HW orange.

HABITAT Ponds and lakes, including brackish ones.

SEASON All year.

COMMENTS Forages from tips of twigs. Males perch on emergent sticks, and establish territories about 15 yards long, hovering about every 3 yards when on patrol. It ranges to Argentina and Chile, including Baja California, and in the FL Keys, Bahamas, and Greater Antilles.

Four-Spotted Pennant *Brachymesia gravida*
Plate 42

IDENTIFICATION 2.0 in., mostly coastal from NM to NJ, common southward. Our only dragonfly with entirely white stigmas. Mature individuals easily identified by black slender body, large black spot between nodus and stigma of each wing, and white stigmas. Juveniles have white spots on sides of face, brown thorax, no wing spots, and a black zigzag dorsal stripe on orange-brown S4–S9. Inconspicuous narrow red bands cross S4–S7 (bands disappear in dry specimens). Females darken more slowly than males, and retain white facial spots. Abdomen as long as a wing, and slender beyond ventrally bulging S2–S3.

BODY FEATURES FW have 4 rows of cells beyond triangle, Tawny Pennant has 3 rows. These 2 species were formerly classified in the now unused genus *Cannacria.*

SIMILAR SPECIES Tawny Pennant has tan face and stigmas, and brown-yellow abdomen. Band-Winged Dragonlet either has bands across wings, or pale lateral spots on S4–S7.

HABITAT Ponds, lakes, and ditches, often with brackish or fertilized water.

SEASON All year.

COMMENTS Perches on tips of tall weeds, twigs in trees, and telephone wires. It often feeds in swarms early or late in the day, and ranges into the FL Keys and Dry Tortugas.

SKIMMERS

Tawny Pennant *Brachymesia herbida* Plate 42

IDENTIFICATION 1.9 in., south TX and south FL, resident? Resembles juvenile Four-Spotted Pennant, but face and stigmas tan, abdomen brownish yellow laterally, and wings tinted brown but without spots. Legs black.

SIMILAR SPECIES Juvenile Four-Spotted Pennant has a mostly black face, white stigmas, and orange-brown abdomen. Black-Winged Dragonlet females have brown wingtips, and abdomen neither notably swollen basally nor definitely striped. Band-Winged Dragonlet females have S4–S7 appearing spotted. Some female King Skimmers are similar, such as Comanche Skimmer, but are larger, with a wider abdomen bearing a straight-edged dorsal stripe, and thorax darker on front than sides. Rainpool Gliders have a tapering, rather than parallel-sided, abdomen. Scarlet Skimmer of FL has a straight-edged dorsal abdominal stripe, pale shoulder stripes, and pale legs.

HABITAT Ponds, lakes, marshes, ditches, and slow rivers, including brackish waters.

SEASON All year.

COMMENTS Probably breeding FL 1997. Forages from tips of stems, but may fly continuously while feeding. Males at water perch on stems, periodically patrolling about 10 yards of shore. It ranges to Argentina, and in the West Indies and Galpagos Islands.

Whitefaces
(genus *Leucorrhinia*)

Small, mostly black, northern dragonflies easily recognized as a group by the combination of white faces, small black basal wing spots, and black legs. However, some species and variations are confusingly alike, difficult or impossible to separate. Juveniles have yellow mottling on the hairy thorax, and in the majority of species, a series of yellow to red dorsal spots on S1–S7 or S8. Mating pairs perch for 3–20 min., usually on low vegetation near water. Males usually hover-guard egg-laying females, and in at least 3 species (Dot-Tailed, Frosted, Red-Waisted) males may "karate-guard" by holding rival males in tandem until their mates have laid eggs! Of the 17 species, 7 are North American and the others are Eurasian. Our species are transcontinental in Canada, except for the eastern Frosted Whiteface.

Dot-Tailed Whiteface *Leucorrhinia intacta* **Plate 43**

IDENTIFICATION 1.3 in., southern Canada and northern 2/3 of U.S., common. Mature male easily identified by all-black body, except for white face and yellow dorsal spot on S7. Female has dorsal yellow spots on S2–S7, the spots of S4–S6 extending nearly the full length of each segment, the spot of S7 wide and square. Abdomen darkens with age so that only dorsal spot of S7 remains bright, but only a few females darken as much as males. Lateral yellow stripes of S4–S5 persist longer than dorsal spots of S2–S6. About 1 in 6 females has a notable amber tint in basal 1/5 of wings, to beyond nodus late in season. Juveniles of both sexes cannot always be distinguished from Hudsonian Whiteface as described below.

BODY FEATURES Male epiproct forked with widely divergent sides. Female subgenital plate 2 parallel pegs 1/4 as long as S9, separated by a distance equal to their length. Hybrids with Crimson-Ringed Whiteface are known.

SIMILAR SPECIES Juveniles not separable from Hudsonian Whiteface unless Hudsonian shows: (1) red abdominal spots (rarely red in Dot-Tailed), (2) a pale dorsal spot on S8, or (3) dorsal spots of S4–S5 as wide as those of S6–S7. The female Hudsonian lacks amber in the wings. Juvenile female Dot-Tails can be told from female Red-Waisted and Crimson-Ringed Whitefaces when: (1) Dot-Tailed has a lateral yellow stripe on S4 rather than a lateral basal spot or no lateral spot, (2) dorsal spots of S4–S5 are 1/2 length and narrow in the others, or (3) abdominal spots are red in the others. The female Crimson-Ringed never has amber wing bases, but has a black chin (chin pale sided in female Dot-Tailed). Female Canada Whitefaces have only a narrow dorsal streak on S7. Boreal Whitefaces are larger, with a full-length red or yellow dorsal spot on S7, and males have a dorsal spot on S8.

HABITAT Marshy ponds, lakes, and slow streams. Commonly farm ponds with water lilies, but sometimes bog ponds.

SEASON Mid-April to early Sept., stragglers to mid-Oct.

COMMENTS Basks on the ground in sunny clearings, obelisking on twigs on hot days. Males perch on sparse low stems or floating vegetation, often in the middle of a pond. They maintain territories of 2–4 yards diameter, but the same male may be territorial or a wanderer on the same or different days.

Hudsonian Whiteface *Leucorrhinia hudsonica*
Plate 43

IDENTIFICATION 1.2 in., Canada and northern half of U.S., abundant northward. Abdomen has wide pale dorsal spots from 2/3 to nearly
as long as segments on S1–S6, a shorter spot on S7, and sometimes a spot on S8 (spots reduced or even absent on S4–S5 in
some western males). These spots yellow in juveniles, becoming red in males and **Red Form** females, paler yellow in **Yellow Form** females. Thorax turns red before abdomen. Chin
may be white laterally, or all black. Individuals with yellow
spots cannot always be separated from Dot-Tailed Whitefaces.
Black basal HW spot may include pale veins, this not noted in
other Whitefaces.

BODY FEATURES In ventral view, posterior branch of male hamule curves anteriorly, and sides of epiproct are slightly divergent. In male Boreal
Whiteface posterior branch of hamule is straight. Female subgenital plate of Hudsonian is rounded in outline, 1/3 as long as
S9, split by a hairline cleft down midline to base.

SIMILAR SPECIES For individuals with yellow markings, see Similar Species under
Dot-Tailed Whiteface. Boreal Whiteface is larger, with dorsal
abdominal spots forming a nearly continuous stripe, and male
always has a spot on S8. Canada Whiteface lacks a pale spot on
S7. Frosted Whiteface has no spot on S7 in males, only a streak
in females. Female Hudsonian, Crimson-Ringed, and Red-
Waisted Whitefaces are very similar, but Hudsonian may have a
pale lateral stripe on S4, or dorsal spots of S4–S5 may be only half
length in Crimson-Ringed and Red-Waisted. The female Red-
Waisted also may have amber wing bases.

HABITAT Boggy or marshy ponds, sloughs, and sand-bottomed lakes,
most common in bogs and fens.

SEASON Early May to mid-Oct., about 6 weeks at each locale. One of the
earliest dragonflies, emerging as pitcher plants (*Sarracenia pur-
purea*) begin flowering.

COMMENTS Perches with wings depressed on low vegetation or the ground.
Males defend territories of about a square yard, but may shift
locations during a day.

Boreal Whiteface *Leucorrhinia borealis* Plate 43

IDENTIFICATION 1.5 in., Alaska to near Hudson Bay, uncommon; local in Rocky
Mountains of U.S. Our largest Whiteface, and with the most red
or yellow on the abdomen. Juveniles have a nearly continuous

yellow dorsal stripe on S2–S7 in females, S2–S8 in males, which turns red at maturity in both sexes. Chin all black.

BODY FEATURES   Has 4–8 cells at ankle of anal loop, no more than 4 cells in our other Whitefaces. In ventral view male hamule has posterior branch straight and very hairy, and epiproct is parallel-sided. Female subgenital plate 30% as long as S9, split to its base by a narrow hourglass-shaped cleft.

SIMILAR SPECIES   Like Hudsonian Whiteface, but larger, with larger pale dorsal abdominal spots, and in males with spot of S8 always present.

HABITAT   Deep sedge marshes, mossy fens, bog ponds, and prairie ponds and lakes.

SEASON   Late May to early Aug., ending sooner than other Whitefaces.

COMMENTS   Behavior presumably like that of Hudsonian Whiteface.

Frosted Whiteface *Leucorrhinia frigida* Plate 43

IDENTIFICATION   1.2 in., northeastern, common. No red coloration. Thorax yellow with small black spots, rapidly becoming brown with age. Male abdomen black, becoming pruinose white on S2–S4. Female abdomen has yellow dorsal spots on S2–S6 and a streak on S7. Some become pruinose like male. Female wings tinted amber in basal 1/5. Chin black.

BODY FEATURES   Two rows of cells beyond FW triangle, usually 3 rows in Red-Waisted Whiteface. Male hamule in lateral view has anterior branch nearly straight, posterior branch prominent and curving anteriorly, without a posterior lateral angle. Male epiproct has convergent sides, twice as wide at base as tip. Female subgenital plate 1/2 as long as S9, narrowly V-split to base to form 2 long, pointed, triangular lobes.

SIMILAR SPECIES   Male very like male Red-Waisted Whiteface, but latter develops red markings at least between wing bases, has less dense or no pruinosity, is a little larger with a longer, more slender abdomen, and has more black mottling on thorax. Female separated from other Whitefaces by smaller size, streaklike pale spot on S7, and amber wing bases. Other female Whitefaces have spot of S7 either wide or absent, and only Dot-Tailed and Red-Waisted may have amber wing bases.

HABITAT   Boggy, sometimes marshy, ponds and lakes.

SEASON   Early May to early Sept.

COMMENTS   Forages from low plants along edges of wetlands. Males mature in 4 days, and defend territories of 1–2 square yards from perches on lily pads or twigs, usually in low dense vegetation and near shore.

Red-Waisted Whiteface *Leucorrhinia proxima*
Plate 43

IDENTIFICATION   1.4 in., Canada and northern U.S., common, except local southward. Thorax yellow mottled with black, becoming brown, then
red at maturity. In males, S4–S10 are black (hairline pale dorsal
streaks may be present). Mature males of the **Red Form**, red at
S1–S3, cannot usually be separated from male Crimson-Ringed
Whitefaces, although red of Red-Waisted is duller. Mature males
of the **White Form** are pruinose white on S1–S4 or up to S6,
and dark red between wing bases. Females have S4–S7 with pale
dorsal spots, the spots of S5–S6 narrow and 1/2–3/4 length of
each segment, but cannot usually be separated from female
Crimson-Ringed. Some females develop red markings, and
some become pruinose like White Form males. About 1 in 6
females has amber wing bases. Chin has white lateral spots, or
may be all black in males.

BODY FEATURES   In ventral view, male hamules lack a medial projection on posterior branch, in side view anterior branch curves smoothly posteriorly (straight to hooked tip in Crimson-Ringed Whiteface).
Male epiproct is parallel-sided and 2/3 as long as cerci. Female
subgenital plate very short, 1/6 length of S9, and widely V-
notched to form 2 rounded lobes. The female Crimson-Ringed
has chin all black, subgenital plate even more shallowly
notched, and 2 rows of cells in radial planate (usually 1 row in
Red-Waisted).

VARIATION   Males from Ontario eastward mostly White Form, only Red
Form males westward.

SIMILAR SPECIES   White Form males look like Frosted Whitefaces but are larger,
with more black mottling on thorax; longer, more slender
abdomens; and dull red between wing bases. Red Form males
are identical to Crimson-Ringed Whitefaces, but latter have
not been found in northern Canada and Alaska. Canada
Whiteface, not yet found in the U.S., is smaller with a slender
abdomen.

   Female Red-Waisted cannot be separated from Crimson-
Ringed Whitefaces except by amber wing bases if those are present, pruinosity, white chin spots, or range. A few female
Red-Waisted have a streaklike spot on S7 and thus look like
Frosted Whitefaces, but are larger with more black mottling on
thorax. Female Dot-Tailed and Hudsonian Whitefaces are separable if they have a pale lateral stripe on S4, and they usually

have longer, wider abdominal spots. Canada Whiteface females are smaller and lack a pale spot on S7, while female Boreal Whitefaces are larger with a wide dorsal stripe on S1–S7.

HABITAT   Marshy or boggy ponds and lakes up to 2200 ft. Also fen ponds.

SEASON   Mid-May to early Sept.

COMMENTS   Forages from weeds and bushes, mostly in small forest openings. Males defend territories of 1–2 square yards from perches near shore that are slightly higher and in less dense vegetation than those of the Frosted Whiteface.

Crimson-Ringed Whiteface *Leucorrhinia glacialis*
Plate 43

IDENTIFICATION   1.4 in., southern Canada/northern U.S., common. Males identical to Red Form of Red-Waisted Whiteface. Males have S1–S3 yellow, becoming bright red at maturity, and S4–S10 black. Juvenile females have yellow dorsal spots on S1–S7, narrow and 1/2–3/4 length on S5–S6. In **Yellow Form** females the yellow spots become paler, in **Red Form** females the spots turn red. Chin all black or nearly so.

BODY FEATURES   Male hamule in side view resembles the jaws of a turtle, the anterior branch straight to its hooked tip, the posterior branch curved to point ventrally. Male epiproct is parallel-sided and 1/2 as long as cerci. Female subgenital plate very short and hinged; when horizontal 1/5 as long as S9 and shallowly V-notched, when folded vertically it is seen as 2 small bumps separated by a shallow V-notch. Compare with Red-Waisted Whiteface.

SIMILAR SPECIES   Mature males cannot be told from male Red-Waisted Whitefaces, but from Ontario eastward the Red-Waisted is usually pruinose white on S1–S4. The female Red-Waisted has a white lateral spot on the chin, difficult to see, but some have amber wing bases. Also see Similar Species under Red-Waisted Whiteface.

HABITAT   Boggy, sometimes marshy, lakes and ponds.

SEASON   Early May to late Aug., emerging as pitcher plants begin flowering.

COMMENTS   Forages from the ground or shrubs in open areas, often in shade. Males at water and mating pairs perch on low plants, including water lily leaves where those exist.

Canada Whiteface *Leucorrhinia patricia*
(see Plate 43)

IDENTIFICATION   1.1 in., Canada (probable ME), uncommon. Our smallest and most slender Whiteface. Female and juvenile male have S1–S3 yellow, S4–S6 with dorsal yellow spots, and S7–S10 black, thus our only female Whiteface without a pale spot on S7. Abdomen of mature males red from S1 to S3 or S4, black beyond. Chin black.

BODY FEATURES Two rows of cells beyond FW triangle, usually 3 rows in Red-Waisted and Crimson-Ringed Whitefaces. Male hamule in side view has anterior branch smoothly curved posteriorly, and posterior branch barely visible but very slender and projecting anteriorly. Hamule lacks posterior lateral projection of Hudsonian Whiteface. Male cerci in lateral view have a toothlike ventral angle near the upturned tip, and male epiproct is parallel-sided. Female subgenital plate 1/4 as long as S9, widely U-notched to the base.

SIMILAR SPECIES Male Crimson-Ringed Whitefaces and Red Form Red-Waisted Whitefaces are larger with thicker abdomens. The female Canada differs from our other Whitefaces by her smaller size and lack of a pale spot on S7. Hudsonian Whiteface is a little larger and more robust, and has a pale dorsal spot on S7, sometimes also on S8.

HABITAT Bogs, fens, and lakes with either mats of floating moss, or shallow pools.

SEASON Mid-June to mid-Aug., but may be only 2 weeks at each locale.

COMMENTS Perches on tips of low twigs.

Small Pennants
(genus *Celithemis*)

All 8 species of this genus are eastern North American. They are mostly small with a delicate build and cling jauntily like miniature flags to tips of plant stems. They allow a breeze to raise the wings, the FW more so than the HW. In spite of their reduced thorax they are extraordinarily adroit dodgers. Face and body markings are yellow, changing to red or black in mature males, while S8–S10 and the legs are always black. Mating pairs perch on weeds or shrubs in or near water for 4–5 min., after which the pair lays eggs in tandem. The larvae seem to be poor competitors against other dragonflies, so Small Pennants are mostly found at newly created or infertile still-water habitats.

Halloween Pennant *Celithemis eponina* Plate 44

IDENTIFICATION   Medium, 1.5 in. Eastern and central, common. Our most but-
terfly-like dragonfly, this resplendent species is easily identified
by the halloween motif of its orange wings, spotted and banded
with black. Juveniles bear yellow body markings, including a
dorsal yellow stripe on S3–S7. In males the yellow becomes pale
red, including the face, wing veins, stigmas, and body markings.
Some females also develop faintly red markings.

SIMILAR SPECIES   Other dragonflies with a similar pattern of dark wing markings,
such as the Banded and Calico Pennants, and Painted Skimmer,
have at least parts of the wing transparent.

HABITAT   Ponds, borrow pits, lakes, and marshes.

SEASON   All year in FL, mid-June to mid-Aug. in Ontario.

COMMENTS   Forages from tips of tall weeds in open fields. It often perches
with FW vertical and HW horizontal, and on hot days may raise
the abdomen while the wings shade the thorax. Almost all
reproductive activity takes place from 8 to 10:30 A.M. It ranges
into the FL Keys, Dry Tortugas, Cuba, the Bahamas, and Nuevo
León, Mexico.

Banded Pennant *Celithemis fasciata* Plate 44

IDENTIFICATION   1.3 in., eastern, local. Readily identified by the sharply defined
black wing pattern, even though pattern is extremely variable. It
includes black wingtips, a spot between nodus and stigma, and a
partial or complete ring occupying the basal half. Body with yellow markings, including face, side of thorax, and dorsal spots on
S3–S7, becoming all black in males. In females the extreme
wingtips are often clear.

VARIATION   Maximum wing coloration consists of basal half of wing black,
and spots in outer half joined posteriorly into a wide U. Mini-
mum wing coloration consists of a black tip, the nodal spot separated into 2 small spots, and an anterior stripe and posterior spot
in basal half of wing. Individuals with near-minimal coloration,
generally found northward, have been called the *monomelaena*
form. Southern individuals usually have an amber area within a
complete basal ring in the HW.

SIMILAR SPECIES   Halloween Pennant has wings orange between dark wing markings. Calico Pennant has basal wing markings restricted to basal

1/4, and male has red abdominal spots. King Skimmers are much larger, with pale lateral abdominal stripes.

HABITAT Permanent ponds and lakes, especially clear-water borrow pits or sand-bottomed lakes.

SEASON Early April to late Oct. in FL, late May to early Sept. in NJ.

COMMENTS Usually feeds from tops of high shrubs or trees. Males are most active in the morning, when they perch on tips of emergent plants adjacent to open water.

Calico Pennant *Celithemis elisa* Plate 44

IDENTIFICATION 1.2 in., eastern, common. Readily recognized by wing pattern of brown markings, including wingtips, a round spot between nodus and stigma, and the basal 1/4 of the HW, which encloses an amber spot or stripe. Rarely, markings in outer halves of wings may be absent. Face, stigmas, and triangular dorsal spots on S2–S7 yellow, becoming bright red in males.

SIMILAR SPECIES Banded Pennant has black basal wing markings extending to nodus, small or absent abdominal spots, and no red markings. Spot-Winged Form of Red-Veined Pennant lacks brown spot *between* nodus and stigma. King Skimmers are much larger, with pale lateral abdominal stripes.

HABITAT Ponds, borrow pits, and lakes with emergent plants or marshy borders, including boggy ponds. Occasionally slow parts of streams or brackish marshes.

SEASON Mid-March to late Oct. in U.S., mid-June to late Aug. in Canada.

COMMENTS Forages from weed tips in open fields. Males active at water primarily in the morning. They are not territorial, and perch facing away from the water or in fields nearby to intercept incoming females.

Double-Ringed Pennant *Celithemis verna* Plate 44

IDENTIFICATION 1.3 in., southeastern to NJ, local. Only wing marking is a small black basal HW spot. Juveniles differ from other Small Pennants in that S5–S7 lack yellow dorsal spots (rarely a small spot on S5). Juvenile has yellow face, side of thorax, and a double ring on S3–S4. Face and body become smoky pruinose black in both sexes; it is the only Small Pennant that becomes pruinose. Thorax has 2 black or brown lateral stripes and blackens from anterior to posterior.

SIMILAR SPECIES Male Martha's Pennants of the northeast have a much larger basal HW spot, while male Seaside Dragonlets lack a basal HW spot. Other similar black dragonflies are much larger, and either lack a HW spot or have a large spot.

HABITAT Ponds, borrow pits, lakes, and occasionally ditches and streams, with scattered emergent plants or a marginal zone of grassy plants, including bogs with emergent sedges.

SEASON Early April to mid-Aug., most common in spring.

COMMENTS Forages in open fields. Males perch on tips of emergent plants, usually along forested shores but closest to open water, and patrol areas about 20 ft. in diameter, hovering occasionally. They are less wary and have smaller territories than male Faded Pennants.

Martha's Pennant *Celithemis martha* **Plate 45**

IDENTIFICATION 1.2 in., northeast coast, common. Mature males easily identified by all-black body and large black HW spot. Females and juvenile males have basal 1/5 of HW with an amber spot containing 3 black stripes, and yellow face, side of thorax, and dorsal spots on S1–S7. Side of thorax may have a black anterior spot and posterior stripe, and sides of S3–S4 are mostly black. In males yellow markings become red, then black, including face and HW spot.

BODY FEATURES FW have 2 rows of cells beyond triangles, and an incomplete cross-vein at basal side of nodus; Faded Pennant has 3 rows and a complete cross-vein.

SIMILAR SPECIES Double-Ringed Pennant has only a small HW spot. The male Marl Pennant and Black Saddlebags are notably larger. Considering females and juvenile males, the Faded Pennant is very similar, but has 2 black lateral thoracic stripes that are connected dorsally, a smaller HW spot, and narrower dorsal abdominal spots. Amanda's Pennant has 2 dark anterior spots and a posterior stripe within the amber basal HW spot, and the sides of at least S3–S4 are each at least half yellow or red. The female Marl Pennant is larger, with S4–S7 mostly yellow. Band-Winged Meadowhawk lacks dark markings in basal HW spot.

HABITAT Boggy, marsh-bordered ponds, borrow pits, and lakes.

SEASON Early May to late Sept.

COMMENTS Named for Mattie Wadsworth, amateur American entomologist. Males perch on tips of emergent vegetation near open water or fly sustained patrols, mostly from 10 A.M. to 12 noon.

Red-Veined Pennant *Celithemis bertha* **Plate 45**

IDENTIFICATION 1.2 in., southeastern, common FL. Juvenile marked with yellow, including side of thorax, dorsal spots on S1–S7, side of S3, and a lateral stripe on S4 (plus S5 in some females). In males all markings turn bright red, along with veins in the basal 1/4 and near the front of each wing. In females the abdominal markings turn orange, then red, first dorsally, then laterally. Side of thorax has square black anterior spot and posterior stripe, generally not joined. HW has an amber to black basal spot, usually very small. Midfrontal black thoracic stripe triangular in males, rectangular in similar Small Pennants.

BODY FEATURES   Normally 2 rows of cells for a short distance beyond FW triangle, 1 row for a short distance beyond HW triangle. Faded Pennant usually has 3 rows and 2 rows, respectively.

VARIATION   South FL males may have a large basal HW spot, amber with 2 dark stripes, covering 1/5 of wing. A distinctive **Spot-Winged Form**, variety *leonora*, occurs from LA to NC. It has round brown spots near the wingtips, varying from a dot in one wing to a large spot in all four wings.

SIMILAR SPECIES   Mature males can be told from similar Small Pennants by their red wing veins and extensively bright red face and body. Faded Pennant has lateral thoracic black stripes connected dorsally, side of S4 mostly black, HW spot usually bigger, and females without red markings. Mature male Faded Pennants have a brown face, dull red abdominal spots, a longer abdomen, and dark wing veins. Martha's and Amanda's Pennants have HW spots covering basal 1/5–1/4 of wing, and side of thorax nearly unmarked. The female Seaside Dragonlet has thorax either black or with many black lines. Meadowhawks that might occur in the southeast have pale spots on S8–S10 and no black lateral thoracic stripes. See also Similar Species under Faded Pennant.

HABITAT   Lakes, borrow pits, and ponds, especially sand-bottomed ones with a fringe of sparse emergent grass. Sometimes spring-fed rivers.

SEASON   Early April to late Dec.

COMMENTS   Forages from tips of plants from weeds to trees. Males and mating pairs perch on tips of emergent plants nearest open water.

Faded Pennant *Celithemis ornata* **Plate 45**

IDENTIFICATION   1.3 in., coastal, TX to NJ, common. Females and juvenile males marked with yellow, including face, sides of thorax, and dorsal spots on S1–S7. Side of thorax has 2 black stripes connected dorsally, S3 has a black lateral stripe, S4 is mostly black laterally. Basal HW spot variable, usually an amber spot containing 3 black stripes and covering 1/5 of wing (spot may be small, anterior stripe may be absent, or spot may be nearly all brown). In mature males face and thorax become brown, the abdominal spots dull red.

SIMILAR SPECIES Amanda's Pennant has a different HW spot, 1/4 of wing and amber with 2 dark anterior spots and a single posterior stripe or spot. Amanda's also has a paler thorax, S3 and basal half of S4 pale, and males are brighter red with a shorter abdomen. Female Martha's Pennants have side of thorax nearly unmarked, and slightly larger HW and abdominal spots. Red-Veined Pennants have lateral thoracic stripes normally separate, a pale lateral stripe on S4, and usually small HW spots. Male Red-Veined is brighter red, and has red veins along front of wings and a shorter abdomen.

HABITAT Ponds, lakes, ditches, and slow streams with emergent grass.

SEASON All year.

COMMENTS Forages from tips of weeds in sparsely vegetated open places. Males perch on tips of emergent plants near open water in marshy situations, not necessarily at the outermost edge of weed beds.

Amanda's Pennant *Celithemis amanda* Plate 45

IDENTIFICATION 1.1 in., southeastern, mostly coastal, common FL. HW has large amber spot covering basal 1/4, containing 2 anterior dark spots and 1 posterior spot. Females and juvenile males have face, thorax, and dorsal spots on S1–S7 yellow. Side of thorax nearly unmarked, with at most a dark anterior spot and narrow posterior stripe. S3 mostly pale, basal half of S4 pale. In mature males face becomes brown to red, thorax becomes brown, and abdominal spots change to pale red.

BODY FEATURES HW base has many extra cross-veins, with 11-plus cells within anal loop on basal side of midrib, seldom as many as 11 in similar Small Pennants. FW has 2 rows of cells beyond triangle.

SIMILAR SPECIES Faded Pennant has smaller HW spots containing 2 or 3 dark stripes, and a black lateral stripe on S3. The male Faded has a brown face, dull red abdominal spots, and a longer abdomen. Female Martha's Pennant has 2 or 3 dark stripes within HW spot, and sides of S3–S4 mostly black. Also see Similar Species under Faded Pennant.

HABITAT · Ponds, borrow pits, and lakes, edged by sparse emergent plants. Sometimes semitemporary ponds, brackish water, or even rivers.

SEASON · Early April to late Nov.

COMMENTS · Amanda's last name, for whom this species was named, is not known. No behavioral differences known from Faded Pennant.

Setwings
(genus *Dythemis*)

Slender, medium-size southern dragonflies that typically perch alertly in a sprinter's "get-set" stance, with abdomen raised and wings lowered. Male abdomen slightly clubbed. North America has 4 species, only 1 east of AR, while 3 more are tropical American.

Mayan Setwing *Dythemis maya* Plate 46

IDENTIFICATION · 1.8 in., TX Big Bend, local. Very distinctive, slender-bodied with basal 1/5 of wings orange. Juveniles brown, becoming bright red on abdomen, then thorax, in males. Males develop a brown tint within the orange wing band, females may have dark wingtips.

SIMILAR SPECIES · Flame and Neon Skimmers have a similar color pattern but are much larger and heavy-bodied. Red Rock Skimmer has abdomen mottled with black. Band-Winged Meadowhawk is much smaller and has a black lateral stripe on abdomen.

HABITAT · Streams in arid country, usually in narrow canyons, cottonwood grove oases in the U.S.

SEASON · Early July to early Dec. in Mexico.

COMMENTS · Perches in hot weather on shaded tree twigs from 1 to 10 ft. up, the males over stream pools. While male Flame Skimmers will share a pool with a male Mayan, male Neon Skimmers apparently will not. The Mayan ranges south to Honduras.

Checkered Setwing *Dythemis fugax* Plate 46

IDENTIFICATION · 1.8 in., south-central, common. Readily identified by combination of brown lacy basal 1/5 of wings, and white-green dorsolateral spots on S3–S7. Thorax pale green with a brown lateral *III* pattern (sometimes *HII*). In mature males face becomes bright red, while thorax becomes brown beginning on front. Females have a green face, and large lateral pale spots on abdomen in addition to dorsolateral spots. Females also have brown wingtips, and occasionally brown nodal spots.

SIMILAR SPECIES None of our other dragonflies with brown wing bases also has the abdomen checkered with pale green spots. Marl Pennant has base of FW clear.

HABITAT Streams, rivers, lakes, and ponds.

SEASON Late April to early Dec.

COMMENTS Forages from stems 2–6 ft. up in fields, on hot days obelisking nearly vertically. The jumpy males perch on tips of waterside stems, sometimes flying lengthy patrols over open water. Males have incredibly fast parallel contest flights, during which they appear only as a dark blur, that last at least 3 min. It ranges south into Tamaulipas, Mexico.

Swift Setwing *Dythemis velox* **Plate 46**

IDENTIFICATION 1.6 in., southern, common TX. The only Setwing in the south-east, recognized there by its slender form, brown wingtips, and usual perching posture of wings down, abdomen up. Side of thorax white to pale green with a *YIY* pattern of dark stripes. Abdomen has pale green dorsolateral spots on S3–S7, most conspicuous on S7, often lacking on S5–S6 in males. Forehead brown in males, dull green in females. In males the body may darken with age, especially in the east.

BODY FEATURES Outer row of spines on middle thigh of males long; spines short and sawtoothlike in male Black Setwing. HW has 3–4 rows of cells between anal loop and rear margin in Swift Setwing, 4–5 rows in Black Setwing.

SIMILAR SPECIES Black Setwing has a metallic-violet forehead in males, while females have lateral pale streaks on S4–S7, and an *HII* or *HIY* thoracic pattern. Female and juvenile male Blue Dashers have an *III* thoracic pattern, and thicker abdomens with yellow streaks. Clubskimmers are larger with unbranched thoracic stripes, no brown wingtips, and they hang from perches. Tropical Dashers of the far south are smaller, with an *III, IYI,* or *WII* thoracic pattern. Mature males develop metallic-green eyes and gray pruinosity between wing bases. Ivory-Striped and Jade-Striped Sylphs are much smaller, the males with green frontal thoracic spots and widely clubbed abdomens. Some King Skimmers have brown wingtips but are larger and stouter, without thoracic stripes but with abdominal stripes.

Two similar Setwings may turn up along the Mexican border. The Blue-Browed Setwing (*D. multipunctata*) has a metallic-blue forehead and develops metallic-green eyes, while the Brown Setwing (*D. sterilis*) has a tan forehead and long streaklike dull yellow spots on its very slender abdomen.

HABITAT   Rivers, streams, ponds, and lakes. Currently extending its range northward.

SEASON   Late March to early Nov.

COMMENTS   Feeds from twigs along forest edges, and males perch on twigs near the water's edge, sometimes high and in shade, on hot days obelisking vertically. Male parallel flights are like those of Checkered Setwing. It ranges south to Durango and Veracruz, Mexico.

Black Setwing *Dythemis nigrescens* Plate 46

IDENTIFICATION   1.8 in., southwestern, common south TX. Females and juvenile males have face and thorax dull greenish yellow, the thorax with a *HII* or *HIY* pattern of brown lateral stripes. Abdomen has pale dorsolateral streaks on S3–S7, and females also have lateral streaks on those segments. Males have a metallic-violet forehead and become entirely pruinose black at maturity. Wingtips possess a touch of brown.

SIMILAR SPECIES   Swift Setwing has a nonmetallic forehead, *YIY* thoracic pattern, no pale lateral streaks on S4–S7, and more brown in wingtips. Male Slaty Skimmer is larger, with a black forehead and tapered abdomen. Marl Pennant is stouter bodied and has a large black basal HW spot. Also see Similar Species under Swift Setwing.

HABITAT   Rivers, streams, lakes, and ponds.

SEASON   Late April to mid-Sept., all year in Mexico.

COMMENTS   Forages from twigs in open forest, often in shade, and males perch on twigs at the water's edge. At large open-water habitats, males make long patrols. It ranges south to Baja California and Oaxaca, Mexico.

Clubskimmers
(genus *Brechmorhoga*)

Body brown or black striped with pale green, the males with clubbed abdomens. They breed in flowing water, where patrolling males look remarkably like Clubtails. However, Clubskimmers hang from perches, never perching horizontally like most Clubtails, and Clubtails have separated eyes. Our 2 species are western, while 12 others are tropical American.

Pale-Faced Clubskimmer *Brechmorhoga mendax*
Plate 46

IDENTIFICATION   Medium-large, 2.2 in. Common southwest, local to SD. Face and forehead pale green (sometimes fuzzy dark area present on forehead). Side of thorax brown with 3 pale green stripes. Abdomen slender, widely clubbed at S7–S9 in male, black with interrupted dorsolateral pale green stripes enlarged to cover most of S7. Sides of S2–S3 mostly green, S8 usually with a small pale basal spot. Some females have tips of FW, and rarely tips of HW, tinted orange-brown.

BODY FEATURES   Male hamule hooked like a question mark or ?-shaped in side view, with a flattened blunt tip twisted to face dorsolaterally.

SIMILAR SPECIES   Masked Clubskimmer of AZ has a sharply defined black forehead, S2–S3 mostly black laterally, and stripes of S7 each about 1/4 as wide as the segment. Clubtails have separated eyes. Setwings are smaller, perch horizontally, and most have dark faces and wingtips. Tropical Dashers are much smaller, perch horizontally, and males are pruinose gray between wing bases.

HABITAT   Clear streams and rivers.

SEASON   Early April to early Nov.

COMMENTS   Feeds with a sustained flight, often in restricted areas, from ground level to treetops. It often flies and perches in shade, sometimes hanging up well back under overhanging branches. When cool they may bask on rocks. Males fly short to long beats low over rippling water with the abdomen raised 30°. It ranges south to Baja California and Morelos, Mexico.

Masked Clubskimmer *Brechmorhoga pertinax*
Plate 46

IDENTIFICATION 2.1 in., southeastern AZ, local. Like Pale-Faced Clubskimmer, but forehead sharply defined metallic black, sides of S2–S3 mostly black, and dorsolateral stripes of S7 narrow, each about 1/4 width of the segment. S8 lacks pale spots. Females may have tips of FW orange-brown.

BODY FEATURES Male hamules nearly straight in side view, the tips bent rearward and cupped dorsally.

SIMILAR SPECIES See Similar Species under Pale-Faced Clubskimmer.

HABITAT Clear streams and rivers.

SEASON Known late June in AZ, but season probably similar to that of Pale-Faced Clubskimmer. Probably all year in tropics, primarily in rainy season.

COMMENTS Males patrol 2–8 yards of stream edge containing egg-laying sites of barely submerged patches of sand or fine gravel. They patrol from about 8 A.M. to 3:30 P.M., for an average of 15 minutes at a time. It ranges south to Bolivia.

Narrow-Winged Skimmers
(genus *Cannaphila*)

The HW of these dragonflies is not much wider than the FW. Accordingly the foot of the anal loop in the HW is reduced or absent, causing the loop to be sac-shaped as in the Emeralds. Only 1 species enters our area, while 2 others are tropical American.

Narrow-Winged Skimmer *Cannaphila insularis*
Plate 47

IDENTIFICATION Medium, 1.6 in. South TX, rare in U.S. HW narrowed in basal half is distinctive among North American Skimmers. Juveniles have a black thorax with 2 or 3 lateral yellow stripes. Abdomen rusty brown to black with narrow lateral and dorsal yellow stripes on S1–S8, in female with wide black lateral flaps on S8. In mature males and some females body becomes black, with base of abdomen gray pruinose. Face white, forehead rusty brown in females, metallic green or blue in males. Eyes red-brown, becoming dark metallic green. Wingtips sometimes brown; occasionally females have wings almost entirely deep brown. Subspecies found in our area is *C. i. funerea*, which has chin nearly all yellow, without a large black central spot.

SIMILAR SPECIES   Mature male Black Setwings and Slaty Skimmers have black faces. Blue Dasher juveniles have *dorsolateral* interrupted abdominal stripes, and females lack flanges on S8. Roseate Skimmer females are larger, with brown faces, a network of thoracic stripes, and S9–S10 brown (black in Narrow-Winged Skimmer).

HABITAT   Marshy pools, sloughs, and streams, including temporary ones.

SEASON   All year.

COMMENTS   Forages from tips of vegetation from low to 10 ft. up, sometimes in shade. Males perch on tips of waterside vegetation. Females lay eggs among dense vegetation. It ranges south to Panama, and in Cuba, Hispaniola, and Jamaica.

Metallic Pennants
(genus *Idiataphe*)

Metallic black or brown Skimmers that resemble Emeralds, but which perch horizontally on stem tips and do not develop green eyes. Only 1 species enters our area, but 3 others are tropical American.

Metallic Pennant *Idiataphe cubensis* Plate 47

IDENTIFICATION   Small, 1.4 in. South FL, common. Slender, metallic black, with face, side of thorax, and lateral abdominal stripes bronzy brown. Lateral abdominal stripes extend from S1 to S5 in males, to S9 in females. HW has small dark amber spot at base. Eyes red-brown.

SIMILAR SPECIES   Seaside Dragonlet male is smaller and entirely black. Tawny Pennant and female Four-Spotted Pennant are larger, with mostly brown abdomens. Pin-Tailed Pondhawk has abdomen very slender beyond a swollen base. Baskettails have yellow lateral abdominal stripes, a paler and hairier thorax, and dark brown basal HW spots.

HABITAT   Fresh or brackish ponds and lakes.

SEASON   All year.

COMMENTS   Forages from tall weeds to treetop twigs, and sometimes flies high in feeding swarms. Males perch with elevated wings on tips of emergent grasses well out from shore, from where they make extensive low and erratic patrols with occasional hovering. Females deposit their green eggs while in tandem. It ranges from Mexico to Costa Rica, and in the FL Keys, Bahamas, Greater Antilles, and Cayman Islands.

Sylphs
(genus *Macrothemis*)

Slender dragonflies that breed in flowing water, differing from our other Skimmers in having forked claws (except Jade-Striped Sylph). Our 3 species are southwestern, while at least 35 others are tropical American.

Straw-Colored Sylph *Macrothemis inacuta* **Plate 47**

IDENTIFICATION   Medium, 1.7 in. Mexican border, scarce in U.S. Yellowish-brown very slender abdomen is distinctive. Thorax bears pale green markings, including 2 inverted L's on front, an interrupted anterior lateral stripe, and 3 posterior lateral spots. Eyes red-brown, becoming blue-violet to whitish aqua in males. Females often have amber tips on FW and an amber basal HW spot. Forehead silver-gray, in males metallic blue dorsally.

SIMILAR SPECIES   Species with similar coloration have thicker abdomens, and some have brown or black basal HW spots.

HABITAT   Streams and rivers.

SEASON   All year.

COMMENTS   Feeds during high sustained flights, and sometimes perches on rocks. Males patrol edges of flowing water. It ranges south to Brazil.

Ivory-Striped Sylph *Macrothemis imitans* **Plate 47**

IDENTIFICATION   Small, 1.4 in. Central TX, scarce in U.S. Thorax black with a distinctive lateral pattern, a whitish-green anterior stripe, and 2 or 3 posterior lateral spots. Males have 2 prominent "headlight" spots on front of thorax, but in females these are small or absent. Abdomen has interrupted pale stripes, with a broad flat club at

females. Eyes red-brown, becoming aqua-blue in males. Wings
often tinted yellow. Subspecies in our area is *M. i. leucozona.*

SIMILAR SPECIES   Jade-Striped Sylph has side of thorax pale green with black
stripes, and front of thorax striped.

HABITAT   Clear and rocky streams and rivers.

SEASON   All year in tropics, probably summer in TX.

COMMENTS   Feeds during sustained flights. Males fly back and forth for a few
yards low over shallow flowing water near the bank. It ranges
south to Argentina.

Jade-Striped Sylph *Macrothemis inequiunguis*
Plate 47

IDENTIFICATION   Small, 1.4 in. Central TX, rare in U.S. Side of thorax pale green
with black stripes in an *IY* or *YY* pattern; front of thorax with a
pair of green stripes that are enlarged dorsally. Abdomen black
with pale green dorsolateral streaks on S1–S5, and a pair of
round to oval spots on S7. Male abdomen clubbed. Forehead
metallic blue and eyes green in both sexes. Some females have
amber wing bases, brown wingtips, or both.

SIMILAR SPECIES   Ivory-Striped Sylph has spots on front of thorax in male, and
essentially lacks frontal markings in female. Three-Striped Dash-
er perches horizontally on twig tips. Clubskimmers are much
larger, with straight lateral thoracic stripes. Blue Dasher has
abdomen not clubbed in males, short in females. Other similar
Skimmers have more dark lateral thoracic stripes in a different
pattern.

HABITAT   Streams, sometimes rivers.

SEASON   All year in tropics, probably summer in TX.

COMMENTS   Feeds in sustained flights, usually in groups of mostly females. It
sometimes perches flat on sunny leaves. Males patrol low over
the middle of a stream. It ranges south to Argentina, including
Baja California.

Tropical Dashers
(genus *Micrathyria*)

Mostly small and black with pale green markings, including a striped thorax and spotted abdomen. S10 is very short, so that the large pale spot on S7 superficially seems to be on S8. Our 3 species are far southern, while at least 40 others are tropical American.

Thornbush Dasher *Micrathyria hagenii* Plate 47

IDENTIFICATION 1.4 in., fairly common south TX, strays? to AR. Thorax pale green with brown *IYI* pattern on side. Male abdomen decorated with dorsolateral pale green spots on S1–S7, the spots of S7 square. In juveniles pale markings are white; in females abdomen can be either mostly black or mostly rusty brown. Face white, eyes red-brown becoming bright green in both sexes. In males area between wing bases, and sometimes S1–S3, become pruinose white-gray.

SIMILAR SPECIES Blue Dashers have a *III* lateral thoracic pattern, and streaks instead of spots on S7. Three-Striped Dasher has an *III* lateral thoracic pattern. Spot-Tailed Dasher is smaller, with a *WII* pattern on side of thorax until it becomes pruinose gray in males, and triangular spots on S7. The female Seaside Dragonlet has a projecting ovipositor, and either an all-black thorax or more black stripes on side. Checkered and Black Setwings are larger, with black wingtips, and a *YIY, HII*, or *HIY* lateral thoracic pattern. Their eyes do not become green, and males have dark faces and do not become pruinose. Pale-Faced Clubskimmer is much larger, with abdomen conspicuously clubbed in males.

HABITAT Ponds, lakes, and canals, including temporary and saline ones.

SEASON Early May to mid-Nov. in TX, all year in Mexico.

COMMENTS Away from water perches on twigs of bushes, often with wings down, abdomen up. Males at water may perch on shore vegetation but within sight of the surface. They are present mostly from 6:30 A.M. to 4:30 P.M., in the morning flying continuously to generate body heat. Females lay eggs before 8 A.M., using two unusual methods. Some hover a foot over the water, extruding clumps of eggs that are released by an upward flick of the abdomen; others drag the tip of the abdomen while they crawl over barely submerged vegetation. It ranges south to Costa Rica, including Baja California, and in the Greater Antilles.

Three-Striped Dasher *Microthyria didyma* Plate 47

IDENTIFICATION 1.4 in., southernmost TX and southernmost FL, scarce in U.S. Thorax pale green with a black *III* pattern on side, and becoming pruinose blue between wing bases. Abdomen black with pale green dorsolateral spots or streaks on S2–S7, the spot of S7 largest and trapezoidal. Face white, eyes red-brown becoming metallic blue-green in males and dark metallic red in females. Forehead metallic green in males, brown in females. Some females have brown wingtips. Pale markings in juveniles yellow.

BODY FEATURES Male hamule unlike that of any other North American dragonfly, in side view with a long club-shaped branch that slants anteriorly.

SIMILAR SPECIES Blue Dasher has streaks instead of trapezoids on S7, and abdomen either has a pale spot on S8 or is pruinose blue. Thornbush Dasher has an *IYI* lateral thoracic pattern. Spot-Tailed Dasher is smaller, with triangular spots on S7, and a *WII* pattern on side of thorax until it becomes pruinose gray in males. The female Seaside Dragonlet has a projecting ovipositor, and thorax is either all black or has more than 3 black lateral stripes. Checkered and Black Setwings are larger, with black wingtips, and a *YIY, HII,* or *HIY* lateral thoracic pattern. Their eyes do not become green, and males have dark faces and do not become pruinose. Pale-Faced Clubskimmer is much larger, with male abdomen conspicuously clubbed.

HABITAT Shady ponds, sloughs, and canals, including saline ones. First found in FL in 1985.

SEASON All year.

COMMENTS Usually perches inconspicuously with lowered wings in the shade, when feeding often on tips of twigs high in trees. It ranges south to Ecuador, including Baja California, and in the Bahamas and West Indies.

Spot-Tailed Dasher *Microthyria aequalis* Plate 47

IDENTIFICATION 1.2 in., south TX and southernmost FL, fairly common. Females and juvenile males have a dull yellow-green thorax with an irregular brown *WII* pattern on the side. Abdomen brown with wide interrupted dorsolateral stripes on S1–S7 or S8. Face white, eyes pale gray. Males develop bright green eyes, and become pruinose gray on thorax and S1–S5, leaving whitish-green triangular spots on S7. Males darken and become pruinose simultaneously, from dorsal to ventral on thorax, and from base toward tip of abdomen. Females may become dusty gray with age, and some have brown wingtips.

BODY FEATURES Male anterior lamina unlike that of any other North American dragonfly, expanded laterally into rounded, shiny brown "Mickey Mouse" earlike flaps that can be mistaken for hamules.

SIMILAR SPECIES Other Tropical Dashers are larger, have an *IYI* or *III* lateral thoracic pattern, and males do not become pruinose on side of thorax. Blue Dasher has an *III* lateral thoracic pattern, and yellower abdominal streaks rather than spots. Checkered and Black Setwings are larger, with black wingtips, and a *YIY, HII,* or *HIY* lateral thoracic pattern. They also have red-brown eyes, and males have dark faces and do not become pruinose. Pale-Faced Clubskimmer is much larger, with male abdomen conspicuously clubbed. The female Seaside Dragonlet has a projecting ovipositor.

HABITAT Lakes, ponds, and sloughs, including temporary ones.

SEASON All year.

COMMENTS Forages from twigs of bushes or trees, sometimes in shade. Males at water perch on stems. The female perches on a floating leaf, curling her abdomen to lay a patch of eggs on its underside. It ranges south to Ecuador, including Baja California, and in the Greater Antilles, Martinique, and Grenada.

ABOUT THE PLATES

Mature males are shown unless otherwise specified.

Available general data are given for each photograph, with dates given as month/day/year. Where it is known that the individual photographed was posed by the photographer, that fact is stated.

Only basic identification can be given on the facing page; please also consult the species accounts. The phrase "As above" refers to the same sex of the immediately preceding species.

RANGE MAP COLORS

SPRING OR EARLY FLIGHT SEASON

SUMMER, LONG, OR ALL-YEAR SEASON

FALL OR LATE SEASON, OR A STRAY

1 Gray Petaltail *Tachopteryx thoreyi.* **p. 31**
1975 Alachua Co., FL, posed   3 in.
Large size, mostly gray, usually perches on tree trunks.
Separated eyes and long narrow stigma.

2 Black Petaltail *Tanypteryx hageni.* **p. 32**
7/7/77 Nevada Co., CA   2.3 in.
Black spotted with yellow.
Separated eyes and long narrow stigma.
Seepage bogs.

3 Common Green Darner *Anax junius.* **p. 33**
1974 Alachua Co., FL, posed   3 in.
Thorax all green, bull's-eye on forehead.
Male abdomen striped blue laterally, including S2.
Female abdomen usually striped pale green.

4 Giant Darner *Anax walsinghami.* **p. 34**
Male. 7/27/97 Brewster Co., TX   4.3 in.
As above but much larger and abdomen spotted laterally.
Abdomen longer than a wing and carried arched in flight.

5 Female. 7/27/97 Brewster Co., TX, posed   3.7 in.
Abdomen thicker and shorter than male, marked green or
tan, and carried straight.

6 Comet Darner *Anax longipes.* **p. 34**
Male. 1977 Alachua Co., FL, posed   3.2 in.
Thorax green, abdomen red.
Forehead and eyes all green.

7 Female. 1975 Alachua Co., FL, posed   3.2 in.
Abdomen spotted pale blue or orange, and eyes blue.

8 Amazon Darner *Anax amazili.* **p. 35**
Female. 7/11/76 Mazatlán, Sinaloa, Mexico, posed   2.8 in.
Stray, TX to FL.
Broken bull's-eye on forehead.
Like Common Green Darner but abdomen looks ringed in
side view.
Male similar but abdomen blotched green laterally, including
S2.

PLATE 1

1 Gray Petaltail

2 Black Petaltail

3 Common Green Darner

4 Giant Darner ♂

5 Giant Darner ♀

6 Comet Darner ♂

7 Comet Darner ♀

8 Amazon Darner ♀

1 Regal Darner *Coryphaeschna ingens*. **p. 36**
Male. 3/26/75 Alachua Co., FL, posed   3.6 in.
Very large size, green eyes.
Thorax green with wide brown stripes.
Abdomen black with narrow green rings.

2 Juvenile female. 5/17/75 Alachua Co., FL, posed   3.6 in.
Streaming cerci.

3 Mature female. Alachua Co., FL, posed   3.1 in.
Eyes become blue and cerci break off.

4 Mangrove Darner *Coryphaeschna viriditas*. **p. 36**
12/13/87 San Isidro, Cortes Dept., Honduras, posed   3.4 in.
As above but thorax nearly all green.
Face green in both sexes.

5 Blue-Faced Darner *Coryphaeschna adnexa*. **p. 36**
12/13/87 San Isidro, Cortes Dept., Honduras, posed   2.7 in.
As above but smaller, and male face blue.

6 Malachite Darner *Coryphaeschna luteipennis*. **p. 37**
8/6/97 Pima Co., AZ, posed   3.2 in.
Thorax has wide brown stripes.
Abdomen has dorsal green triangles.
Female cerci always short.

7 Phantom Darner *Triacanthagyna trifida*. **p. 37**
10/5/75 Clay Co., FL, posed   2.6 in.
Like Regal Darner but much smaller.
Abdomen spotted, and narrowed at S3.
Mature males have blue eyes, blue between wings and on
   S2–S3.

8 Swamp Darner *Epiaeschna heros*. **p. 38**
Female. 5 April Alachua Co., FL, posed   3.4 in.
Like Regal Darner, but thorax brown with green stripes.
Eyes blue in both sexes.
Female cerci leaflike, do not break off.

PLATE 2

1 Regal Darner ♂

2 Regal Darner ♀

3 Regal Darner ♀

4 Mangrove Darner

5 Blue-Faced Darner

6 Malachite Darner

7 Phantom Darner

8 Swamp Darner ♀

1 Cyrano Darner *Nasiaeschna pentacantha.* **p. 39**
1974 Alachua Co., FL, posed   2.7 in.
Thorax brown with green stripes.
Abdomen striped with blue-green.
Projecting blue forehead.
Male has tapered abdomen and patrols with raised wings.

2 Harlequin Darner *Gomphaeschna furcillata.* **p. 40**
Male. 4/14/74 Rapides Par., LA, posed   2.2 in.
Small Darner with green mottled thorax.
Abdomen cylindrical with green spots on S2–S9.
Bright green eyes.

3 Female. 1/22/74 Clay Co., FL, posed   2.2 in.
White lateral spots on middle abdominal segments, rusty
    orange dorsal spots on S2–S6.
Orange tint in outer half of FW.

4 Taper-Tailed Darner *Gomphaeschna antilope.* **p. 41**
Male. 4/8/74 Perry Co., MS, posed   2.2 in.
As above but abdomen tapered with obscure posterior spots.
Eyes with only a green sheen.

5 Female in egg-laying position.
3/29/76 Leon Co., FL, posed   2.2 in.
As above but abdomen has rusty orange lateral spots on mid-
    dle segments, and orange dorsal spots only on S2–S3.
FW often has orange cloud at nodus.

6 Twilight Darner *Gynacantha nervosa.* **p. 41**
1974 Alachua Co., FL, posed   3 in.
Large size, wide brown-tinted wings.
Plain brown and dull green.

7 Bar-Sided Darner *Gynacantha mexicana.* **p. 42**
Juvenile male. 10/25/98 Hidalgo Co., TX   2.8 in.
As above but has wide dark lower rear thoracic stripe.
Abdomen narrowed at S3 with blue markings on S1–S3.
Brown costal wing stripes often present.

8 Ocellated Darner *Boyeria grafiana.* **p. 43**
1981 NC, posed   2.6 in.
Gray-brown with 2 lateral yellow thoracic spots.
Female eyes partly blue.

9 Fawn Darner *Boyeria vinosa.* **p. 43**
Female. 1974 Alachua Co., FL, posed   2.6 in.
As above but browner, more slender, abdominal spots dot-
    like.
Brown spot at base of each wing.
Female eyes green.

PLATE 3

1 Cyrano Darner

2 Harlequin Darner ♂

3 Harlequin Darner ♀

4 Taper-Tailed Darner ♂

5 Taper-Tailed Darner ♀

6 Twilight Darner

7 Bar-Sided Darner

8 Ocellated Darner

9 Fawn Darner ♀

1 Springtime Darner *Basiaeschna janata*. **p. 44**
1981 FL, posed   2.4 in.
Lateral thoracic stripes straight and yellow to white.
Brown spot at base of each wing.

2 Shadow Darner *Aeshna umbrosa*. **p. 45**
Eastern Form. 10/16/96 Johnson Co., IN, posed   2.9 in.
Lateral thoracic stripes yellowish, straight, and narrow.
Abdominal spots small and green, often lacking on S10.
No face stripe and lower rear of head brown.
Male cerci of wedge-type.

3 Western Form. 9/10/77 Fresno Co., CA, posed   2.9 in.
Abdominal spots larger and blue.

4 Lance-Tipped Darner *Aeshna constricta*. **p. 47**
Male. 1983, posed   2.8 in.
Anterior lateral thoracic stripe yellow-green below, slightly
    notched on front and rear borders.
Posterior lateral thoracic stripe expanded dorsally.
No face stripe and S1 without vertical pale streak.
Spots of S9 separate, and cerci of wedge-type.

5 Green Form female. 1991.   2.8 in.
Abdomen long, slender, and constricted at S3.
S9 longer than S8, pale spots of S10 vestigial.

6 Paddle-Tailed Darner *Aeshna palmata*. **p. 48**
1977 CA, posed   2.8 in.
Male as above but has larger abdominal spots, usually has
    black upper face line, S1 with vertical pale streak, spots of
    S9 fused.
Female abdomen normal for genus.

7 Walker's Darner *Aeshna walkeri*. **p. 49**
1978 CA, posed   2.7 in.
As above but thoracic stripes white below, S1 and S10 dark.
Posterior spots of each abdominal segment fused, midlateral
    spots of S7 vestigial, those of S8 lacking.

8 Persephone's Darner *Aeshna persephone*. **p. 49**
10/23/76 Chiricahua Mountains, Cochise Co., AZ, posed   3 in.
Like Paddle-Tailed Darner but lateral thoracic stripes wide
    and all yellow.
S4–S9 with only posterior spots well developed.

PLATE 4

1 Springtime Darner   2 Shadow Darner   3 Shadow Darner

4 Lance-Tipped Darner ♂   5 Lance-Tipped Darner ♀

6 Paddle-Tailed Darner   7 Walker's Darner   8 Persephone's Darner

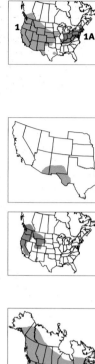

1 Blue-Eyed Darner *Aeshna multicolor*. **p. 50**
8/5/97 Pima Co., AZ, posed   2.7 in.
Male has sky-blue eyes and forked cerci.
Lateral thoracic stripes whitish blue.

1A Spatterdock Darner (not shown) is identical to above, but
eastern with an early season.   2.8 in.
Green Form female has bright blue eyes.

2 Arroyo Darner *Aeshna dugesi*. **p. 51**
6/8/94 Pima Co., AZ, posed   2.8 in.
As above but anterior lateral thoracic stripe has dorsal posterior extension, and male cerci are not forked.

3 California Darner *Aeshna californica*. **p. 52**
5/2/82 Placer Co., CA, posed   2.5 in.
Smallest and earliest western Mosaic Darner, has pale blue
spots.
Anterior lateral thoracic stripe pointed at upper end.
Upper black face line present, frontal thoracic spots small.

4 Variable Darner *Aeshna interrupta*. **p. 52**
Pair in Wheel, male Striped Form and female Spotted Yellow
Form.
8/26/83 BC   2.9 in.
Four lateral thoracic spots of Spotted Form diagnostic.
Striped Form has narrow straight lateral thoracic stripes.
Black upper face line present, short or absent frontal stripes.

5 Black-Tipped Darner *Aeshna tuberculifera*. **p. 53**
Male. 9/95 Barnstable Co., MA, posed   3 in.
Lateral thoracic stripes broad and straight.
S10 black, no face line.

6 Female laying eggs. 8/24/86 Centre Co., PA   3 in.
Like Lance-Tipped Darner (Plate 4) but posterior lateral tho-
racic stripe not widened dorsally, and S9 not longer than
S8.

7 Sedge Darner *Aeshna juncea*. **p. 54**
8/5/83 AB, posed   2.7 in.
Anterior lateral thoracic stripe wide, straight, tapered above,
and greenish yellow below.
Black upper face line present.

8 Subarctic Darner *Aeshna subarctica*. **p. 55**
8/5/83 AB, posed   2.8 in.
As above but both lateral thoracic stripes bent forward in
upper halves.
Two narrow yellow spots between lateral thoracic stripes.

PLATE 5

1 Blue-Eyed Darner

2 Arroyo Darner

3 California Darner

4 Variable Darner

5 Black-Tipped Darner ♂

6 Black-Tipped Darner ♀

7 Sedge Darner

8 Subarctic Darner

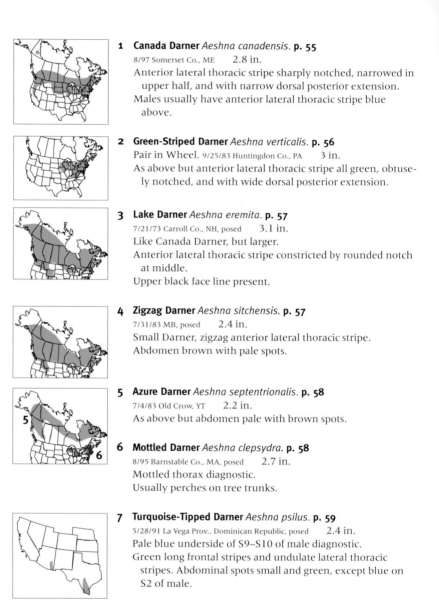

1 Canada Darner *Aeshna canadensis*. **p. 55**
8/97 Somerset Co., ME   2.8 in.
Anterior lateral thoracic stripe sharply notched, narrowed in upper half, and with narrow dorsal posterior extension.
Males usually have anterior lateral thoracic stripe blue above.

2 Green-Striped Darner *Aeshna verticalis*. **p. 56**
Pair in Wheel. 9/25/83 Huntingdon Co., PA   3 in.
As above but anterior lateral thoracic stripe all green, obtusely notched, and with wide dorsal posterior extension.

3 Lake Darner *Aeshna eremita*. **p. 57**
7/21/73 Carroll Co., NH, posed   3.1 in.
Like Canada Darner, but larger.
Anterior lateral thoracic stripe constricted by rounded notch at middle.
Upper black face line present.

4 Zigzag Darner *Aeshna sitchensis*. **p. 57**
7/31/83 MB, posed   2.4 in.
Small Darner, zigzag anterior lateral thoracic stripe.
Abdomen brown with pale spots.

5 Azure Darner *Aeshna septentrionalis*. **p. 58**
7/4/83 Old Crow, YT   2.2 in.
As above but abdomen pale with brown spots.

6 Mottled Darner *Aeshna clepsydra*. **p. 58**
8/95 Barnstable Co., MA, posed   2.7 in.
Mottled thorax diagnostic.
Usually perches on tree trunks.

7 Turquoise-Tipped Darner *Aeshna psilus*. **p. 59**
5/28/91 La Vega Prov., Dominican Republic, posed   2.4 in.
Pale blue underside of S9–S10 of male diagnostic.
Green long frontal stripes and undulate lateral thoracic stripes. Abdominal spots small and green, except blue on S2 of male.

8 Riffle Darner *Oplonaeschna armata*. **p. 59**
7/18/77 Coconino Co., AZ, posed   2.6 in.
Upper 1/3 anterior lateral thoracic stripe nearly separated, and abdominal spots small.
Male cerci of wedge-type.
Female abdomen short and stout, cerci break off.

9 Dragonhunter *Hagenius brevistylus*. **p. 61**
Male eating a female Shadow Darner. 1991.   3.3 in.
Darner size, with separated green eyes and long legs.
Male flies with abdomen bent in downward J-shape.

PLATE 6

1 Canada Darner

2 Green-Striped Darner

3 Lake Darner

4 Zigzag Darner

5 Azure Darner

6 Mottled Darner

7 Turquoise-Tipped Darner

8 Riffle Darner

9 Dragonhunter

1 Pacific Clubtail *Gomphus kurilis*. **p. 63**
6/4/77 Stanislaus Co., CA, posed   2.1 in.
Thorax gray-green, without an anterior black lateral stripe, and legs all black.

2 Pronghorn Clubtail *Gomphus graslinellus*. **p. 63**
5/21/96 Bandera Co., TX, posed   2 in.
S7 mostly black laterally, and S9 all yellow dorsally.
Both black lateral thoracic stripes present, complete.
Shins pale; hind thigh black in male, streaked green in female.
Compare with Plains Clubtail (Plate 11).

2A Tennessee Clubtail (not shown) is identical to above but has isolated range in south-central TN.   2 in.

3 Sulphur-Tipped Clubtail *Gomphus militaris*. **p. 65**
5/22/96 Kerr Co., TX   2 in.
As above but yellower, with definite pale shoulder stripe.
S7–S9 deep yellow, with S7 pale laterally, and dorsal and lateral yellow of S9 only narrowly separated.
Thighs mostly pale in both sexes.

4 Clearlake Clubtail *Gomphus australis*. **p. 66**
4/5/75 Putnam Co., FL, posed   2.1 in.
Slender club with S9 longer than either S7 or S8, black.
Early spring on sand-bottomed southeastern lakes.

5 Diminutive Clubtail *Gomphus diminutus*. **p. 66**
4/22/89 Chesterfield Co., SC   1.7 in.
As above but much smaller, with S9 longer than S8 but shorter than S7.
Shins pale, area between lateral thoracic stripes darkened.

5A Westfall's Clubtail (not shown) is nearly identical to above but has isolated FL Panhandle range.   1.7 in.

6 Rapids Clubtail *Gomphus quadricolor*. **p. 67**
Male. 6/16/84 Lauderdale Co., AL   1.7 in.
Small-medium size and bright coloration.
S9 black dorsally, and legs all black.

7 Female. 6/19/76 Lincoln Co., WI, posed   1.7 in.
Side of S7 not striped, and S9 as long as S8.

8 Harpoon Clubtail *Gomphus descriptus*. **p. 68**
6/26/96 North Bay, ON, posed   2 in.
S8–S9 slender and all black dorsally, and eyes green.
Legs all black, except streaked hind thigh of female.

9 Beaverpond Clubtail *Gomphus borealis*. **p. 68**
6/28/96 Charlotte Co., NB, posed   1.9 in.
As above but midfrontal dark stripe narrow, legs all black in both sexes, and eyes gray-blue.

PLATE 7

1 Pacific Clubtail

2 Pronghorn Clubtail

3 Sulphur-Tipped Clubtail

4 Clearlake Clubtail

5 Diminutive Clubtail

6 Rapids Clubtail ♂

7 Rapids Clubtail ♀

8 Harpoon Clubtail

9 Beaverpond Clubtail

1 Ashy Clubtail *Gomphus lividus*. **p. 69**
5/3/97 Morris Co., TX   2 in.
Dully colored, thorax brown with 2 pale lateral stripes.
Male epiproct as wide as cerci.

2 Dusky Clubtail *Gomphus spicatus*. **p. 70**
1996 MI Upper Peninsula   2 in.
As above except usually blacker.
Male epiproct spreads wider than cerci.

3 Lancet Clubtail *Gomphus exilis*. **p. 70**
7/97 Medina Co., OH   1.7 in.
Lateral dark thoracic stripes fused, and lower rear dark thoracic stripe present.
Abdomen has full-length dorsal yellow stripe.

4 Oklahoma Clubtail *Gomphus oklahomensis*. **p. 71**
5/3/97 Morris Co., TX   1.9 in.
As above but with a more southwestern range, and male has
lateral teeth on cerci.

5 Hodges' Clubtail *Gomphus hodgesi*. **p. 72**
4/5/94 Santa Rosa Co., FL, posed   1.7 in.
S8–S9 slender with narrow yellow dorsal streaks, with S10
of male dorsally black.
Legs striped green.

6 Cypress Clubtail *Gomphus minutus*. **p. 72**
1975 Alachua Co., FL, posed   1.8 in.
Like Lancet Clubtail but lateral thoracic stripes not fused, no
lower rear dark thoracic stripe.

7 Sandhill Clubtail *Gomphus cavillaris* **p. 73**
Black Form. 4/14/94 Liberty Co., FL   1.7 in.
As above but with a dark facial cross-line, lateral teeth on
male cerci, on sand-bottomed lakes.

8 Brown Form. 1975 Putnam Co., FL, posed   1.7 in.
FL Peninsula only.

PLATE 8

1 Ashy Clubtail

2 Dusky Clubtail

3 Lancet Clubtail

4 Oklahoma Clubtail

5 Hodges' Clubtail

6 Cypress Clubtail

7 Sandhill Clubtail

8 Sandhill Clubtail

1 Mustached Clubtail *Gomphus adelphus*. **p. 74**
1996 WI, posed   1.7 in.
Small chunky Clubtail, abdomen nearly all black.
Thorax gray-green with 1 or 2 black lateral stripes.
Face with more than 1 black stripe.

2 Green-Faced Clubtail *Gomphus viridifrons*. **p. 75**
6/1/85 New River, Grayson Co., VA, posed   1.8 in.
As above but larger lateral abdominal spots, no complete lateral thoracic stripes (except in AL), and no face stripes.

3 Twin-Striped Clubtail *Gomphus geminatus*. **p. 75**
1981 FL Panhandle, posed   1.6 in.
Small chunky Clubtail with bright yellow sides on club.
Thorax has 2 black lateral stripes, and face has 1 black stripe.

4 Piedmont Clubtail *Gomphus parvidens*. **p. 76**
6/19/84 Caldwell Co., NC   1.7 in.
As above in AL and GA, but northward the anterior lateral black thoracic stripe is incomplete and face is unstriped.

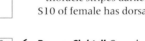

5 Spine-Crowned Clubtail *Gomphus abbreviatus*. **p. 77**
5/14/83 Chatham Co., NC, posed   1.5 in.
Like Carolina individuals of above, but area between lateral thoracic stripes darkened.
S10 of female has dorsal yellow spot.

6 Banner Clubtail *Gomphus apomyius*. **p. 77**
5/15/82 Moore Co., NC, posed   1.5 in.
Like Carolina individuals of Piedmont Clubtail but male club wider.
Lateral thoracic stripes complete and area between them darkened.
Face brownish green.

7 Cherokee Clubtail *Gomphus consanguis*. **p. 78**
6/13/94 Washington Co., VA, posed   1.9 in.
Abdominal club slender with S8–S10 black dorsally.
Thorax has 2 black lateral stripes.
Face has 1 black stripe, and legs are all black.
Male thorax gray-green, female thorax yellow-green.

8 Sable Clubtail *Gomphus rogersi*. **p. 79**
7/11/94 Huntingdon Co., PA, posed   2 in.
As above but anterior lateral thoracic stripe incomplete, and face has 2 black stripes.
Black **dorsal** surface of occiput diagnostic.

PLATE 9

1 Mustached Clubtail

2 Green-Faced Clubtail

3 Twin-Striped Clubtail

4 Piedmont Clubtail

5 Spine-Crowned Clubtail

6 Banner Clubtail

7 Cherokee Clubtail

8 Sable Clubtail

1 Skillet Clubtail *Gomphus ventricosus*. **p. 80**
1996 WI, posed   1.9 in.
Club wider than thorax and striped yellow on sides.
S8–S10 black dorsally.
Side of thorax lacks stripes.

2 Cobra Clubtail *Gomphus vastus*. **p. 81**
Black Form, obelisking. 6/22/88 Union Co., NC   2.1 in.
Wide club with yellow lateral spot of S8 not touching edge of
    segment, and smaller than on S9.
Face has wide black stripes, and thorax has 2 usually com-
    plete lateral black stripes.

3 Brown Form. 7/26/77 Gonzales Co., TX, posed   2.1 in.
Face stripes may be absent, pale basal ring on S7 may be pre-
    sent, mostly TX range.

4 Blackwater Clubtail *Gomphus dilatatus*. **p. 82**
1974 FL, posed   2.7 in.
Like Black Form of above, but lateral spots of S8–S9 small,
    and neither is in contact with edges of segments.

5 Gulf Coast Clubtail *Gomphus modestus*. **p. 82**
6/17/92 Benton Co., MS, posed   2.4 in.
As above but lateral yellow spots of S8–S9 both prominent.
One narrow black face line.

6 Splendid Clubtail *Gomphus lineatifrons*. **p. 83**
6/12/83 Lauderdale Co., AL, posed   2.6 in.
As above, but club narrower with vertical sides.
Midfrontal dark stripe usually parallel-sided.

7 Midland Clubtail *Gomphus fraternus*. **p. 84**
Dark Form. 6/23/83 Green Co., KY, posed   2.2 in.
Eyes green, anterior lateral black thoracic stripe incomplete,
    posterior lateral stripe variable.
S8–S9 have large yellow lateral spots, S9 black dorsally in
    most of range.
Legs black except female hind thigh usually has pale lateral
    stripe.
Pale Form of upper midwest may have yellow dorsal spot on
    S9 and yellow shins.

8 Handsome Clubtail *Gomphus crassus*. **p. 84**
1983 TN, posed   2.2 in.
As above but eyes blue, S9 usually has yellow dorsal spot,
    and female hind thigh usually black.

PLATE 10

1 Skillet Clubtail

2 Cobra Clubtail

3 Cobra Clubtail

4 Blackwater Clubtail

5 Gulf Coast Clubtail

6 Splendid Clubtail

7 Midland Clubtail

8 Handsome Clubtail

1 Septima's Clubtail *Gomphus septima*. **p. 85**
5/10/82 Chatham Co., NC, posed   2.3 in.
Lateral brown thoracic stripes nearly absent.
Wide brown shoulder stripes fused dorsally.
Club small, with small lateral pale spots on S8–S9, and
    S8–S10 brown dorsally.

2 Ozark Clubtail *Gomphus ozarkensis*. **p. 86**
Male. 6/12/96 McCurtain Co., OK   2 in.
Shoulder and lateral thoracic stripes each nearly fused with
    neighbor.
S8–S9 have large yellow lateral spots, S9–S10 dorsally black
    or with narrow yellow stripes.

3 Female. 6/12/96, McCurtain Co., OK   2 in.

4 Plains Clubtail *Gomphus externus*. **p. 86**
Male. 4/19/97 Love Co., OK, posed   2.1 in.
Abdomen has dorsal yellow spots or stripes on all segments.
Dark lateral thoracic stripes complete, with dark area
    between them.
Shins yellow, thighs black in males, often yellow dorsally in
    females.
In west TX/NM, looks like Tamaulipan Clubtail, and compare
    with Pronghorn Clubtail (Plate 7).

5 Female. 1974 NM, posed   2.1 in.

6 Tamaulipan Clubtail *Gomphus gonzalezi*. **p. 87**
1997 Starr Co., TX   1.9 in.
As above but paler, brown marked with pale yellow.
Lower rear thoracic brown stripe present.
Yellow bands on S8–S9, all-brown lower legs.

7 Columbia Clubtail *Gomphus lynnae*. **p. 87**
1971 Benton Co., WA   2.3 in.
Dark lower rear thoracic stripe.
Thorax and S1–S2 become pruinose gray.
Shoulder and lateral thoracic stripes each nearly fused with
    its neighbor.

8 Cocoa Clubtail *Gomphus hybridus*. **p. 88**
1981 AL, posed   2 in.
Dully colored like Septima's Clubtail, but lateral thoracic
    stripes well developed and area between them darkened.
Lateral pale spot of S8 nearly isolated from edge of S8, and
    S9 brown dorsally.

PLATE 11

1 Septima's Clubtail

2 Ozark Clubtail ♂

3 Ozark Clubtail ♀

4 Plains Clubtail ♂

6 Tamaulipan Clubtail

5 Plains Clubtail ♀

8 Cocoa Clubtail

7 Columbia Clubtail

1 Zebra Clubtail *Stylurus scudderi.* **p. 89**
1994 WI, posed   2.3 in.
Alternating black and pale green or yellow markings.

2 Arrow Clubtail *Stylurus spiniceps.* **p. 89**
7/28/94 Richland Co., WI, posed   2.5 in.
S9 longer than S8.
Wide black lateral thoracic stripes.

3 Olive Clubtail *Stylurus olivaceus.* **p. 90**
7/5/77 Stanislaus Co., CA, posed   2.2 in.
Thorax gray-green, with wide shoulder stripes, but no lateral
   stripes.

4 Brimstone Clubtail *Stylurus intricatus.* **p. 90**
7/17/98 Cherry Co., NE, posed   1.9 in.
Mostly yellow-green, with front of thorax and abdomen
   more pale than dark.
S3–S7 have pale basal rings.

5 Russet-Tipped Clubtail *Stylurus plagiatus.* **p. 91**
Eastern Form. 1974 FL, posed   2.4 in.
Gray-green thorax, rusty orange club, green eyes.

6 Western Form. 9/3/83 Yavapai Co., AZ, posed   2.4 in.
S8–S9 brown or black with yellow spots or bands, blue eyes.

7 Shining Clubtail *Stylurus ivae.* **p. 92**
10/12/74 Columbia Co., FL, posed   2.2 in.
Thorax mostly dark on front, with yellow-green sides.
Club mostly pale orange, on sand-bottomed streams and
   rivers.

8 Yellow-Sided Clubtail *Stylurus potulentus.* **p. 92**
6/24/74 Calhoun Co., FL, posed   2 in.
Slender and mostly black, with sides of thorax and club yellow.
Face brown and eyes blue, on sand-bottomed streams.

PLATE 12

1 Zebra Clubtail

2 Arrow Clubtail

3 Olive Clubtail

4 Brimstone Clubtail

5 Russet-Tipped Clubtail

6 Russet-Tipped Clubtail

7 Shining Clubtail

8 Yellow-Sided Clubtail

1 Laura's Clubtail *Stylurus laurae.* **p. 93**
8/7/76 Gadsden Co., FL, posed   2.3 in.
Area between lateral thoracic stripes darkened.
Side of S2 pale, and S9–S10 usually red-brown dorsally.
Eyes green, face dark brown.
Male thoracic markings green, those of female yellow.

2 Riverine Clubtail *Stylurus amnicola.* **p. 93**
6/21/82 Houston Co., GA, posed   2.1 in.
Front of thorax has 3-pointed star and wide nearly parallel
    pale stripes, and eyes are green.
Male club wide with large lateral yellow spots on S8–S9.
Female yellower with black lateral edge on S8.

3 Townes' Clubtail *Stylurus townesi.* **p. 94**
7/27/74 Okaloosa Co., FL, posed   2 in.
As above but frontal stripes narrow and strongly divergent.
S8 of female has yellow lateral edge, on sand-bottomed
    streams.

4 Elusive Clubtail *Stylurus notatus.* **p. 95**
7/28/94 Richland Co., WI, posed   2.4 in.
Two complete black lateral thoracic stripes, blue eyes.
Male has legs and upper face black.
Almost never seen perched.

5 Black-Shouldered Spinyleg *Dromogomphus spinosus.* **p. 95**
Male. 5/23/96 Bandera Co., TX   2.5 in.
Wide black shoulder bands on pale green thorax.
Black lateral thoracic stripes usually absent, long black legs.
Club small with small pale lateral spots.

6 Juvenile female. 1974 FL, posed   2.5 in.
Shiny yellow markings in juveniles.
Club nearly absent in females.

7 Southeastern Spinyleg *Dromogomphus armatus.* **p. 96**
10/11/74 Alachua Co., FL, posed   2.6 in.
Eyes green, legs long, S4–S6 striped.
Male club slender, compressed vertically, and rusty orange.
Female club nearly absent, marked pale green to rusty
    brown.

8 Flag-Tailed Spinyleg *Dromogomphus spoliatus.* **p. 97**
8/19/97 Travis Co., TX   2.3 in.
Eyes blue-gray, legs long, S4–S6 with pale basal rings.
Male club vertically flattened, pale yellow to rusty orange on
    sides.
Female club slender and yellowish to rusty brown.

PLATE 13

1 Laura's Clubtail

2 Riverine Clubtail

3 Townes' Clubtail

4 Elusive Clubtail

5 Black-Shouldered Spinyleg ♂

6 Black-Shouldered Spinyleg ♀

7 Southeastern Spinyleg

8 Flag-Tailed Spinyleg

1 Lilypad Clubtail *Arigomphus furcifer*. **p. 98**
Male. 7/13/83 Oscoda Co., MI, posed   2 in.
S8–S9 black dorsally with rusty brown lower edges.
Eyes blue, legs all black.
Male abdomen widest at S8.

2 Juvenile female. 1996 MI, posed   2 in.
S10 narrow and occiput level with eyes.

3 Horned Clubtail *Arigomphus cornutus*. **p. 98**
6/25/96 Chippewa Co., MI, posed   2.2 in.
As above but male abdomen widest at S10.
Female has S10 normal and occiput extending above eyes.

4 Unicorn Clubtail *Arigomphus villosipes*. **p. 99**
7/97 Lorain Co., OH   2 in.
Like Lilypad Clubtail, but S8–S9 almost entirely black, and
eyes green.

5 Stillwater Clubtail *Arigomphus lentulus*. **p. 99**
6/1/81 Franklin Co., AR, posed   2.1 in.
Thorax grayish yellow-green, with 2 equally wide shoulder
stripes.
S7 and S9 brown, paler than S8.
Eyes gray-blue.
Male has S3–S6 ringed.

6 Jade Clubtail *Arigomphus submedianus*. **p. 100**
5/10/98 Bastrop Co., TX   2.1 in.
As above but eyes green, thorax grayish green, and anterior
shoulder stripe wider than posterior.
Abdomen has gray-green rings, and S7–S9 are rusty brown.

7 Bayou Clubtail *Arigomphus maxwelli*. **p. 100**
5/22/81 Sharkley Co., MS, posed   1.9 in.
As above but thorax more extensively striped, and S7–S9
dark brown.
Thorax contrasts with yellow-green abdominal rings.

8 Gray-Green Clubtail *Arigomphus pallidus*. **p. 101**
1974 FL, posed   2.3 in.
Thorax gray-green and practically unmarked.

PLATE 14

1 Lilypad Clubtail ♂

2 Lilypad Clubtail ♀

3 Horned Clubtail

4 Unicorn Clubtail

5 Stillwater Clubtail

6 Jade Clubtail

7 Bayou Clubtail

8 Gray-Green Clubtail

1 Least Clubtail *Stylogomphus albistylus*. **p. 101**
1983 TN, posed   1.5 in.
Very small size, white cerci.
Abdomen usually has narrow pale rings.

2 Northern Pygmy Clubtail *Lanthus parvulus*. **p. 102**
6/17/88 Huntingdon Co., PA   1.5 in.
Very small size, black cerci.
Abdomen nearly all black.
Two black lateral thoracic stripes.

3 Southern Pygmy Clubtail *Lanthus vernalis*. **p. 102**
1986 PA, posed   1.4 in.
As above but only one black lateral thoracic stripe.

4 Grappletail *Octogomphus specularis*. **p. 103**
6/27/76 Marin Co., CA   2 in.
Thorax has wide black shoulder stripes but no other stripes.
Abdomen nearly uniform black, widest at S10 in male.

5 Gray Sanddragon *Progomphus borealis*. **p. 104**
6/13/94 Cochise Co., AZ   2.3 in.
Side of thorax gray with one brown stripe.
Small brown spot at each wing base, on sand-bottomed
    streams.

6 Common Sanddragon *Progomphus obscurus*. **p. 104**
Alachua Co., FL   2 in.
Thorax has two lateral brown stripes.
Brown spot at each wing base.
Pale spots of S8–S9 small or lacking.

7 Belle's Sanddragon *Progomphus bellei*. **p. 105**
6/5/83 Calhoun Co., FL, posed   2.3 in.
As above but S8 with 2 squared yellow lateral spots.

8 Tawny Sanddragon *Progomphus alachuensis*. **p. 105**
7/5/74 Alachua Co., FL, posed   2.2 in.
FL Peninsula, usually at sand-bottomed lakes.
As above but S8–S9 mottled yellow laterally.
Female dorsal abdominal markings orange.

PLATE 15

1 Least Clubtail

2 Northern Pygmy Clubtail

3 Southern Pygmy Clubtail

4 Grappletail

5 Gray Sanddragon

6 Common Sanddragon

7 Belle's Sanddragon

8 Tawny Sanddragon

1 Boreal Snaketail *Ophiogomphus colubrinus.* **p. 106**
1983 MI, posed   1.9 in.
Face has black stripes, thorax has 1 black lateral stripe.
Narrow green dorsal spots on dark brown abdomen, mostly
    pale thighs.

2 Extra-Striped Snaketail *Ophiogomphus anomalus.* **p. 107**
6/30/96 Washington Co., ME, posed   1.7 in.
Black facial stripes, legs, and N-shaped lateral thoracic mark-
    ing.

3 Bison Snaketail *Ophiogomphus bison.* **p. 107**
1977 CA, posed   2.1 in.
Wide brown shoulder stripe on yellow-green thorax, lower
    legs black.

4 Arizona Snaketail *Ophiogomphus arizonicus.* **p. 108**
8/7/95 Catron Co., NM   2.1 in.
Anterior black shoulder stripe an elongate spot.
No abdominal rings and shins pale.

5 Pale Snaketail *Ophiogomphus severus.* **p. 108**
An especially pale individual. 8/24/94 Edmonton, AB   2 in.
As above but anterior black shoulder stripe often absent.
Identical to Great Basin Snaketail if dark midfrontal thoracic
    stripe present.

6 Sinuous Snaketail *Ophiogomphus occidentis.* **p. 109**
7/18/71 Benton Co., WA   2 in.
Narrow wavy black anterior shoulder stripe on yellowish-
    green thorax, dark gray eyes, and narrow male cerci.

7 Great Basin Snaketail *Ophiogomphus morrisoni.* **p. 110**
6/18/98 Inyo Co., CA, posed   2 in.
As above but anterior shoulder stripe wider, straighter, and
    more separated from posterior stripe.
Thorax grayish green, eyes usually blue, and male cerci
    stout.
Identical to Pale Snaketail if anterior shoulder stripe isolated
    and midfrontal thoracic stripe absent.

8 Pygmy Snaketail *Ophiogomphus howei.* **p. 111**
5/31/85 Grayson Co., VA, posed   1.3 in.
Very small size, yellow HW bases.

PLATE 16

1 Boreal Snaketail

2 Extra-Striped Snaketail

3 Bison Snaketail

4 Arizona Snaketail

5 Pale Snaketail

6 Sinuous Snaketail

7 Great Basin Snaketail

8 Pygmy Snaketail

1 Rusty Snaketail *Ophiogomphus rupinsulensis.* **p. 111**

7/90 Clearwater Co., MN   2 in.

Thorax stripes reduced except for 2 brown shoulder stripes.
Abdomen mostly rusty brown with black markings on
    S7–S9.
Obscure rings on S4–S6, and club crooked between S8 and
    S9.
Male eyes yellow-green to blue-green, browner in female.

2 Acuminate Snaketail *Ophiogomphus acuminatus.* **p. 112**

6/16/83 Lewis Co., TN, posed   2 in.

As above but abdomen either browner or blacker and not
    ringed.
Male eyes blue, female eyes gray.

3 Westfall's Snaketail *Ophiogomphus westfalli.* **p. 113**

6/2/90 Fulton Co., AR, posed   2 in.

As above but essentially only posterior brown shoulder stripe
    present.

4 Appalachian Snaketail *Ophiogomphus incurvatus.* **p. 113**

5/13/83 Caswell Co., NC, posed   1.7 in.

Small Snaketail, lateral thoracic stripes vestigial or absent.
Side of club deep yellow to orange.

5 Southern Snaketail *Ophiogomphus australis.* **p. 114**

4/9/87 Washington Par., LA, posed   1.7 in.

Thorax bright green with two black lateral stripes, LA/MS.

6 Edmund's Snaketail *Ophiogomphus edmundo.* **p. 115**

6/4/94 Burke Co., NC   1.8 in.

As above but southern Appalachian Mountains.

7 Maine Snaketail *Ophiogomphus mainensis.* **p. 115**

6/30/96 Washington Co., ME, posed   1.8 in.

Abdomen has narrow dorsal streaks and yellow sides on
    club.
One black lateral thoracic stripe, legs all black.

8 Riffle Snaketail *Ophiogomphus carolus.* **p. 116**

1983 MI, posed   1.7 in.

As above but thorax usually paler green and club less yellow.
Dorsal abdominal spots wide, with a lengthwise rectangle on
    S8 and a crosswise basal rectangle on S9.
Thighs sometimes green-sided.

PLATE 17

1 Rusty Snaketail

2 Acuminate Snaketail

3 Westfall's Snaketail

4 Appalachian Snaketail

5 Southern Snaketail

6 Edmund's Snaketail

7 Maine Snaketail

8 Riffle Snaketail

1 Brook Snaketail *Ophiogomphus aspersus*. **p. 116**
1982 VT, posed   1.9 in.
One black lateral thoracic stripe, thighs have green sides.
Half-length spot on S9, usually triangular dorsal spot on S8.
Compare with Riffle Snaketail (Plate 17).

2 Sand Snaketail *Ophiogomphus* sp. **p. 117**
6/16/96 Eau Claire Co., WI, posed   1.8 in.
As above but dorsal pale stripe of S9 full length, IA/WI.

3 Wisconsin Snaketail *Ophiogomphus susbehcha*. **p. 117**
1991 WI   2 in.
As above but S10 yellow and legs black.

4 Eastern Ringtail *Erpetogomphus designatus*. **p. 118**
6/22/88 Union Co., NC   2 in.
Anterior shoulder and anterior lateral thoracic stripes incomplete.
S1–S2 yellow dorsally, wing bases amber.

5 Dashed Ringtail *Erpetogomphus heterodon*. **p. 119**
8/16/87 Grant Co., NM   2 in.
As above but all thoracic stripes poorly developed.
S1–S2 green dorsally, S8 with black stripes, no amber at wing
   bases.

6 Yellow-Legged Ringtail *Erpetogomphus crotalinus*. **p. 120**
8/13/97 Eddy Co., NM, posed   2 in.
Thoracic stripes vestigial, shins striped yellow.

7 White-Belted Ringtail *Erpetogomphus compositus*. **p. 120**
8/10/95 Cochise Co., AZ   2 in.
Thorax yellow-green, whitish on front and between lateral
   dark stripes.

8 Serpent Ringtail *Erpetogomphus lampropeltis*. **p. 121**
Green Form. 8/10/97 Cochise Co., AZ   2 in.
Thorax pale green with complete brown stripes.
S8–S9 usually dark brown dorsally.
Gray Form of CA has thorax gray with wider brown stripes.

PLATE 18

1 Brook Snaketail

2 Sand Snaketail

3 Wisconsin Snaketail

4 Eastern Ringtail

5 Dashed Ringtail

6 Yellow-Legged Ringtail

7 White-Belted Ringtail

8 Serpent Ringtail

1 Blue-Faced Ringtail *Erpetogomphus eutainia*. **p. 121**
Male. 7/24/77 Gonzales Co., TX, posed   1.7 in.
Small size and blue markings.
Rings around **centers** of middle abdominal segments.

2 Female. 7/24/77 Gonzalez Co., TX, posed   1.7 in.
Club smaller and browner.

3 Four-Striped Leaftail *Phyllogomphoides stigmatus*. **p. 122**
1977 TX, posed   2.7 in.
Large size, yellow-green thorax lacks a lower rear stripe.
Middle abdominal segments ringed, and male club widely
    flanged.
Compare with Serpent Ringtail (Plate 18).

4 Five-Striped Leaftail *Phyllogomphoides albrighti*. **p. 122**
8/18/94 Kerr Co., TX, posed   2.5 in.
As above but thorax gray-green with a dark lower rear
    stripe.

5 Two-Striped Forceptail *Aphylla williamsoni*. **p. 123**
1974 FL, posed   2.8 in.
Thorax mostly brown with 2 greenish-yellow lateral stripes.
No pale shoulder stripe, and male has S8 widely flanged.

6 Broad-Striped Forceptail *Aphylla angustifolia*. **p. 124**
Male. 8/21/97 Zapata Co., TX   2.5 in.
As above but thorax has a narrow midlateral pale stripe and
    pale shoulder stripe.
Male has S8 only narrowly flanged.

7 Female. 1997 Starr Co., TX, posed   2.5 in.

8 Narrow-Striped Forceptail *Aphylla protracta*. **p. 124**
7/5/76 Mazatlán, Sinaloa, Mexico, posed   2.6 in.
As above but thorax has 3 equally narrow pale lateral stripes.
Both sexes have S8 widely flanged.

PLATE 19

1 Blue-Faced Ringtail

2 Blue-Faced Ringtail ♀

3 Four-Striped Leaftail

4 Five-Striped Leaftail

5 Two-Striped Forceptail

7 Broad-Striped Forceptail ♀

6 Broad-Striped Forceptail ♂

8 Narrow-Striped Forceptail

1 Pacific Spiketail *Cordulegaster dorsalis.* **p. 126**
7/10/77 Nevada Co., CA, posed   3.1 in.
Blue eyes touch at one point.
Abdomen has yellow saddlelike dorsal spots.

2 Apache Spiketail *Cordulegaster diadema.* **p. 126**
7/19/77 Coconino Co., AZ, posed   3.3 in.
As above but abdomen banded.

3 Tiger Spiketail *Cordulegaster erronea.* **p. 126**
9/3/75 Towns Co., GA, posed   2.9 in.
As above but eastern, with green eyes, and black upper face.
Female ovipositor extends length of S10 beyond abdomen.

4 Say's Spiketail *Cordulegaster sayi.* **p. 127**
Female. 4/6/90 Alachua Co., FL   2.6 in.
As above but thorax marked white and magenta, and upper
    face yellow.
Ovipositor extends just to end of abdomen.

5 Twin-Spotted Spiketail *Cordulegaster maculata.* **p. 127**
Female of Southern Form. 3/22/88 Alachua Co., FL, posed   2.8 in.
Short yellow abdominal spots.
Body brown with pale yellow markings, and eyes blue.
Ovipositor extends length of S9 + S10 beyond abdomen.
Northern Form has black body, bright yellow markings,
    green eyes.

6 Delta-Spotted Spiketail *Cordulegaster diastatops.* **p. 128**
7/82 Essex Co., VT, posed   2.4 in.
Like Northern Form of above but S6–S8 have long pointed
    triangular spots.
S2 has yellow stripes.
Side of thorax usually has 3 yellow stripes, middle stripe nar-
    rowest, posterior widest.
Female ovipositor extends length of S10 beyond abdomen.

7 Brown Spiketail *Cordulegaster bilineata.* **p. 128**
Female. 1974 MS, posed   2.5 in.
As above but brown with blunt abdominal spots, and thorax
    has 2 equally narrow yellow lateral thoracic stripes.

8 Arrowhead Spiketail *Cordulegaster obliqua.* **p. 129**
Southern Form. 6/28/78 Alachua Co., FL, posed   3.3 in.
Pale yellow arrowhead markings on abdomen, blue eyes.
Northern Form, 3.1 in., has brighter yellow markings, green
    eyes.

PLATE 20

1 Pacific Spiketail

2 Apache Spiketail

3 Tiger Spiketail

4 Say's Spiketail ♀

5 Twin-Spotted Spiketail ♀

6 Delta-Spotted Spiketail

7 Brown Spiketail ♀

8 Arrowhead Spiketail

1 Stream Cruiser *Didymops transversa.* **p. 130**
6/24/96 Marquette Co., MI, posed   2.2 in.
Thorax brown with 1 pale yellow lateral thoracic stripe.
Small brown spot at base of each wing, costa veins pale
    brown.
Eyes green, male abdomen clubbed.

2 Florida Cruiser *Didymops floridensis.* **p. 131**
Alachua Co., FL, posed   2.6 in.
In spring at FL/AL sand-bottomed lakes.
As above but but larger, grayer, no wing spots, costas yellow.

3 Western River Cruiser *Macromia magnifica.* **p. 132**
6/77 Madera Co., CA, posed   2.8 in.
As above but thorax has half-length pale frontal stripes.
Eyes opalescent brown.

4 Bronzed River Cruiser *Macromia annulata.* **p. 132**
Pair in Wheel. 8/9/97 Travis Co., TX   2.8 in.
As above but frontal stripes nearly full length.
Side of S1 yellow, eyes usually tinted green.

5 Gilded River Cruiser *Macromia pacifica.* **p. 133**
1974 McClennan Co., TX, posed   2.8 in.
S2–S8 have half-length yellow spots, thorax has full-length
    yellow frontal stripes.
Eyes brilliant green, male abdomen clubbed.

6 Illinois River Cruiser *Macromia illinoiensis.* **p. 133**
Southern Form. 1978 FL, posed   2.8 in.
As above but with half-length frontal stripes.
Yellow band on S2 complete.
Northern Form lacks frontal stripes, has yellow band of S2
    broken dorsally and laterally, and has small abdominal
    spots except on S7. Line across map shows approximate
    separation of Forms.

6A Mountain River Cruiser (not shown, no map) of southern
    Appalachian area, see p. 134.

7 Allegheny River Cruiser *Macromia alleghaniensis.* **p. 134**
6/13/87 Cumberland Co., TN, posed   2.8 in.
Like Northern Form of Illinois River Cruiser but yellow band
    of S2 complete laterally, S7 banded, and thorax often
    browner than abdomen.

8 Royal River Cruiser *Macromia taeniolata.* **p. 135**
FL, posed   3.3 in.
Like Southern Form of Illinois River Cruiser but yellow band
    of S2 broken dorsally, S7 has pair of spots, male abdomen
    not clubbed.

PLATE 21

1 Stream Cruiser

2 Florida Cruiser

3 Western River Cruiser

4 Bronzed River Cruiser

5 Gilded River Cruiser

6 Illinois River Cruiser

7 Allegheny River Cruiser

8 Royal River Cruiser

1 American Emerald *Cordulia shurtleffii.* **p. 136**
Male. 1977 CA, posed   1.9 in.
Thorax unmarked, abdomen black beyond S4 and widest at
  S8.

2 Female. 6/22/96 Oneida Co., WI, posed   1.9 in.
Abdomen cylindrical with white spot on lower edge of S3.
Cerci as long as S9 + S10.

3 Racket-Tailed Emerald *Dorocordulia libera.* **p. 137**
Male. 6/20/96 Forest Co., WI, posed   1.6 in.
As above but S7–S9 a wide flat club.

4 Female. 6/20/96 Oneida Co., WI, posed   1.6 in.
As above but abdomen clubbed, and orange at base of S3.

5 Petite Emerald *Dorocordulia lepida.* **p. 138**
Juvenile male. 6/26/94 Barnstable Co., MA   1.5 in.
As above but abdomen only slightly widened beyond S3.

6 Female. 8/96 Middlesex Co., MA, posed   1.5 in.
As above but abdomen cylindrical with orange-brown lateral
  basal spots on S4–S7.

7 Ringed Boghaunter *Williamsonia lintneri.* **p. 139**
5/96 Norfolk Co., MA   1.3 in.
Small size, yellow face, orange posterior bands on S2–S9.
Local at northeastern bogs and fens in early spring.

8 Ebony Boghaunter *Williamsonia fletcheri.* **p. 139**
6/29/96 NB, posed   1.3 in.
Small size, all dark with white rings on S2–S4.

9 Selys' Sundragon *Helocordulia selysii.* **p. 140**
4/8/74 Perry Co., MS, posed   1.7 in.
Nearly complete orange basal ring on S3, face yellow.
Small orange lateral basal spots on S4–S7.
Brown spot and dots at base of each wing.

10 Uhler's Sundragon *Helocordulia uhleri.* **p. 140**
1996 NB, posed   1.6 in.
As above but has amber next to basal wing spots.

PLATE 22

1 American Emerald ♂

2 American Emerald ♀

3 Racket-Tailed Emerald ♂

4 Racket-Tailed Emerald ♀

5 Petite Emerald ♂

6 Petite Emerald ♀

7 Ringed Boghaunter

8 Ebony Boghaunter

9 Selys' Sundragon

10 Uhler's Sundragon

1 **Prince Baskettail** *Epitheca princeps.* **p. 142**
1974 FL, posed   3.2 in.
Size varies from medium (2.2 in.) in north to Darner size in
  south.
Wings have brown tips, usually also basal and nodal spots.
Males have green eyes and patrol without perching.

2 **Common Baskettail** *Epitheca cynosura.* **p. 142**
1975 FL, posed   1.6 in.
Basal HW spot varies from tiny spot to large triangle.
Abdomen usually rather stout, and female cerci short.

3 **Mantled Baskettail** *Epitheca semiaquea.* **p. 143**
4/8/88 Clay Co., FL   1.3 in., no map, Eastern.
As above, but in the southeast basal half of HW is brown.

4 **Stripe-Winged Baskettail** *Epitheca costalis.* **p. 144**
Dot-Winged Form male. 1996 Collin Co., TX, posed   1.7 in.
As above but usually more slender, in TX area Dot-Winged
  Form has row of brown dots in wings.
See text for 5 additional similar species.

5 **Whitehouse's Emerald** *Somatochlora whitehousei.* **p. 148**
7/8/83 Old Crow, YT   1.9 in.
Brown spot at base of HW (in addition to membranule).
Thorax has only anterior pale lateral stripe.
Abdomen widest at S7 in male, S6 in female.
Female has oblique ovipositor, cerci longer than S9 + S10.

5A **Muskeg Emerald** (not shown) as above but abdomen widest
  at S5 and female lacks ovipositor.   1.8 in.

6 **Treeline Emerald** *Somatochlora sahlbergi.* **p. 149**
7/6/83 Old Crow, YT   2 in.
As above but no spot in HW, no thoracic stripes, and male
  abdomen widest at S6.
Female lacks ovipositor and has cerci as long as S9 + S10.

7 **Ringed Emerald** *Somatochlora albicincta.* **p. 150**
7/82 Grafton Co., NH, posed   1.9 in.
Thorax brassy green with only anterior pale lateral stripe.
White rings between all abdominal segments and pale spots
  at bases of cerci.
Female has pale epiproct and lacks ovipositor.

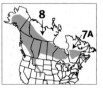

7A **Quebec Emerald** (not shown) lacks spots at bases of cerci and
  nearly lacks rings on S3–S7.   1.9 in.

8 **Hudsonian Emerald** *Somatochlora hudsonica.* **p. 151**
7/6/83 Old Crow, YT   2.1 in.
As above but thoracic stripe more obscure, larger pale spots
  anterior to bases of FW, and no pale spots at bases of cerci.
Female has black epiproct and a short oblique ovipositor.

PLATE 23

1 Prince Baskettail

2 Common Baskettail

3 Mantled Baskettail

4 Stripe-Winged Baskettail

5 Whitehouse's Emerald

6 Treeline Emerald

7 Ringed Emerald

8 Hudsonian Emerald

1 Lake Emerald *Somatochlora cingulata.* **p. 152**
7/97 Mt. Carleton Prov. Park, NB, posed   2.5 in.
Thorax brown and usually unmarked, and white rings
    between all abdominal segments.
Female lacks ovipositor, and males patrol far out over lakes.

2 Mocha Emerald *Somatochlora linearis.* **p. 152**
8/13/75 Franklin Co., FL, posed   2.6 in.
Thorax unmarked and wings tinted brown.
Male cerci straight, female has perpendicular ovipositor as
    long as S9.

3 Fine-Lined Emerald *Somatochlora filosa.* **p. 153**
1978, posed   2.4 in.
Thorax dark green with narrow curved anterior lateral
    stripe, posterior stripes meet under thorax.
Male cerci straight, female ovipositor skidlike, juvenile
    female has orange wingtips.

4 Texas Emerald *Somatochlora margarita.* **p. 154**
6/23/85 San Jacinto Co., TX, posed   2.1 in.
Two pale lateral thoracic stripes, posterior ones join under
    thorax.
Face pale, pale rings between S8–S10, S10 all brown, male
    cerci bent downward.
Female ovipositor horizontal, extending to tip of S10.

4A Treetop Emerald (not shown) appears identical to above.
    2 in.

4B Ozark Emerald (not shown) also appears identical to above.

5 Calvert's Emerald *Somatochlora calverti.* **p. 155**
Male. 1974 Okaloosa Co., FL, posed   2.1 in.
As above but with pale rings between middle abdominal seg-
    ments, and usually a white dorsal spot on S10.

6 Female. 8/16/75 Gadsden Co., FL, posed   2.1 in.
Brown stripe from nodus to stigma in each wing is diagnos-
    tic.

7 Clamp-Tipped Emerald *Somatochlora tenebrosa.* **p. 156**
Male. 9/13/74 Transylvania Co., NC, posed   2.3 in.
Circular gap between male cerci and epiproct in side view is
    diagnostic.
Two yellow lateral thoracic stripes fade with age, the anterior
    first.

8 Female. 9/13/74 Transylvania Co., NC, posed   2.3 in.
Ovipositor longer than S9 and slanting slightly posteriorly.
Compare with Williamson's Emerald (Plate 25).

PLATE 24

1 Lake Emerald

2 Mocha Emerald

3 Fine-Lined Emerald

4 Texas Emerald

5 Calvert's Emerald ♂

6 Calvert's Emerald ♀

8 Clamp-Tipped Emerald ♀

7 Clamp-Tipped Emerald ♂

1 **Williamson's Emerald** *Somatochlora williamsoni.* **p. 157**
7/83 MI, posed   2.3 in.
Like Clamp-Tipped Emerald (Plate 24) but male has straight cerci.
Female ovipositor slender, longer than S9, and perpendicular.

2 **Ski-Tailed Emerald** *Somatochlora elongata.* **p. 157**
Male. 8/95 Berkshire Co., MA, posed   2.3 in.
As above but lateral thoracic markings remain bright yellow.

3 Female. 9/6/86 Huntingdon Co., PA   2.3 in.
Ovipositor in side view an equilateral triangle as long as S9.

4 **Ocellated Emerald** *Somatochlora minor.* **p. 158**
6/29/96 Charlotte Co., NB, posed   1.8 in.
A small Striped Emerald with a short abdomen and black face.
Thorax has 2 oval yellow lateral thoracic spots.
Female ovipositor perpendicular and as long as S8.

5 **Brush-Tipped Emerald** *Somatochlora walshii.* **p.159**
7/83 MI, posed   1.9 in.
As above but thorax has anterior lateral stripe and face is yellow.
Male cerci enlarged at tip, and female ovipositor oblique.

6 **Plains Emerald** *Somatochlora ensigera.* **p. 160**
7/16/98 Cherry Co., NE, posed   2 in.
Face and 2 lateral thoracic stripes bright yellow, male cerci straight.
Female has wide yellow lateral stripes on S2–S6, ovipositor perpendicular and as long as S8, cerci shorter than S9 + S10.

7 **Hine's Emerald** *Somatochlora hineana.* **p. 160**
Male. 7/24/94 Door Co., WI, posed   2.4 in.
As above but cerci hooked downward.

8 Female. 7/24/94 Door Co., WI, posed   2.4 in.
Wings tinted brown, ovipositor oblique, and cerci longer than S9 + S10.

PLATE 25

1 Williamson's Emerald

2 Ski-Tailed Emerald ♂

3 Ski-Tailed Emeraldd ♀

4 Ocellated Emerald

5 Brush-Tipped Emerald

6 Plains Emerald

7 Hine's Emerald ♂

8 Hine's Emerald ♀

1 Forcipate Emerald *Somatochlora forcipata.* **p. 161**
Juvenile male. 6/96 Scotch Ridge, NB, posed   2 in.
Thorax has 2 pale oval lateral spots.
S5–S8 of male and S3–S7 of female have small yellow lateral
     spots.
Female ovipositor horizontal.

2 Incurvate Emerald *Somatochlora incurvata.* **p. 162**
Male. 7/27/94 Jackson Co., WI, posed   2.4 in.
As above but abdomen more elongate, anterior lateral tho-
     racic spot elongate, and pale lateral spot present on S4.

3 Female. 7/27/94 Jackson Co., WI, posed   2.4 in.

4 Kennedy's Emerald *Somatochlora kennedyi.* **p. 162**
Male. 6/25/96 Baraga Co., MI, posed   2.1 in.
Only anterior lateral thoracic spot present, and pale spots
     posterior to S3 tiny or absent.

5 Female. 1996 WI, posed   2.1 in.
Large orange basal spot on S3, ovipositor horizontal.

6 Mountain Emerald *Somatochlora semicircularis.* **p. 163**
8/83 AB, posed   2 in.
Thorax metallic green with 2 large ovoid pale yellow lateral
     spots, face dark.
Female lacks ovipositor.

7 Delicate Emerald *Somatochlora franklini.* **p. 163**
8/27/95 Warner Bog, AB   2 in.
Brown spot at HW base, upper face black, no posterior lateral
     thoracic spot.
Male abdomen 1/2 longer than a wing and widest at S9.
Female has abdomen 1/5–1/3 longer than a wing, ovipositor
     horizontal.

8 Coppery Emerald *Somatochlora georgiana.* **p. 164**
7/28/74 Okaloosa Co., FL, posed   1.9 in.
Small Striped Emerald, brown-orange with 2 lateral pale
     thoracic stripes, and red-brown eyes.

PLATE 26

1 Forcipate Emerald

2 Incurvate Emerald ♂

3 Incurvate Emerald ♀

4 Kennedy's Emerald ♂

5 Kennedy's Emerald ♀

6 Mountain Emerald

7 Delicate Emerald

8 Coppery Emerald

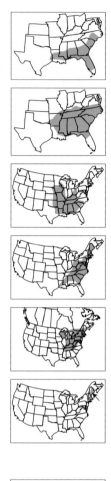

1 Alabama Shadowdragon *Neurocordulia alabamensis.* **p. 165**
Female. 7/2/74 Alachua Co., FL, posed   1.7 in.
Brown-orange with side of thorax waxy white to yellow.
Row of amber dots along entire front edge of each wing.

2 Cinnamon Shadowdragon *Neurocordulia virginiensis.* **p. 165**
Female. 1973 Alachua Co., FL, posed   1.8 in.
As above but side of thorax mostly brown, and only a few
   dark dots near wing bases.

3 Smoky Shadowdragon *Neurocordulia molesta.* **p. 166**
7/26/74 Liberty Co., FL, posed   1.9 in.
As above but generally browner, with smoky gray wings and
   olive green eyes.

4 Umber Shadowdragon *Neurocordulia obsoleta.* **p. 166**
4/4//76 Alachua Co., FL, posed   1.8 in.
Body brown, and each wing has a basal brown spot connected by dots to spot at nodus.

5 Stygian Shadowdragon *Neurocordulia yamaskanensis.* **p. 167**
6/29/96 Charlotte Co., NB, posed   2 in.
Basal amber spot of HW has network of brown veins.
Body brown, and S4–S8 with yellow lateral stripes.

6 Broad-Tailed Shadowdragon *Neurocordulia sp.* **p. 167**
6/29/96 Charlotte Co., NB, posed   1.6 in.
ME and New Brunswick.
Abdomen wide and inflated at base, with yellow lateral
   dashes on S2–S8.
Eyes yellowish, veins near wing bases outlined with amber.

7 Orange Shadowdragon *Neurocordulia xanthosoma.* **p. 168**
Male. 6/7/92 Sevier Co., AR, posed   2 in.
Body brownish orange, basal 1/4 of wings orange.
Row of amber dots along front edge of each wing.

8 Female. 5/21/92 Collin Co., TX, posed   2 in.
Body brown; brown spots along front of wings, particularly
   at base, 1/4 length, and nodus.

PLATE 27

1 Alabama Shadowdragon ♀

2 Cinnamon Shadowdragon ♀

3 Smoky Shadowdragon

4 Umber Shadowdragon

5 Stygian Shadowdragon

6 Broad-Tailed Shadowdragon

7 Orange Shadowdragon ♂

8 Orange Shadowdragon ♀

1 Evening Skimmer *Tholymis citrina.* **p. 169**
Female. 6/24/91 Loreto Dept., Peru, posed   1.9 in.
Like a Shadowdragon (Plate 27) but with amber spot at
nodus of HW.

2 Widow Skimmer *Libellula luctuosa.* **p. 170**
Male. 1995 Collin Co., TX   1.8 in.
Black basal half of wings and white wing bands diagnostic.

3 Female. 9/1/97 Collin Co., TX   1.8 in.
Black wing bases and lateral yellow abdominal stripes diagnostic.

4 Common Whitetail *Libellula lydia.* **p. 171**
Male. 1975 FL, posed   1.7 in.
Wide brown band between nodus and stigma of each wing.
Abdomen white, small white basal spot in HW.
Juvenile male abdominal pattern like female.

5 Female. 7/97 Medina Co., OH   1.7 in.
Brown spots at base, nodus, and tip of each wing.
Abdomen has oblique white lateral dashes.

6 Desert Whitetail *Libellula subornata.* **p. 172**
Male. 8/18/87 Grant Co., NM, posed   1.7 in.
As above but most of wing base white, center of wing bands
paler.

7 Female. 6/2/74 San Diego Co., CA, posed   1.7 in.
Two brown bands in each wing, abdomen has lateral yellow
stripes.

8 Eight-Spotted Skimmer *Libellula forensis.* **p. 173**
1977 Fresno Co., CA, posed   1.9 in.
Wings have brown stripe at base, band at nodus, and clear
tips.
Males and some females have white spots near nodus and
stigma.
Forehead black in males, yellow in females.

PLATE 28

1 Evening Skimmer

2 Widow Skimmer ♂

3 Widow Skimmer ♀

4 Common Whitetail ♂

5 Common Whitetail ♀

6 Desert Whitetail ♂

7 Desert Whitetail ♀

8 Eight-Spotted Skimmer

1 Twelve-Spotted Skimmer *Libellula pulchella*. **p. 173**
Male. 6/97 Collin Co., TX   2 in.
Alternate black and white wing spots including dark wingtip
   is diagnostic.

2 Female. 1973, posed   2 in.
Dark spots at base, nodus, and tip of each wing.
Abdomen has straight yellow lateral stripes.
Compare with female Common Whitetail (Plate 28) and
   Prince Baskettail (Plate 23).

3 Painted Skimmer *Libellula semifasciata*. **p. 174**
1975 FL, posed   1.7 in.
Wing pattern diagnostic, with amber at base and tip, brown
   streaks at base, brown spot at nodus, and brown band at
   stigma.

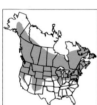

4 Four-Spotted Skimmer *Libellula quadrimaculata*. **p. 174**
1996 Forest Co., WI   1.7 in.
Wings have small black nodal spots, HW has black basal triangular spot.
Abdomen has basal half brown, posterior half black, and yellow lateral stripes.

5 Hoary Skimmer *Libellula nodisticta*. **p. 175**
6/9/74 Catron Co., NM, posed   1.9 in.
Each wing has brown stripe at base and brown nodal spot,
   with basal stripe edged white in males.
Thorax has 4 lateral yellow spots.
Forehead black in male, yellow in female.

6 Chalk-Fronted Corporal *Libellula julia*. **p. 176**
Male. 6/19/96 Lincoln Co., WI, posed   1.6 in.
Small King Skimmer, with front of thorax and base of
   abdomen white.
HW has small triangular brown spot.

7 Mature female. 1991   1.6 in.
Dull plain dark brown, abdomen relatively short and blunt
   with grayish base.

8 Juvenile female. 6/20/96 Oneida Co., WI, posed   1.6 in.
Thorax has white shoulder stripe, and abdomen has wide
   black dorsal stripe.

PLATE 29

1 Twelve-Spotted Skimmer ♂

2 Twelve-Spotted Skimmer ♀

3 Painted Skimmer

4 Four-Spotted Skimmer

5 Hoary Skimmer

6 Chalk-Fronted Corporal ♂

7 Chalk-Fronted Corporal ♀

8 Chalk-Fronted Corporal ♀

1 White Corporal *Libellula exusta.* **p. 176**
Male. 7/20/73 Lincoln Co., ME, posed   1.4 in.
Small size, white abdomen, and narrow white shoulder
 stripe.
Each wing has 1 basal brown stripe.

2 Female. 6/94 Barnstable Co., MA   1.4 in.
Abdomen brown with narrow black dorsal stripe.

3 Blue Corporal *Libellula deplanata.* **p. 177**
Male. 5/3/97 Morris Co., TX   1.4 in.
As above but front of thorax and abdomen pale blue.
Each wing has 2 brown basal streaks.

4 Female. 1975 FL, posed   1.4 in.
As above but abdomen bears chain of dorsal black triangles.

5 Spangled Skimmer *Libellula cyanea.* **p. 177**
Male. 5/3/97 Morris Co., TX,   1.7 in.
Dark blue, with black-and-white stigmas and black face.
Each wing has black basal streak.

6 Female. 5/27/79 Habersham Co., GA, posed   1.7 in.
Wingtips brown, face tan, yellow anterior lateral diamond on
 thorax, yellow lateral abdominal stripe.

7 Comanche Skimmer *Libellula comanche.* **p. 178**
Male. 7/25/97 Concho Co., TX,   2.1 in.
As above but gray-blue, face white, no wing streaks.

8 Female. 1977 TX, posed   2.1 in.
As above but only extreme wingtips brown, and stigmas may
 be black-and-brown.

PLATE 30

1 White Corporal ♂

2 White Corporal ♀

3 Blue Corporal ♂

4 Blue Corporal ♀

5 Spangled Skimmer ♂

6 Spangled Skimmer ♀

7 Comanche Skimmer ♂

8 Comanche Skimmer ♀

1 Yellow-Sided Skimmer *Libellula flavida.* **p. 178**
Male. 4/14/74 Rapides Par., LA, posed   1.9 in.
Like Spangled Skimmer (Plate 30) but pale blue, stigma yellow to brown and usually with a black outer tip.

2 Female. 7/27/74 Okaloosa Co., FL, posed   1.9 in.
Like Spangled Skimmer but side of thorax more extensively yellow.

3 Golden-Winged Skimmer *Libellula auripennis.* **p. 179**
Male. 1974 FL, posed   2 in.
Mostly orange body, pale costa veins, black lower hindleg.

4 Female. 1974 FL, posed   2 in.
Thorax has diffuse pale lateral stripes.
Abdomen yellow with black dorsal stripe.
Yellow Form Female of Purple Skimmer (FL) is identical.

5 Needham's Skimmer *Libellula needhami.* **p. 180**
Male. 9/8/74 Alachua Co., FL, posed   2.1 in.
As above but redder, more of posterior wing veins dark, brown lower hindleg.

6 Female. 6/10/97 Chambers Co., TX   2.1 in.
As above but pale side of thorax extends anterior to shoulder, costas dark from base to nodus.

7 Purple Skimmer *Libellula jesseana.* **p. 180**
Male. 7/74 Putnam Co., FL, posed   2.1 in.
Blue body, orange wings, black head, FL sand-bottomed lakes.

8 Mature Purple Form female. 5/11/94 Clay Co., FL   2.1 in.
Most are Yellow Form, identical to female Golden-Winged Skimmer.

PLATE 31

1 Yellow-Sided Skimmer ♂

2 Yellow-Sided Skimmer ♀

3 Golden-Winged Skimmer ♂

4 Golden-Winged Skimmer ♀

5 Needham's Skimmer ♂

6 Needham's Skimmer ♀

7 Purple Skimmer ♂

8 Purple Skimmer ♀

1 Flame Skimmer *Libellula saturata.* **p. 181**
Male. 8/5/97 Pima Co., AZ   2.1 in.
Thick-bodied, thorax brown, abdomen orange-red.
Each wing has basal half orange and a basal brown streak.

2 Female. 8/6/97 Pima Co., AZ, posed   2.1 in.
Brown body, each wing has an amber stripe that darkens
toward base.

3 Neon Skimmer *Libellula croceipennis.* **p. 181**
9/1/97 Collin Co., TX   2.2 in.
As above but front of thorax and abdomen brilliant red.
Wings amber in basal 1/4 and lack brown streaks.
Female lacks wing stripes.

4 Bleached Skimmer *Libellula composita.* **p. 182**
Male. 6/11/74 Chaves Co., NM, posed   1.8 in.
Each wing has a white costal vein, brown-amber basal spot,
and often a nodal spot.
Body pale blue, especially on front of thorax and S1–S3.

5 Female. 8/22/73 Inyo Co., CA   1.8 in.
Side of thorax white with one black stripe.
Abdomen has dorsolateral broken yellow stripes.

6 Great Blue Skimmer *Libellula vibrans.* **p. 183**
Male. 1974 FL, posed   2.2 in.
Abdomen and front of thorax pale blue, face white, eyes
blue.
Each wing has black stigma, streak at base, nodal spot, and
tip.

7 Mature female. 1975 FL, posed   2.2 in.
More black in wingtips, body brown with black dorsal
abdominal stripe.

8 Juvenile female. 1975 FL, posed   2.2 in.
Eyes red-brown, side of thorax nearly unmarked, abdomen
yellow with black dorsal stripe.
Compare Slaty and Bar-Winged Skimmers (Plate 33).

PLATE 32

1 Flame Skimmer ♂

2 Flame Skimmer ♀

3 Neon Skimmer

4 Bleached Skimmer ♂

5 Bleached Skimmer ♀

6 Great Blue Skimmer ♂

7 Great Blue Skimmer ♀

8 Great Blue Skimmer ♀

1 Slaty Skimmer *Libellula incesta*. **p. 183**

Male. Jackson Co., IN   2 in.

All black with clear wings, abdomen tapered.

2 Juvenile female. 1974 FL, posed   2 in.

Like juvenile female of Great Blue Skimmer (Plate 32) but face brown and side of thorax has brown triangle at base of FW.

Wing pattern varies from absent to identical to Great Blue or Bar-Winged Skimmers.

In mature female body becomes brown and eyes remain brown.

3 Bar-Winged Skimmer *Libellula axilena*. **p. 184**

6/97 Clay Co., FL   2.2 in.

Wings have a black bar or spot between nodus and stigma, but Great Blue and female Slaty Skimmers can have identical pattern.

Male has touch of white at HW base, black face, and gray-blue front of thorax and base of abdomen.

Female identical to some female Slaty Skimmers, but in juveniles center of face is darker than contrasting border.

4 Roseate Skimmer *Orthemis ferruginea*. **p. 185**

Pink Form male. 1974 FL, posed   2 in.

Pale blue thorax and pink abdomen are diagnostic.

5 Red Form male. 11/9/74 Alachua Co., FL, posed   2 in.

All red body, larger than male Scarlet Skimmer (Plate 34). South FL.

6 Female. 1974 FL, posed   2 in.

Thorax brown with white *HIII* pattern on side and white dorsal stripe.

Abdomen rusty brown with lateral flange on S8.

7 Filigree Skimmer *Pseudoleon superbus*. **p. 187**

Male. 8/15/94 Bandera Co., TX, posed   1.6 in.

Wing pattern unique, body brown with pale chevrons on abdomen.

Compare with Black-Winged Dragonlet (Plate 36).

8 Female. 8/11/95 Cochise Co., AZ, posed   1.6 in.

Wing pattern less extensive than male's.

Abdomen bears ovipositor perpendicular to S9.

PLATE 33

1 Slaty Skimmer ♂

2 Slaty Skimmer ♀

3 Bar-Winged Skimmer

4 Roseate Skimmer ♂

5 Roseate Skimmer ♂

7 Filigree Skimmer ♂

6 Roseate Skimmer ♀

8 Filigree Skimmer ♀

1 **Red Rock Skimmer** *Paltothemis lineatipes.* **p. 188**
Male. 6/5/74 Gila Co., AZ, posed   2 in.
Abdomen mottled dull red, basal 1/4 of wings orange, perches on rocks.

2 Female. 5/9/74 Cochise Co., AZ, posed   2 in.
Abdomen mottled gray, clear wings.

3 **Scarlet Skimmer** *Crocothemis servilia.* **p. 189**
Male. 2/21/81 Broward Co., FL, posed   1.6 in.
Body all bright red, amber basal HW spot.
Compare larger Red Form male Roseate Skimmer (Plate 33).

4 Female. 2/21/81 Broward Co., FL, posed   1.6 in.
Pale yellow with white shoulder stripe and black dorsal
     abdominal stripe.
Abdomen has oblique ovipositor.

5 **Black Meadowhawk** *Sympetrum danae.* **p. 190**
Juvenile male. 1983 AB, posed   1.2 in.
Side of thorax has chainlike marking, face and body quickly
     become all black.
Seaside Dragonlet (Plate 37) is more slender and has denser
     wing venation, while Double-Ringed Pennant (Plate 44)
     has dark spot at HW base.

6 Female. 8/24/94 Edmonton, AB   1.2 in.
Face remains yellow and body darkens less completely.
Abdomen bears short ovipositor.

7 **Blue-Faced Meadowhawk** *Sympetrum ambiguum.* **p. 191**
Pair in wheel. 9/2/96 Anne Arundel Co., MD   1.4 in.
Forehead nonmetallic blue or green, thorax gray, legs tan.
Abdomen black-ringed, mostly red in males and some
     females, brown in other females.

8 **Cardinal Meadowhawk** *Sympetrum illotum.* **p. 192**
1977 CA, posed   1.4 in.
Thorax brown with 2 white lateral spots.
Wings have brown basal streaks, and basal 1/4 amber.
Parallel-sided abdomen lacks black markings and becomes
     bright red in males.
Female mostly brown with spoutlike ovipositor.

PLATE 34

1 Red Rock Skimmer ♂

2 Red Rock Skimmer ♀

3 Scarlet Skimmer ♂

4 Scarlet Skimmer ♀

5 Black Meadowhawk ♂

6 Black Meadowhawk ♀

8 Cardinal Meadowhawk

7 Blue-Faced Meadowhawk

1 Variegated Meadowhawk *Sympetrum corruptum*. **p. 192**
Male. 9/9/97 Reeves Co., TX   1.5 in.
Mostly gray body, anterior wing veins orange, face red.
Thorax has 2 white stripes yellow below, stripes age to yellow spots.
Abdomen has chain of lateral white spots, irregular red dorsal stripe to black S8–S9.
Legs black with yellow stripes.

2 Female. 4/28/97 Cooke Co., TX, posed   1.5 in.
Face tan, S2 black dorsally, abdominal stripe orange.

3 Striped Meadowhawk *Sympetrum pallipes*. **p. 193**
7/19/77 Coconino Co., AZ, posed   1.4 in.
Thorax brown with 2 all-white lateral stripes.
Abdomen pale red without dorsal black or lateral white markings.
Face brown and legs black.
Juveniles have yellow-brown abdomen and tan legs.

4 Red-Veined Meadowhawk *Sympetrum madidum*. **p. 194**
6/25/77 BC   1.6 in.
Face and body red, wings tinted brown with anterior and basal veins red, legs black.
Juvenile female's wings have amber base and costal stripe, veins yellow in those areas, face and body brown-gray with 2 all-white lateral thoracic stripes, and abdomen has white lateral stripe bordered dorsally by black stripe.

5 Yellow-Legged Meadowhawk *Sympetrum vicinum*. **p. 195**
Male. 10/19/97 Collin Co., TX, posed   1.3 in.
Slender pale red abdomen has little black.
Legs yellow to red-brown, forehead red.
Juveniles have brown abdomen, tan forehead.

6 Female. 1989   1.3 in.
Abdomen bears trumpet-shaped ovipositor.

7 Spot-Winged Meadowhawk *Sympetrum signiferum*. **p. 196**
Juvenile male obelisking. 1978 Durango, Mexico   1.5 in.
As above but HW has triangular brown basal spot.

8 Saffron-Winged Meadowhawk *Sympetrum costiferum*. **p. 196**
8/27/95 Edmonton, AB   1.4 in.
Face and abdomen pale red, little black on abdomen, legs partly to entirely black, anterior wing veins orange.
Juveniles have amber stripe along front of each wing, face and abdomen dull yellow.

PLATE 35

1 Variegated Meadowhawk ♂

2 Variegated Meadowhawk ♀

3 Striped Meadowhawk

4 Red-Veined Meadowhawk

5 Yellow-Legged Meadowhawk ♂

6 Yellow-Legged Meadowhawk ♀

7 Spot-Winged Meadowhawk

8 Saffron-Winged Meadowhawk

1 Band-Winged Meadowhawk *Sympetrum semicinctum.* **p. 197**
7/29/73 Broome Co., NY, posed   1.3 in.
Basal halves of wings amber, abdomen pale red (brown in
    juveniles), legs black, face brown.
Western Forms have black lateral W on thorax.

2 Cherry-Faced Meadowhawk *Sympetrum internum.* **p. 198**
Western Form. 7/96 Montrose Co., CO   1.3 in.
Abdomen dark red with black lateral stripe, legs black, ante-
    rior wing veins orange, face dark red.
Juveniles have brown abdomen and yellow face, and some
    females have basal halves of wings amber.

3 Ruby Meadowhawk *Sympetrum rubicundulum.* **p. 200**
7/97 Medina Co., OH   1.4 in.
As above but wing veins dark and face yellow to brown.
Eastern Form of above is identical.
Some of both sexes west of OH have basal halves of wings
    amber.

4 White-Faced Meadowhawk *Sympetrum obtrusum.* **p. 201**
Male. 9/96 Lincoln Co., ME, posed   1.3 in.
As above except face white when mature.

5 Female. 1973, posed   1.3 in.

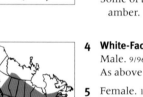

6 Band-Winged Dragonlet *Erythrodiplax umbrata.* **p. 202**
Male. 4/74 TX, posed   1.7 in.
Slender black body, black band between nodus and stigma of
    each wing.

7 Brown Form female. 1988 FL, posed   1.7 in.
Dull brown body, brown wingtips, tan rectangular lateral
    spots on at least S5–S7.

8 Black-Winged Dragonlet *Erythrodiplax funerea.* **p. 203**
Male. Mazatlán, Sinaloa, Mexico, 1976, posed   1.7 in.
Stray to AZ and TX.
As above but wings black from near base to halfway between
    nodus and stigma.
Spotted Form female has slender black body, round black
    spot at HW base.
Brown Form female has front of thorax darker than sides.

PLATE 36

1 Band-Winged Meadowhawk

2 Cherry-Faced Meadowhawk

3 Ruby Meadowhawk

4 White-Faced Meadowhawk ♂

5 White-Faced Meadowhawk ♀

6 Band-Winged Dragonlet ♂

7 Band-Winged Dragonlet ♀

8 Black-Winged Dragonlet

1 Little Blue Dragonlet *Erythrodiplax minuscula.* **p. 204**
Male. 1974 Alachua Co, FL, posed   1 in.
Very small size, face and basal HW spot black, thorax and
    S1–S7 pale blue, cerci usually white.

2 Female. 1974 Alachua Co., FL, posed   1 in.
Abdomen tan with black dorsal and interrupted lateral
    stripes on S1–S6, black on S7–S9; face tan; scooplike
    ovipositor; thorax tan with diffuse dark shoulder stripes.

3 Plateau Dragonlet *Erythrodiplax connata.* **p. 205**
Male. 7/28/97 Brewster Co., TX   1.3 in.
As above but thorax becomes black, basal spot of HW
    remains amber, and cerci usually dark.

4 Female. 7/28/97 Brewster Co., TX, posed   1.3 in.
As above but abdomen browner, especially on S7–S9, and
    dark dorsal abdominal stripe reduced.

5 Red-Faced Dragonlet *Erythrodiplax fusca.* **p. 205**
Male. 1990 Zamorano, Francisco Morazan Dept.,
    Honduras, posed   1.1 in.
Very small size, red face, blue abdomen.

Female. 7/18/96 Napo Prov., Ecuador, posed   1.1 in.
As above but dorsal abdominal stripe prominent, and
    abdomen may be pale red.

6 Seaside Dragonlet *Erythrodiplax berenice.* **p. 206**
Male. 6/11/74 Chaves Co., NM, posed   1.3 in.
Small, slender, all black, no basal wing spots.
Eastern salt marshes and mangroves, and southwestern
    saline lakes.

7 Male-like Form female. 8/12/75 Franklin Co., FL, posed   1.3 in.
Abdomen has ovipositor, and S1–S7 remain yellow longer
    than in male.

8 Juvenile Spotted Form female.
    6/16/94 Reeves Co., TX, posed   1.3 in.
Thorax has narrow black and yellow stripes, and wings have
    brown nodal spots.
Unspotted Form females lack nodal spots, and abdomen
    becomes black before thorax.

PLATE 37

1 Little Blue Dragonlet ♂

2 Little Blue Dragonlet ♀

3 Plateau Dragonlet ♂

4 Plateau Dragonlet ♀

5 Red-Faced Dragonlet

6 Seaside Dragonlet ♂

7 Seaside Dragonlet ♀

8 Seaside Dragonlet ♀

1 Elfin Skimmer *Nannothemis bella.* **p. 207**
Male. 6/22/96 Oneida Co., WI   0.8 in.
Tiny size, pale blue body, face edged white, abdomen
clubbed.
Juvenile male has black thorax and abdomen, local in bogs
and fens.

2 Female. 6/22/96 Oneida Co., WI   0.8 in.
Wasplike pattern, basal 1/3 of wings orange.

3 Eastern Amberwing *Perithemis tenera.* **p. 208**
Male. 6/97 Collin Co., TX   0.9 in.
Very small, stubby shape, thorax mostly brown with 2 pale
lateral stripes, orange wings.

4 Female. 7/97 Lorain Co., OH   0.9 in.
Wings banded or spotted with clear and brown areas, usually
also amber areas.

5 Mexican Amberwing *Perithemis intensa.* **p. 209**
Male. 1974, posed   1.1 in.
As above, but thorax not striped.

6 Female. 1976 Mazatlán, Sinaloa, Mexico, posed   1.1 in.
Wings variably marked with amber and brown, but no
brown wingtips.

7 Slough Amberwing *Perithemis domitia.* **p. 209**
Male. 7/3/90 Francisco Morazan Dept., Honduras, posed   0.9 in.
As above but side of thorax pale with narrow brown stripes,
and abdomen has straight brown stripes.

8 Female. Francisco Morazan Dept., Honduras, 3/7/90, posed   0.9 in.
Wings variably marked with clear and amber areas, and
often brown spots or bands, and HW has brown tip.

PLATE 38

1 Elfin Skimmer ♂

2 Elfin Skimmer ♀

3 Eastern Amberwing ♂

4 Eastern Amberwing ♀

5 Mexican Amberwing ♂

6 Mexican Amberwing ♀

7 Slough Amberwing ♂

8 Slough Amberwing ♀

1 Blue Dasher *Pachydiplax longipennis.* **p. 210**
Male. 6/97 Collin Co., TX   1.0–1.7 in.
White face, metallic-green eyes, black and yellow striped
   thorax, pale blue tapered abdomen.
Outer halves of wings often tinted brown.

2 Juvenile female. 6/97 Collin Co., TX   1.0–1.5 in.
Eyes red-brown, black and yellow striped abdomen.
Female abdomen short and blunt.

3 Eastern Pondhawk *Erythemis simplicicollis.* **p. 211**
Mature male. 6/22/97 Montgomery Co., TX   1.7 in.
Pale blue with green face and white cerci.
Abdomen narrowed slightly at S4–S5.

4 Semimature male. 1974 FL, posed   1.7 in.
Juvenile male green, side of thorax one of last areas to
   become pruinose.

5 Female. 1974 FL, posed   1.7 in.
Green, with black rectangular dorsal spots on middle abdominal segments, and spoutlike ovipositor.

6 Western Pondhawk *Erythemis collocata.* **p. 212**
Male. 6/29/97 San Diego Co., CA, posed   1.6 in.
As above but darker blue, with black cerci and tapered
   abdomen.

7 Female. 1974, posed   1.6 in.
As above but abdomen has black dorsal stripe.

8 Great Pondhawk *Erythemis vesiculosa.* **p. 213**
7/76 Mazatlán, Sinaloa, Mexico, posed   2.4 in.
As above but larger, both sexes green, and with complete
   dark bands across middle of slender abdomen.
Green stigmas of juveniles diagnostic.
Female ovipositor short and inconspicuous.

PLATE 39

1 Blue Dasher ♂

2 Blue Dasher ♀

3 Eastern Pondhawk ♂

4 Eastern Pondhawk ♂

5 Eastern Pondhawk ♀

6 Western Pondhawk ♂

7 Western Pondhawk ♀

8 Great Pondhawk

1 Pin-Tailed Pondhawk *Erythemis plebeja*. **p. 214**
Male. 7/76 Mazatlán, Sinaloa, Mexico, posed   1.8 in.
Black body, HW has small black basal spot.
Abdomen as long as a wing, very slender beyond swollen
base, with tan cerci.

2 Female. 2/27/90 Francisco Morazan Dept., Honduras, posed   1.8 in.
Dark brown with front of thorax tan.
Abdomen has ovipositor and tan bands across middle seg-
ments.

3 Black Pondhawk *Erythemis attala*. **p. 214**
Male. Loreto Dept., Peru, posed   1.6 in.
Stray? to AL.
As above but abdomen less slender and shorter than a wing,
and HW has larger basal spot.

4 Juvenile female. Loreto Dept., Peru, posed   1.6 in.
As above but front of thorax dark, and S4–S7 have square
pale dorsal spots.

5 Wandering Glider *Pantala flavescens*. **p. 215**
FL, posed   1.9 in.
Yellow tapered abdomen, long broad wings, sustained flight.

6 Spot-Winged Glider *Pantala hymenaea*. **p. 216**
7/25/97 Coleman Co., TX, posed   1.9 in.
Shaped as above but abdomen mottled gray-brown.
HW has small round dark spot near posterior corner.

7 Black Saddlebags *Tramea lacerata*. **p. 217**
Male. 1973, posed   2.1 in.
Body black, with white dorsal spots on S3–S7 that darken
but persist longest on S7.
Basal 1/4 of broad HW black, flight sustained.

8 Female. FL, 1974, posed   2.1 in.
Like male but pale markings more persistent.

PLATE 40

1 Pin-Tailed Pondhawk ♂

2 Pin-Tailed Pondhawk ♀

3 Black Pondhawk ♂

4 Black Pondhawk ♀

5 Wandering Glider

6 Spot-Winged Glider

7 Black Saddlebags ♂

8 Black Saddlebags ♀

1 Carolina Saddlebags *Tramea carolina.* **p. 218**
6/97 Clay Co., FL   2 in.
Abdomen bright red with S8–S9 mostly black, and forehead violet.
Basal 1/4 of HW brown, including all of anal loop.
Female has brownish-red abdomen, and only basal half of forehead violet.

2 Red Saddlebags *Tramea onusta.* **p. 219**
4/97 TX   1.8 in.
As above but male abdomen paler red and sides of S8–S9 red.
Smaller HW spot with clear sole in foot-shaped anal loop.
No violet on forehead.

3 Striped Saddlebags *Tramea calverti.* **p. 219**
Male. 4/97 Santa Ana NWR, TX   1.9 in.
Thorax has 2 wide pale lateral stripes.
Face and abdomen red, brown basal HW band.

4 Female (with mite under abdomen).
1987 Honduras, posed   1.9 in.
Face yellow and abdomen brownish red.

5 Antillean Saddlebags *Tramea insularis.* **p. 219**
5/22/97 Brewster Co., TX, posed   1.8 in.
Dark face and forehead, red abdomen, narrow basal HW band.
Females have brown face and body, posterior forehead violet. Female and juvenile male Sooty Saddlebags are identical.

6 Sooty Saddlebags *Tramea binotata.* **p. 220**
6/11/95 Napo Prov., Ecuador, posed   1.8 in.
Strays? to FL.
As above but mature male all black.

7 Vermilion Saddlebags *Tramea abdominalis.* **p. 220**
1985 Dade Co., FL, posed   1.9 in.
Like Antillean Saddlebags but face and forehead red.
Females have yellow face and lack violet on forehead.

8 Hyacinth Glider *Miathyria marcella.* **p. 221**
Juvenile male. 1974 FL, posed   1.5 in.
Smaller than Saddlebag Gliders, abdomen orange-brown with black dorsal stripe.
Thorax has 2 white lateral stripes, and HW has brown basal band.
Old males have pruinose violet front and top of thorax.

PLATE 41

1 Carolina Saddlebags

2 Red Saddlebags

3 Striped Saddlebags ♂

4 Striped Saddlebags ♀

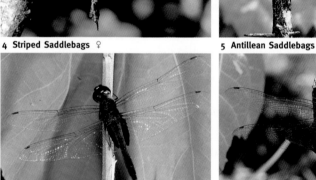
5 Antillean Saddlebags

6 Sooty Saddlebags

7 Vermilion Saddlebags

8 Hyacinth Glider

1 Garnet Glider *Tauriphila australis*. **p. 222**

Loreto Dept., Peru, posed   1.7 in.

Violet forehead, black front of thorax, red abdomen, brown basal HW spot, short cerci.

Female all brown, with dorsal black line on abdomen, and HW spot often just an amber smudge.

2 Aztec Glider *Tauriphila azteca*. **p. 223**

7/76 Mazatlán, Sinaloa, Mexico, posed   1.7 in.

Stray? to south TX.

Thorax brown and unstriped, abdomen yellow-brown with black bands, brown basal HW spot, male has violet forehead.

3 Marl Pennant *Macrodiplax balteata*. **p. 223**

Male. 6/11/74 Chaves Co., NM, posed   1.6 in.

All black, with round black basal HW spot.

Southern, at mineralized or saline waters.

4 Female. 6/11/74 Chaves Co., NM, posed   1.6 in.

White face, gray thorax, S1–S7 dull yellow, S8–S10 black.

5 Red-Tailed Pennant *Brachymesia furcata*. **p. 224**

Male. 4/97 Hidalgo Co., TX, posed   1.7 in.

Red face and abdomen, brown thorax, amber basal HW spot.

6 Juvenile female. 5/26/96 Starr Co., TX, posed   1.7 in.

Brown with a dorsal white stripe between wings and on base of abdomen, and a short black dorsal stripe on S8–S9.

7 Four-Spotted Pennant *Brachymesia gravida*. **p. 225**

1974 FL, posed   2 in.

Black slender body, white stigmas, round black nodal spots.

Juveniles mostly orange-brown with white spots on sides of face.

8 Tawny Pennant *Brachymesia herbida*. **p. 226**

10/12/88 Napo Prov., Ecuador, posed   1.9 in.

Resident? in south TX and southernmost FL.

Like juvenile of above but face and stigmas tan, abdomen brown-yellow with irregular black dorsal stripe, brown-tinted wings.

PLATE 42

1 Garnet Glider

2 Aztec Glider

3 Marl Pennant ♂

4 Marl Pennant ♀

5 Red-Tailed Pennant ♂

6 Red-Tailed Pennant ♀

7 Four-Spotted Pennant

8 Tawny Pennant

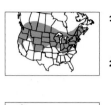

1 Dot-Tailed Whiteface *Leucorrhinia intacta*. **p. 227**
Male, eating beetle. 6/20/96 Forest Co., WI   1.3 in.
Small, black, with white face and yellow dorsal spot on S7.

2 Female. 6/22/96 Oneida Co., WI, posed   1.3 in.
Dorsal yellow spots of abdomen full length on S4–S6, wide
   and square on S7, absent on S8.
S4 has lateral yellow stripe.

3 Hudsonian Whiteface *Leucorrhinia hudsonica*. **p. 228**
6/22/96 Oneida Co., WI   1.2 in.
Both sexes like female of above, but abdominal markings
   become red in males and Red Form females.
A pale spot may be present on S8, but wings lack amber.

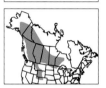

4 Boreal Whiteface *Leucorrhinia borealis*. **p. 228**
7/1/95 Devon, AB   1.5 in.
As above but larger, and dorsal abdominal spots form a nearly continuous stripe.
Males always have a spot on S8, females have a full-length
   spot on S7.

5 Frosted Whiteface *Leucorrhinia frigida*. **p. 229**
Male. 1973, posed   1.2 in.
Black, with white face and S2–S4.

6 Female. 7/94 WI, posed   1.2 in.
S7 has yellow streak, wing bases amber.

7 Red-Waisted Whiteface *Leucorrhinia proxima*. **p. 230**
White Form male. 6/19/96 Lincoln Co., WI, posed   1.4 in.
As above but slightly larger, and develops red markings at
   least between wings.
Red Form male is identical to male Crimson-Ringed White-
   face.

8 Female of White form.
   6/19/96 Lincoln Co., WI, posed   1.4 in.
Like Dot-Tailed Whiteface but spots of S5–S6 narrow and less
   than 3/4 length.
Female Crimson-Ringed Whiteface identical but not known
   to be pruinose or have amber in wings.

9 Crimson-Ringed Whiteface *Leucorrhinia glacialis*. **p. 231**
Male. 6/22/96 Oneida Co., WI   1.4 in.
Mostly black with white face and red S1–S3.
Red Form male of above is identical.

10 Female. 1977 CA, posed   1.4 in.
Identical to some females of above.

10A Canada Whiteface (not shown) like above, but smaller
   (1.1 in.) and more slender, female has pale spot of S7
   absent or reduced to a streak.

PLATE 43

1 Dot-Tailed Whiteface ♂

2 Dot-Tailed Whiteface ♀

3 Hudsonian Whiteface

4 Boreal Whiteface

5 Frosted Whiteface ♂

6 Frosted Whiteface ♀

7 Red-Waisted Whiteface ♂

8 Red-Waisted Whiteface ♀

9 Crimson-Ringed Whiteface ♂

10 Crimson-Ringed Whiteface ♀

1 Halloween Pennant *Celithemis eponina.* **p. 233**
Pair in wheel. 7/97 Medina Co., OH   1.5 in.
Orange wings patterned with black are diagnostic.
Juveniles have yellow body markings.

2 Banded Pennant *Celithemis fasciata.* **p. 233**
Male. 5/11/89 Alachua Co., FL, posed   1.3 in.
Sharply defined black wing pattern diagnostic but variable.
Body all black.

3 Female. 1973 Putnam Co., FL, posed   1.3 in.
Body marked with yellow.

4 Calico Pennant *Celithemis elisa.* **p. 234**
7/97 Medina Co., OH   1.2 in.
Wing pattern diagnostic.
Body markings yellow, becoming red in males.

5 Double-Ringed Pennant *Celithemis verna.* **p. 234**
Male. 4/17/76 Columbia Co., FL, posed   1.3 in.
Face and body smoky black, small black basal HW spot.

6 Juvenile female. 6/5/66 Marlboro Co., SC   1.3 in.
Yellow rings on S3–S4, but no spots on S6–S7.

PLATE 44

1 Halloween Pennant

2 Banded Pennant ♂

3 Banded Pennant ♀

4 Calico Pennant

5 Double-Ringed Pennant ♂

6 Double-Ringed Pennant ♀

1 Martha's Pennant *Celithemis martha.* **p. 235**
Male. 7/95 Barnstable Co., MA   1.2 in.
Black, with 1/5 length black basal HW spot.

2 Juvenile (very juvenile = teneral) female.
8/93 Barnstable Co., MA   1.2 in.
Basal HW spot amber with 3 black stripes, body marked yellow, thorax has black lateral anterior spot and posterior stripe, sides of S3–S4 mostly black.

3 Red-Veined Pennant *Celithemis bertha.* **p. 235**
Male. 10/27/74 Alachua Co., FL, posed   1.2 in.
Bright red face, wing veins, and body markings.
HW basal spot very small, but up to 1/5 length in south FL.

4 Spot-Winged Form male. 1977 FL Panhandle, posed   1.2 in.
Tiny to large brown spot near tip of one or more wings.

5 Female. Putnam Co., FL, posed   1.2 in.
Lateral black thoracic markings generally not joined, side of S4 has yellow to red stripe.

6 Faded Pennant *Celithemis ornata.* **p. 236**
1974 FL, posed   1.3 in.
Mature male like Martha's Pennant but face and thorax brown, abdominal spots dull red.
Female like Martha's but 2 lateral black stripes on thorax connected dorsally, and S3 has black lateral stripe.

7 Amanda's Pennant *Celithemis amanda.* **p. 237**
Male. 1974 FL, posed   1.1 in.
As above but HW spot larger and containing 2 dark anterior spots and a posterior spot, and abdomen shorter.

8 Female. 1974 FL, posed   1.1 in.
Side of thorax nearly unmarked, and side of S3 mostly pale.

PLATE 45

1 Martha's Pennant ♂

2 Martha's Pennant ♀

3 Red-Veined Pennant ♂

4 Red-Veined Pennant ♂

5 Red-Veined Pennant ♀

6 Faded Pennant

7 Amanda's Pennant ♂

8 Amanda's Pennant ♀

1 **Mayan Setwing** *Dythemis maya.* **p. 238**
Male. 7/27/97 Brewster Co., TX, posed   1.8 in.
Slender red body, basal 1/5 of wings orange.
Compare with stout-bodied Flame Skimmer (Plate 32).

2 Female. 7/27/97 Brewster Co., TX, posed   1.8 in.
Body brown, wings often black-tipped.

3 **Checkered Setwing** *Dythemis fugax.* **p. 238**
7/24/97 Somervell Co., TX   1.8 in.
Lacy brown basal wing spots, pale green abdominal spots.
Face green, becoming red in males.

4 **Swift Setwing** *Dythemis velox.* **p. 239**
6/97 Collin Co., TX   1.6 in.
YIY pattern on side of thorax, brown wingtips.
Forehead brown in males, dull green in females.
Both sexes lack pale **lateral** abdominal streaks.

5 **Black Setwing** *Dythemis nigrescens.* **p. 240**
Male. 5/12/97 Hidalgo Co., TX, posed   1.8 in.
Pruinose black with slightly clubbed abdomen, forehead
    metallic violet.

6 Female. 5/12/97 Hidalgo Co., TX, posed   1.8 in.
As above but thorax dull greenish yellow with HII or HIY pat-
    tern.
S4–S7 have lateral pale streaks, wingtips are only narrowly
    brown.

7 **Pale-Faced Clubskimmer** *Brechmorhoga mendax.* **p. 241**
7/26/97 Brewster Co., TX, posed   2.2 in.
Thorax brown with 3 lateral pale green stripes; forehead pale
    green; abdomen mostly green on sides of S2–S3, widely
    clubbed in male.
Female abdomen cylindrical.

8 **Masked Clubskimmer** *Brechmorhoga pertinax.* **p. 242**
8/82 Veracruz, Mexico   2.1 in.
As above but forehead sharply defined metallic black, sides
    of S2–S3 mostly black.

PLATE 46

1 Mayan Setwing ♂

2 Mayan Setwing ♀

3 Checkered Setwing

4 Swift Setwing

5 Black Setwing ♂

6 Black Setwing ♀

7 Pale-Faced Clubskimmer

8 Masked Clubskimmer

1 Narrow-Winged Skimmer *Cannaphila insularis.* **p. 242**
Male. Dominican Republic, posed   1.6 in.
HW narrowed in basal half, body black with base of
abdomen pruinose gray, face white, forehead metallic
green or blue, metallic-green eyes.

2 Juvenile female. Dominican Republic, posed   1.6 in.
Straight yellow thoracic stripes. Abdomen rusty brown,
becoming black at maturity, with narrow dorsal and lateral
yellow stripes, wide black lateral flange on S8.

3 Metallic Pennant *Idiataphe cubensis.* **p. 243**
5/3/81 Dade Co., FL, posed   1.4 in.
Metallic black with bronzy brown face, thorax, and lateral
abdominal stripe.

4 Straw-Colored Sylph *Macrothemis inacuta.* **p. 244**
1976 Sinaloa, Mexico, posed   1.7 in.
Slender yellow-brown abdomen, pale green lateral thoracic
spots, aqua eyes. Females often have amber FW tip.

5 Ivory-Striped Sylph *Macrothemis imitans.* **p. 244**
1987 Honduras, posed   1.4 in.
"Headlight" frontal thoracic spots, broad club, aqua eyes,
metallic-blue forehead. Female has side of thorax with
pale green anterior stripe and 2 or 3 posterior spots, frontal
spots small or absent, red-brown eyes, brown forehead.

6 Jade-Striped Sylph *Macrothemis inequiunguis.* **p. 245**
6/12/67 Puntarenas Prov., Costa Rica   1.4 in.
Side of thorax pale green with *IY* or *YY* pattern, front with
wedge-shaped green stripes, forehead metallic blue and
eyes green in both sexes, male abdomen clubbed.

7 Thornbush Dasher *Microthyria hagenii.* **p. 246**
Male. 5/12/97 Cameron Co., TX, posed   1.4 in.
IYI pattern of dark lateral thoracic stripes, square pale green
spot on S7, face white, eyes green. Juveniles have red-
brown eyes, females may have abdomen rusty brown.

8 Three-Striped Dasher *Microthyria didyma.* **p. 247**
1987 Dade Co., FL, posed   1.4 in.
As above but more slender, with *III* thoracic pattern and
trapezoidal spot on S7.

9 Spot-Tailed Dasher *Microthyria aequalis.* **p. 247**
Male. 1988 Dade Co., FL, posed   1.2 in.
Small size, pruinose gray with triangular pale green spot on
S7, face white, eyes green.

10 Female. 1976 Mazatlán, Sinaloa, Mexico, posed   1.2 in.
Thorax dull yellow-green with lateral dark *WII* pattern.

PLATE 47

1 Narrow-Winged Skimmer ♂

2 Narrow-Winged Skimmer ♀

3 Metallic Pennant

4 Straw-Colored Sylph

5 Ivory-Striped Sylph

6 Jade-Striped Sylph

7 Thornbush Dasher

8 Three-Striped Dasher

9 Spot-Tailed Dasher ♂

10 Spot-Tailed Dasher ♀

Further Reading

Acorn, J.H. 1995. "Acorn, the Nature Nut." Episode No. 20: *Dragonflies*. (Video, Great North Productions, #012, 11523- 100 Ave., Edmonton, AB, Canada T5K OJ8.)

Cannings, R.A., and K.M. Stuart. 1977. *The Dragonflies of British Columbia*. B.C. Prov. Museum Handbook 35, 254 pp.

Carpenter, V. 1991. *Dragonflies and Damselflies of Cape Cod*. Cape Cod Mus. Nat. Hist., Nat. Hist. Ser. 4. 79 pp.

Corbet, P.S. 1963. *A Biology of Dragonflies*. Chicago: Quadrangle Books. 247 pp.

Corbet, P.S. 1980. "Biology of Odonata". *Annual Review of Entomology* 25:189–217.

Corbet, P.S. 1999. *Dragonflies, Behavior and Ecology of Odonata*. Ithaca: Cornell Univ. Press. 829 pp.

Corbet, P.S., S.W. Dunkle, and H. Ubukata, eds. 1995. *Proceedings of the International Symposium on the Conservation of Dragonflies and Their Habitats*. Japanese Soc. for Preservation of Birds, Kushiro. 70 pp.

Corbet, P.S., C. Longfield, and N.W. Moore. 1960. *Dragonflies*. London: Collins. 260 pp.

Dunkle, S.W. 1989. *Dragonflies of the Florida Peninsula, Bermuda, and the Bahamas*. Gainesville, Florida: Scientific Publishers. 154 pp.

Holder, M. 1996. *The Dragonflies and Damselflies of Algonquin Provincial Park*. Algonquin Park Tech. Bull. 11. 40 pp.

Legler, K., D. Legler, and D. Westover. 1998. *Color Guide to Common Dragonflies of Wisconsin*. 429 Franklin St., Sauk City, WI, 53583.

Miller, P.L. 1995. *Dragonflies*, 2nd Ed. Slough, England: Richmond Publishing. 118 pp.

Moore, N.W. 1997. *Dragonflies— Status Survey and Conservation Action Plan*. IUCN/SSC Odonata Specialist Group, Cambridge, UK. 28 pp.

Needham, J.G., and M.J. Westfall, Jr. 1955. *A Manual of the Dragonflies of North America*. Berkeley: Univ. California Press. 615 pp.

252   Paulson, D. 1999. *Dragonflies of Washington*. Seattle Audubon Soc. 32 pp.

Paulson, D.R., and S.W. Dunkle. 1999. *A Checklist of North American Odonata*. Univ. Puget Sound Occ. Pap. 56:1–86.

Pilon, J.-G., and D. Legace. 1998. *Les Odonates du Quebec*. Entomofaune du Quebec, Chicoutimi. 367 pp.

Walker, E.M. 1953. *The Odonata of Canada and Alaska*, Vol. 1. Univ. Toronto Press. 292 pp.

Walker, E.M. 1958. *The Odonata of Canada and Alaska*, Vol. 2. Univ. Toronto Press. 318 pp.

Walker, E.M., and P.S. Corbet. 1975. *The Odonata of Canada and Alaska*, Vol. 3. Univ. Toronto Press. 307 pp.

Walton, R.K., and R.A. Forster. 1997. "Common Dragonflies of the Northeast." (Video, NHS, 7 Concord Creene #8, Concord, MA 01742.)

West, L. and J. Ridl. 1994. *How to Photograph Insects and Spiders*. Mechanicsburg, Pennsylvania: Stackpole. 118 pp.

Westfall, M.J., Jr., and K.J. Tennessen. 1996. "Odonata," in R.W. Merritt and K.W. Cummins, eds. *An Introduction to the Aquatic Insects of North America*, 3rd ed. Kendall/Hunt, Dubuque, Iowa, 862 pp.

Photographic Credits

Index and Checklist

Note: A box (□) is placed next to the common name of each resident species, listed under the last word of the English name. The checklist contains 302 species, of which the Scarlet Skimmer is introduced; 5 other species are considered strays to our area. Numbers in **boldface** refer to colored plates.